LIFE BETWEEN THE LINES:

A MEMOIR

JOHN IZBICKI

UMBRIA PRESS

Cover image by Paul Izbicki

Umbria Press,
2 Umbria Street,
London SW15 5DP
www.umbriapress.co.uk

Printed and bound by
Ashford Colour Press Ltd, Gosport

ISBN 978-0-9541275-7-2

*I dedicate this book to my son, Paul,
my stepson and stepdaughter Patrick
and Anna, my grandchildren, Tyler and
Chloe and my step-granddaughter,
Robyn*

*And I should also like to dedicate it to
the memory of the many who perished in
the holocaust.*

CONTENTS

	PREFACE BY CHARLES MOORE	VII
	INTRODUCTION	1
CHAPTER 1	KRISTALLNACHT	3
CHAPTER 2	ESCAPE	24
CHAPTER 3	A NEW LIFE	35
CHAPTER 4	MOVE TO MANCHESTER	50
CHAPTER 5	PEACE	60
CHAPTER 6	ON CAMPUS	65
CHAPTER 7	RETURN TO GERMANY	72
CHAPTER 8	NATIONAL SERVICE	86
CHAPTER 9	REAL WORK BEGINS	113
CHAPTER 10	PARIS LOVES	120
CHAPTER 11	MY NAKED HEROINE	140
CHAPTER 12	TAKEOVER	157
CHAPTER 13	THE TORYGRAPH	174
CHAPTER 14	THE TORYGRAPH (2)	190
CHAPTER 15	ON TO EDUCATION	217
CHAPTER 16	THE THATCHER YEARS	231
CHAPTER 17	SADNESS AND LIGHT	259
CHAPTER 18	BACK TO PARIS	278
CHAPTER 19	FAREWELL SQUABBLES	305
CHAPTER 20	FROM POLY TO UNI	314
CHAPTER 21	HEADHUNTED AT 62	327
CHAPTER 22	EPILOGUE	341
	INDEX	344

PREFACE

When I joined the *Daily Telegraph* as a young reporter in 1979, the paper had a reputation for being stuffy and staid. The odd thing was that no words could have been less appropriate for the journalists who worked there. The place was a charming madhouse of genius, drunkenness, wit and eccentricity.

Even in this gallery, though, no figure was more exotic than that of John Izbicki (though he was, I hasten to add, sober). Snappily dressed, with attractive dark looks and a sort of mock courtliness in his manner, he looked like the compere of a variety show. It was typical of the unexpectedness of the paper that John was, in real life, its education correspondent. It surprised me that this was his job. It did not surprise me to hear that his legendary charm had persuaded Margaret Thatcher, then Education Secretary, to join him after a dance to admire Scarborough beach in the moonlight.

John was one of those clever men who, while always busy, always have time to talk, so I learnt a good deal of the lore and language of Fleet Street from him. But when one works with people, one tends not to ask them their life history; and so I never knew John's – until now. It is a tragic, touching, comic and inspiring tale.

From the horrible moment on the *Kristallnacht* in 1938 when the Nazis smashed his father's Berlin haberdashery shop while young Horst (John) hid, through his life as refugee, as a foreign correspondent, as a saviour of the Open University and as a specialist reporter, to his retirement in rural Kent, John Izbicki vividly takes us through the extraordinary changes and chances of the 20th century.

For me, two things stand out. One is the unique contribution made to the life of this country by the generation of Jews of whom John is a leading example. The other is that this book explains to the reader why newspapers are – or should I say were? – fun. His has been a life well lived, and here it is, well told.

Charles Moore

INTRODUCTION

For many years, I have been asked and encouraged to pen my memoirs. People, whether they were my readers, my professional contacts or simply my friends, told me that I had a story to tell – the story of a little Jewish refugee boy who came to England on the day the Second World War was declared, unable to speak a single word of English, and who became the education correspondent (editor) of the *Daily Telegraph* and the head of its Paris office, and later helped the country's polytechnics become universities. I hope you will find the book filled with enjoyable anecdotes, humour and pathos and, yes, sadness.

My thanks go out to June, my wife, who not only showed great patience during the many months I sat closeted in my study to write these pages, but who also helped by checking for literals and the odd (I hope very odd) grammatical error.

My thanks are also extended to Demitri Coryton, editor and proprietor of *Education Journal*, the informative monthly magazine, for which I have been contributing regular columns, and who urged me to write these memoirs.

Now turn the page – and enjoy!

John Izbicki
Horsmonden, 2012

CHAPTER ONE:

KRISTALLNACHT

"*Ich bin ein Jude!*" "I am a Jew!" I shouted the words to the sky and they ricocheted from the tall houses and the trams that stood abandoned and silent in the middle of Invalidenstrasse, the street where I lived and which was now totally deserted. Nothing seemed to stir – except for me, a small five-year-old, who had woken from his afternoon nap and was making his way along the silent street. I had no idea why I was so completely alone or why the trams that usually clanked their way up and down the middle of this, one of Berlin's busiest streets, were now motionless.

I did not see that there were men and women staring out from the shops that lined both sides of the road. All I knew was that, for the first time in my life, I was alone in this long and empty street and that I was free to shout words I would normally not even dare to whisper. To admit aloud and in public to being Jewish was just asking for trouble. I danced along the pavement and repeated with increasing glee: "I am a Jew….I am a Jew…I am…"

My happiness was cut short as a firm hand clasped my shoulder and dragged me away. "Be quiet! Be quiet at once!" my father blurted out as he pulled me the last few metres into the shop. "What the hell d'you think you're doing, yelling like that. You'll have us all arrested. Is that what you want? Well?"

But by now I was crying. The hot tears flowed freely. How could I tell him that I had only dared to confess my faith aloud because I was so alone and no one was listening? No one. By now my mother was already clasping me to her warm bosom. "Hush, hush, Horstchen. Don't cry. Everything will be all right. Hush now."

Only then did my father explain that there had been an air raid alarm. It was just a test but the whole of Berlin had to come to a standstill. Passengers were ordered off trams and took shelter in the nearest houses or shops until the all clear sounded. "You were not alone, Horst. Everyone could hear you from one end of the street to the other. They were all watching from their windows. You were very lucky that there wasn't a police or Gestapo patrol. Otherwise…well, I don't know what would have happened. But, believe me, it would not have done us any good."

My father was a good, hardworking man, quick of temper but also quick to replace it with gentleness. He was born Luzer Ber Izbicki, the son of a baker, in Lenczyca, a small town in the Russian part of Poland in 1898. He was called up to fight with the Russian army during the Great War but, shortly after Armistice was declared, made his way out of the country on foot, tunnelling his way beneath the thick snow that enveloped the border and entering East Prussia. He earned his daily bread by doing odd jobs. His bronzed, handsome face and easygoing manner appealed to the German *Hausfrau* and work was readily offered. By the time he reached Kolberg, a popular north German seaside resort, he had managed to learn enough of the language to seek more permanent employment. A small shoe manufacturer was looking for designers. Luzer Ber knew nothing of shoes or art, but applied for the job and was promised a trial period. The job would start at the beginning of the month – two weeks away.

He spent every spare moment examining shoes in every Kolberg shop that sold them and studied books about them in the local reference library. By the time he started his job, he was able to draw the designs he had invented. They appealed to his new employer – and so did he. He managed to save enough to move out of the garret that had become his home and rent a small flat but lived mostly on bread, cheese and fruit, spending whatever was left on German books. These would go with him, tightly packed in a shoulder bag, wherever he went, accompanied by the hope that, somehow, the language would be transferred to him through some form of osmosis.

My father neither drank alcohol nor smoked. "A Russian officer once gave me three green cigars and I smoked them one after the other," he would tell anyone who offered him a cigarette. "I was violently ill and haven't touched tobacco since." Only many years later would he sip at a glass of lager – to mark the first day of a family holiday. It became a tradition.

One Saturday, while drinking a coffee at a beach bar, he got talking to a pretty young woman at the next table. He and Hedwig Alexander went dancing or to a cinema or restaurant for more than a month and the relationship was on the point of becoming serious. Then Hedwig, Heti to her friends, took him home to meet Mum. Berta Alexander was a war widow. Hermann, her husband, had fought for the Fatherland and met his death by a bullet from a Russian rifle. Berta sold the small but lucrative cigar and cigarette factory he had started in the East Prussian town of Czersk and moved to Kolberg with her family of two daughters, Hedwig and Selma, and three sons, Isidor, Karl and Georg.

Heti's introduction of Luzer to the Alexander family was a mistake on her part. But not as far as my future was concerned. It was in Berta's comfortable home that he met Heti's sister, Selma, and did not hesitate to ask her out. It took a while for Heti to forgive her younger sister, but forgive her she did. The Alexander family did not bear grudges. Selma had already had plenty of young admirers pestering her for a date, but this one, she felt, was different. For one thing, he had not tried to kiss her for weeks. And when they danced, he held her correctly, not too close. He brought flowers whenever he came to the house but presented them not to her but to her mother. He had learned German etiquette well and knew that patience was a virtue that would one day be rewarded.

They had met in the early part of 1921 and "courted" for nearly two years before Luzer popped the question. Selma accepted and her fiancé was welcomed into the Alexander family. It was not until 1925 that they were married at the local Kolberg synagogue, where Isidor, "Isi", the eldest brother, replaced their war hero father in giving her away.

The honeymoon was brief and deliriously happy. Luzer had saved as much as he could from the wages he earned but there was not really enough to splash out. So they decided to spend a few days in Germany's capital. It was on their second day in the cheap but clean Pension they had found close to the Stettiner Bahnhof, where they had arrived from Kolberg that Luzer produced a bombshell suggestion.

"Listen, Selma Liebling, I've been thinking. Kolberg is all very well but I'll never get much further in the shoe business. It's not what I want to do all my life. Why don't we move here to Berlin?"

Selma was disturbed by the announcement. "But what on earth will we do here. It's a big city. We don't know a soul. Anyway, I can't just up and leave my mother and family back there in Kolberg. What can you be thinking of?"

"Of course you can't my darling. Of course you can't. I don't expect you to. First I shall take a closer look at what openings there are for me to start a small business here. It doesn't have to be anything spectacular. I couldn't afford anything too risky…Why don't we at least try?"

And try he did. With the help of mother-in-law Berta, he rented a small ground floor apartment in the Invalidenstrasse, a busy street off the Friedrichstrasse in North Berlin, bought himself a long trestle table and filled it with small articles of haberdashery, zips, buttons, multi-coloured ribbons, handkerchiefs, as well as ladies' underwear, men's socks and ties. He insisted on stocking that table only with the best quality goods and selling them at low prices. The year was 1926.

Every morning he would get up at six and by seven o'clock had his table of wares open just inside the big double doors that led to the courtyard of No. 33 Invalidenstrasse. The crowds hurrying along the street to their places of work or to the nearby Stettiner Station would first glance at the available wares as they passed by, then stop and look more closely. By the end of the first month, the "stall" was a going concern and starting to make a profit.

In the winter of 1930 Selma became pregnant and on November 8 that year I came into the world, opening my eyes in the labour ward of the Berlin Jewish Hospital. Looking back at those early photographs, I can only describe myself as thoroughly ugly. How could such an abominable baby have been born to such an attractive couple? I looked Japanese, with little slit eyes, and my complexion was more brown than pink. I was, my parents later told me, jaundiced. But I was loved. And thoroughly spoiled.

Among the earliest memories I treasure, is waking up in the half light and watching my father tugging big boxes as quietly as possible towards the front door of our apartment, then still on the central courtyard of the house, and from there dragging them to the big double doors that opened to the busy street with its noisy trams, cars and horse-drawn carts.

My mother would also be up, busy brewing the coffee and cutting slices from a big brown loaf. For me there was milk and more milk as well as some porridge oats. When I was big enough to walk, I would skip around the courtyard and watch as my parents sold the wares from their stall.

At weekends, Grandma Berta and my uncles and aunt would come to visit. By now they had all moved to Berlin and some of them had married. Isi, the eldest, had created a veritable stir by bringing Mary to the house and introducing her as his fiancée. Mary was not only ravishingly beautiful but she was also a Roman Catholic. To marry "out" was regarded with distaste bordering on repulsion and fear. But Isi was adamant and Mary was reluctantly accepted into the family. Their daughter, Liane, was born on December 18, 1930. She was just one month younger than me and was to become a close and lifelong friend.

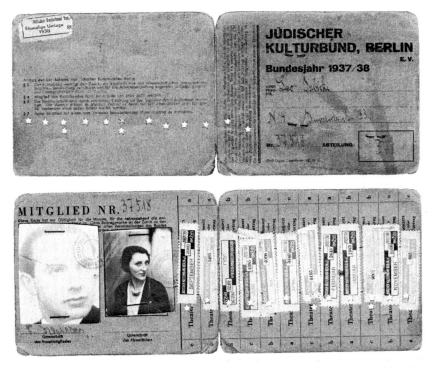

My parents (pictured) *could not enter theatres or cinemas unless they were Jewish theatres or cinemas. They joined the one remaining Berlin Jewish Cultural Association, of which this is their membership card.*

Heti, too, found the love of her life and married a young electrician called Benno Itzig. Their son, Heini, who was a year older than me and Liane, also became a close friend to both of us. But, alas, I am unable to add "lifelong". Heini, along with his mother and father, as well as my darling Oma (grandma) and all her children, except my mother, met their deaths in the Nazi extermination camps of Theresienstadt, Bergen Belsen and Auschwitz.

But I go too fast. My childhood – at least, the first five years of it – was a happy one. My father's haberdashery stall became so successful that he rented a small shop just along the road at No. 31. It stood opposite the Nordland Hotel, which was always packed with tourists from Scandinavia, and next to the area's busy main post office. My mother was put in charge of the shop and was even given an assistant, while Dad continued to work the stall. But by 1933, both businesses had grown so much that the stall was abandoned and my father joined my mother, whom he would always address as "Fräulein" in front of customers. "It makes a good impression and shows that the business has several assistants," he would explain.

That same year, Germany's unemployment had reached critical proportions. A man named Adolf Hitler was making trouble. People took little notice. He had, after all, been trying to muscle in on politics for some years and had never been successful. Only a year after Germany's defeat in the Great War he had joined a small, inconsequential party which he renamed the National Socialist German Workers' Party and in 1923 he tried, again unsuccessfully, to overthrow the Bavarian government and ended up in prison.

There, this young and ambitious man, who was born Schicklgrüber in Upper Austria and could not rise beyond the rank of corporal in a Bavarian regiment, wrote a book called *Mein Kampf* (My Struggle). He didn't actually write it as he was not a very talented writer, but dictated it to one of his closest friends, Rudolf Hess.

The book became his political will and testament and, after his release from jail, he continued to tour the country, speaking on street corners and promising those who would care to listen, full employment, food in their bellies and a world without Jews.

He failed to beat Germany's President, General Paul von Hindenburg, in the 1932 elections, but to everyone's surprise and to the shock of the country's Jewish population, he was elected Chancellor shortly after Hindenburg's death in August, 1934. It was a cue for total mayhem. He ordered a suspension of the German constitution, made capital from the burning down of the *Reichstag* building and brought the NSDAP (the Nazi party) to power. Any opponents he might still have had within the party were murdered on his orders by his personal bodyguards – the SS – in what became widely known as the Night of the Long Knives.

For Jews it was the beginning of the end. My father decided to change his name – but only unofficially. To family and friends he became known, not as Luzer, but as Hans. It was "more German", less foreign. My own name, Horst, was of course as German as *Leberwurst*. I later came to hate it as I always associated it with the *Horst Wessel Lied* – the Nazi marching chorus that was sung with gusto at every rally and was always accompanied with arms outstretched in the *Heil Hitler* salute. It had become even more popular than Germany's own jingoistic national anthem: *Deutschland, Deutschland Über Alles*.

By the time I was four, we had moved out of our ground floor flat at the other end of the courtyard to a larger, more comfortable one on the first floor, with a balcony that overlooked the Invalidenstrasse. From there, I recall seeing uniformed guards in front of my parents' shop. A placard was pasted on their window: *Deutsche Wehrt Euch: Kauft nicht bei Juden!*, it commanded (Germans Defend Yourselves: Don't buy from Jews). Danish and Swedish tourists from the Nordland Hotel took no notice and continued to enter the shop to buy things they didn't even need. "I cannot understand what or why this is happening, Herr Izbicki," one Swede told my father. "All I know is that it's wrong and cannot continue like this for long."

But continue it did. As early as 1934, Jews were forbidden to possess health insurance. They were also barred from qualifying for legal professions. A little later, they were unable to serve in Germany's armed services and, if they were artists, actors or comedians, they could not join any "Aryan" association but were confined to a "Jews only" cultural union.

A few years later, on August 17, 1938, we were presented with yet another name. An order went out: all Jewish men had to add "Israel" and all women "Sarah" to their names on legal documents, including passports. My mother's name on her identity card became Selma Sarah Izbicki, while my father's was Luzer Israel Izbicki and mine, the card of a little child, stated: Horst Israel Izbicki.

Shortly after Hitler's election as *"Führer"* a special brigade of Hitler Youths was founded. Schoolchildren were given well pressed khaki uniforms with swastika armbands and made to join these regiments. They were proud to serve the Führer, and march round the streets of Berlin carrying pots of white paint and brushes. On my parents' shop window and on the windows of hundreds of other Jewish shops and department stores throughout Germany, a huge letter "J" was painted. It stood for *Jude* and acted as a "stop" sign to any would-be customer.

My parents were aghast. They would sit for hours in the evenings speaking in whispers, wondering what the future held for them. All their hard work was being drained away by the actions of the new Nazi government. Like so many Jews in Nazi Germany, my father felt that it could not go on much longer. Reason would prevail. But the years passed and the persecution continued. By 1935, Jews started to disappear. News got round that they had been arrested in the middle of the night and dragged away to prison. Why?

"There must be some mistake," my father said one evening as he heard of yet another friend's arrest. "Perhaps they didn't pay their tax properly. Or maybe they were caught listening to a foreign radio station" (listening to anything other than the German radio had been strictly forbidden).

People started talking of hearing loud banging on the doors of apartments occupied by Jewish neighbours and seeing men being dragged down the stairs and packed into Gestapo vans. The Gestapo – short for *Geheime Staatspolizei* (secret police) – in their black uniforms, highly polished leather boots and caps whose leather bands were surmounted by a silver skull and crossbones, became the most feared of all Nazi officials.

No one knew for certain the destination of those who disappeared in the middle of the night. Prison was all one heard to begin with. Then there were rumours that those arrested had ended up in a camp. I think I was five when I first heard the word *Konzentratsionslager* (concentration camp), later abbreviated to the more simple yet ominous KZ. One uncle had been taken to a place called Dachau He was never seen again.

As a child, I can recall my parents speaking in low voices after the evening meal. But I did not share their fear. Far from it. Like most children, I found the smart uniforms of the Nazis, whether it was the brown of the Hitler Youths or the black of the Gestapo, exciting and when I saw them marching down the street, I would stand and wave and even give the *Heil Hitler* salute. When it was returned, I felt proud.

"Why can't I join the Hitler Youths?" I asked my mother when I was about seven. "You're too young, Horstchen," she would reply. "So when will I be old enough to join them, Mutti?" I insisted. "I don't know my Liebling, we'll have to see…later…later maybe."

But later never came and I grew up in a Berlin full of bunting and music. Swastika flags flew from thousands of windows and I could not understand why our windows stayed flagless. Martial music blared from loudspeakers attached to lamp posts lining the streets along which people strode giving each other the Nazi salute with a barked accompaniment of *Heil Hitler!*

There was a cinema in our street and I would stand outside its doors admiring the still photographs of scenes from the film being shown. But I could not enter the cinema to see the film. Jews were not allowed to enter any place of entertainment other than a Jewish theatre. I simply failed to understand why – not even after I had learned to read and could see for myself. The notices outside the cinemas were very clear: *Juden Verboten* (Jews Forbidden).

I learned to read and write at a Jewish school which I attended from the age of six. Our teachers were, of course, all Jewish. From January 1937, they were no longer allowed to teach non-Jewish, German children, but were confined to Jewish educational establishments. That same month, Jews could no longer practise accountancy or dentistry ("A Jew's hand inside an Aryan mouth is unthinkable!" the Nazi "house journal" *Der Stürmer* declared).

I enjoyed school and loved my teachers. They coached me with affection and patience and made sure that I could do joined-up writing almost from the very beginning. German teaching was by rote but it was drummed in not by threat of punishment or, worse, the cane, as in so many English schools, but by gentle persuasion. By the time I was seven, I could read and write reasonably well.

In the summer of 1937 the school took the children on a week's holiday to the seaside. My father gave me five marks to spend during the week and on the train, children lined up to hand their pocket money to a teacher who noted down the amounts against the children's names in the register. When it came to my turn, I searched through all my pockets but the five mark coin had gone. I was distraught The teacher was sympathetic but could do nothing other than to note a "Nil" against my name.

At the seaside, whenever the children were asked: "Who wants an ice cream?" I shot up my hand amongst the others. But I couldn't have an ice cream as there was no money to pay for it. For days I was miserable. But it was no use crying about it. Class friends let me have a lick of their cornets and wafers and others handed me the odd sweet. Then, on the Saturday, there was a surprise. My father came to visit. He had bought a large bag of peaches and we went for a walk along the promenade and sat down on a bench to eat them. The juice dribbled down our chins and we both dissolved into spasms

The author as a young man of two years in Berlin.

Hold the Front Page: The author in Berlin in 1932 – before the troubles started.

of laughter. It was a glorious afternoon and, to this day, remains among my happiest childhood memories. The fact that he also gave the teacher some pocket money for me was an added bonus.

I treasure one other happy memory – also from that same holiday. We had spent part of the afternoon splashing about in the sea and were then called back to the beach and told to lie down on our towels and rest. I found myself lying close to a little girl about the same age as myself but from another class. She had long black hair that flowed across her shoulders and down to her waist. I found myself wanting to touch it. I reached out my hand and gently stroked her hair. It was, oh so silky. There was no reaction, either positive or negative, from her. My eyes closed and I fell fast asleep. When I awoke, I was alone on the beach. The children were all up – and queuing for their ices. I have had a thing about long hair ever since.

Back in Berlin, such happy memories are replaced by those of a more gloomy nature. The post office adjoining my parents' shop had a long hall leading to the entrance. Showcases containing a large variety of goods, including sparkling jewellery, leather goods and toys, lined each side. There was also one large window in which stills for films showing at the cinema across the road flicked on a rotary arm, so that a picture would hold the onlooker's attention for several seconds before being replaced by the next one. This and the toys could sometimes occupy me for many minutes on end.

One day as I was watching the picture show for the third or fourth time round, I felt a man's face close to mine. With a start, I turned and saw this gnarled, ugly, pock-marked, hairy face with piercing eyes. I could smell the man's stale breath and felt his hand clasp my wrist in a grip of steel. I could not move and was terrified. "Listen little boy," the man rasped, spittle spraying my face. "I am going to go into that post office and I want you to wait for me here. You understand? You're not to move from this spot. And when I get back," he looked round furtively to make sure no one else was listening, "and when I get back I shall cut your throat from here (the thumb of his free hand touched my ear) to here (and it crossed along the throat to the other ear). Understand?"

The tears of fear welled up and I nodded my head. He let go of my wrist and produced a knife from the pocket of his long, smelly greatcoat. He waved the knife in front of my face and turned to stride to the post office. I was rooted to the spot. What was I to do? He had ordered me to stay there. But to have my throat cut on his return? I looked to the post office doors. There was no sign of him. I turned and looked towards the end of the hall and the exit. If I made a run for it, would he catch me? I had to take a chance and ran as fast as my legs would carry me, into the street, turned right and sprinted, panting and screaming into my parents' shop.

Customers were shocked to see this little boy in such genuine anguish. My mother rushed to me and escorted me to the store room at the back of the shop. "There's...there's a man," I blurted out between sobs, "who's going to cut my throat!" "What man? Where? Horstchen, there's no one and no one is going to cut even a single hair from your head," my mother said, hugging me and trying to calm me down. But she was perturbed. There were madmen lurking in Berlin who might well murder children. And it wasn't even anything to do with being Jewish or non-Jewish.

My father telephoned the police and then left the shop to make a search for the man with the long overcoat and pock-marked face. But he had clearly got away. The police said they had made a search. Maybe they had, but even the police, who should not be confused with the Gestapo, did not burn any midnight oil to assist Jews.

On another occasion, I had taken myself off to a pretty little park a few hundred metres south of the house in the Invalidenstrasse. It was a crisp autumn afternoon and the gold-red leaves had created a colourful carpet across the paths that criss-crossed the park from one end to the other. There was a sandpit for children and I loved to build my castles and bake sand pies. Somehow, although I was often alone there, I was never lonely.

On this occasion, I had hardly been there for more than ten minutes when I was joined by a group of eight boys and two girls One of the boys, a lad of about my age, seven or possibly eight, addressed me: "We're playing cowboys and Indians. D'you want to join us?" I was thrilled and readily accepted the offer. We split into two teams, but I seemed to be the only one chosen to be an Indian.

"Tell you what," the leader said, "you'll be the Red Indian we've just captured. So we're going to tie you to a tree. Later, we'll all be Red Indians and we'll come and rescue you."

It sounded all right to me. I didn't mind a bit when they produced a roll of strong string and bound me, hands, feet and neck to one of the slimmer trees within the thicker undergrowth of the park. "We'll be back soon," they cried as they rode away on their imaginary horses, leaving me to await my rescue. Minutes slipped away and turned into what seemed like hours. I became worried – and started to shiver from the cold. What little light there had been was now rapidly fading. I could hear a handbell being rung – the signal for the park's closure – and I started to call for help. "Help! Help me! Oh, help me, please...pleeeease!" But no one heard. No one came. I was now completely alone and very, very scared. Darkness enveloped the wood and I could hear the scrabble of animals as they came to explore their territory. I had visions of wild beasts, tigers, lions and bears coming to tear me to pieces. I could feel huge imaginary rats gnawing away at my legs. I screamed and screamed.

I was not heard and was left untouched and alone. I was unable to move. The knots the boys had tied were extremely tight and seemed to get even tighter the more I wriggled. At last, cold and weary from crying, I fell fast asleep, only to be further tortured by nightmares in which I was running away from a cluster of devils, whose cloven hooves were rapidly advancing on me, their fangs ever-closer to my face. I awoke several times, each time in an ice-cold sweat.

Meanwhile, my parents, frantic with worry, had contacted the police and a search party was organised. But where could they look? My friends had all been contacted, all safe and sound having their supper at home with their mothers and fathers. My favourite haunts, such as the rear of the post office, where I used to go and "direct traffic", beckoning the postal delivery vans as they rushed from their parking lots, and the station which, though out of bounds as a prospective place of danger to little children, still managed to lure me to its platforms to watch the steam trains coming and going. The park was totally ignored. Its gates were firmly shut and its fence too high for a little boy to climb.

It was about eight o'clock in the morning, shortly after the park had reopened, that one of the two girls arrived at my side. She produced a pair of scissors and proceeded to cut away the string that had kept me so firmly bound. "There. Now run home. You must not tell anyone that I came to free you. D'you understand? No one must know. You've got to promise," she said over and over. I was so relieved, so very happy to be alive and at liberty that I would have promised her anything. As it was, all I could do, my teeth chattering from the bitter cold, was to blurt out: "Thank you…oh, thank you so very, very much!" I ran all the way home and into the arms of my parents. Neither of them had slept that night and they were as weary and haggard as I – and, for the first time since the launch of the shop, it opened late.

Bad memories always last longer than the good ones but my childhood was by no means an unhappy one. Far from it. Oma, my lovely grandmother, came to live with us at No.33 Invalidenstrasse in 1936, and looked after me as only a Jewish grandmother can. While my own Mutti and Papa were busy working in the shop, she would sit me on her lap and tell me the most beautiful stories. She and my mother were gifted story tellers, weaving wonderful yarns about little boys and their adventures on mountains and the high seas. Their love of language must have rubbed off on me and might even have sparked off my own attraction to spoken and written words.

Oma also owned a pretty little yellow canary to whom she would speak for long periods of the day. "He understands every single word, you know Horstchen," she would say earnestly. And I believed her, for the bird would hop from rod to rod inside his cage and look Oma in the eye and chirp as he passed. "You see, Horstchen. He's answering me." "What did he say, Oma?" "He said that he is very happy to be chatting with me but please could I give him some more of those lovely seeds to eat." And she would go and fetch his seeds and pour some into his feeding bowl.

During the day, we would put the cage out on the balcony that looked down on the Invalidenstrasse "Let him see all the people and the trams. He'll enjoy that," Oma used to say. That summer was exceedingly hot. Oma had taken a trip to see friends in the country outside Berlin; my parents were in the shop; I was at school; and the canary was on the balcony. He had tried desperately to keep cool and had gone into his birdbath. But the water was practically boiling and, when I came back home from school, the poor little thing lay dead, its feet pointing up to heaven. I dissolved in tears and ran to the shop with the news.

What would Oma say? Her best friend, dead? And through our negligence! My father immediately took charge. He ran back to the apartment, took the cage into the room and the bird out and sprinted to the nearest pet shop. He put the canary on the counter. "Please have you got a canary exactly like this one? We must have it immediately." The pet shop owner understood the problem at once and produced two or three canaries. One of them was an almost perfect match. He was transported back to the house and into the cage to await Oma's return.

She strode to the cage and started her conversation. "There now, there, did you miss me?" she said soothingly. "I've brought you some nice little seeds. Here…" and she poured a few into the pot. The canary stared but did not chirp and did not fly from perch to perch. Oma could not understand it. "What is the matter with you today? Not speaking to me? If I didn't know any better, I'd think you were a stranger." Papa chipped in: "It was rather hot today, Berta, and the poor thing was outside too long and has probably caught a bit of sunstroke." This was accepted but Oma and the canary never seemed to renew their old close relationship.

My cousins Liane and Heinz often came to visit and stay over weekends and we would play for hours with my toys and board games. I did not get many toys, but once a year on my birthday, I would always be given one "super present" and lots of smaller ones from friends and family. So one year, I awoke on the 8th November, to be called into the dining room where the table was laden with my favourite foods for breakfast and a big birthday cake (to be eaten later when my friends would come for the party) and at one end of the room stood a beautiful Punch and Judy theatre. I stood and stared in wonder when two puppets would poke their wooden heads over the edge of the stage and wish me a happy birthday. It was my father who stood behind the theatre and manipulated the glove puppets. A great present that provided me with hour upon hour of make-believe and provided a foretaste of my lasting love for the theatre.

On another birthday, there was a pedal car which I would ride around the courtyard and in the park (under Oma's supervision!); and on another, there was an indoor swing with all the trimmings – rings, bars, ropes. It was fixed to the opening between the dining room and the lounge for me to perform my acrobatics.

My eighth birthday on the 8th November 1938 was comparatively disappointing. I was presented with a watch. I had always wanted a watch but, when it was given to me, I felt that it was somehow too utilitarian. I couldn't play with it. On this occasion the table was not laden with goodies, but just a few little cakes. It was all a bit down-key, almost solemn. My parents were apologetic. "This year, Horstchen, we cannot give you as good a present as we should have liked. Things are not looking very good. But we will make it up to you. Believe me," Papa said and gave me a hug. Mutti kissed me and I noticed that there were tears in her eyes. "*Na, mein braver Junge, mein Liebling*" (My brave boy, my darling) she whispered.

The next day would make me understand what they had meant.

They had kept one or two things from me. They had not told me, for instance, that in April of that year, they, along with all other Jews in Germany, had to register what wealth and property they owned. This did not just mean money and bank balances, but any valuable paintings or books or heirlooms. My father was an ardent coin collector and possessed coins from the ancient Roman era as well as from Victorian England; he had also bought some exquisite paintings, not by the Masters but by reputable painters whose names would one day become famous. These items had all to be registered. The Nazis needed to know what loot they could expect. The following month, Jews had to register their businesses. On July 15, Jewish doctors were barred from practising medicine and on August 11, the big synagogue at Nüremberg was destroyed by fire.

For Germany's Jews, life was becoming decidedly sickening.

November 9th started with a persistent ring of the doorbell. It was just after seven o'clock in the morning. Mutti went to open the door and let one of our neighbours in. Herr Schultz was a neat little man with a thick moustache and was a known member of the Nazi party, wearing the little swastika insignia in his lapel. But, for all his political gesturings, he had remained decent and friendly towards my parents and would often run his hand through my hair affectionately when we met in the street and say: "Na, how's Horst? Be good. You've got good parents."

This time, I could hear him tell my parents in almost a whisper: "I've just heard. Your shop will be done tonight, around seven. I'm so very sorry. You've not heard it from me. You've not even seen me." "Please wouldn't you like a coffee, Herr Schultz?" my mother asked. "No. No thank you, Frau Izbicki. I must go. I really am sorry." And with that he slipped out of the door and away.

My parents sat at the table with Oma, discussing their next move. "We must open the shop as usual," my father decided. "Otherwise it would look suspicious. We must act as though nothing is going to happen. But then, this afternoon, we shall start taking all stock to the back room (the store room) and finally, we shall take every article out of the window and the showcase and bring everything to the back. That way, there'll be no damage to the stock."

I had no idea what was going to happen. I could not even have imagined it. But a few minutes later, I was to realise what horror awaited us. I ran to the window when I heard a kind of choral sloganising: *Juden Raus! Juden Raus! Juden Raus!* ("Jews Out") was chanted over and over by a group of about thirty Hitler Youths armed with batons and bricks. Immediately across the road from our house was a leatherware shop called Stiller.

Their shopwindow was painted with a big white "J", because the owner was a Jew. The gang stopped in front of the shop and started to smash the window. Glass sprayed into the road. They then ransacked the leather goods still on show in the window and continued on their way, still chanting their dreadful slogan. Policemen stood a few yards away at the corner of Invalidenstrasse and Chausseestrasse. They were watching but did nothing. One of them smiled.

I looked at the broken window and trembled. Is that what was going to happen at seven tonight? Just then, an old woman, almost doubled with arthritis, hobbled along the pavement outside Stiller's shop. She went close to the window and started screaming: "Serves you right, you Jewish swine. You should all be dead. All be dead, d'you hear? Heil Hitler!" Her scream had reached a crescendo. Its pitch made one big jagged sliver of glass quiver in its putty casing. And, as she threw in an additional "Heil Hit—!" and began to move on, the glass dropped, cutting through her skull. Her salutation to the Führer stuck in her throat as she collapsed in a rapidly growing pool of blood.

I vomited. And when I had finished vomiting, I believed in God.

I did not go to school that day. Or the next. Indeed, I have no recall of having gone back to school ever again in Germany.

My parents did as they had planned. The shop was opened and some customers even came to buy. Then, in the afternoon, they started moving goods from the many shelves, cabinets and glass show counter to the store room at the back of the shop. The clock was moving fast towards the appointed hour. At about 6.30 p.m. they began to clear the window. This is a slow process, as many articles were decoratively arranged and pinned down. I had put on a pullover and a coat, for it was cold and I wanted to see what was happening from the balcony. I was scared for my parents who were alone in the shop.

Somehow, word must have got round, for the street – a busy, bustling main road – was rapidly filling with people. A large crowd had gathered. The traffic had been brought to a standstill and there was an eerie silence. People stood and stared. And waited. My parents were popular, as was the shop. They had always been friendly and helpful to their customers and their neighbouring shopkeepers. The people were making their sympathy felt – but could do nothing to prevent what was about to happen.

At 6.55p.m. a large group of Hitler Youths, accompanied by squads of SA troops, marched their way from the Stettiner Station, past the post office, to the shop and started chanting their mantra: *Juden Raus! Juden Raus!* At the same time, they flung their bricks at the shop's window. The bricks bounced back. There was laughter from the crowd and some people applauded. The Nazi hooligans grew angry and attacked the glass with their thick batons. Nothing even cracked. More applause and laughter. They had not reckoned on the thickness of the curved glass of that window.

Three of the leaders broke away and marched into the butcher's shop two doors away. "Give us your heavy weights," they demanded of the butcher, a burly bearded man of 45 with heavily tattooed arms. "What the hell for?" he wanted to know. "What d'you think? We want to smash that Yid's windows next door!" "Then you can fuck off. You're not getting my weights. Leave the poor bugger alone!" For his pains, the butcher had his head bashed by one of the batons and his glass counter smashed. And as he lay cut on his sawdust floor, the Hitler Youths dragged away his 10 kilo weights and returned to the task in hand.

This time the window gave way with a roar of splintering glass. There was a loud groan from the crowd and several whistles (German equivalent of booing). I saw some women openly weeping in that otherwise silent street and I wept with them. But my tears turned to screams when I saw the Nazi thugs picking up large splinters of glass and hurling them into the shop. I knew my parents were inside and that these deadly missiles were meant for them. They could be killed. I screamed and screamed. Oma rushed me inside and hugged me to her. "Horstchen, Horstchen, it will be all right. You'll see. Hush, hush, now" and she cradled me in her arms and rocked me like a baby. But I could feel that she, too, was frightened.

When I awoke, Mutti and Papa were standing, stroking my hot brow and rubbing my arms. They were alive and unharmed. Unharmed, that is, physically. Mentally, however, the damage would last them a lifetime.

That same day, some 7,500 Jewish businesses throughout Germany had their windows smashed and their stocks looted. The SA murdered around 100 Jews who had tried to defend themselves against the onslaught. Another 30,000 Jewish males were arrested and transported to the concentration camps of Dachau, Buchenwald and Sachsenhausen. And, as if all this was not enough, hundreds of synagogues were set on fire, their holy scrolls burned or torn into shreds, their Torahs vandalised and cemeteries desecrated.

Among the synagogues to be attacked was the one my parents and I used to attend in the nearby Oranienburgerstrasse. It was a beautiful building topped by a large golden dome. Inside, I would join Mutti and Oma upstairs where all the women had to sit, but would also slip downstairs to join Papa among the men. Although one mad Nazi arsonist set fire to the Oranienburger Tempel as it was called, a courageous policeman recognised this mindless vandalism and rushed to put out the flames. He called the fire brigade and ordered the rest of the fire to be extinguished. His bravery has never been properly recognised.

Many years later, when the synagogue was rebuilt and reopened as a museum, I attended its launch. In the entrance hall stood a large glass-covered photograph of men at prayer in the old Tempel. I produced my camera to photograph the picture when to my amazement I saw a ghost. There in the third row of the worshipers stood my father. It was, to say the least, an emotional moment.

But back to November 1938. The Nazis, not satisfied with their vandalism, plunder and murder, blamed the entire episode on the Jews themselves and demanded payment for the damage caused. They cashed in one billion

Reichsmarks (about £200 million in 1938 money) from Jewish pockets. To this day I still possess the receipt my father was given for paying 2,000 Reichsmarks *Judenbusse* (literally, a fine for being a Jew).

My screaming had damaged my vocal chords and I was unable to speak for many days. My father took me to the Jewish hospital, where they looked into my throat and found the chords covered in papiloma, knots formed from overstraining the voice. They decided to operate. But most of the experienced doctors had already left the country. They had been barred from practising medicine anywhere other than at the few Jewish clinics and hospitals that were dotted about the country. The ones that were left were not exactly quality surgeons. Instead of curing my condition, they made it worse.

My father was advised to take me to Professor Dr Carl von Eicken, Berlin's eminent ear, nose and throat specialist. It was a risk. But the professor saw us and even called in a number of his students to see my throat. He carefully picked out several of the papilomae. "This is most interesting. Most interesting. How long will you be here, Herr Izbicki?" My father replied that we were shortly going to emigrate to Palestine. "Good. Good. I'll give you the name of a colleague over there, in Tel Aviv. He's the man for this. He'll be able to help your boy." And he wrote down the Jewish doctor's name and address. "You realise that the only other person who has suffered from this vocal chord condition was Adolf Hitler. He got it from over-shouting his speeches. And I, so help me, operated on him in 1935 and gave him back his voice."

My father thanked him and took out his wallet. But the professor pushed it away. "No, my dear Sir. Please don't pay me. You people have paid quite enough already."

Thank God there were still many people like him in Germany. But there weren't enough and it was time to be rational. Oma, for her own safety, was moved to a Jewish old age home where we visited her every weekend. Meanwhile, my father had already applied for visas from the United States and the United Kingdom as well as for an entry permit to Palestine. Although many German Jews still believed that "there must be some mistake, which will surely be put right soon…" many others decided to call it a day and get out while it was still possible to do so. One needed a great deal of patience.

Meanwhile, however, Papa went into hiding, spending days and nights in the ruins of burned out synagogues and returning home only to have a shower and change his clothes.

The reason? Almost every day the Gestapo would come to our apartment and ask to see him. And every time Mutti told them that they were unlucky, that he wasn't in. "You've just missed him. He was here until a few minutes ago but has had to go out on business. I'm not sure what time he'll be back." That would normally be that.

There was a day when a neighbour, Dr Löwenstein, paid us a visit. Like Papa, he was also in hiding and had come home for a change of shirt. He joined Mutti for a cup of ersatz coffee and an exchange of news. He was a widower and no longer saw many people. He wasn't allowed to treat patients any more, so felt lonely and depressed. While he was in the apartment, the doorbell rang followed by insistent knocking. It meant only one thing – the Gestapo. Mutti took immediate control. She ordered Dr Löwenstein to get under a small coffee table and threw a large cloth over it, hiding the man below. "Horst, sit on the table, hurry," she commanded and cleared the coffee cups, taking them rapidly to the kitchen on the way to opening the front door.

"Frau Izbicki, Heil Hitler," the officer said. "Good morning, Herr Officer," responded my mother calmly. "Herr Izbicki? Is he in this time?" "I'm so sorry, you're out of luck again. He has just left." "Well," said the Gestapo officer with a slight smile, "you won't mind if I come and take a quick look?" And he stepped past her and marched into the lounge where I was sitting, legs crossed, on the coffee table. As he approached, I got up. It was, after all, the proper thing to do. "So, my boy," the officer said, taking my chin in his hand and squeezing it. "Is your Papi in?" "No, Sir, he's not here. He has left on business," I replied, feeling myself blush with embarrassment and pain for his fingers were hurting me. Beneath the table, a fully grown man in his fifties, was cowering like a dog, not even daring to breathe or scratch the itch that was troubling his nose.

The Gestapo seemed satisfied and, after a glance into the dining room and kitchen, he turned to the door and, with another "Heil Hitler", marched out.

Dr Löwenstein crawled out from under the table, the sweat pouring from his face and tears from his eyes. "Thank you, Horst. You're a good boy." And he slipped me five marks. I shrank away. "No, no, really Herr Doctor, that is not necessary," I exclaimed with all the authority of an eight-year-old. My mother backed me. "No, Dr Löwenstein. Horstchen is right. There cannot be any payment for an act of humanity. Wait a few more minutes, then go in peace. May the good Lord preserve us all."

Two days after that incident, there was another that I shall never forget. Whenever Papa came home, I would have to stand on the balcony and keep a watch for the arrival of the Gestapo. This had actually happened a couple of times and Papa would then leave the apartment and climb the stairs to an upper floor and wait until the coast was clear. On this occasion, I had fallen down on my duty. I had watched from the balcony but then, as my father was ready to leave, I ran in to kiss him goodbye and be hugged by him.

This little ritual had obviously taken longer than usual for when Papa left and was proceeding down the stairs, he came face to face with the Gestapo officer. Both stopped and stared at each other. "Heil Hitler, Herr Izbicki," the officer mouthed, then added: "What the hell are you doing here?" My father stammered his reply: "I – I was just leaving. I – I must make a number of – of visits…business visits, Herr Officer." The Gestapo officer looked at Papa, then looked up and down the stairs to see whether anyone else might be within hearing. "I've not seen you. Now fuck off. And for God's sake, get out of the country while you still can!"

My father stuttered his thanks and ran the rest of the way down the stairs and out of the house, while the Gestapo officer continued up to our apartment, rang the bell and knocked his threatening knock, to be told by Mutti: "You've just missed him…"

Even the Gestapo possessed the odd human being.

While my father continued the cat-and-mouse game, hiding himself under the ruins of synagogues, my mother was left to take care of me and look after what little remained of the business. The Chamber of Commerce was now sending "interested parties" to look at the shop and make "offers". Several such offers were received and these would be discussed by my parents, when Papa was home for those short periods. There were also times when he would go to the old age home to see Oma and Mutti and I would meet him there.

The so-called offers were, of course ludicrously low, but one of them, the best of a bad lot, had to be accepted before December 3. From that day, all Jewish businesses became "Aryanised", taken over by full-blooded Germans, many of them Nazi party members. What little we received for the shop and all its stock was further taxed. The result was not even worth banking, but at least we were all alive and still at liberty. Hermann Göring was put in charge of "The Jewish Question" and made sure that his own pockets would be lined with Jewish savings and treasures.

Around February, 1939, all items made of silver or gold had to be surrendered to Göring's Ministry. Anyone who was caught hiding some treasured piece of jewellery was immediately arrested and sent to a camp. Wedding and signet rings were allowed to be kept. My father, even at that highly critical and dangerous time, decided to take a risk. His coin collection contained a number of English gold sovereigns and half sovereigns. These he took to a friendly jeweller who melted them all down and turned the resulting lump of gold into a large signet ring. It was heavy and the only article of value that came out of Germany with us. It was to be kept for "a rainy day".

Even in England, where it rained a great deal, the ring was never sold. It is with me to this day and will be passed on to my son and, I hope, by him to his son in memory of a period that showed man's inhumanity to man. A memorial to a period that should never be repeated.

CHAPTER TWO:

ESCAPE

S ometimes waiting for a visa is like that proverbial wait for a bus. You can stand for hours and hours, then suddenly three turn up. So it was with our visas. The first to surface was one for the United States. It had certainly been my parents' first choice so they were overjoyed when it popped through the letter box in December 1938, a month after *Kristallnacht*, which became known throughout the world as "the night of broken glass".

"We're saved, Selma, we're saved," Papa shouted as he opened the envelope and Mutti gave me the biggest hug I had had in years and we all started to cry, but for once they were tears of joy and sheer relief. Even I could by that time, at the mature age of eight, understand why living in Germany was no longer considered fun. My school had closed; the shop had been all but destroyed; I could only see my father for short periods; my darling Oma was living in an old age home that we could only visit occasionally; my friends, especially my cousins, Liane and Heini, did not visit us any more, having to deal with their own problems; my voice could hardly make itself heard through painful hoarseness; I could no longer go and play outside as it wasn't safe… Things just weren't the same any more.

Papa booked us flights to New York. We would leave Tempelhof Airport on September 1, 1939. There was still plenty of time to arrange all the packing and say our goodbyes. But it is strange how fast time flies when a deadline beckons.

In March, Hitler marched into Czechoslovakia. Papa was furious. "There you see, I was right. That bastard has broken his own agreement with the

British. I said at the time that Chamberlain should not trust this Nazi bastard."

He was referring to an occasion the previous September, less than two months before the Nazis smashed Jewish shops and burned down their synagogues. Neville Chamberlain, the British prime minister, had flown to Munich to meet with Hitler, Benito Mussolini, the Italian Fascist dictator and Edouard Daladier, the French premier, to sign an act of appeasement that became known as the Munich Agreement. It presented the German-speaking Sudetenland on a plate to Hitler on the understanding that he would not touch Czechoslovakia or Poland.

On that occasion, Papa and my uncle Georg were deep in conversation. "How can a man like Chamberlain come over to Germany? He is the leader of Great Britain. *Great* Britain, with its huge empire and a well-fed, happy people who defeated Germany in the 14-18 War...It is unheard of for such a man to come crawling to a shit like Hitler. What can he be thinking of? Does he realise what's going on here? Has he not heard of the concentration camps? Does he really believe that Adolf Hitler is anything other than an asshole?"

At the time of Munich, Eduard Benes, the Czechoslovak president, had not been invited to join the Hitler-Chamberlain-Mussolini round table talks and protested the moment the agreement was signed. But Chamberlain had told him in a curt message that Britain was not prepared to go to war over the Sudetenland and that Hitler would keep to the agreement. After Chamberlain's return to London, when he marched from his plane waving his little piece of worthless paper bearing Hitler's less-than-worthless signature, he came under attack from both Anthony Eden and Winston Churchill. Neither of them trusted the Führer and both felt that Chamberlain had acted dishonourably towards Czechoslovakia.

The invasion of Czechoslovakia hammered another nail into the coffin of European Jewry. Czech Jews were now being rounded up and sent to camps along with German Jews. And notice went out that, from September 1, 1939 – the day of our intended departure to the USA — Jews could not even leave their homes to go for walks in the street after 8 p.m.

In July, it was Oma's 70th birthday and we went to the home to celebrate it. Everyone had gathered – Mutti's brothers, Georg, Karl and Isi, and sister Hedwig (Heti), Uncle Benno, her husband, cousin Heini, their son, my aunt Maria (Isi's wife) and my cousin, Liane, their daughter, Georg's lady friend, Lonni, various other members of Oma's relations, Hertha and Ernst Lewandowski, who was a cantor with a magnificent baritone voice that could shatter glasses and a few hearts, and Flora Katz, Oma's sister and Hertha's mother. A big cake complete with candles had been baked at home and there

Grandmother Bertha's 70th birthday, Berlin, summer 1939.
Pictured L - R (front row): Horst, aged 8, Grandma Bertha, Aunt Hetwig, Uncle Benno;
(back row): Father, Mutti, Aunt Maria Alexander, Uncle Georg.

(*Note: Bertha died of starvation, Theresienstadt concentration camp; Georg, mother's youngest brother, murdered at Auschwitz; Aunt Maria, survived because she was a Roman Catholic; her husband Isidor, mother's oldest brother, who took the picture, died of poisoning, probably self-inflicted; Hetwig, mother's sister, and husband Benno, both murdered at Auschwitz; Father, Mother and Horst saved by Britain*)

was even a bottle of Sekt which was sparingly consumed as well as coffee and soft drinks for us children.

It was a beautiful day, filled with sunshine and a garden of flowers. Oma was presented with a large bouquet of red roses and presents of scarves and stockings and perfumes. A photograph was taken in the garden of the group, all smiling to fit the happy occasion.

It was to be the last time I was to see Oma smile. The next time we visited was to say goodbye.

"As soon as we are in America, we shall send for you," Papa told Oma. "We shall try to get everyone out," Mutti said and added: "Don't worry. We shall be all right and you will all come to join us in New York."

We waved goodbye to each other and cried all the way home.

Papa had booked the flights and the packing was in full swing. Several crates had already been sent for safe keeping to Asher, Papa's brother in Palestine. Asher had been one of the true pioneers and had walked all the way from Poland to Turkey from where he hitched a lift on a cargo boat to Haifa.

He arrived there with one change of clothes and two pairs of shorts, joined a Kibbutz and spent his days digging the desert to help make it bloom and the nights dancing the Hora around a camp fire. The crates went at the time Papa still thought we might be going to the Promised Land. But the American visa was the first to appear.

Then, after tickets had been bought and seats reserved, the Palestinian permit arrived, followed close at heel by the visa from the British foreign office. Asher had helped this along by depositing the necessary £1,000 with the Bank of England as a guarantee that we would not be a burden to the British state.

Still, we were all happy with the prospect of life in America and my parents settled down every evening to study English. They had bought a course *Tausend Worte Englisch* (One Thousand Words English), which comprised a set of ten colourful booklets assembled in an even more colourful cardboard box. It provided grammar and vocabulary and they both struggled their way through it, page by page, testing each other and laughing at the dreadful pronunciations. Someone had told them that, to speak English properly, especially with an American accent, they should put a hot potato in their mouths. They pretended to have the potato and laughed even more.

The almost daily visits by the Gestapo had ceased some time ago. Had they given up? Or was this some kind of lull before a storm? Each day, Papa would hear of more arrests but he would also hear of many more who had managed to get out. By 1938, some 38,000 had left Germany to go to France, Holland or Belgium. By September 1939, when we were due to leave, 95,000 had flown to the United States, 60,000 had reached Palestine and 40,000 Great Britain. By the end of that year, 202,000 Jews remained stuck in Germany and a further 57,000 in Austria (in 1933 a total of 523,000 Jews, less than one per cent of the German population, had lived in Germany, one third of them in Berlin).

Even children (a total of about 10,000) were sent away by their parents on something called a *Kindertransport*, trains that would take them, complete with labels tied from their necks, out of the country to England. Would my parents send me away like some parcel to an unknown destination? The thought worried me and I would cry myself to sleep at night.

One day I plucked up the courage to ask Mutti: "Will you send me on a train with other children?" She looked at me in shocked surprise. "Why do you ask? Do you want us to send you away?" "No! No! No!" I cried, bursting into tears. Mutti clutched me closely to her and stroked my hair: "Oh, *mein liebling Hortschen*…How can you even think that we would let you go anywhere without us? Parents who have done this haven't got any visas and cannot leave the country, so they are saving their children. They are making such terrible sacrifices. But with us it is different. We have visas and we are going to America – all three of us together. You will see that we shall have a wonderful life over there where people are free and no one will ever make our lives a hell because we are Jewish. So don't cry. Don't cry." But I noticed that she, herself, was weeping.

September was rapidly drawing near. Soon it would be time to leave. On the appointed day, September 1, we got up early and prepared to leave. Suitcases stood ready packed, just waiting to be taken downstairs to a waiting taxi, ordered to transport us to Tempelhof. No one said anything. We dressed in total silence.

Papa had turned the wireless on to hear the news – an automatic reflex action that had been repeated every morning for many years. The announcer, in brisk, guttural tones, told us that all our plans lay shattered.

"Polish troops have invaded the German Reich in an act of total aggression. The Führer, in a statement early this morning, said that our troops would fight to the last drop of blood." The voice droned on an on. Then it stated: "All air transport into and out of Germany has been halted."

We were trapped. Visa and tickets were useless. My parents could hardly speak. What was there to say? Was God willing us to stay? "We still have our British visa," Papa exclaimed. "I shall go back to the travel agency and get the tickets changed." And he ran out of the house while Mutti and I sat down and waited.

Papa ran all the way to the agency which had only just opened its doors. He was the first customer. "Please you must help me," he blurted out to the assistant. "Flights have been stopped because of Poland's war on the Reich. Please, here are the tickets you sold me some weeks ago. Would you please refund the money and I shall buy new tickets – this time to England."

The assistant told my father to wait and went into a back room, presumably to speak to his superior. A squat little man with a moustache and a Nazi membership badge in his lapel came to the counter and looked my father up and down. "This cannot be done. Your request is denied. You can't just come here and juggle with our bookings and tickets. It is typical of you Jews. You think you can just play with us, eh?"

"No, no, of course not, *mein Herr*, I have no wish to play with you or the tickets or offend you in any way. But the flights have had to be cancelled because Germany is now at war. Have you not heard the news? I simply want to provide you with alternative business and am simply asking for tickets to England. Two-and-a-half tickets by train and boat, please."

The squat man stroked his moustache as he thought this through. "Right, I'll tell you what I am prepared to do – and I am already proposing far more than I should, you understand. I shall take back these flight tickets and I shall issue two-and-a-half boat tickets to Great Britain. There will, however, be no refund. On the contrary, you will have to pay a further 100 *Reichsmarks* for the inconvenience you have caused us with this additional administration."

There was no alternative but to pay up, clutch the tickets and run back home.

Train times were checked and, as dusk fell, we made our way on foot to the Stettiner Bahnhof. We had to reach the station and catch our train before the curfew. As we walked, the air raid siren wailed an alarm. We were supposed to get off the street into shops or houses to await the all clear. Instead, we ran the last 200 or so metres and managed to enter the station – and await a train to Cologne.

The suitcases that had been packed for New York were left abandoned at our deserted home. Each of us carried just one suitcase (I had a small one and my school satchel on my back). We just wanted to get out of Berlin, out of Germany, where we were not wanted.

I slept most of the way to Cologne and, apart from a ticket collector, there were no inspections. So far, so good.

The train, which continued its way to Holland, was slowing down and came to a grinding halt. I looked out of the window and saw a long stretch of green fields. But from the window to the other side of the compartment door I could see a wooden platform on which stood a large group of green uniformed police and a smaller party of dreaded Gestapo officers. They started to mount the train and enter compartments, rasping out their orders. Would they come to us? I grew scared and clung to Mutti.

"Now Horst," my father said quietly. "They will be coming to see our papers. If they ask you any question – any question at all – remain polite and say you don't know. D'you understand? Mutti and I will answer any questions they have to ask, but you will say nothing. Yes?" I nodded and clung still closer to Mutti.

I heard doors slam and, from a distance, I could make out people crying, and some children screaming. I felt my heart pounding. Everyone must be able to hear my heart pounding. I looked out of the window and saw people lined up on the embankment that bordered the green fields. They had been pushed out of the doors of the train and their luggage had been thrown out after them. There they now stood, huddled together, pale and shaking with the cold and fear.

Suddenly our compartment's sliding door slammed open and there stood a policeman and a Gestapo officer. "Heil Hitler!", both shouted and saluted. "Papers!" My father already had our documents ready, along with the British visa. "Here, please," he said quietly and handed them over to the policeman. The Gestapo officer looked at our few cases up on the rack, and pointed to the largest of them. "This one. Open. Quick, quick, we haven't all day!" My father lifted down the suitcase and fumbled with the key.

When it was opened, the Gestapo rummaged through its contents, spilling women's underwear, socks and a suit onto the floor. He went through each pocket of the suit. Apart from a handkerchief, he found nothing.

Meanwhile, the police officer had stamped our identity papers and waited for the Gestapo to finish his inspection of our luggage. "Right. You can pack it," he said before snatching the papers from the police. He looked at each closely, then put his face down close to mine. "So, little boy, what's your name," he said gently. Was I to answer? Papa had told me not to answer, just to remain polite. "Na, Horst, answer the nice gentleman. Give him your name," my father said. "Horst," I said. "Horst Izbicki".

"Yes, Horst Israel Izbicki, isn't it?"

"Yes, Sir," I said.

"Well, Horst, tell me, have your parents packed any nice things to take away from Germany?"

I looked at my father for advice but the Gestapo pulled my chin back so that I would once again be facing him. "I – I don't know, Sir."

"What do you mean, you don't know. You must have seen what has been packed. Come now, Horst, you can tell me."

"I'm very sorry, Sir," I replied. "But I really do not know. I have left all my toys at home." I could feel my eyes starting to burn, the tears ready to pour from them.

He looked at me hard for a while, then rose, handed the papers back to my father, gave the Nazi salute and, with another "Heil Hitler!" stamped out of the compartment, followed by the policeman.

My parents repacked the suitcase in silence and put it back on the rack. "Are we going now?" I asked.

"Quiet, Horst. Quiet. Just sit quietly and wait," my father said and Mutti sat down beside me and put her arm round my shoulders.

We waited for what seemed hours. The line of Jews on the embankment did not rejoin the train. After more guttural orders rasped by Gestapo officers, they were marched away and loaded into lorries that had suddenly appeared at the end of the wooden platform.

"Those poor people," Mutti whispered through her tears. "What could they possibly have done?"

"Their papers can't have been in order. Or perhaps they were trying to smuggle something. You can be sure there must have been some crime committed," my father said. He still believed that Germans would only arrest people who had broken the law. As if to prove his point, he added: "We have not done anything wrong and our papers are in order. That's why they have not taken us off the train."

But we were still not certain and continued to speak in whispers. After further door slamming, there was a shrill whistle and the train started to move on. We sat close together, still refusing to believe that it was all over.

It wasn't. Not many metres further, the train stopped once again and there was more slamming of doors and the stamp of approaching boots. What had they come back for? We sat there holding hands, not daring to voice our fears.

Our door slid open and there stood a police officer. But the colour of his uniform was grey, not green. And his hat was a different shape. He saluted. But it was not the Nazi salute, just an ordinary hand raised to the peak of his hat. And he did not say "Heil Hitler". Instead, he said in quiet German: "Good morning. May I see your papers, please?"

My father gave him our documents, which he studied for a few moments, then stamped them and handed them back with a smile. "Welcome to the Netherlands," he said, saluting once again and closing the door behind him.

After he had gone, all three of us burst into tears. But they were tears of joy and relief.

Now it was really over. We had escaped.

The ferry from Flushing was packed and set sail for Harwich at about 9 p.m. on September 2, 1939. For a child still two months from his ninth birthday, it was all very exciting. Although I had been taken on one or two Rhine river cruises during holidays, when Jews were still permitted on such small boats, I had never before been on a big ship on the high seas. It was choppy to say the least, but I was too thrilled to notice the roll. We ate some sandwiches after the ship had been sailing for about three hours. I had a little sleep but was awakened by the noise of people running and shouting.

I followed the runners out onto the deck. There was a moon and the sea was reasonably calm. When I reached the rail and stood on tiptoe, I could see what all the commotion was about. There, silhouetted against the horizon, were many ships. It looked like hundreds. Big ships. Someone said they were destroyers. Someone else chipped in with: "It's the entire British Navy. Good

God in Heaven, the entire Navy!"

What were they doing, these ships? And why were we not moving?

True, our ferry had come to a halt, here in the middle of the ocean. I could feel the roll now, but it was gentle. My father was by my side. "Come inside, Horstchen. You mustn't catch cold," he said and took me by the arm.

"What are all those ships, those destroyers, doing Papa?"

"I don't know, but it looks like they might be ready for a war. Perhaps they will fight against Hitler and we shall soon be able to go back to Berlin and live in peace again."

"But I want to go to England, Papa. I don't want to go back to Berlin. Things were not very nice there," I said hoarsely.

Once we were away from the deck and back in the warmth, we heard why the ship had stopped. An officer came to explain and was immediately surrounded by a crowd of men and women, all eager to learn the reason for the delay.

"The captain has been on the ship to shore telephone for the past half hour," the young Dutch officer said in almost perfect German. "The British immigration people are reluctant to allow us to dock. There is an emergency about which I cannot tell you anything. But a German boat which arrived at about this same point a couple of hours ago has been sent back. We are trying our best but can make no promises. It's entirely up to the British authorities."

And so we had to sit and wait…and pray that we would not be sent back to Germany. It would mean certain arrest, possibly even death. We had heard of people disappearing from their homes in the middle of the night and being transported to a "KZ", a concentration camp, never to return. Relatives spoke of them having been killed. It was only a rumour but such rumours were believed.

At about four o'clock, there was an announcement over a loudspeaker. "Good morning ladies and gentlemen," the voice said in German and later repeated it in English. "This is your captain speaking. I am deeply sorry that you have had this long delay and know how unhappy this must have made you all feel. I have been in long discussions with the British immigration authorities and they have at last agreed to let us enter Harwich."

There was a loud and prolonged cheer from everyone on the ship and people hugged each other, whether they were strangers or not. Many wept openly.

"The reason…" the captain continued over the cheering…"the reason in the end was that we are a Dutch ship. Had we been a German ferry, we should certainly have been turned back, as was the case of a previous ship that tried to enter Harwich. The many battleships that you might have seen from the decks are sections of the Royal British Navy. They are prepared to defend the British Isles against any possible attack from Nazi Germany. I am no politician, but I shall go as far as to say that Hitler would be very foolish to attempt to do to this great nation what he has done to Czechoslovakia and is now doing to Poland."

There was more cheering. The ship was already moving forward and soon we entered the port of Harwich. We had arrived at our new home. It was overwhelmingly exciting – and also very frightening, for none of us knew what awaited us, where we would live, *how* we would live and what we would live on. We had almost no money, very few clothes and no precious possessions except my father's heavy gold signet ring and my parents' wedding rings, a necklace or two, a watch each and a decent Leica camera, of which Papa was very proud.

We were immediately introduced to something very British – the queue. Everyone had to be interviewed by immigration officers and have their passports and papers stamped. At last it was our turn and the three of us carried our suitcases to the desk behind which sat a man of about my father's age. He wore glasses, a small moustache and a huge smile.

"Your passports, please," he said in English.

My father handed him our various documents but said: "Please, we not speaking English. I speaking German, Polnish, Russisch…"

"All right," the immigration officer said with a smile and holding up his hand in mock protest. "I shall try my German." And he did. It was quite good. He asked us how long we were hoping to stay and we explained that we were refugees. "Ah, *Flüchtlinge*. So, all right." He looked at the visa and again at our passports and asked us whether we had anything to declare. My father said that we had nothing except our bits and pieces of jewellery and a camera.

"May I see the camera?" the officer asked and my father opened the suitcase in which he had packed the little 35 mm joy of his life. He was a keen photographer.

"Hm, I'm sorry but I shall have to confiscate that," said the officer. "Don't worry, it won't be lost but kept safely and returned to you at a later date. I shall give you a proper receipt." This he did. After all the other losses, this additional loss was almost gladly accepted by my parents.

Some six years later, after my parents had totally forgotten the camera, my father received a letter from Customs and Excise, to say that a Leica camera, believed to be his, could be collected from the Manchester Excise office. It had remained in perfect condition and is still in my possession.

The immigration officer continued his questioning. "What is your nationality? Are you German?"

"No!" my father exclaimed. "We are *staatenlos* (stateless)," he said.

"Stateless? Stateless? We don't have that over here. No such thing. Dear me, stateless. Well, Mr Izbicki, where were you born?"

"I was born in Lenczyca, which is in Poland but, at the time of my birth, belonged to Russia."

"Russia, eh? So that makes you Russian." And he wrote it down on the form and stamped it before handing it to my father, who took it as in a daze. "Thank you," he said in German and in English and shook the officer's hands warmly.

"Good luck," the officer said and waved to the next people in the queue. The interview was over and we moved towards the waiting train.

We were in Great Britain. It was official. And we were Russian. Suddenly, within a few minutes and one rubber stamp, we were no longer stateless but Russian. That immigration officer had no idea of the favour he had bestowed upon us.

Unlike the many thousands of German Jewish refugees, we were not interned to the Isle of Man during the 1939-45 war. We were not "enemy aliens" and, as long as we informed the local police of our movements, could travel around the country.

And so it was that my father, mother and I were among the comparatively few refugees to have received a visa to enter the United Kingdom. Between May 1938 and March 1939, the British Foreign Office had issued a total of 45,566 such life-saving visas – a slight surplus to the laid-down quota. Ours was just one of them.

Six hours after we had arrived at Harwich, Mr Chamberlain broadcast to the nation and announced that Britain was at war with Germany.

CHAPTER THREE:

A NEW LIFE

Another train. This time, a British train with upholstered, comfortable seats into which I sank and immediately fell asleep. Outside it was still dark so I could not have seen the beautiful English countryside even if I had kept awake. My sleep was so deep that it was not even interrupted by dreams. The next thing I knew was someone gently shaking my shoulders until I opened my eyes.

"Come, Horstchen, it is time to leave the train." It was Mutti, who made sure that my coat was pulled right up so the collar almost touched my nose. "It is cold outside, so I must wrap you up like a cuddly little doll. Come now, Horstchen, my darling."

The platform of Liverpool Street Station was heaving with a mass of babbling men, women and children, all strangers in a strange land, heaving suitcases and bulging cardboard boxes containing their precious belongings. We just had the three suitcases and my school satchel. Papa carried the biggest of the three, a heavy, light brown leather case; Mutti heaved the middle-sized case, also brown, up to her left shoulder and held my left hand tightly; I carried the small case, which, due mainly to my tiredness, now seemed very heavy, and bent down slightly under the weight of the satchel on my shoulders.

"*Achtung, Achtung!*" A loudspeaker had sprung into action and we stiffened momentarily with fear on hearing guttural German being shouted at us once again. The woman's voice on the loudspeaker continued in German: "Welcome to Great Britain. Please make your way as quickly as possible to the centre of the station, opposite the platform of your arrival where you will

[35]

be met by members of the Jewish Refugee Committee and allocated to coaches that will transport you to your various hotels…*Achtung, Achtung!*" The voice on the loudspeaker repeated the same message over and over again.

The *Jewish Refugee Committee*! Was such an organisation possible? Here was freedom indeed. On an English railway station, the word "Jewish" could be spoken for all to hear in a manner that did not immediately induce antagonism on the part of the speaker and fear in the Jew to whom it might have been addressed.

There, indeed, in the middle of the freezing station stood a dozen or so young men and women who wore armbands with the letters J R C boldly emblazoned on them. How different from those red, white and black armbands we had left behind in Germany, bearing the dreaded swastika.

Our names were on a list and were ticked off by the German-speaking JRC guide. We were on a list. We existed! "Please go to bus Number Three – Number Three. D'you understand?" "Yes, thank you. Thank you so very much," my father said, his voice shaking with emotion. We joined the others who had also received their bus numbers and made our way, half walking, half running to the station forecourt where six or seven coaches stood, their engines already running.

"There…there…over there! Number Three. That's our bus. Hurry. It might leave without us." Papa quickened his pace and Mutti and I stumbled after him. The bus was warm and the seats were so luxurious. Never had I sat in a more comfortable seat Mutti and I sat together. Papa sat in front, next to an elderly man who was quietly crying. I looked up at Mutti and found that she, too, was wiping the tears from her eyes. Why was everyone crying? Should we not be laughing with happiness?

When the coach was full, the driver shut the doors and drove off through the early gloom of the City of London. It was a Sunday and the streets were almost empty. The coach lurched past St Paul's and down Ludgate Hill to Fleet Street. At that time, none of these names meant anything to me. Little did I then know that one day I would come back to Fleet Street and join one of the country's greatest newspapers.

On went the bus, down towards the Aldwych and past the Courts of Justice. Everything looked very beautiful in the early morning sunlight. We turned right at Holborn and drove along Southampton Row to Bloomsbury, stopping at last outside the Bloomsbury Hotel. "Right," said the driver – in English, which only a few of his passengers appeared to understand. "Right, this is as far as we go, ladies and gents." Then, as he grasped that he was not being understood by more than three or four people, he spoke more slowly and mimed: "Every-body – must – now – git – orf - the – bus – 'cause – we – 'ave – arrived – at – your – 'otel – savvy?"

We all smiled and started to leave. Papa shook the driver's hand and helped Mutti and me off the steps. Hotel porters were already lifting the luggage from the coach and lining it up on the pavement from where we retrieved our suitcases and entered the warmth of the hotel. There was a queue which we joined in front of the reception desk. After the queue at Harwich, it was the first proper queue we experienced in England – the first of very many we were to encounter. My father would always praise the British queuing system. "It is a sign of good order and discipline without it being autocratic," he would say. "It is one of the best things British society has invented."

We were given a lovely room with three beds – a double for Papa and Mutti and a single for me. We got undressed and fell into our beds with hardly a word being spoken. Sleep came quickly – but it did not last long. We were woken up by a familiar sound – a sound that we had last heard as we had made our way in blackout from our home in the Invalidenstrasse to the station on our hurried departure from Berlin. It was the wail of an air raid siren. As with the one in Berlin, the alarm in London was just a practice run.

While we slept, Mr Neville Chamberlain, the prime minister, had broadcast to the nation. Great Britain had declared war on Germany.

We only discovered this when we made our way downstairs. It was too late for breakfast but the hotel served us coffee in the lounge and gave me some biscuits and a glass of milk. There was great elation among the other guests, all refugees. "Have you heard? England has declared war on Germany! Now we shall see what will happen to that bastard's Thousand Year Reich!" Thus, a man with a little greying beard who sweated into his spectacles. Others readily agreed. "It can't last more than a few weeks," one woman ventured. "Then we'll all be able to go back and pick up our lives and be reunited with all our loved ones. That swine Hitler won't know what has hit him once the British take Berlin!" There was a chorus of "hear-hear".

Of one thing everyone was certain: Great Britain, the mother of such a vast empire, would soon make mincemeat of Adolf and his insufferable gang of murderers. Hitler was cursed with every gruesome name people could bring to their lips, names they could only pronounce in their minds but never so much as whisper out loud in public back in Nazi Germany. He was described as a "shit-eating asshole", a "decomposing lunatic" and a "beady-eyed pig". My parents, always so keen to protect me from foul language while we lived in Berlin, didn't even attempt to put their hands across my ears on this occasion but joined in the general merriment.

One thing was clear. We could not have timed our departure from Germany and our arrival in Britain any better. We had just made it. For that, we thanked God and the King of England.

We stayed at the Bloomsbury Hotel for just over a week, paid for by the Jewish Refugee Committee. We had very little money but Papa was too proud to accept charity. He was determined to find himself a job and lodgings for Mutti and me. And so he made his way to the East End of London, the only place he could think of where he might make himself understood. The East End was known as the Jewish ghetto. Its residents would speak Yiddish, which bears a close resemblance to German. German Jews had always refused to learn to speak or even understand Yiddish. They considered themselves to be first and second as Germans and only third as Jews and considered Yiddish as the language of East European *nebbichdicks*, paupers to be pitied. But needs must. In any case, Papa had relatives somewhere in the East End. He would seek them out. Maybe they could help.

But first, he would look for somewhere to live. He would not appear before relations like a down-and-out beggar. Off Brick Lane, where the crumbling houses huddled side by side, kneeling towards their identical terraces across a narrow road, he found a single furnished room up one flight of stairs for half a crown a week. There was gas lighting and a rusty gas cooker in the corner, fed by a meter that took pennies and sixpences. A sagging double bed was the room's centre piece and there was an occasional table bearing a porcelain jug and bowl and a small sink whose single cold water tap dripped incessantly.

It was to this miserable room that we made our way by public transport late one afternoon, lugging our suitcases with us. When we arrived, it was already evening and the street seemed to be alive with women of varying sizes who sat on stools and chairs outside their front doors gossiping with their neighbours on both sides of the road. The first Yiddish word I ever learned was *yachnying* – gossiping. I thought they were speaking English. But Papa corrected me. "That's Yiddish, Horst. Can you not make out some of the words as German?" It was difficult, but when I listened very, very closely, I managed to make out the odd word.

Our arrival created immediate interest. We were obviously foreigners. We were too well dressed to be East Enders. Yet what the hell were we doing in *their* street going up the stairs of one of *their* houses to a room that was… well, that probably wasn't suitable?

Their thoughts were accurate. The room was small, but it was a room, and we started to get undressed. By now darkness had fallen. There were no curtains, so we could not light the gas lamp. All we had was a small torch containing a Number 8 battery. This we now switched on for short periods of time, enough to look round for somewhere to put our clothes.

From below, we could hear the voices of the *yachnying* women saying in Yinglish (a mixture of Yiddish and English): "What are they doing? They're putting on the light; they're putting off the light. They're supposed to have blackout on the windows. Oy, what people are they? And did you see the little boy with them? A *nebbichdicker bocher* (a pitiful lad)."

By now Mutti had put on her nightdress and had gone to the bed, torch in hand. She pulled back the sheets, lit the torch and let out a piercing scream. "Oh no, never! I'm not sleeping in that bed and nor are you, Hans and Horstchen. Never!"

We rushed to her side and looked at the bed. It was alive with bugs.

Never have three people got dressed as quickly as we did that night. We grabbed our suitcases and almost ran down the stairs and into the street. Under the bewildered stares of our short-lived neighbours, we walked briskly away towards Aldgate and hailed a taxi. It was the first taxi we were to take in our new country. Mutti started to argue with Papa that we could not afford such an extravagance. "Selma, be quiet. We can't afford it. That's true, but I cannot see us all going by the tube with all these cases again. The boy needs his sleep and a taxi is the quickest way he'll get to a bed."

"But where are we going, Hans?" The taxi driver was waiting for instructions. "Pliss, vee going nach ze Bloomsbury Hotel," Papa told the driver in the best English he could muster. When we arrived and paid off the taxi, we went quietly into the hotel. To our luck there was no one at the reception desk and no porter or waiter within sight. So we climbed the carpeted stairs on tiptoe, carrying our cases so that they would not bump against the steps and made our way to the room we had vacated earlier that day. Our hearts were thumping as we tried the door which, to our amazement,was not locked. We entered and stood for a while in the dark, listening. No sound could be heard. The blackout curtains had been drawn and Mutti switched on the lights. The room was unoccupied.

Mutti and I went to bed, while Papa returned to the reception desk, rang the bell and explained to the young woman who answered the call that we would be staying on a little while longer after all – if that would be all right. The woman, who spoke very little German but seemed to understand my father, was not in the least put out by the request. "Of course, Sir. That'll be perfectly all right. What was your room number again?" And she made a note in the ledger. Once again, we had been saved.

Our early days in London were reasonably happy. The Blitz had not yet started, so everything appeared peaceful. Everyone was saying that "Mr Schicklgrüber" (the name they gave Hitler, whose father, a minor Austrian customs official, was originally called Schicklgrüber) would be well and truly beaten by Christmas. Mutti missed her mother, sister and brothers and I missed my favourite cousins, Liane and Heini. But Christmas was not far off so we would not have to wait too long before we would all be reunited in a free Berlin.

Meanwhile, this was like a holiday When November 8 came we all went to Lyons Corner House at Oxford Street for lunch. My parents thought they would "splash out" to celebrate my birthday. I had reached the ripe old age of nine. My present was a big bag of sweets – not as exciting nor as expensive as the little pedal car or the Punch and Judy theatre with its puppets from previous birthdays – but money was scarce and the sweets tasted wonderful.

We sat at a table for four and were handed menus by an efficient waitress. In the background an orchestra conducted by Albert Sandler played a waltz. We studied the menu carefully, unable to understand any of it. The waitress returned.

"Right, m'dears. What can I do you for? Will you be having a nice lunch then?"

"Yes," said Papa.

"D'you want to start with the soup? Nice tomato soup today," said the waitress.

"Yes," said Papa, smiling broadly.

"Or there's the sardine salad as a starter. That's nice, too..." said the waitress helpfully.

"Yes," said Papa.

The waitress was quick to grasp the problem and brought us a set menu which we found "very nice".

I needed to go to the toilet and went off to search for it Strung across a staircase leading to the basement, was a long rope in the middle of which hung a notice with just one word: *CLOSED*. The German for lavatory is *Klosett*. I thought it strange, but climbed under the rope and made my way down the stairs into the darkness below. It was scary and I eventually returned to the light and asked *our* waitress: "Bitte, Klosett...Toilette"

"You want the toilet? Come on then sweetheart, I'll show you." And she took me to the *Gents*. It was probably the first English word I learned that would stick with me always.

Papa continued searching for work and for lodgings so that we did not need to live off charity. He found both almost immediately after my birthday.

In the East End he was offered a job sewing buttonholes for a tailoring firm that produced greatcoats for the Finnish army. Finland was fighting Russia at the time and Britain was supporting the Fins with aid of one sort and another. Papa had never sewn anything in his life, but Mr Kornfeld, the tailor, assured him that it was easy.

"I have *rachmoniss* with you (I pity you) and try to help my fellow Jews whenever possible. That's why I'm offering you the job and I shall pay you..." and his voice dropped to a conspiratorial whisper "thirty-five shillings a week!". His voice dropped another octave: "Don't tell any of the others, or they will all want me to pay them as much as that."

Papa was overjoyed. A job at last and good pay as well! It took him about two months to discover that no one else in the factory was being paid thirty-five shillings a week. They were all being paid at least two pounds and even forty-five shillings! So much for a Jew helping his fellow Jews for whom he felt such pity.

But it was a job and my father worked hard and long hours that brought him overtime pay which all went towards the rent of our new home. This was a garret in a four-storey Edwardian house in Belsize Park Gardens, Hampstead, a part of London which had become the centre for German Jewish refugees. The rest of the house was occupied by German Jews. Our landlord was one Herbert Sulzbach, a Frankfurt banker, who had come over with his family; then there was a delightful actor called Stiller who secured himself a permanent post with the BBC's German service, an actress cum singer who later moved on to the United States and a writer and his wife who had come from Potsdam. Not all their names have remained in my memory but their presence will always be remembered.

Herbert Sulzbach's story is worth a mention at this point. When all Germans were interned as "enemy aliens" and sent to camps on the Isle of Man, Sulzbach was among them. There he joined the Pioneer Corps, the only section of the British army that was open to "enemy aliens" who weren't really enemies at all. The Corps performed all the nasty jobs, such as digging ditches, emptying latrines and so on. Sulzbach was soon commissioned and later sent as a Captain to M18, a prisoner of war camp for high-ranking Nazi officers. His job: to interrogate and help "de-nazify" them. Not only did he manage to accomplish this feat successfully, he also turned many of his prisoners into lifelong friends.

After the war, Herbert Sulzbach was appointed cultural attaché to the first post-war German Embassy in London – the only former Jewish refugee to hold such a prestigious position. He continued in this job for many years, well beyond the normal retirement age. Shortly after he left the embassy, he died at the age of 75. His funeral was attended by hundreds of his old friends, including a dozen or so of the officers he had "de-nazified". Captain Sulzbach's name still lives on in the annals of the German Foreign Office and London's German Embassy.

We, of course, were not interned. Although we were aliens we were not enemy aliens but Russians. As such, we were able to hire a wireless from Radio Rentals at sixpence a week. This we would switch on every evening at seven for the BBC news in German. We would open the door of our little attic room so that the rest of the house, including all the Sulzbachs, could cram in to listen. After that, we would normally be invited downstairs for a good coffee and a chat about "the bad old days".

Mutti became acquainted with a delightful little old lady called Helene Burg. She was a refugee from Vienna and had found work as a secretary to a large West End shop. She spoke three or four languages fluently and had lived in England long enough to be naturalized. So she, too, was not among those to be interned. She turned out to be a great help and a good friend.

It was "Miss Burg" (she always insisted on that handle to show that she had never found it necessary to have a man in her life) who found me a place at a school. It happened to be a Roman Catholic school – Bartram's Convent School on Haverstock Hill, which was in easy walking distance from Belsize Park Gardens.

The nuns were exceptionally kind and understanding and made sure that I was not bullied too much. It was here that I learned my first English and here, too, that I learned some basic mathematics. "I shall give a prize to the first boy or girl who comes out having correctly written their six-times table," our arithmetic teacher, Sister Angela, said one morning. The entire class leaned over their slates (yes, it was still slates in those days) and began to work at the task.

I was the first to rush to Sister Angela and proudly handed her my slate. She looked at it, then at me, at first with astonishment crossing her face, then anger, then…then she laughed and laughed. I had written my six-times table: TABEL TABEL TABEL TABEL TABEL TABEL.

Although the children had been told that I was a refugee from Hitler's Germany and that they should be nice to me, there was nevertheless a certain amount of bullying. Young children are often wary of the "odd one out" and I was it. They would mimic my accent and call me a dunce because I was unable to follow all the lessons properly. Some of the boys would try to goad me into fighting them. Only when I was hit would I hit back and not only gave as good as I had got but returned blows with ferocity. That was usually the end of the matter and by the time I had been at Bartram's Convent for four or five months, I had made a small group of friends – boys and girls.

By now the German Blitz with its nightly bombings had begun and the occupants of the Belsize Park Gardens house would congregate in the Anderson shelter which had been erected in the back garden. It was a small shelter with enough room for five or even six persons comfortably. But for the eight or nine of the house, there was not really sufficient space. So we took it in turns to remain behind in the house and lie under the kitchen table or in the narrow closet under the stairs. We were assured that if a bomb were to hit the house, those would be the safest places to be.

One day, this refuge division became unnecessary. When I returned home from school, Mutti told me: "The house is empty, except for us. Everyone has been arrested and taken away. They said they would be all right and were only going to some island with other German Jews. It's terrible."

She was in tears. At that point she had no idea that the internment was not the same as the Nazi camps. People would be treated like human beings, not like animals. But this did not become clear until Herr Sulzbach had sent us a picture postcard from the Isle of Man telling us that everything was reasonably civilized. Papa had also read an article in the *Daily Express* which described conditions on the island. He was a regular reader of Lord Beaverbrook's newspaper ever since it started publishing a daily column in German which gave the main points of the news for refugee readers. The *Daily Express* used to be a great newspaper in those days.

So it was that for a period we were able to occupy the Anderson shelter just by ourselves and listen to the bombs hailing down on London. Their sound lives with me still. The German bombers had a hum all their own. It would rise and fall quite gently – *wroom…ram…wroom…ram* – but the bombs, that was something else. First there would be a loud *shush* sound, the kind we make when we demand silence, followed by a shrill whistle until it hit its target and exploded: *shhhushhh…eeeeeeeehhh…karamm*! The air raid siren giving the alert of a raid was equally frightening in its repetition of some high-pitched scale. When it started, it would shock everyone into a race for the shelters, for there seemed little interval between the siren and the *wroom…ram* of the first bombers. The All Clear, usually in the morning, would be far gentler on the ear.

Despite the heavy bombing, the people of London never lost their cool. Their good humour shone through all the adversity. Like the woman who was intent on brushing clean a settee standing alone amidst the rubble of a destroyed house; or the other woman who was seen scrubbing her front steps, the only thing left of her house, while the rag-and-bone man came past on his horse-drawn cart and shouted to her: "'Ere, darlin', d'you want me to come clean yer winders?" and receiving the answer: "You ain't got the guts to clean any windahs; you couldn't even polish yer own balls!"

The language was new to my young ears. And Cockney was completely incomprehensible. But I began very gradually to feel that people were speaking more slowly than at first. Perhaps my ears were becoming attuned.

Every Saturday, Papa and I used to walk from our Hampstead home to Camden Town to do the shopping. At the busy market, we would buy chicken giblets at sixpence a pound – five pounds for two bob. We always took the discounted five pounds. Then it was off to Woolworth, the 3d and 6d store, where we would obtain a two-pound jar of strawberry jam for sixpence and a large loaf of white bread. We would then get some cast-off vegetables – cauliflowers that were not selling because of the odd small mark, some over-ripe tomatoes, potatoes that were growing roots and moth-eaten cabbage. For a total of about four shillings, we would carry home the food that would last us about a week. Mutti would create wonders with the chicken livers and she would stuff the neck. There was a daily plate of chicken soup with *lokchen* (vermicelli). We lived like kings.

But the bombs were getting dangerously close and each night we continued lying in the Anderson shelter, wondering whether the house would still be standing the following morning.

It was the day I went to school and found that it was gone that I started to panic. Two of our lovely nuns had been killed by a direct hit. The shell of the school and the burned out classrooms were a pitiful sight. When I heard of the death of my teachers, my mind raced back to the sight of the old woman whose head was split open by a sheet of glass from Stiller, the leatherware shop opposite our house in the Invalidenstrasse. She had been killed because she had screamed curses against the Jewish owners of the shop. It was to my mind an act of God. But this, how could this have been an act of God? To kill two nuns who were themselves the representatives on earth of God was surely not possible. They had been free of sin. I was beginning to lose faith and ran back home to scream against heaven.

It was time to get out of London. My mother and I had been found a residential place with a family in Steventon, a village near Abingdon. We weren't exactly evacuated, but were evacuees of a sort. I believe the placement had been found by the Jewish Refugee Committee, although the lady to whom we were assigned, a Mrs Rogers, was not Jewish. My father continued to work in London, but there was talk of his firm being relocated well away. They were now making greatcoats and uniforms for the British army and my father had been given a rise to the princely sum of £2.10s a week.

Now that he was "in the money" and could speak some English, he went in search of his relations, and tracked them down, all cousins, in the East End. There was Mary Turatsky and an Izbicki family, whose two sons, David and Eddie had joined a whaling ship, and daughter Polly who had married an all-in wrestler called Len Ring who later became an international authority and lecturer on back problems. They were a wonderful family and we spent many happy Sundays together. The two boys ended up in New Zealand where they married and had families. They changed their names from Izbicki to Isbie.

Goodness knows why, but it clearly was a move that helped them get on, for one became leader of New Zealand's dockers' union while the other became a socialist politician, and made it to Minister of Labour in the late 'Seventies, early 'Eighties. Polly and Len followed them to Auckland and would have celebrated their Golden Wedding in the year 2001 but for the demise of Len, one of the sweetest, best humoured men I've ever known. Both Dave and Eddie died earlier and have both been sorely missed by New Zealand society.

Mutti and I got on a train bound for Oxford. It was a lengthy, rattling journey and, after one change, we eventually arrived just after 11 p.m. at Steventon. The station was deserted and in total darkness. We made our way to the entrance and stood alone, not knowing which way to turn or whom to ask. There was no one. Then suddenly, a kindly but authoritative voice behind us boomed: "Hello, hello, what be you two doin' 'ere at this time of the noight, eh?" Even in the dark we could see it was a policeman. Now, we had never been able to see eye to eye with the police. If anything, we were very much afraid of the police. They represented the first move to concentration camps.

My mother still spoke hardly any English, so it was left to me to speak up. "Pliss Sir, we must go to Mrs Rogers."

"Mrs Rogers? Goodness lad, Mrs Rogers'll be asleep be now. But I'll tell you what. You and your Mummy – it is your mummy ain't it? (I nodded) – you come with me to the station and you'll be made comfortable."

"But zis is doch the station, Sir," I argued.

He laughed. "Yes, of course it is lad. But Oi mean the police station, d'you see?"

And he took Mutti's case and led the way with us reluctantly following on behind, clutching each other's hand. Our memories of "police" rekindled our fear.

At the police station it was warm and there was another policeman. The one who had brought us was a sergeant with three stripes on his arm. Both were very kind and made us tea. Then they opened a cell door and we looked at the interior with trepidation. The sergeant noticed. "Oh, don't worry. We won't lock ye up. But you'll be quite comfortable, Oi can assure ye." And sure enough, the two policemen made up the bunk beds inside with sheets and blankets, showed us where we could wash and use the toilet and bade us good night. We slept like logs.

In the morning, the sergeant woke us with steaming mugs of tea. "When you're ready, come and have your breakfast," he invited.

We were treated to fresh eggs, toast, butter – real butter – and jam and more tea. It was a feast. Rationing had started and we weren't used to this kind of spread. The sergeant sat down with us and drank tea.

"So now tell me, young feller m'lad, what's your name?"

"Pliss Sir, it is Horst. Horst Izbicki."

"'Ors? 'ORS? Nay, that's not a name that a h'animal. 'Ors you say?"

"No, Sir, Horst – H-o-r-s-t."

"Good 'eavens. Why don't you call yourself by a proper name like my boy. He's called John. Now John's a proper name. 'Orst indeed!"

From that moment on, whenever someone asked me my name, I'd reply: "John. My name is John Izbicki."

And no one ever laughed again.

We stayed several months with the dear Mrs Rogers. Her husband was in the army but her son Tony was still at school. Mutti and I slept over the barn on a pile of straw. It was like some great adventure and we would go down to the house to eat with Mrs Rogers and Tony. Mutti helped in the kitchen and cleaned the house. As for me, I joined the local scout troop and learned all about knots and being prepared. We went camping and I used to go scrumping for apples, once being caught by our police sergeant who gave me a far-too gentle clip around the ear. "Don't you ever let me catch ye pinchin' apples or anything else ever again, d'you hear, Orse?" I told him my name was John and he just laughed and laughed.

One day, Papa telephoned to say that his tailoring firm was moving to Llandudno in North Wales and we should come and join him there as soon as he had found some lodgings.

And so it was that we ended up at the seaside in Wales. Llandudno is a fabulous place and was to become a great influence in my life. I must have become a pupil at every primary school in the town because we kept moving to different flats, each one slightly bigger than the last. I went to Dyffryn Road

*With my parents
in Llandudno,
North Wales,
in May 1944.
I was 13.*

School and Lloyd Street School, where I took and failed my 11-plus.

So then I was sent to the Central School, a secondary modern, where I spent one year before being transferred to the John Bright's County School – a grammar school. The teachers at Central School had decided that I should never have been sent to them but was grammar school material.

My English had shown vast improvements since my arrival in Britain at the age of eight and a half. I was now 13 and was virtually having to look after myself. Dad's firm had closed and he had taken himself off to Manchester and found a job making ammunitions at the R O F factory at Risley. It was there that one of the many Cockneys who had been sent "oop north" to the ammunitions factory asked him one Friday afternoon: "'Ere, Len," (his names of Luzer and Hans had long been abandoned along with Horst, and he called himself Leonard) "'ere Len, 'ave you 'ad yer pie?" "No," replied my father. "I don't like pies." "No, not that sort of pie! Your pie, your pie," and he mimed the payment of money. "Oh, my pay!" said my father. "Yes, I've had my pay – er, my pie." And both enjoyed the joke.

My mother had found a job as a cook at the Granville Restaurant on Mostyn Street. Her bosses were Jewish – a Mr and Mrs Fainlight – and she worked from 10 a.m. until nearly midnight, when she would come home and slip into bed. I would go to the restaurant for meals at weekends but for the rest of the time, hardly saw her. I took myself to school each morning – a short walk from Trinity Square where we now lived to the John Bright's County School. Afterwards, I would go home to do my homework and make myself something to eat.

I was mercilessly bullied at school. The biggest of the bullies, an overweight, redheaded lad would repeat whenever he saw me: "Why don't you go back to Jerusalem, you fuckin' Yid?" At first I told him that I had never been to Jerusalem and so couldn't return there. "Well then go back to fuckin' Germany," he'd say. "No thank you. If I did go back there, I'd be killed." "Fuckin' good job. They should kill all the fuckin' Yids," he'd say and I would lash out but would usually end up with a bloody nose. It was almost a routine.

One weekend I was walking round the Daganwy swimming pool with Michael Myers, my best friend. Suddenly, someone pushed me and I fell into the deep end. I could not swim and went down and down, trying to hold my breath. When I thought I would surely drown, someone put their arms around my body and started pulling me upwards and almost threw me out of the pool. When I recovered my wind, I looked around me. "Who pulled me out," I asked Michael.

"You'll never believe it," he said and named my arch enemy – the red-headed bully.

Later that evening, I went round to his house and asked his mother whether I could speak to him. He came to the door. "I just wanted to thank you for saving my life," I said and held out my hand. He was surprised but took my hand and shook it. "That's all right," he said and went back in.

The next day I was told that my rescuer had pushed me in in the first place. But the bullying stopped and he never again made a nasty remark to me.

Michael and I would play on the Great Orme, making fires and building secret camps. We were a gang of two. Michael's parents ran a kosher hotel in Llandudno. His father, the chef, was huge and must have weighed at least 20 stone. His mother, on the other hand, was a petite little thing. I often ate at the hotel along with Michael and his sister, Pauline.

But one day, Michael and I had a fight. A terrible fight. It was to do with sex. We were discussing how babies are made. I had been doing a lot of background reading in the public library and knew Havelock Ellis' books off by heart, so I was able to tell Michael exactly how babies are made. We were outside in the hotel's back garden. "The woman lies down on a bed or something and the man gets on top of her and puts his penis into her," I said with all the authority of a professor. "You're lying. You're lying," he said, tears welling in his eyes. And he lashed out at me. We both fell to the ground, rolling over and over as he kept pummeling me with his fists.

"I'm not lying Michael. Honestly, I'm not. I'll show you if you like. I'll take you to the library and you can see for yourself."

But he would have none of it and sobbed his heart out. The reason was clear. The thought of his father lying on top of his little mother proved too much for my friend. But we remained best friends, even when the Myers family sold up and moved to open another hotel – the Stanmore – in Brighton. Later, Michael left the country and flew to Canada. We have since lost touch. More's the pity.

In the summer, Llandudno came alive. There was brass band music on the prom every evening and conducting contests. I entered once and even won a ten shilling prize.

There was more music on the pier and I would go regularly to listen. It opened my ears to classical music.

And up on the Great Orme there were regular shows on the stage at Happy Valley – the Happy Valley Follies. I would climb to see those shows religiously. During the winter season, the Manchester Repertory Company would come and occupy the Pier Pavilion Theatre. I scraped together every penny of my pocket money so that I could see each production. I had fallen in love with the theatre.

CHAPTER FOUR:

MOVE TO MANCHESTER

As the war started drawing to a close, Llandudno suddenly became "occupied" by American forces. It certainly seemed like an occupation, for the "Yanks" appeared to be everywhere, doling out chewing gum and nylon stockings and "courting" the local girls. Some of them were billeted at Michael's dad's hotel and they would keep us excited with their tales of "back home" where everything was bigger and better than here in Wales. They kept Michael and me supplied with gum and "life savers" (little boiled sweets) that had to be sucked for a long time before they disappeared. With chocolate and sweets rationed (along with other foodstuffs, clothes, even furniture) those sticks of gum and sweets proved a godsend to us boys and we gladly ran errands for "our Yanks soldiers" whenever they asked us to.

I used to take notes to the houses of young women, inviting them to a dance or dinner and wait for a reply. Only once was there a negative response. This drew a mouthful of angry epithets from the disappointed soldier. "Ah, sheet...ah, fuck that...Now what the fuck am ah goin' t'do tonight? Jeez... goddammit...Well, fuck her...Jeez!" And he'd tear up the reply note, which had been very apologetic and merely said: "Sorry, can't tonight. Mum needs me to be home. How about tomorrow?"

My father used to spend one weekend a month with us in Llandudno. As he had to travel more than 50 miles away from his lodgings in Manchester, he had to report to the police station and have his registration book marked and stamped. The Yanks used to take themselves off on trips to the Lake

District, even Scotland, and I would ask them whether they had to go to the police to report their journeys.

"What in the heck for?" I would be asked.

"Well, every foreigner has to tell the police they're going somewhere more than 50 miles away," I'd reply.

"Goddammit, John, we're no goddamn foreigners. We're Americans. We don't have to tell your fuckin' police where we're wantin' to go, goddammit! Jeez, d'you get that kid?"

Over the four years we spent in North Wales, my English had become near fluent and I was no longer betrayed by an accent. My ear for music had also helped me pick up English. My thanks were mainly due to my regular visits to the theatre and cinema and my listening to radio plays such as *Saturday Night Theatre* and variety shows such as Music Hall, where I would criticise the strange accents displayed by such comedians as Vic Oliver and Issy Bonn. Strangely enough, I did not find the broad Lancashire accent of Frank Randle or the Cockney of Tommy Trinder in the least bit strange. To me, they were totally English, as indeed they were.

My other language aid was the ordinary comic. I devoured *Beano, Dandy, Radio Fun* and *Film Fun* from cover to cover and was also a regular reader of *Hotspur* and *Adventure*. Every two or three weeks, I would pack my entire collection under one arm and hawk them around the houses of every schoolmate I knew. "Any swaps?" I would ask and would let them sift through the pile of books and comics spread before them. They would pick those they had not read, then fetch their own pile and let me go through it eagerly. We would swap on a one-to-one basis.

Throughout my years as a writer on education, I never decried the reading of comics. Indeed, I advised parents to let their youngsters read comics. Words, however simple, alongside pictures can only help. "Reading comics is better than reading nothing at all," would be my recommendation. I did and do, however, draw the line at some so-called comics these days that glorify the violence of knives and guns. The "play-fighting" of Lord Snooty and Our Gang or the punches delivered by Desperate Dan on a villain cannot compare with the horrors displayed in some of our current children's publications.

The Llandudno period, like the war, was coming to an end. My father (by now I had replaced Papa with Dad) had rented a small flat in the Hightown area of Manchester and wanted us to come and join him. Germany lay defeated and my mother (now Mum rather than Mutti) was praying that she would be reunited with her family from whom we had heard almost nothing throughout the war years. "Almost nothing" …there had been two postcards, received via neutral Switzerland, from Lonni Mühl, a non-Jewish family friend who had been madly in love with Georg, my mother's youngest brother. He loved her too, but had refused to marry her because he felt that this would only heap unnecessary trouble upon her head.

She told us in one of the two cards that he had gone to Holland and had met a young Jewish doctor. They were married (and later had a baby daughter, whom they named Beatrice after the Dutch princess). The other card told us that Karl, Hedwig, Benno and Heini as well as Oma had all "gone on holiday". This was the code for disappeared, presumably taken to a concentration camp. But there was nothing that ever suggested that they were not still alive. Mum lived in constant hope.

So we packed our bags and took the train to Manchester. I had been there two or three times already to visit Dad and stay with him at a B & B lodging house run by a fellow German refugee, Helga Birkenfeld and her gorgeous daughter, Ilse. Ilse was a couple of years older than me and we soon became close friends.

I liked Manchester. It had some of the bustle reminiscent of Berlin, although it seemed much dirtier and always appeared to be enveloped in fog if it wasn't drenched in rain. But there were lots of cinemas and a couple of theatres and many shops including two exciting department stores, Lewis's and Kendal Milne, whose lifts and escalators I would use with glee.

Beech Street, where our "house" was, could not be described as a welcoming road. It was a long row of back-to-back terraced houses, dirty grey with two stone steps leading from the pavement into the front room or parlour. We didn't have a parlour. Instead, there was a small shop through which we had to walk to find the stairs that would take us up to two rooms, one overlooking the street, the other looking out onto a small backyard. That's where the lavatory was. Throughout the year, this was damp and in the winter it was freezing. Instead of toilet paper, old newspapers were carefully cut into pieces long and wide enough to make for a comfortable wipe.

I was given the rear room, which contained a single bed and a table on which I would do my homework. My parents occupied the front bedroom, which had a double bed, a large table, where we would all eat, and a grease-laden cooker, which my mother scrubbed until it shone as new.

The shop belonged to an old man, a Jew who had originally come from Poland and who still spoke with a thick accent despite the fifty or so years he had lived in Manchester. All he sold was eggs. There weren't many of them, just enough to keep him alive, along with our rent of 12s6d a week.

There was no bath, just a large bowl that was fed from a jug with cold water (boiled by a kettle in the winter). To get to the lavatory, one would have to climb down the steep stairs to a short corridor that led to the back door which opened onto the yard. Apart from the cooker, the flat was clean and my mother kept it spotless.

It was by no means the best address but it was home. "We shall find something better soon, don't you worry," Dad would say. "I've saved a bit of money from my munitions pay and I shall put it towards a house of our own as soon as a suitable one comes along." He believed it and I, for one, believed him. Mum seemed a little more sceptical.

There was the immediate question of school. Someone had suggested Manchester Grammar. My reports from John Bright County in Llandudno had been good and Dad, who had left the Risley munitions factory and found a job with a soap manufacturer called Sankey in Salford, made an appointment with the school's High Master and took me along for an interview. It was a long way and required two buses to get there, one into the city centre, another to the school in Old Hall Lane, South Manchester.

My first impression was not a good one. The school appeared too clinically clean and the boys I saw were somehow too quiet. It was unreal. The Head was kind enough and gave me a fairly simple test to do. He appeared satisfied and told my father that he would let us know his decision, but that we could be sure it was favourable. We traipsed back to our Hightown ghetto having tasted a little of another world. That night I prayed that Manchester Grammar would turn me down.

It did not. But the fees we would have to pay made my father gasp. We simply did not have this kind of money and the letter made clear that the school could not offer me a scholarship. My parents were desperately disappointed and could not understand why I had so lightly shrugged the whole matter off. Schools in the Hightown area had a poor reputation, but someone had told my mother of a boys' school in New Moston whose name was held in high esteem but where places were hard to get.

So once again we set off on a trek to keep an appointment with the headmaster of North Manchester High School for Boys. Again it required two buses to make the journey, one from Queen's Road, a fair ten-minute walk from Beech Street, to the Oldham Road, and another for a 20-minute journey to New Moston and the school.

J. C. Burnett was a formidable character, tall yet rotund with rosy cheeks beneath a balding head of white hair. But his eyes betrayed a twinkle that immediately endeared him to me. He asked me a few questions about my likes and dislikes, seemed to appreciate my love of the theatre and agreed with my hatred of spinach ("I've never much liked it myself, although it is supposed to be so good for you," he said). He did not test me but asked a couple of masters to take me away and put me "through my paces".

I was taken to an empty classroom and stood in front of a blackboard. One of the masters set me a couple of mathematical problems to work out on the board and this I managed to accomplish without too much bother. Then I was asked two or three questions about English grammar. I was still not sufficiently knowledgeable to answer everything correctly but I remember even now one of the questions posed by the master, a slender fellow with long hands and fingers that might have been ideal for mastering the violin:

"What is wrong with this sentence – Between you, me and the gatepost, the boat will sail without a captain in charge — ?"

I thought about this for a while. I could see nothing wrong with it, and yet there had to be something. At last I felt I had solved it. "Please Sir," I said. "Is it the use of between?"

"Explain. You're right, but explain it to me," he said, trying to hide a little astonishment in his voice.

"Is it because between can only be – er – between two things or people, while you, me and the gatepost is – er – are three people...or two people and one thing...?"

"Well done, young man. Well done. Exactly right. Between really is 'by twain'. So what should it really be?"

I was stumped there. I tried 'Between you and me, the boat..."

"No, no. It's 'among' when you have more than two. Among three is the division. Although I'll grant you that we probably wouldn't say, 'Among you, me and the gatepost.' We'd probably continue using between as it has become common usage..."

He was in his element and had just given me my first proper English lesson. His name was Tom Crossley and he was to give me and others many more lessons. He would open my ears to poetry and my eyes to the beauty of nature and language. If there is any man to whom I owe whatever talent I might have gathered over the years for the written and spoken word, it is Thomas A. Crossley – or TAC as he was known to the boys who were lucky enough to have been taught by him.

I was accepted at North Manchester which, alas, has turned into one of the country's worst comprehensives. But when it was still a grammar school (indeed, it changed its name to North Manchester Grammar School a little later) it was a happy and beautiful place of learning. One often hears the expression that schooldays were "the happiest days of your life". I cannot say

As Tony Lumpkin in
"She Stoops To Conquer"
a North Manchester High
School production, 1947 or 48

that about John Brights County School in Llandudno or any of the other North Wales schools where I suffered merciless bullying. But of North Manchester High in New Moston, I willingly echo that sentiment.

TAC not only taught us English. He also produced the school plays and edited the school magazine. On its stage in the Great Hall I played the prime minister in *R U R*, a play about robots and based my character on Disraeli and in André Obey's *Noah*. I was given a small but delicious character part – the Wild Man. The entire role took up no more than ten or fifteen minutes at the end of Act 1, but I loved every second of it. After the second night's performance, TAC came up to me.

"A friend of mine wants to meet you," he said very simply and took me over to a woman who was sipping a sherry just outside our dressing room. She turned to greet me and I was stunned. It was Sybil Thorndike.

"Young man," she said, "I liked what you did out there. Nice little performance. Ever thought of taking up the stage professionally?"

I could almost hear Lady Bracknell in her voice but I stammered: "I'd love to, Lady…er…Dame Sybil. Thank you so much for your kindness."

"Good. Well, if you like and, of course, if it's all right with your parents, I could recommend you for a RADA scholarship. Just let Tom Crossley know and I'll do the rest. Now go along and keep working hard."

That night I almost flew home, my head buzzing with music of the spheres. I ran into the house and blurted out the news. "You'll never guess what happened at school tonight…" I spluttered to Mum and Dad, who just ordered me to sit and calm down. "Dame Sybil Thorndike, one of Britain's greatest actresses saw me in the play tonight and said…and said…she would recommend me for a RADA scholarship – a RADA scholarship!!!"

I then had to explain exactly who this "Dame Sorndik" was and what on earth "Radar" had to do with anything. They had never heard of the Royal Academy of Dramatic Art nor of Dame Sybil...but once I had made it all clear to them, my father said to me quietly:

"So Horst (they insisted on calling me Horst while at home), first of all many congratulations on having such a fine actress make you such a great compliment. That must have given you much pleasure and it gives your mother and me much pleasure too. We are always glad to hear of any success you make. Of that please be sure. Always! But taking up the theatre when you are only 14 years old is a very serious move, not something that can be taken lightly. And it would mean you going to London on your own and leaving us behind here in Manchester.

"I'll tell you what. We're not going to say, 'No, you can't do it and that's that.' We won't forbid you to do this at any time, only for now. First, carry on in your schooling and do well in your examinations. Then, if you can, do something which neither your dear mother nor I, nor any other member of our family has ever managed to do, and that is to go to a university and get a degree. When you have done that, and if you still want it, then we shall be happy to discuss your move to the theatre."

And that is where it was left. Some few years later, when I was about to enter university, I saw exactly how right my father had been. I used to go to Manchester's Central Library every evening to study for my Higher School Certificate (the pre-runner of GCE A-levels). Its reference library is among the finest in the country. In the basement there is the Library Theatre and I was among its regular patrons. I met some of its highly talented actors and often bought cups of coffee for one of them. His acting was his life, but he could hardly afford a coffee and had to rely on a schoolboy to help him out.

I took part in other productions at school and travelled to Stockport to see TAC and the Stockport Players in their productions. He was as good an actor as he was a teacher and I often wondered why he had not become a professional in the theatre rather than in schools.

I also showed promise on the sports field – not in either football or cricket but in athletics, beating records in the high and long jumps as well as in races (100 and 220 yards...these were the days before the metric system was introduced). But my housemaster, a geographer named Jennings, helped ruin any long-term chances I might have had by insisting that I took part in the cross country.

"I'm no good at long distance running, Sir," I protested.

"Go on, Izbicki, you'll beat everyone easily," he persisted. And so I had to enter the race for the sake of Clynes, the house I was to help come top of the lot. After two or three miles I collapsed with a stitch. I continued to run and came in last. My sprinting went to the dogs as a result, though I could still excel at the long jump.

J. C. Burnett retired and was sadly missed by us all. He was replaced by a small, weedy man called R. M. Sibson, who lectured boys on rainy days when football or other field sports had to be cancelled, on his experiences in Palestine where he had run a school for Christian children. It was already a time of fighting between Jew and Arab.

"There they were, shooting at each other from one school wall to the other. I went out into the school field and called to them to stop. 'You lot stop it now, at once,' I shouted and blew my whistle. I also told them to go and shoot in someone else's field."

"What did they do, Sir?" several of us would call out, knowing full well what was said to have happened since we had heard the story several times over. "Why, they obeyed me, of course and dispersed quietly – just as you are going to do now!" He always managed to time things neatly with the sounding of the bell.

My father was as good as his word regarding the Beech Street flat only being temporary. He suddenly announced that he was buying a house in nearby Heywood Street. This meant a move to Cheetham Hill, certainly a step up from Hightown. The house at No.22 had three floors, several rooms – and a real bathroom and lavatory *inside the house*. No longer would I need to take my weekly trip to the public baths in Herbert Street where I would be given a small slab of soap and a towel and made to wait for one of a dozen cubicles where a hot bath was being run.

After I had been in for 12 minutes, the keeper would bang on the door with his fist. "Cum on out now, lad. You've 'ad enuf. 'urry oop."

I was also afraid of losing one of my good friends. Barry Brown, who lived in Oak Street, a few roads away from Beech, with his Mum, went to my school and we would meet every morning and walk to the bus together. But our new house was closer to the bus stop in Queen's Road and Barry and I continued to meet.

It was farewell to Beech, Elm, Cedar and Oak – all streets that figured in Louis Golding's delightful novel *Magnolia Street*. My father's purchase had a snag – but it was a snag that would eventually turn to our advantage. In order to obtain No. 22 Heywood Street at a cost of £650, he had also to accept the house next door – No. 24, which was "thrown in" for free. The two stood together, thus making one detached house of two semis. No.24 had a sitting tenant, a man of some 76 years, who had recently become a widower.

First peacetime holiday with parents in
Blackpool, 1945

My parents would spend one morning a week at an auction house in central Manchester, buying up second hand beds, tables, chairs, curtains, sofas, pictures, carpets, rolls of lino, cutlery, pots, pans, ornaments and so on. My father had received a good mortgage on the houses, so was able to spend quite a large amount on furnishing No. 22. We had no real money to speak of but there was enough to make the place look and feel comfortable.

A year later, the tenant at 24 died and the house became "vacant". The trips to the auction house started all over again and this time, my parents turned No. 24 into a series of little flats. Our tenants came mainly from the nearby Jewish Hospital in Elizabeth Street, which ran parallel to Heywood. There was one young doctor and two hospital ward sisters – Sister Williams and Sister Garbutt who used to entertain me to tea on a regular basis.

Ilse Birkenfeld and the B & B run by her mother stood in Morton Avenue which ran from our backgate to Cheetham Hill Road. We were now able to meet often. I lost my virginity to her when I was not yet 16 and she was about 18. I was madly in love with her – until her mother announced that they were packing up and emigrating to America. We kept corresponding, sending each other passionate letters – until I received her "Dear John". She married a lawyer and settled in one of the swankier suburbs of New York. I recall sending her new husband a letter wishing him well and asking him to look after her. He wrote back to say that this is exactly what he would do.

They were divorced four years later, leaving Ilse with a little boy. The next and last time I saw her was many years later when I was investigating New York city schools for *The Telegraph*. She had turned into a shrill New York matron. But she was a good mother and the little boy was a sheer delight.

My father and I still used to go shopping every Saturday. But we had come a long way from those excursions to Camden market for giblets and jam. Now it was to Lewis's food hall for nice bread and some fresh vegetables. Whenever we would see a queue, Dad would order me to stand in it while he would go to the front to see what was being sold. Rationing was still very much on and people did not queue for nothing. Sometimes it was cigarettes, which we did not need and so I would be called away from the queue, but at other times it might be cartons of matches or candles or torch batteries, all of which we needed and would buy.

Any food which did not require coupons was always welcome – such as spam or rabbit or fish.

Even after the war had finished, rationing remained and continued for some years.

When the Germans surrendered, there was rejoicing throughout the land. But the war in the Far East was still in full swing. Japan was not yet beaten. When in 1945 the last All Clear sounded, everyone danced in the streets. There were parties in every village.

Oh we had all heard of the reason why Japan had at last surrendered. The atom bomb had been the last straw for Emperor Hirohito. "Serves him bloody right," the people cried – until they saw the pictures of Hiroshima and Nagasaki. Somehow, the dancing ceased. People were aghast at what had been caused by that great big mushroom in the sky.

But was it any worse than the pictures that had come out of Bergen Belsen, Buchenwald and, God help us all, Auschwitz?

There's a line in Ernst Toller's *No More Peace*, in which I played the part of Socrates. It is a song and it goes: "This is the war to end war…the last war, really…or very nearly…the very last war of all."

CHAPTER FIVE:

PEACE

Peace turned out to be a mixture of high elation and deep depression. The "boys" were coming home, too many of them on crutches, some of them blind or without an arm or a leg. But there were many who had been spared the war and whose families were once again reunited.

My parents were busy writing to the Red Cross in an attempt to discover what had happened to Mum's family. Silence, though ominous, still gave a little space for hope. The telephone call from Hertha Lewandowski provided that first tiny ray of hope. She was my mother's cousin and was married to the cantor, Ernst Lewandowski, whose magnificent baritone thrilled the Liberal Jewish congregations of West London.

"I have news, Selma. My mother is alive. She will be coming to live with us in London. Isn't that wonderful?"

Mum was overjoyed. If her auntie Flora was alive, then maybe Flora's sister, Berta, Mum's mother, my darling Oma, might also be alive still. "Ach, Hertha, this is marvellous. I am so very, very happy for you," she said, weeping for joy. "You must bring her up to Manchester to stay with us – please!"

And so it came to pass. Two months or so later, Tante Flora, now in her early 70s, and Hertha came to stay. But something was not quite right. My mother, who had always been a bit of a clairvoyant, "knew" that Flora was keeping something from her. At last, Flora could no longer keep up the pretence of happiness and joy.

"Selma, as you know, I was in a concentration camp. Theresienstadt. They took me there in 1941. They also transported all the inmates of the old age home, including your dear mother…

Mum let out a gasp and immediately buried her head in her arms and sobbed "I knew it. I know what you are about to say. She's dead isn't she? Isn't she!"

Flora remained silent and, after a while, picked her handbag from the floor and opened it. She pulled out an envelope and handed it to my mother whose trembling hands slowly withdrew a small sheet of paper, frayed at the edges. The paper was covered in a faint scrawl, written in pencil by Oma. Mum recognised the hand even though it had been written by someone who was too weak and too distressed to consider calligraphy.

"My dearest darling Selma," the letter began.

"I am always thinking of you and of my sweet little Horstchen and dearest Hans and hope you are well. Yesterday I exchanged my wedding ring, the only thing of value left to me, for two raw potatoes Oh, they were so good… Please take care of yourself, Horstchen and Hans. I love you all so very much."

There were some other words but they were so faint that they had all but faded completely. It was the last letter she would ever write. She gave it to Flora in the hope that she would be able to deliver it one day. Two days later she died. The cause of death: starvation.

This was just the start of a tragic roll call. Apart from my cousin Liane and her mother, Maria, both of whom were Roman Catholics, none of Mum's brothers and sister, their families, aunts, uncles, cousins, had survived the Hitler holocaust.

The eldest brother, Isi, who had given his sister away at the wedding ceremony, had died in curious circumstances. He was at home and complained of a burning sensation in his stomach. He drank glass after glass of water to try to still the pain. Maria called a doctor, but by the time he arrived, Isi was dead. There was talk of his having swallowed poison, either poison that was given to him or that was self-administered. I have always opted for the latter theory, believing his untimely death to have been suicide, despite there having been no "farewell note", nor any last message to his wife and daughter.

When Liane was arrested and taken away as a half Jew, Maria rushed to the police station and screamed her protests at the arresting officer. "She is a good Christian," she shouted. "She and I believe wholeheartedly in the Führer. We are followers of National Socialism…" and so on in increasing vehemence and volume. After some three hours of this harangue,

My beautiful cousin, Liane, Berlin.
Liane was saved from the Nazis
because of her Roman Catholic religion.

a frightened and shaking Liane was freed.

Only a mother would be able to understand, even agree with the fuming fight Mary had put up for her daughter's life.

Mum's youngest brother, Georg, who thought he had managed to escape the Nazi tentacles by fleeing to Holland, was arrested together with his wife, a doctor, and their baby daughter, and transported to Auschwitz, where they were gassed on January 2, 1944 – just one day before his 38th birthday.

Her "middle" brother, Karl, together with his wife and two small boys, were taken to Bergen Belsen, where they died of "causes unknown" in 1944.

Hedwig (Heti), Mum's sister and my father's first real girlfriend, together with her husband, Benno, and their son, my cousin and best friend, Heini, were dragged from their home at No. 14 Pestalozzi Strasse and transported to Auschwitz on December 9, 1942. There they were separated, told to strip for a "communal bath". They were crammed into a vast building that looked like a hangar. Shower heads hung from the ceiling. The doors were shut and the showers opened. But instead of water, it was gas that flowed down upon the heads of several hundred people. Outside, laughing soldiers revved up a series of motorbikes. The noise helped to dull the screams from within.

The list went on.: Dagobert Katz, Hertha's brother and Mum's cousin:

Auschwitz: *Verschollen*, which meant "missing presumed dead". Often, neither the Red Cross nor any of the other researchers who had gone into the camps to try to identify the survivors and the corpses, could find anything left of the cadavers to identify. Hair, shaven from the heads of a million women, lay in heaps, still waiting to stuff cushions or be made into wigs. Gold teeth extracted from hundreds of thousands of men and women were gathered, a glittering hill, ready to be melted down and line the pockets of the SS troopers or even the camp commandant. The Nazis were able to turn everything to profit, even skin and bones, the former to become lampshades while the bones made excellent glue.

What intrigued me at the time and has continued to do so, was that those in charge of the administration of camps and prisons kept such meticulous records, noting down the most minute details such as the amount of water and vegetables that were mixed to produce an indescribably weak soup to feed an entire camp. It was a sort of research project: how little of each "ingredient" does one need to mix to obtain the least nourishing meal?

My mother did not receive the entire list at once. It took more than ten years to be completed and each note brought renewed anguish that would last for weeks. How she managed to cope with it all without going insane said much for her stamina and resolution. Instead of displaying the pain she felt, she threw herself into helping other refugees to trace their loved ones – dead or alive. As a literate woman, she wrote letters for them to the Red Cross and, later, to solicitors based in Germany who took up cases for "restitution".

The question of restitution was spooky. Here was Germany, the new, post-war Germany, trying to make amends by throwing money at those who had suffered at the hands of the Nazis. I automatically qualified for a cheque of £500 in compensation for "loss of education". Later, I could have applied for still further money to compensate me for humiliating persecution but I responded with a letter to the German authorities, which made my feelings clear: "Thank you for your offer but I am not interested in accepting blood money."

The German description of their generous offer was *Wiedergutmachung* – literally "making good again". The dictionary translates the word as "compensation" or "making reparations" but I could see it only in its literal meaning and there was no way the then Bonn government could ever "make good" the evil their predecessors had inflicted on an entire race.

And there was another reason for my refusal: to qualify for restitution, applicants had to be examined by a doctor on the German Embassy's list. Each examination entailed a thorough medical to see whether Nazi persecution had affected the applicant in one way or another. If the doctor could show that the applicant was suffering from depression or some other nervous disorder, the claim would pass and be rubber-stamped. My parents as well as many thousands of others qualified for a pension, paid regularly every month. But every refugee within our circle of friends who had "successfully" passed their medical, became ill. Some died shortly after such an examination. It was clear that the claim forms they had to complete and the medical they had to undergo had re-awakened bitter memories that had until then been filed in their subconscious.

My priorities lay elsewhere. Examinations loomed and I was determined to pass them. The School Certificate, in which one had to pass with at least a credit grade English language and mathematics – or, if one failed to make that grade in one or both, re-take the lot, was the first hurdle. I cleared it without too much difficulty. It provided me with the opportunity of going into the Arts Sixth or the Science Sixth. I chose Arts because it would allow me to study my favourite subjects – English, French, German and History – for the second of the hurdles: the Higher School Certificate.

Lo and behold, two years in the Upper Sixth of the North Manchester Grammar School brought me not only a pass in all four subjects but a distinction in the English Scholarship paper. It was 1949. To think that just 10 years earlier I was unable to speak a single word of English.

There was a bonus. I was awarded a Manchester City Council Scholarship of £250 a year. It might not sound like a lot these days but then it paid for my board and lodgings at university, my books and even my entertainment (cinema, theatre once a week). The fees were also paid by Manchester.

I had applied to three universities to read German and French: Leeds, Birmingham and Nottingham. I was interviewed by each and offered a place at each. In the end I chose Nottingham for two reasons: it had the most beautiful campus and it boasted a ratio of four women to each man.

Oh, and its German department also enjoyed an excellent reputation.

CHAPTER SIX:

ON CAMPUS

Nottingham University's campus stretches across more than 300 rolling acres of luscious green parkland briefly interrupted by a large, shimmering lake and to see it for the first time knocks one's breath away. There's a long uphill walk from the bus stop just outside the main gates on University Boulevard to the white Trent Building that overlooks and commands the lake. When I arrived in October 1950, the Trent Building was where everything happened – registration, teaching, eating, congregating, playing – the lot.

Lower corridor belonged to the students. The student union's office; the junior common room; an almost endless notice board that advertised some 180 clubs and societies; at the end of the corridor was The Refectory where one queued for snacks and meals and where one chatted up students of the opposite (or same) sex. Up one flight of stairs to the ground floor – and one was in the administrative part of the building. Here was the Registrar and, opposite his office, was the realm of the Vice-Chancellor, then the amazing Bertrand Hallward, a historian and classicist who had been headmaster of Clifton College throughout the war years. At one end of the long corridor was the Library, which always smelled of lacquer, and at the other end the entrance to the Great Hall where concerts, plays and general assemblies were held.

Higher up the next floors held the lecture rooms where most of the teaching took place. Additional teaching was to be found in prefabricated huts on various parts of the campus. The university was, after all, young. Although it had been inaugurated in 1837 as the Mechanics Institute and had become a university college in 1881, it had to wait until 1903 for its royal charter of incorporation. It did not become a "proper" university until 1948, twenty years after it had moved three miles west of the city centre to the site to which I was introduced. And it was not until 1956, a couple of years after my graduation, that it opened the Portland Building, almost a reflexion of the Trent Building, to house student facilities, cafeterias and an art gallery. Indeed, when I return to the campus today, I can hardly recognise it. The halls of residence have snowballed and teaching is now performed in dozens of well designed buildings. There is a superb library and an attractive music centre, to say nothing of a gigantic teaching hospital that has sprung up over the years.

But it was the embryonic campus I entered in 1950. I was just one of a comparative handful of students – some 1,200 undergraduates (compared with today's 15,000 plus 8,000 part-timers and 8,000 postgraduates). It was an intimate, friendly atmosphere and yet I felt nervous. I was the first in my family who had ever entered higher education. My father's pride could not contain itself. He broadcast the news to everyone he met. "My son has gone to university. He has won a scholarship. Now he is at the University of Nottingham. I cannot speak English proper but my son is in the university…"

My father had always been my best publicist. He would have made a good public relations officer. When I had gone hitch hiking through Europe with Bill Houfe, my school friend, after we had sat our Higher School Certificate (that's pre-A-levels), we had left a number of poste-restante addresses behind so that our results could be posted to us. It was just a question of reaching certain destinations and going to general post offices in Geneva, Lyon, Dijon and Versailles. There weren't any mobile telephones or email facilities in those days. Internet cafés had not even been dreamed of. My father had opened the letter addressed to me that contained the results and had forwarded them, along with Bill's, to the various post offices, as we had agreed. But he went further. He telephoned the *Manchester Evening News*, one of our two local newspapers and had managed to get through to the news desk.

"Yes, hello, pliss can you help? My son, John Izbicki, ist somewhere in Europa hitchhiking mit a frient. I have no idea vehr they are and am vorrit. Zey haf both done very vell in ze Higher School Zertifikat but zey don't know anysink…"

A reporter was despatched to see my father at home along with a photographer and he was pictured holding the paper showing my results under the headline:

Refugee Boy with high HSC scores missing 'somewhere on Continent'

With my German cousin, Liane,
at home in Manchester's Heywood Street.

Alongside the double column picture of my father and the HSC results was a smaller one of me, borrowed by the reporter from one of the many picture albums kept by my parents.

Later, when I was awarded the scholarship and had my application to Nottingham accepted, he had passed on the information to the *Evening News* as well as the *Jewish Telegraph*, one of Manchester's Jewish papers which, of course, gave a page lead to the story of the lad who could speak no English on arrival to Britain in the dark and dangerous days of 1939 having now gained top marks (98 per cent) in an English scholarship paper and awarded a City Council Scholarship etc etc etc...

But this did not help me become less nervous during those first few days at Nottingham. Everyone else I saw seemed so very self assured. And a number of students *owned cars*! I had found digs on the Mansfield Road, a room in a nice little semi with a doctor's surgery on the ground floor. My landlady, a kindly soul called Molly Walker, cooked decent meals – breakfast and dinner every day and full board at weekends, all for £3 a week. I made my way to the university by bus and a walk (often a run if I was late) up that long road from University Boulevard to the Trent Building whose clock would announce the time and help increase my pace. Students and academics with cars would pass me (and many others) and beat us to the car park.

My nervousness did not last more than a few days. I encountered none of the snobbery and certainly none of the anti-Semitism I had feared. And I joined as many clubs and societies as I fancied. The very first was Dramsoc. My memory of the encounter with Sybil Thorndike was not forgotten and my love of the theatre and acting had not diminished. Then there was Ensoc – the Entertainment Society, which put on shows and cabarets as opposed to plays. It would stand me in good stead for many a year to come.

The others were: the International Society; the German Society; the French Society and the Film Society.

I did not join the Jewish Society. Was it because I did not feel particularly Jewish? Or was it perhaps because I had never managed to feel at ease within other Jewish groups I had tried to join? In Manchester I visited the Habonim and the Maccabi, both fairly respectable associations with particularly good reputations in the fields of sport and athletics. My visits were disasters. I found the other young people present noisy, snobbish and unfriendly. The girls seemed more interested in what cars young men had available than in their opinions. As I didn't have a car and had come by bicycle, I didn't count, so I just sat in a corner and observed. And when I had observed enough, I rose and left, never to return. My Jewish school friend, Norman Morris, was different. He and I saw eye to eye and came to each other's houses to sit and talk or play the piano – Norman was a superb pianist and I was a good and willing listener.

So I didn't join anything Jewish at Nottingham. I was kept busy enough with Dramsoc and Ensoc. At the former, I met Gamini Salgado, a Sri Lankan student of English who would sit cross-legged in a corner of the junior common room, chain smoking and blowing the biggest smoke rings I had ever seen. Gamini turned out to be a talented director and picked me to play Socrates in his production of Ernst Toller's brilliant anti-war play *No More Peace*. It was my Dramsoc debut and I found myself playing the lead in Gamini's production of Marlowe's *Dr Faustus* and later a leading role in Shakespeare's *Richard III* produced by a young woman called Rosemary England, who made use of the entire Great Hall, having characters abseil from the circle down to the stalls and run onto the stage. In one scene on the first night, I led a group of characters down from the stage for a trip to the Tower of London. We were meant to march up the centre aisle, then round to the aisle Left and down to the stage which, by that time, had been transformed to the Tower. I suddenly noticed that I was being followed by only two characters; three others were calmly marching towards the Left aisle. I had to do something.

"My Lord of Hastings! Has't forgot the way to the Tower? This is by far the shorter route." And I marched on…all characters now behind me. Members of the audience howled with laughter and cheered the impromptu addition to the play.

In the review that appeared later that week in the *Nottingham Guardian*, the headline read: *Uni actor improves on Shakespeare and saves scene.* The reviewer gave the production a thumbs up.

Another Rosemary England production saw me playing *Volpone*, Ben Jonson's avaricious character. My leading lady was an exceptionally beautiful young student in the French department, so when it came to the line: *Come, my Celia, let us prove, while we can, the sports of love*, we went to it with such realism that it left the audience – and us – gasping.

I even managed to try my hand at a Dramsoc production. I translated Wedekind's *Erdgeist* (*Earth Spirit*) from the German and produced it on the Great Hall stage, giving it its British premiere and even playing the part of Schwarz, the artist who paints and seduces the gorgeous Lulu. It received a rave review but it proved to be my swan song for Dramsoc.

Ensoc proved even longer lasting. While taking part in its shows, I met another highly talented undergraduate called Charles Griffiths. Charles was a gifted mime artist and I not only learnt a great deal from him about the art of mime but have to confess without a great deal of shame that I pinched one or two of his sketches to add to my own repertoire used later at teacher union cabarets.

All this time I was of course going to lectures and trying to keep up with my other, far keener fellow students. The lecturers were superb and often very funny. Horton Green was a well built man who towered over everyone at around six foot seven. He took size 12 shoes and prided himself in his ability to run. Despite his energy and his concentration on exercise and maintaining a healthy lifestyle, he died not many years after I had graduated. Another lecturer, Dr Schweizer, spoke with a high pitched German accent, adored everything that Goethe had written and impregnated each of his students with a love for the German language. About once a month, he would invite us to his house, play records of Mozart and serve us decent tea and cakes. We always left him reinvigorated and determined to get Firsts.

We didn't get Firsts. I just about scraped a 2:2, having concentrated more on my social life than on my books. My parents came to the graduation ceremony in the city centre and my mother cried. My father's smile stretched from ear to ear. Both were extremely proud and a little embarrassed to be introduced to my tutors. My father kept giving little bows as he shook hands.

It was his way of showing respect for academe.

I had two lots of digs at Nottingham – the first with Mrs Walker on the Mansfield Road; the second in a German household on the Bilborough Estate, where George, my landlord turned out to be an alcoholic, poor sod. He was a Brit. His wife, Milly, was German and would discuss politics with me. She had a great sense of humour and was a good cook to boot. I had a brief affair with a blonde who ran an ironmongers in Bilborough village. While with Mrs Walker, I noted that the doctor, a GP, was a chain smoker. I tackled him about this: "Isn't smoking supposed to be bad for you?" I asked one day. "Yes, it is," he replied. "I use fags as an antiseptic against all the microbes my patients bring to the surgery." I was grateful for this piece of advice as I was a fairly heavy smoker myself in those days.

At my Bilborough digs I recall having to walk home from a party. It was well after midnight and I didn't have enough cash to afford a cab – and my stomach was in a bad way. I had the runs – but there was nowhere to stop and relieve myself. I flagged down a police car and pleaded with them to take me home. I gave them the reason and the two coppers collapsed laughing. "Jump in then, son," they said and switched on their siren, racing me to my digs. I ran in and straight to the lavatory. Milly obviously heard me and knocked at the door. "Would you like a cork?" she asked – but later brewed me a cup of black tea to help things settle down. I've never forgotten those two policemen. I doubt whether such service would be given to a young student these days.

My sex life was healthy. I dated some of the prettiest girls on campus. Some lived in Florence Nightingale Hall, whose warden, a Miss Beecham, was extremely protective and strict with her tenants. Men were barred from the hall after 10 p.m. and, even during the day, if they visited their girlfriends in their rooms, the girl had either to be chaperoned by another woman friend or had to wheel the bed outside into the corridor. The warden would patrol the hall's floors regularly and at night, if she heard a man and woman "snogging" in the grounds outside the hall, she would lean out of a window and shout: "You two! Stop disturbing everyone. Go to the bikesheds round the back!"

Today Florence Nightingale is mixed, as are all the other halls. But the ghost of Miss Beecham still continues to stalk the corridors.

I thoroughly enjoyed Nottingham and later sat on the committee that organised reunions. I also edited a magazine for alumni and called it *GONG – Gazette of Nottingham Graduates* – containing a page of readers' letters called *Your Write* and a couple of pages called *Where Are They Now*, filled with news and pictures of past students. Both were later adopted by university alumni magazines and newspapers in various parts of the country. The reason for the title, Gong, was a nostalgic echo of the Fifties and Sixties when the Nottingham students' arty and glossy magazine was called *Gong* and the newspaper *Gongster*. "My" *Gong* didn't last many years. Other glossier journals are now being produced to feed the memories of alumni and seek their cash and legacies. As long as governments deprive higher education of their much needed funds, universities and colleges will have to continue milking their well-to-do alumni.

CHAPTER SEVEN:
RETURN TO GERMANY

One part of my German degree course stipulated that at least one semester should be spent studying at a university in the country where that language is spoken. In my case, I returned not once but twice – first for the conditional semester, the second to take up a one-year British Council research scholarship. In 1951 I agreed to a place at the University of Göttingen, one of the oldest and finest of the country's universities. Ironically, it was founded by a British king – George II, Elector of Hanover – in 1734. He even gave it his name: Georgia Augusta and it was among the very first institutions of higher education in Germany. Like other German universities, it suffered humiliating blows during the Nazi period. It has spawned more than 40 Nobel Prize winners yet some 50 professors and lecturers were forced to leave its employment in 1933 when the Nazi party came to power. Max Born and James Franck, two Jewish Nobel Prize winners were among those sacked. It cost the university its worldwide renown for mathematics and the natural sciences. What, I wonder, would Otto von Bismarck, one of the university's many famous alumni, and the Brothers Grimm, two others, have thought of the Nazi actions?

I went to Hanover by boat and train with some understandable fear and trepidation. How was I going to regard the people around me? How would I feel to hear German spoken – the German of the streets, rather than that of the university lecture theatre? The war had only ended a little over five years before. Rationing was still in full swing in the UK. Tea continued to be rationed until 1952; sweets, sugar, cream and eggs remained rationed until

1953; butter, cheese, margarine, cooking fats, meat and bacon stayed rationed until 1954. Bread and jam had come off the ration in 1948 and points for clothes were finally abandoned in 1950.

The first thing I noticed as I stepped off the train at Hanover was the shop windows. They were crammed with goodies: rows upon rows of sausages and salamis; chocolate and sweets; wines and beers; coffee and tea…I could hardly believe my eyes. Who had won this war? Was it really us? I could not think of myself as German. I was British through and through and I was suddenly filled with a desire to smash some of those windows – not in order to eat the food they displayed, but to avenge the Kristallnacht 13 years before. I could feel tears of anger welling up in my eyes. Sod them! Sod the lot of them! I felt like turning round and taking the next train back home.

Instead, I stamped into the station restaurant, found a table and ordered *Ein Paar Wiener Würstchen mit Kartoffelsalat und ein Bier* (a pair of Vienna sausages, potato salad and a beer). The waiter, very polite, brought the beer at once along with knife, fork and serviette. I sipped the Dortmunder. It was excellent and I drank down about half the glass. The meal was soon served and I helped myself to a dollop of the *Düsseldorfer Löwensenf* (mustard) from the jar already on the table. I tucked in. A glorious taste. There was clearly no shortage of decent food and drink here. Not like us at home, still queuing up for a few sausages at the butchers and hoping he might find us a morsel of steak from under the counter.

I noticed that people at nearby tables were watching me eat. They weren't so much looking as glaring. What on earth was the matter? How dare these bastards stare at me! Did they recognise my "Jewishness", my longish nose? I tried not to stare back but could not help myself throwing them the odd angry glance. At this they looked away but seemed to be muttering to each other, clearly about me.

It was not until a few days later when I was having another fine meal in a restaurant with Helmut, a newly found young German friend, that I experienced the same strange stares "What on earth are people glaring at me for?" I asked him. He smiled. "It is because you are cutting your potatoes with a knife. They are crazy."

These Germans who had lost the war, who had plundered Jewish homes and shops, who had cheered Hitler and helped him and his Nazi henchmen murder so many millions of innocent people, now had time to bother their little heads with stupid etiquette. I resisted the temptation to stick my tongue out at them.

Göttingen turned out to be a remarkable city with medieval buildings sensitively mixed with more modern architecture. I quickly learned that it dated back to AD 953 when a village called Gutingi was presented to a Magdeburg monastery by Emperor Otto. In the 14th century Göttingen became a commercial centre and part of the Hanseatic League. The Thirty Years' War almost saw the death of the town, turning it back into what it had been at the start, a sleepy village. So it remained until 1734 when George II decided to pull it up by its roots and build a university. He obviously succeeded because Göttingen never looked back – although it had to wait until some 13 years after my visit to win city status. Like most German towns and cities, it holds tight to its many traditions. So, for example, every graduate who attains a doctorate is obliged to kiss the lips of a goose girl whose smiling statue stands proudly in the centre of a fountain in front of the old town hall. The *Gänseliesel* boasts of being the most kissed girl in the world.

I made my way to the Fridtjof Nansen Haus, the address which was to be mine for the semester. As the name suggests, this student hall of residence was founded and run by Norwegians and named after the Norwegian explorer who managed to reach 86 deg.14', then the highest latitude ever reached in the Arctic. But the name given to this student residence was far more appropriate, for Nansen became High Commissioner for refugees with the League of Nations after World War One and in 1922 was awarded the Nobel Prize for Peace for the superb relief work he had performed after the war. The atmosphere I encountered inside FNH immediately put me at my ease. About 70 men and women, all fellow students from countries throughout the world, lived there. The "working language", alas, was English – not the best for those wishing to perfect their German, but we all managed to get together regularly in the large sitting room to debate "issues of the day".

At the university I signed myself up for more subjects than I could cope with: Literature from the Niebelungen to Goethe and Schiller; Middle High German; Poetry in the 19th Century; History of the Second World War... Yes, History of the Second World War.

This weekly two-hour lecture was, believe it or not, the most popular provided by the university. It was delivered by Professor Ernst von Schramm and filled not only the biggest lecture theatre (with seating for about 300 students, although I'm sure many more managed to cram themselves into it) but was relayed to three other big lecture theatres.

Before Professor von Schramm had become an "academic" he was General von Schramm of the Wehrmacht and had fought alongside Field Marshal Rommel. At least one was fairly certain that he knew more than many others about the history of the Second World War. The lectures were held on

Tuesday evenings from 7 – 9 p.m. – a good time to make one's retreat to one of the many nearby taverns for a few beers. Von Schramm spoke in the clipped tones of what could be described as a typical German officer. But it became increasingly clear that he had never been a Nazi – just a soldier doing his normal duty. I introduced myself to him and found him almost human. Could it be that I was over-generalising about "the Germans"?

Indeed, hardly a day went by without Germans approaching me in pubs and clubs, once they discovered that I was British and a Jew, to engage me in long and involved conversations (in German) that went something along these lines:

"Ach, you know, I was never ever a member of the Nazi party. In fact, I was never a Nazi sympathizer. I knew nothing, really, hand-on-heart, *nothing* about concentration camps. Yes, it is true that I could see Jewish people suddenly disappearing from their homes. But I thought that they were emigrating, leaving Germany. Believe me, I would have also left Germany if I could have afforded it. Ach yes, there were times when I saw a Jew or two being arrested. Again, I thought that they must have broken the law and would have to go to jail. That they ended up in those awful death camps…that never even occurred to me. Please have another beer…"

So it would go on. And on. And all I could do was to nod or shake my head slowly and give the odd tut-tut, neither agreeing nor disagreeing.

But when I sat in a bus or a train or a café and looked around me at German men and women aged around 30 or 40, I could not help wondering. "What were you doing between 1933 and 1945? Did you throw the odd brick at a Jewish shop window on November 9, 1938? Did you help set fire to your local synagogue? Did you throw up your arm in a Nazi salute? Did you spit at some old Jew in the street? Look at you now, quietly reading the paper or tucking into a delicious piece of apple cake smothered in whipped cream…

And then I met Bernhardt. Bernhardt Silber was a student of medicine. He was 22 years old and extremely pale I discovered why, when he told me that he was financing himself through university and was selling his blood to blood banks in Göttingen as well as at hospitals in towns as far off as Kassel. His blood group was rare and he was often called to come and provide a quick pint in emergencies. Each hospital would pay him 25 DM, enough to help him pay for food and lodgings. No one bothered to check whether he was perhaps selling more blood than was healthy.

One evening, when we were having a quiet drink in my room in the Nansen Haus, Bernhardt undid the button on his shirt sleeve and rolled it up to his elbow. He turned his arm towards me and there, tattooed on his skin, was a long number – **5879649.** Bernhardt was a Jew who had survived Auschwitz. We spoke until three o'clock in the morning, during which time I tried to comfort him. But what comfort is there for a young man who is going through a living nightmare?

Bernhardt truly believed that he had killed his parents.

He was not quite 13 years old and preparing for his Bar Mitzvah when he, his mother and father, were dragged from their apartment in Dortmund, bundled into a truck already bursting at the seams with other arrested Jews and driven to a camp. Two days later, they were transferred to a train and pushed into one of the wagons normally used to transport cattle. There were no windows and hardly any ventilation. The train rattled on for two days and nights.

"Babies cried endlessly. Old people groaned and complained of pains in their heads, stomachs, legs, arms, backs. There was nowhere to lie down properly. We leaned against each other. Our asses went numb from sitting on the hard, cold floor of the wagon for so long. Some people were sick. Others kept farting. People shat themselves and peed in their pants…there was nowhere else, no latrines, not a fucking thing in the entire carriage. The stench of vomit, urine and shit was dreadful. I tell you, I can still smell it now.

"When we arrived and the doors were thrown open, it was a relief. Some of us even cheered. We had air to breathe. Can you believe it? We welcomed the air of the place we had now reached at last. And when we jumped down and were ordered to form ranks and keep our belongings at our sides, we did so willingly. As long as we were out of that fucking wagon with its stench, we were satisfied.

"Then, from the distance came the sound of music. An orchestra was playing to greet us. An orchestra, would you believe it? They were playing Beethoven – I can't remember whether it was the Eroica or the Pastoral. I think it was the Pastoral. Beautiful. It was like arriving at some holiday camp. Holiday camp…huh…" and Bernhardt began to cry, the tears rolling down his cheeks very quietly. There were no sobs, just quiet tears.

"It was Auschwitz. That's what the holiday camp was. Auschwitz. And the orchestra was formed of Jewish prisoners who in their real lives had been members of the Berlin Philharmonic and other well known orchestras and who were now forced to play for the camp commandant – and us newcomers. It was a neat piece of Nazi humour, God damn them."

Bernhardt continued to shed his tears in silence and I felt my own eyes burning. "What happened then?" I asked, breaking the silence.

"Then? Well, then we were marched to the camp's reception area by these goddamn guards in their green uniforms, who did nothing but shout at us to hurry. '*Schnell, Schnell, Mach's los!*' Some carried truncheons and sort of whips and they just lashed out at the older people who found it difficult to march or walk fast. Some fell down and were kicked until they got up again. By now many of the women were screaming and holding on tightly to their children and husbands or brothers. They knew that this was no holiday camp but some fucking awful hell hole manned by devils.

"We were then ordered to leave our suitcases and other bits of luggage at the side of the square. 'You'll get it later' we were told by one smirking guard. We had to get into three groups – men on the left, women and girls on the right and boys aged 12 and over on the far right. The screams of women grew louder and louder as they were parted from their menfolk and sons.

"A more senior officer stepped out of a hut and came to inspect us new arrivals. He was joined by a couple of adjutants holding clipboards on which to take special notes – though what notes they were hoping to take eluded me then and continues to elude me now. The men were closely inspected and the younger, healthier, better built specimens were told to form another separate group on one side of the square. The older, physically less able were ignored.

"The routine was different for the women. Any decent looking ones were made to form a side group. Next to them came those women who were not particularly attractive but who looked as though they'd be good workers. The feeble and old were also ignored. The girls formed a group of their own. Why? What was to become of these groups?

"And the band played on...

"The process of dividing us all up took hours. At last we were sent off to our so-called living quarters, each group marched away by storm troopers or whatever they were, with their sticks and whips and constant shouts. The elderly and old were also marched away. They were to be given the privilege of taking a communal shower, while the water was still warm." There was a long pause, while Bernhardt's breathing grew heavy. We had been drinking a few bottles of beer that evening and I quickly opened another bottle and poured the contents into his glass. He downed it in one before continuing his narrative.

"I don't need to tell you what kind of showers those poor people were treated to. Everyone knows now what the showers at Auschwitz were. But then, no one suspected that they were anything other than showers. A real luxury for some people were showers.

"Even I had no idea of what showers they were when I was given my job. I had to roll these large steel cylinders from one of the big stores to the buildings that contained the showers. Once at the buildings, they were lifted by a mobile crane up to the roof where other prisoners, under the supervision of guards, had to roll them to a central point and attach some rubber hoses to outlets on the cylinders. I must have transported about 20 cylinders a day.

"On about the fourth or fifth day, I spotted my parents queuing up for their shower. I waved to them and they waved back. My father shouted something to me. I couldn't hear but it sounded like 'God bless you, Berni!' He used to call me Berni. I never saw them again." He looked me straight in the eyes. "Don't you see? I killed them. I killed my parents with those fucking cylinders. They contained the Zyklon B gas that was poured from the roof down into the shower rooms that exterminated so many thousands of Jews, including my parents. And I helped to murder them. Fuck it. I murdered them!"

And now he let it go and broke down in sobs. I put my arms around him and tried to comfort him. But what comfort could anyone offer a young man who for years had genuinely thought and would continue to think for the rest of his life that he had been instrumental in gassing his parents to death in one of the world's worst concentration camps.

Life at the Fridtjof Nansen Haus went blissfully on. I recall two of my fellow inmates in particular. One was a young Scot called Hector Mackenzie, a helluva nice guy but an awful miser. I have never met any Scottish people who resembled anyone even vaguely associated with the many jokes told about Scots. They are nowhere near as thrifty as the average Yorkshireman. But Hector was an exception and I often suspected that he was deliberately putting on an act for us Sassenachs.

Hector would regularly enter into conversation with me about nothing in particular, then say: "John hav'ye got a cigarette?" I would take out a packet and let him pick one, even two. But one day, I was myself out of cigarettes, so when Hector approached me with his usual: "John, hav'ye got a cigarette?" I told him: "Sorry, can't help you today. I've run out myself..." Hector then delved into his pocket and pulled out a packet of cigarettes. "Och well, I'll hav'te smoke one of me own then," he would say and, without offering me one, would turn his back and stalk away.

He had won himself quite a reputation, not so much as a miser, but more as a Scottish patriot and "freedom fighter". He was among the small party of students who whipped away the ancient Stone of Scone from Westminster Abbey on Christmas Day, 1950, carried all 152 kilos of it to the boot of their somewhat ancient car and brought it back to Scotland. About four months later it was recovered and returned to London – but it is believed that the students, including Hector, had managed to make a replica and that the stone now at Westminster Abbey is a fake. The original, on which the kings of Scotland were crowned from around the year AD 900, is said to be safely in the keep of Arbroath Castle.

The other memorable student was a man called William King, an American – a black American. Now, Germans in 1951, other than those living in the American zone of Germany, had hardly seen let alone met a black American – or, for that matter, any black man or woman. So wherever Bill went, there was no end of interest. I was with him when we were walking through some of the narrow streets of the old section of Essen, a pleasant city we were visiting one weekend. It was in the early afternoon, a time when many people were sleeping off their heavy lunch. Suddenly a first floor window burst open and a little girl of about nine or ten, looked out and shouted: "*Mama, Mama, komm schnell. Da ist ein Neger in der Strasse*" (Mum, mum, come quickly. There's a Negro in the street). At this Bill, who was well over six foot tall and fairly wide with it, looked up at the girl and acted like an angry gorilla. The girl screamed. "*Mama, er macht mir angst*" (Mum, he's frightening me). Bill and I laughed and he shouted up to the child: "*Mach nix*" (it's okay).

My semester at Göttingen showed me another side of the German psyche. It was the time of the Landtag (state) elections and there were daily public meetings either in halls or in the main square of the city. There was, believe it or not, an ultra-Right wing neo-Nazi party – the *Deutsche Reichs Partei* (German Empire Party) founded in 1950 – only five years after the end of the war. Its leader, Otto Ernst Rehmer came to Göttingen to speak in the hustings. He drew a huge crowd – and a great deal of applause throughout his speech, a speech in which he extolled the beauty and power of Germany and called on its people to support nationalism. I looked at the faces around the square. Were these people zombies? Did they not realize where nationalism had got them? Had they not seen the massive destruction of their towns and cities? And could they not recognize yet another Nazi standing before them and repeating those trite old Hitlerian messages?*

The following day I was again in the same square, this time listening to another politician. This time it was Kurt Schumacher, leader of the SPD –

---

* Dr Konrad Adenauer, leader of Germany's Christian Democrats (equivalent of Britain's Conservatives) tried to ban the Nationalist Party (NPD) which had subsumed Rehmer's Reichs Partei, in 1953. His attempt failed miserably and in 1964 the party managed to win one per cent of the seats in the Bundestag.

Germany's socialist party. Schumacher was a totally different fish from Rehmer. Although he was only 56 years old, he gave the impression of being much older. He was just half a man with one eye, one arm and one leg, having been seriously wounded during the Great War of 1914-18. When Hitler came to power, Schumacher spoke out publicly against him and his followers and was badly beaten up by Nazi thugs for doing so. This did not deter him from continuing to oppose the Hitler regime. His reward was arrest and incarceration in one concentration camp after another. He suffered 10 years in a series of camps, including Dachau. He was at his fourth or fifth camp – Neuengamme – when the British Army liberated it and him in April 1945.

Schumacher's oratory was splendid and he managed to shout as loudly, possibly even louder than Rehmer and attracted the same volume of applause and cheers as the neo-Nazi on the previous day. I looked at the faces around the square. They belonged to the same zombies as those who had cheered Rehmer. It was then that I realized that there was a schizophrenia governing Germany, that Beethoven and Buchenwald, Mozart and Mauthausen, Schiller and Sachsenhausen, appeared to go hand in hand through German history. The people who gave the world literary geniuses like Johann Wolfgang von Goethe also burnt the works of Heinrich Heine and banned the music of Felix Mendelssohn.

I was lucky to hear Kurt Schumacher speak that day for at Christmas that same year he suffered a stroke that laid him low and the following summer, August 1952, he died. He was two months short of his 57th birthday.

Not all my spare time was spent listening to political diatribe. Göttingen had a splendid theatre and was putting on a whole festival of new German plays. The director was Heinz Hilpert, one of Germany's best, whose reputation was already well developed when he was producing plays at the *Volksbühne* in Berlin as early as 1932. I went to the theatre every night, seeing each play in the ambitious repertoire and marvelled at the immense talent shown by their authors. In a way, German playwrights in the immediate after-war years could be likened to the sudden rise in the tide of English poets during the First World War.

I recall in particular Wolfgang Borchert's moving play *Draussen vor der Tür* (which was translated as *The Man Outside*). The author described it as "the play no theatre wants to perform, no audience wants to see". It told the story of a young soldier who returns home from the horrors of the front at Stalingrad, having lost a leg in battle, only to find that he has also lost his wife and his house along with his illusions, his hopes and his beliefs. There was, in fact, nothing left, no open door and nothing worth living for. The play was broadcast in February 1947 to critical acclaim and given its stage premiere in Hamburg that November – the day after Borchert died.

Hilpert's production influenced me so much that I decided to write about it and the other plays I had seen at the *Göttingen Stadtstheater*. I sat down and penned a series of five features on "Post-War German Theatre" and sent them, along with pictures (given to me by the theatre's public relations office), to the *Manchester Evening Chronicle*. To my amazement and delight, I had a letter from the paper's feature's editor to say they not only wanted to publish them all but, unless I objected, would also like to syndicate them to the other papers in the Kemsley group. They paid me £5 for each feature and one guinea for each picture published – that was a total of £30.5s from the *Manchester Evening Chronicle* alone and about another £126 from a further six local Kemsley papers that accepted and published the Monday to Friday series. I felt myself rich. It also represented my very first successful step into the world of journalism. Kemsley was later to become my first employer.

I was to return to Germany once again before graduating from Nottingham, this time for a whole year. I won a British Council Research Scholarship, which I decided to take up at the University of Münster in Westphalia. I must confess that my main research was conducted at Pinkus Müller's wonderful pub in the city's centre. Münster is a devout Catholic city with many churches. But the churches are outnumbered by pubs and Pinkus Müller seemed to attract a large proportion of students who sang bawdy songs and drank his famous *Altbierbowle* (a mature beer in a bowl of various fruits, from strawberries to grapes and apples). This gave it the impression of being nothing more than a fruit cup – but that was deceptive...

I lived at the Aaseehaus, a large students' residence right on the shore of the huge lake (the *Aasee*) whose water laps at the buildings on the edge of the city centre. Again, the tenants were about as international as one could hope for with many hailing from Scandinavia, Italy, Spain, the United States and the UK. But instead of me going for some curvaceous blonde from Sweden, I fell head over heels for a curvaceous blonde who was homegrown in Münster and bearing the poetic name of Barbara Seraphim. We had met at one of those hectic balls held during the *Drei Tolle Tage* (the three mad days) that precede Ash Wednesday and form an annual event in Germany, particularly in the Catholic sections of the country. For three days people go bonkers, dress up in the weirdest of costumes and attend dances (balls) where drinks of every type flow freely and hotdogs are devoured by the ton. Just about anything goes. And I joined in the fun with the gayest of abandon. As did Barbara.

One of the "Three Mad Days" celebrations in Münster, Westphalia,
together with Barbara Seraphim, an early love during student days, 1953

Her father turned out to be Professor of Economics at the university and was anything but stuffy. Her mother was a delightful woman and cooked like a dream. As for Barbara's younger sister, Ulli, she was sensational. But enough. Suffice to say that we all had a very good time but it was becoming all a little too serious and I was far from ready to put down my anchor.

At least Barbara and her family, who introduced me to numerous others in their circle, helped me to shed my anti-German prejudice. I always remembered that Gestapo officer who encountered my father on the stairs of our Berlin home... *"I've not seen you. Now fuck off. And for God's sake, get out of the country while you still can!"* And anyway, one should never make the young pay for the sins of their fathers.

There remained a few episodes that left a bad taste in my mouth, the most bitter of which was the "tradition" of the German *Verbindungen* (fraternities). Although duelling was strictly forbidden, it continued to be practised by certain fraternities, particularly those in the Right-wing sectors of the country (Göttingen certainly had many, of which three or four still fought with sabres). One can still see some *Alte Füchse* (Old Foxes) parading the country's streets, particularly the streets of university towns. They may be recognised by their nasty looking scars – cuts across their cheeks and sometimes foreheads.

I was once invited to a *Verbindung* – all meetings are secret – and witnessed a duel. It would be hilarious were it not so violent and vicious. Two men will stand facing each other, a sabre's length distant. They wore no masks or protective gear of any kind and their swords were real and very sharp. At the signal of the "referee", they would simply hack away at each other. There's no Errol Flynn-type duel, where blows are parried and the fighters jump over chairs and tables in a continuing battle. They simply hack and hack away until one or other draws blood. Then the fight is immediately stopped and a doctor approaches, examines the wound and stitches it. During that time, the wounded student must not flinch or so much as blink. He must "take it like a man" and will be able to show off his scar with pride.

But it isn't just the stupidity of this kind of duelling that turned my stomach. It's the advantages gained by the Fraternity Member. Real academic advantages. Unfair advantages over students who are not members of such fraternities or who belong to the "wrong" fraternity. In those days, students were able to move from university to university, studying their subject for a year or even a semester at, say Essen, another at Cologne, a third at Frankfurt am Main, a fourth at Wuppertal and so on. Before taking their finals, they would examine carefully the list of professors who would be likely to see them for their *viva* and perhaps mark their final papers. A professor who happened to be an Old Fox of the same fraternity as the finalist, would be the one to whose university the student would enrol. If both wore the tell-tale scar, so much the better. It did not mean that an absolute *Dumkopf* (idiot) would be able to pass his examination, but it certainly helped.

Thank goodness this travesty of academe now lies in the tatters it deserves.

On the brighter side, I joined a play-reading circle at *Die Brücke* (the Bridge) in Münster, a branch of the British Council. There I met many young Germans who were decent actors and actresses who wanted to improve their English. We had great fun together reading and discussing plays that ranged from Shakespeare to Arnold Wesker. But the experience brought back my ambition to strut the stage and I decided to write and produce a show for myself and a "supporting cast".

Posters went up proclaiming "John Izbicki – Mimes and Character Sketches (in English, French and German) in *Die Brücke*" with dates. It was a sell-out – and what is more, it was a success. I performed soliloquies from *Volpone, Richard III* and *Dr Faustus* (that last wonderful scene, just prior to his awful death) and sketches of various kinds in which young German men and women students formed the cast, plus mimes ranging from "The Lady

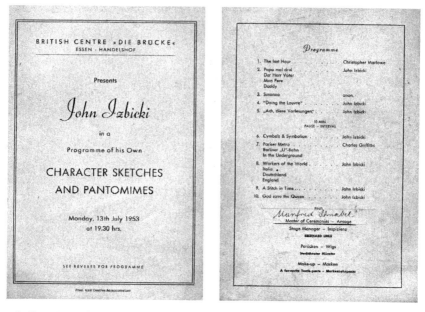

On Tour: Actor Izbicki, tours his own show of character sketches and mimes round Germany, 1953

Character Sketches programme, 1953

Takes a Bath" to "Rush Hour in the London Tube". The 90-minute show reaped a fair income which went into the coffers of the *Brücke* (used for its charitable causes).

Word had got out and the call came for a tour round other British Council "bridges". They paid all expenses and I would rehearse local student actors for a couple of hours before each show. And so it was that performances were given at Göttingen, Essen, Dortmund, Wuppertal, Düsseldorf, Cologne, Frankfurt am Main (the only one in the American zone) and Berlin with ("by special demand") repeats in both Göttingen and Münster.

In Berlin I was reunited with Liane, my lovely cousin, and her mother, Aunt Mary. It was an emotional coming together with tears all-round. The first night at their Tempelhof flat was spent talking and listening into the small hours (I seem to recall getting into bed at about 5 a.m. – with a rehearsal to attend later that day for a performance that same night). They told me of the terrible time they had lived through and of the bitter battle Mary had to wage against Gestapo and police to save Liane from certain deportation to a camp and probable death at the hands of her murderous fellow countrymen. The end of the war was in no way a sudden bed of roses. The Russians were touring the city in droves seeking food to eat and females to rape. There was not much of the former but plenty of the latter and women, including my aunt and cousin had to spend their time seeking safe hiding places, often within the rubble of what was once a beautiful city.

They spoke of my uncle Isi's death and the refusal by doctors to rush to the flat in the middle of the night to try and save him. Jews were expendable.

I was glad my mother, Isi's sister, was not present at that meeting and I never told her about that part of the conversation.

Instead I returned to Münster and my "research" and Barbara and packed my bags for a sad departure and return to Nottingham.

The show had to go on.

CHAPTER EIGHT:

NATIONAL SERVICE

My degree course and its accompanying periods in Germany had brought me a deferment of what in those days was a compulsory two years of National Service. I was not looking forward to it, especially as it meant having to share this long stretch with youngsters of 18. After all, by the time I received my orders to report to Willems Barracks, Aldershot in October 1954, I had reached the mature old age of 24! But it had to be done and so I packed my suitcase, embraced mother and father in a long and tearful farewell and took the train down to Hampshire.

Aldershot – "Home of the British Army" – turned out to be just as miserable a place as I had expected. Everything was grey. The houses were grey, the shops were a dull grey, the barrack gates were grey, the squares that seemed constantly occupied with marching soldiers and screaming NCOs, were grey. Only the barrack huts where we were billeted had their greyness mixed with a dull, rusty red.

We had to report to a hut to be provided with our uniform, comprising a rough khaki battledress that itched and scratched the legs and any other part of the body it contacted, two shirts, equally rough and khaki, a brown knitted tie, a black beret, some badges, a pair of heavy boots – the fact that they turned out to be a bit loose didn't matter ("You'll grow into 'em. Now get on wi' it") – two pairs of khaki socks, two vests, two pairs of pants, a khaki sweater and a kit bag.

The motley crew that I suddenly found myself part of was told to "fall in" (where, I wondered) and were then marched off to a barrack room to await the arrival of our trainer. Corporal Frank Ward was slim, tall, dark and about 35. He made himself comfortable on the edge of a table so that he could look down on his new batch of recruits. There was absolute silence as he glared at each one of us in turn, devouring us with his fiery brown eyes.

"Right," he rasped at long last. "Let me introduce myself. My name is Ward. Corporal Ward. Just think of 'ospitals and blood and you'll immediately think of me." There were a few giggles. "What are you laughing at, eh? I've said nothing funny. Any more giggling, like a lot of bloody little girls, and I'll give you something to really laugh about! My name – sweeping the room of petrified rookies with those blazing eyes – is Ward. And you'll certainly get to know me and remember the name, I can promise you that. I take no nonsense from anyone. You'll address me either as Corporal or Sir. Is that understood?" As there was no response, he shouted: "IS…THAT…UNDER…STOOD?!"

"Yes" we all called back. "Yes, What?" "Yes, Corporal," we shouted. We were learning fast. We were in for ten weeks of the most intensive squarebashing which some of the weaker incumbents were unable to take. They tended to go on sick parade every couple of mornings and managed to get out of the more painful periods of training.

Just before I received my call-up papers, I had been contacted by a young officer back in Manchester who offered me the opportunity of joining the Intelligence Service and going to a camp in Hertfordshire to learn Russian. "You'll be put through an intensive language course and you will speak nothing other than Russian for the few months you'll be there." He made it sound very attractive and I still kick myself to this day for having rejected that opportunity. But frankly, I had just graduated and had had my fill of books and study. At that time it seemed as if I had been able to do nothing other than study from the day we entered England. My English had become accent-free and I simply could not have contemplated another "intensive language course". So I refused.

The result was Willems Barracks, Aldershot – and the Royal Army Service Corps. The RASC, of which I was to become a proud member, was best known to all and sundry as the "Shit and Treacle mob" for they were the soldiers who dealt with transport and supplies, including food, petrol and ammunition for the rest of the British army. The RASC lasted until 1965 when it was amalgamated with the Royal Engineers to form the Royal Corps of Transport. Luckily I was in it for only two years, from 1954 until 1956 – but they were among the most eventful, even enjoyable, years of my life.

Squarebashing was everything one has ever heard or read about it. Not only did it mean a great deal of cross-country marching carrying full kit – together with one's rifle ("The rifle is your best friend and don't you ever forget it or I'll fuckin' brain you" said Corporal Ward) – but it also meant cleaning the square by picking up leaves and rubbish with one's bare hands and scrubbing parts of it clean with a toothbrush. Nights were mainly spent in the barrack room, occupied by an entire platoon of 30, cleaning one's gear. This included burning the end of a spoon over a candle, then smoothing it over the black polish that had been spread on your pair of boots. Boots had to shine so that Corporal could see his ugly face in them. The brass buttons on tunics and clasps of belts were polished with Brasso so that they shone in competition with the sun and the webbing belts and gaiters had to be scrubbed with a product called Blanco until they appeared clear yellow. Everything had to be laid out in a certain order at the bottom of the bed for morning inspection and anything that was not 150 per cent to the inspecting officer's liking would be flicked onto the floor and the name of the "culprit" put on report. This invariably meant extra duties or even jankers (army jail) for a night.

Apart from all the parading, we received training in various fields. Being of a "literary disposition", I was earmarked for clerical tuition, put into an office to type out forms and file documents. It was a boring task but liberation was close at hand.

I was summoned to appear before the barracks commandant. "Ah, Izbicki … have I pronounced the name correctly? .. I've entered you for a WOSB. Think you might be just the chap. All right?"

"Sorry, Sir, the what? I'm afraid – er – I've not heard of a Was Bee…"

"War Office Selection Board. It's a small test they give you to see whether you might be officer material don't chew know … Report to Buller Barracks tomorrow morning 0800 hours sharp. All right? Good. Good luck." He busied himself with something else on his desk. The interview was over. I said "Thank you, Sir," saluted smartly, turned and marched out. War Office Selection Board, eh? What will they expect me to do? How does one become an officer? Should I phone my parents? No. Better not raise their hopes. I might not pass this test, whatever it turns out to be.

The "test" extended to three days and consisted of a variety of exercises. I was by no means alone. There were about 15 other young men, all roughly my age, all graduates as it turned out, though mainly Oxford, Cambridge and Bristol. I was the only one from Nottingham. There were debates on topics which we were given 15 minutes to prepare if we were chosen to propose or oppose the motion; then there were discussions on numerous topical subjects, some heavily political (I told myself not to fall into the partisan trap but remain

*Officer Cadet Izbicki at Buller Barracks,
Aldershot, 1954*

as objective as possible and I think I was right to make this decision), and talks we had to give on subjects literally pulled out of a hat – and without any time for preparation.

The outdoor exercises were more complicated. We were told that such and such a ditch represented a torrential river which had to be crossed in order to rescue two of our men on the other side. All we had were some planks of wood, lengths of rope and a torch. We discussed the matter, closely observed by some officers who were our examiners. They were noting which of us would take a leading role in solving the problem and who, if anyone, would be content to be a follower rather than a leader. I made sure that I did not fall into the passive group.

Finally there was the all-important obstacle race. We were given three minutes to run a course that was riddled with such items as tyres dangling from tree branches through which one was meant to dive; long tubes through which one had to crawl; water jumps; tunnels flooded with water through which one had to inch one's way by holding one's breath – and finally, a tree one had to climb (there were large nails for footholds) until one reached a long branch at the end of which hung a rope. This one had to grab and shimmy down before the timed whistle was blown. I suffer from vertigo and this might well have been my undoing, end of WOSB, end of officer material…I held my breath, climbed, then crawled along the branch. God, it was awful, terrifying. The rope was hanging there, just a couple of feet away – and I knew that I could not have more than a few seconds left. I shut my eyes, jumped for the rope and slid to the ground, touching it as the whistle blew.

I passed!

Buller Barracks. Smarter uniform and a white officer cadet insignia on the beret. On my first spot of leave I rushed home to Manchester in uniform. It gave my parents a thrill and my father cried. He often did when anything moved him deeply – and that included TV films. But on seeing me, the tears were understandable. "Ach, Horstchen, Horstchen, Du bist doch so elegant, so schön!" my mother exclaimed (You are so elegant, so handsome). My mother continued to call me Horstchen (the diminutive of Horst) throughout her life. She had never managed to get properly used to John.

Weeks later, when I had passed the many tests and squarebashing ordeals and arrived at the passing out parade, Mum and Dad travelled down to Aldershot. They joined the many other families in a grandstand to watch as we marched to a military brass band and were inspected by the big wigs, a general and a collection of other senior officers. We were real officers – Second Lieutenants…Subalterns.

Afterwards we had tea with our parents and officers would do their duty by mixing with the visitors. A Major came to chat to my parents who blushed with pride and more than a little embarrassment on account of their "broken English". The Major didn't bat an eyelid. "You must be very proud of your son," he declared. "Oh, yes, certainly, very proud," my father replied. "We never dreamed that an English officer he would be. It is good. So very good."

It was all very understandable. Here we all were, just 15 years after our arrival as refugees from Nazi Germany, unable to utter a single word of English, let alone conduct a conversation; just six years after being naturalised as British citizens, and here was little Hortschen a graduate from a university and an officer in the British army. When I received a parchment bearing golden letters and signed by Her Majesty the Queen to admit me as a loyal officer in her army, my father immediately had it framed and prominently displayed at the house in Heywood Street, Cheetham Hill.

Soldiers are never allowed to stand still for too long and I received my sailing papers. I had to report to the good ship Halladale at Liverpool and sail to – I knew not where. I was asked where I should most like to serve and answered with absolute candour that, as I spoke perfect German and reasonable French, I felt I would be of most use being stationed in Germany (BAOR) or with SHAPE in Paris. But the Halladale, which was not only carrying troops but also their families, was not sailing to Germany or France. We were going to be at sea for 10 days and I took on two jobs for the duration of the cruise: education officer and entertainments officer.

Every morning I would be in charge of teaching children and in the afternoons I would supervise deck sports and swimming galas or act as disc jockey, playing records over the ship's radio. In the evenings I organised entertainments ranging from bingo to ballroom dancing.

The jobs, which I thoroughly enjoyed, turned my head a little, so when I was given yet another form to complete, asking me what I should most like to do in my posting, I answered: "I should like to be an entertainments officer or an education officer". I handed the form in and thought no more about it.

At long last we arrived at our destination – Egypt. The ship stopped well outside Port Said for about an hour and I later discovered that the delay was on account of my presence. The officer commanding had had second thoughts about taking me to Egypt. He was telephoning London for advice and had suggested dropping me off in Cyprus where we also had regiments stationed. He felt that taking a Jewish officer into a country that was hostile to Israel, as Egypt then certainly was, was asking for trouble. London, however, felt otherwise and I was thrown in at, as it were, the deep end.

Port Said has a smell all of its own. As the ship approached the dock, nostrils were besieged by a mixture of aromas. It was not a nasty smell, just something

Young National Service officer
goes to Egypt, 1954

Berlin Wedding: While I was busy doing my National Service on Egypt in 1954, my lovely cousin Liane married a Berlin police officer, Wolfgang Pirsch. My parents (pictured on the right) had never wanted to return to the city of their nightmares but plucked up the courage to attend Liane's wedding in a Berlin Catholic church. Also pictured are Wolfgang's mother (left) and Lonny Mühl, who had been deeply in love with my mother's youngest brother, Georg.

that lodged between a thousand different spices and the sharp tang of fish. The heat hit us in dry waves. The cruise had proved hot enough once the ship had passed Malta and we had already come prepared with a healthy tan, but the scorching, almost overpowering sun of Port Said was new to us and officers and men alike sought the shelter of what little shade the ship allowed.

Then there were the traders. Small boats, motorized and rowed, seemed to fly towards us until they swayed and rocked alongside the Halladale, their owners shouting their wares and promising us "good prices, cheap, cheap, cheap." And what wares they were: rugs and carpets were stacked high in one small boat that looked as though it might sink under their weight at any moment; there were sweetmeats in another; cameras; pictures, which, when packets of them were thrown up to outstretched hands, included "naughty" photographs of naked young girls in curiously acrobatic positions being penetrated by athletic, muscular men; leatherware occupied another rowing boat and the Arab manning it waved handbags aloft promising to "make good price and give presents"; another boat was stacked high with the inevitable crates of Coca-Cola – an awful drink that owed its Middle East success to the cunning of the company's astute marketing department which produced posters showing a happy looking Arab on a bicycle, drinking from a bottle of Coke and bearing across his shoulders a Camel. The slogan read something to the effect: *Coca-Cola for Strength and Virility*! The drink, which had found no success when it was first introduced to Arab countries, suddenly found itself top of the soft drinks league. The slogan – and the illustration – had done the trick.

When the troops had eventually disembarked, they were assailed once again by tradesmen who waved their products, from bags and "priceless" Rolex watches offered at ridiculous prices ("To you Sir, only £20. £20 for Rolex!" When the victim shook his head, the salesman would not give up. "All right Sir, how much you give me for Rolex?" If he said "I'll give you a fiver", the Arab knew he was in for a sale. "Fiver? You make joke, yes? All right. £18. No? £15 and that's my best price." "No way I'll give you £8, not a penny more." "Sir, I am losing money on your price but I will give you also this bracelet for girl friend. £15!" "Okay, here's £10" and the soldier reaches in his pocket and produces a note. "My heart bleeds…but you just arriving, guest in my country, so as welcome, I will give you." And he snatches the £10 note and hands over the watch and bracelet. A good deal. Copywatches are cheap and he will have made a decent profit.

A special coach for officers took us to a transit camp where we were to stay until postings were decided. For three days, we "got our knees brown", sunbathing, lounging, swimming, writing letters, going shopping at the nearby souk or taking military buses to the nearest big city, Ismailia, a place I was to get to know a great deal better during my posting.

On the fourth day at our transit camp, we were gathered together and bussed to Moascar to see the Brigadier who was to issue us with orders to take up more permanent posts. Our motley crew stood around outside the Brig's offices waiting to be called. This procedure was done in alphabetical order. Each man went in and, some five or six minutes later, came out smiling or sullen to announce to the rest of us which was to be his fate. "Water Transport at Suez!" exclaimed the first, clearly delighted with such a plum posting. "Bloody Transport at Azyut, wherever that might be," grumbled another. "Supplies, Port Said," pronounced the next with a skip in his stride.

When it was my turn, I marched into the Brigadier's office, came smartly to attention and produced my finest salute. The Brig was looking at some papers and when he had done, peered at me without a smile. After what seemed an eternity, but must have been all of twenty seconds, he said, almost with disbelief in his voice: "So you're the young man who wants to do just about anything except soldiering, what?!"

I had no idea what he was talking about and replied limply: "Not ex—act—ly, Sir…."

"But here you say," quoth the Brig lifting a sheet of paper and waving it in my direction, "here you say quite clearly that you want to be an *entertainments* officer …or – and I suppose that might be a little better – an *education* officer."

The form I had filled in on the ship, which had probably been the third or fourth of its kind I had been asked to complete since my departure from Aldershot, had been the one document that had actually been read. I felt myself blushing and could only stammer a "Sorry, Sir."

But the Brigadier stood me at ease and started asking me some interesting questions. What had I done before I had joined the RASC…What were my hobbies…and so on. When I explained my love for the theatre and my "experience" in journalism – i.e. my articles on the post-war German theatre, published by the Kemsley Press, and my contributions to the university magazines and newspaper, he started taking notes. I even told him that the editor of the *Manchester Evening Chronicle* had advised me to write to him some three weeks before I was demobbed if I should still be interested in journalism as a career. "Very interesting," he grunted.

At last, after nearly 25 minutes, I was dismissed. Outside, my fellow subalterns looked astounded. "Well, you took your bloody time," one of them said. "Where the hell have you been posted?" The puzzlement on my face only increased their curiosity. "I don't know," I said quietly.

"You don't know!! What d'you mean you don't bloody know?"

"Exactly that," I said. "I honestly have no idea. I've not been given a posting, just told to get out and he'll let me know."

And so it turned out. We all returned to our transit camp and within 24 hours all my companions had disappeared, each to his new posting while I continued to laze on the nearby beach, go for walks, sit in the officers' mess in the evenings or visit restaurants and clubs in Moascar or Ismailia. I soon got to know the best clubs in town – there were three or four to choose from: the French Club; the Italian Club and the Tennis Club. Ironically, there did not appear to be a British Club. But Ismailia had large Italian and French communities. The Brits were all service people living in camps and family living quarters. But both the Italian and French clubs had goodly proportions of Brits – mainly officers and their ladies (that's one thing I learned immediately: it's officers and their ladies; NCOs and their wives and ORs (other ranks) and their women; the periods of enlightenment, women's lib and political correctness had not yet been born).

Those who ran the transit camp were by no means amused at my continued stay. They had to look after me; I cost them money; I was, as far as anyone could tell, totally useless. Nearly three weeks went by and the officer commanding the camp had just decided to put me on the duty roster, when a message was received at the office and passed to me: I was to report to the Brigadier the following morning. A car was to come and collect me at 0830 sharp.

To my surprise and the amazement of all others who were anywhere nearby, the vehicle sent to fetch me was a highly polished staff car, normally occupied only by senior officers. The driver gave me a smart salute as he held open the door and off we whizzed to Moascar and the Brig.

"Ah, Mr Izbicki (subalterns are always addressed as Mr, just like surgeons...) I think we've found you the kind of job you might like."

"Yes, Sir. Thank you, Sir," I said still at attention.

"Stand easy, man, stand easy, I don't bite. Now I want you to report to Colonel Stubbs. My adjutant will show you where he hangs out. If he finds you all right, you'll work under him. Good. Well, off you go."

I again stamped my feet to attention, saluted, thanked him again and made my exit. I had no idea what awaited me just a few Nissen huts away.

Colonel John Stubbs was a remarkable man. Tall, thick-set but not fat, with a bristling moustache and steel-blue eyes. His eyes were astounding. They pierced through you. My salute was dismissed. He got up from behind his untidy desk and shook my hand. I felt no warmth in the welcome. His eyes seemed to burn through me as he commanded me to sit down.

"How d'you pronounce your name and where does it originate," he demanded. I told him. "Is – bi – cki...Think of biscuits. It's Russo-Polish in origin. My father was born in a part of Poland which at the time was a part of Russia..."

"All right, spare me the long history. I've been asked to have a look at you and see what you can do." He rifled through some papers on his desk and pulled out a couple of pages.

"This is a piece I wrote yesterday. I want you to put it into English. You'll find a typewriter over there," and he pointed to a desk in the corner of the room.

I took the piece from him and started to read it as I crossed to the desk. I could see nothing really wrong with it. It seemed like a perfectly reasonable news story about some sporting event at one of the camps. What was I to do? If I rewrote it – putting it "into English" as he had advised – it would appear as if I was criticising his composition. If I did not rewrite it, it would look as if I was incapable of writing. What the hell! I decided to have a go and take the consequences. I rapidly found an alternative intro half way down the Colonel's story and then rewrote the odd sentence. Fifteen minutes later I took

Lieutenant Izbicki,
Army Public Relations Officer,
Suez Canal Zone of Egypt,
1954-55

the piece over to him. I must admit that I could feel myself trembling. Those eyes!

Colonel Stubbs looked at the piece for a few seconds, then up at me. "So, you think I'm not much good, what?"

"No, Sir, not at all, but you did – er – ask me to do a rewrite job. I – er – found it very difficult because – because there was nothing wrong with the piece you wrote," I stammered.

Then an amazing thing happened. John Stubbs stood up, held out his hand to shake mine and his lips parted into a smile that seemed to radiate throughout the room. His piercing eyes twinkled. "Welcome aboard, John Izbicki. Welcome to the madhouse."

He poured me a large scotch and explained the job. And that was the second surprise of the day. Stubbs was the head of public relations for the Canal Zone of Egypt. The military establishment of this unit comprised a lieutenant-colonel, a major, a captain, two sergeants, three corporals (drivers and gofers). There was no establishment for a lieutenant, whether second or full. The captain was being repatriated, so that created the vacancy which I was to fill. So I became an acting National Service captain, billeted in the staff officers' mess, with a personal batman, which meant no more need to polish boots, Blanco webbing or even make beds. This was a dream come true. No, not a dream come true, since I had never even dreamed of anything like this.

I was able to appreciate some of the ill feeling towards me from other members of my mess – all of them officers who had earned their pips and crowns in the normal way, through long service and devotion to Queen and Country. Here was this pipsqueak, a national serviceman by gad, still wet behind the bloody ears, come into a staff officers' mess! He'll soon be telling us all what to do, by gad. I never heard any such comments but could well imagine them. Some might even have thought: trust the bloody Jews to wheedle their way into this elevated position – and a bloody foreigner to boot!

But, as I say, I never heard such a comment expressed by anyone, though some of the looks received spoke volumes. It took several weeks to break the ice. But when that ice was broken, the atmosphere changed dramatically. The first to buy me a drink at the bar was the oldest member, a captain who had joined the regulars 26 years ago, just before the start of the Second World War, had seen service at El Alamein and been wounded. He had made it to quartermaster and had come up through the ranks, a genuine man whose friendship I was to treasure. His approach had triggered others in the mess to drop their aloofness and warm towards me.

There was only one other Public Relations Officer (for that was now my title) in the small but comfortable array of Nissen huts that housed our offices. Major Harold Digby, a short, bronzed, good natured man who spoke in clipped, slightly high-pitched tones, was second-in-command, and took care of much of the administration. He had come out with his wife and family and entertained me to many a decent dinner at his home. The other active – very active – member of this busy crew, was Sergeant David Steen. He was our photographer and a damned good one. No wonder. He had been photographer on the *Picture Post*, which used to be Britain's finest glossy and sold 1,500,000 copies a week after it was founded by Edward Hulton in 1938. But later, Hulton accused the editor, the legendary Tom Hopkinson, of running pro-Communist articles. Hopkinson left in disgust in 1950, followed by several of his best writers and photographers. The magazine struggled on until it folded in 1957, the circulation having dropped to below 600,000.

To tell the truth, I didn't have much of an idea about public relations but I was soon to find out following an unforgettable lesson. John Stubbs handed me my first assignment. "I want you to nip along to El Alamein next Tuesday and cover the commemoration service. Big affair. Probably the last one, you never know, so it should get some decent coverage. See the Digger (his name for Major Digby) and he'll give you a warrant for the train journey. You should enjoy it." He was a man of few words. But just as I was going out of the door he called me back. He was holding a small poster in his hand.

"Damn. The Moascar Players are putting on a show next week. First night Tuesday – just when you'll be in El Alamein. Pity. See if you can't get some little advance on it from the producer, eh?" And he handed me the poster.

The Moascar Players were doing Priestley's *An Inspector Calls*, one of my favourites. I telephoned the producer who said I'd be welcome to attend the first dress rehearsal on the Sunday night. I gladly did so.

The performance, stopped umpteen times for little corrections and changes, ended late and I hurried back to my desk, now resplendent with a name board, a typewriter, a telephone, in and out trays and a small heap of A4 paper and sheets of carbon, to write my first piece. Having gone through a few years of philosophy at Nottingham, my intro went into Priestley's thoughts on time and motion and how these affected the play. I then spent some time on the production, which I praised, and the cast, which I lambasted.

I re-read the article carefully, making sure that grammar and spelling were correct, put it on the desk of the young corporal clerk who would produce copies and send it to whoever was on our list of newspapers, magazines and suchlike, and went to bed at about 2.30 a.m.

The train took me past Alexandria and into the desert to El Alamein where a variety of regiments were already represented and were busily erecting tents, latrines and a Press enclosure (there was even a special tent put up for me!). What surprised me most on that day was how, out of nowhere, in the middle of this vast desert, groups of Arab boys, some of them no more than 10, suddenly appeared pushing carts and wheelbarrows crammed with crates of beer – and yes, Coca-Cola – to sell to thirsty soldiers, despite the fact that we already possessed our own supplies of food and drink.

About 100 metres from the small city of tents was the reason for our being there: a huge cemetery of white stone containing thousands of graves – the graves of those who fell in this, the most decisive battle of the Second World War. British and Commonwealth forces, comprising 250,000 men of the Eighth Army under the command of Bernard Montgomery, were pitted against the German Afrika Korps together with Italian and German infantry of some 90,000 men under General Erwin Rommel who had already captured Tobruk the previous month and were intent on digging themselves in and taking the whole of Egypt.

It was a bitter battle extending from July until September in 1942. Rommel threatened our most vital supply lines across the Suez Canal and El Alamein represented the Allies' last ditch defence. At the end of the battle, 23,500 of Monty's men were either dead or wounded. And Rommel lost 13,000 dead and 46,000 either wounded or taken prisoner.

Now all that remained was the cemetery and its memorial crosses and those thousands of graves.

The story of that commemoration service virtually wrote itself. I filed it as quickly as I could and caught the military train back to Ismailia. There I was met by a staff car and driven at top speed back to Moascar.

"What's the rush?" I asked the driver.

"I've been instructed to take you straight back to the General, Sir," he replied.

"The *General*? What General?"

"Sir, General Richard Hull, Sir."

"General Richard Hull wants to see *me*?! Whatever for?"

"No idea, Sir."

I had never even seen a general, let alone the General Officer Commanding the entire Canal Zone. What could he possibly want? I was getting quite jittery and only hoped I was properly dressed.

I was ushered into the General's plush office, came smartly to attention and saluted. He glared at me and did not ask me to stand easy, so I continued to stay erect and to attention. After an ominous silence he spoke loud enough to let me know that he was angry. Very angry.

"What in the name of God d'you think you're doing, man! Eh?"

"I don't know what..."

"Be quiet! Have you seen this?" He picked up a newspaper and held it close to my face. I had never seen the paper before in my life. It was a copy of the *Egyptian Gazette*, an English language paper printed in Cairo. What on earth had it to do with me?

"See this headline? *Priestley's Inspector Leads Weak British Army Cast.* And there's even your bloody byline underneath it: *By John Izbicki* (he pronounced it John Isbeeky).

Thereupon followed the worst dressing down I have ever received. The General went on and on for a good ten minutes, telling me that this was not what public relations was about. "You had the audacity to say that the actor playing the Inspector had a voice like a rattling dustbin lid! Did you know that that was Frank Gardner? *Major* Frank Gardner! You have insulted him and half the wretched cast. Is that your idea of public relations?"

And so on...I can still hear his voice today. Not only was he the GOC British Troops in Egypt from 1954-56, but he was knighted in 1956 and promoted Field Marshal.

I felt my knees trembling and a cold sweat trickling down my face and neck.

Then the strangest thing happened. After he had finished ranting and raving at me, he just suddenly stopped, opened a cupboard at the side of the room, brought out a bottle of scotch, turned to me, smiled broadly and said quietly: "All right. Stand easy. What'll you have to drink? You could probably do with a stiff one. Young man, I have to say that I like your nerve. What's more, I tend to agree with much of what you wrote. But for pity's sake don't do it again. And try to make your peace with the Moascar Players…"

That last order took more than a while. But I ended up joining them and took a leading part in *Reluctant Heroes*, Colin Morris's satire on the army as seen through the eyes of National Servicemen. I took the part of Gregory, the country yokel, later played by Bernard Cribbins.

But by that time I had learned that public relations meant impressing the public with the product you are trying to sell to them – in this case, the British Army and all who serve in it.

One of the most important things I learned during my posting in Egypt – apart, that is from coming to grips with PR – was how to protect oneself from the *khamsin*, that strong and incredibly hot southerly wind that suddenly descends on you and brings half the sand of the Sahara with it. If one is unfortunate enough to be on the beach in nothing but a swimsuit, it will lash one's back just like a whip and leave its mark. I have even known it to draw blood. The

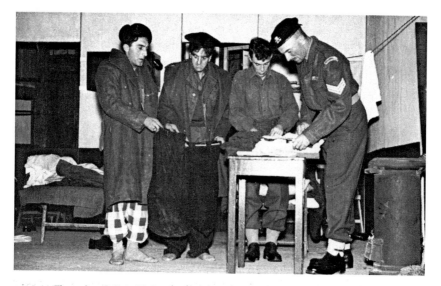

The author (left) in "Reluctant Heroes" with the Moascar Players, Egypt, 1955

Izbicki (centre) in another scene from "Reluctant Heroes," 1955

khamsin (also known as the *ghibli* in other parts of the Arab world) comes without much warning at any time between March and May and attacks everything in its way with great ferocity. It penetrates cracks under doors and gets into every drawer, leaving mounds of sand in neatly folded clothes as well as larders and fridges of food.

The only thing to do, if one has the time to spare, is to fill a bath with lukewarm water, get into it with a book and a bottle of scotch and wait until it subsides. One's hair will still be caked with Sahara sand but at least one will have been able to relax with a leisurely drink and a read.

Public relations proved easy after that first disaster. I drew up a list of twenty questions on a sheet of A4, attached to a board, grabbed David Steen, and visited one company after another, interviewing soldiers at random. Name, Rank, Unit, Where Stationed, Since When, Married, Single, National Service or Regular, Home Town and Address, Brothers/Sisters and What Do They Do, What is Missed Most, What is Liked Best at Posting, Any Ambition, What Message for Those at Home, Favourite Book/Pop Star/Sports/Food... The answers were jotted down and a nice picture taken by Snappy Steen.

Later that afternoon or the next morning, the stories would be written up and posted, together with the pic, to the subjects' local rag, be it the *Newcastle Journal* or the *Northampton Chronicle*, the *Colchester Evening Gazette* or the *Manchester Evening News.* If I came across brothers in the same regiment, I hit the jackpot. They were bound to make a decent story. And there were even times when I managed to find stories that warranted national coverage – like the time someone managed to drive a Land Rover into the Sweetwater Canal and was rescued by a passing young National Serviceman who was to be repatriated and demobbed the following day. Both driver and his heroic rescuer ended up in hospital and received the requisite 20-plus jabs to counteract just about every possible disease. The story made the *Daily Mail,* the *Mirror* and even the *Sunday People* as well as the boys' local papers.

The Sweetwater Canal, it should be pointed out, was the most misnamed waterway in the world. It was a great source of just about every disease under the sun; local Arabs not only pee'd and crapped into it but they threw their dead animals, ranging from dogs to donkeys into it. It looked very still and very beautiful but represented a menace to our forces. There is the tale of a North Londoner who in the late 'Thirties went down with a dreadful illness – terrible headaches, stomach pains, a rash of green and blue pimples, high temperature and constant vomiting. Doctors were stumped and the man grew more and more sick. At last he was sent to London's Hospital for Tropical Diseases. Even there doctors could not identify the symptoms until one of them prised out of the patient some of his past history. During the First World War the man had been in Egypt and had been foolish enough to swim in the Sweetwater Canal. Now, more than 20 years later, the River had its revenge. Doctors pumped into him a veritable cornucopia of antidotes and he was discharged a week later. The story is probably apocryphal but it was drummed into us and certainly persuaded most, though by no means all, to keep well clear of the Not-So-Sweetwater Canal. By now it will have been cleaned up and might even have returned to being a source for pure drinking water. But I still wouldn't risk it...

At one or other of the Ismailia clubs I shared a bottle or two of wine with an FBS (Forces Broadcasting Service) producer and complained that, although this radio station was putting out some decent programmes (mostly from the BBC) and that there was quite a sufficiency of pop programmes, the only classical music that could be heard was the odd record on the weekly *Two-Way Family Favourites* which played requests for "the boys" overseas from their parents or sweethearts. Why, I wanted to know, wasn't there a classical – or semi-classical requests programme.

"Not a bad idea. I'll put it up at conference next week. D'you think you'd be able to run it?"

"What, me! You must be...well – er – yes, I suppose I could. Why not?"

And we uncorked another bottle and toasted the newest (to be) disc jockey for FBS.

The programme ran every Friday evening for an hour. To begin with I made up the requests and prayed that no one would take the trouble to check the existence of Staff Sergeant Joseph Mulley or Lance Corporal Jack Green. But they had asked for Beethoven's Pastoral or Mozart's Requiem Mass – both among my own favourites and I introduced excerpts and made sure to pronounce the various German orchestras and conductors properly. Slowly, letters did come in and genuine requests played. What is more, I started receiving the odd "fan letter". Women said they found my "husky voice attractive". Well, wow! One record that was asked for again and again was one I had played during my second week (and had invented the letter requesting it). It was from the Brecht/Weill *Dreigroschenoper* and had the opening line: *We must be barmy to join the Army...*Clearly a winner.

My PR work also took me to numerous Army cocktail parties and dinners to which leaders of the local Egyptian society had been invited. By this means I met and became friendly with Ismailia's Chief of Police as well as a rather charming Egyptian army Colonel who knew Gamal Abdel Nasser personally. Nasser was then Egypt's prime minister, having been the driving force behind the coup that deposed General Mohammed Neguib a year after the latter had put an end to the monarchy and proclaimed a republic.

Nasser was an intelligent and ambitious man. A product of Cairo's Military Academy, he soon rose to the rank of Colonel and was wounded in the Palestine War of 1948. He was understandably not well disposed towards the formation of the State of Israel and for a period, the 65,000 Jews of Egypt – more than 25,000 of them in Alexandria alone – were being persecuted.

I had visited two or three synagogues in Ismailia and Cairo, though never in uniform, and had no idea that my actions had been spotted and reported by Egyptian intelligence. I recall advising some Jewish tradespeople in the Moascar area to leave the country while it was still possible and safe to do so. Again, I had no idea that my comments were being transmitted to the Egyptian powers that be. It was to become clearer at the beginning of 1956.

Meanwhile, I was making my mark in other areas. A young corporal approached me one day and asked if he could speak to me privately. We went into an empty office in the PR section of the compound.

"Sir, I was wondering whether I could ask you to be my friend in court..."

"A what in court?" I had not come across the expression.

"A friend in court, Sir. I'm being court-martialled and I need someone to speak for me. You did a story about me a few weeks ago and it got in the local paper at home, Sir, so I thought maybe you'd be able to speak for me like..."

"On what charge are you being court-martialled?"

"Sir, I was accused of taking this ring from out a jewellers in town and not paying for it."

"And did you?"

"Yes Sir, I did Sir, but I was goin' to pay for it, honest Sir. I was on my way to the pay desk at the front of the shop but before I got there, I was grabbed and the police was called an' then the redcaps (Military Police) came and took me away and banged me in the slammer, and then I was charged with shoplifting this ring and told I'd be court-martialled, Sir…"

After further discussion I decided to defend the man.

In those days, my leisure reading consisted mainly of crime fiction. My particular favourite was Perry Mason – not the televised version with Raymond Burr acting Mason from an inexplicable wheelchair; that particular series came much later, when I had already outgrown my passion for the courtroom detective and his beautiful secretary, Della Street. I devoured the books of Erle Stanley Gardner while in Egypt and, frankly, the Case of the Shoplifting Corporal intrigued me.

Like Mason, I spent much of my spare time prior to the hearing, finding and interviewing prospective witnesses. I paid particular attention to the manager of the jewellery shop from which Corporal B (I do not wish to publish his name) was alleged to have stolen the ring. I actually got the man to admit that he might not have given the young man much of an opportunity to pay the cash. He reluctantly agreed to give evidence.

I also had an hour's chat with Corporal B's girlfriend, a lovely Greek girl, born and bred in Egypt, for whom the ring had been intended. To introduce a love angle was just the kind of thing Perry Mason would have enjoyed doing.

The day of the court martial arrived and we all filed into the courtroom (one of the larger conference rooms at the camp). The president of the court was a Scottish colonel of the Army's legal branch. Two captains sat on either side of him. The president told me later that he thought this was to be an "open and shut case" and he had already agreed to an invitation to lunch after it was over. He was in for a surprise. John Perry Mason Izbicki was the defending officer and he had a list of witnesses to call.

Courts martial are not like the courtrooms of fiction. Counsel have to speak very slowly so that their words may be noted, verbatim if possible. The case dragged on and had to be adjourned for an all-too-brief lunch break. At around 4 p.m. the President summed up and he and his two aides left to deliberate their findings.

It was unusual for anyone being court-martialled to be found not guilty. Once on a charge so serious that a court martial has to be convened, there's little hope for the prisoner in the dock. The three officers returned after some twenty minutes and the President pronounced the verdict: "NOT GUILTY! You are free to go…"

There were gasps from everyone, including Corporal B, the prosecuting officer – and me. The President and the two captains departed and then a cheer went up. Corporal B, with tears in his eyes, rushed over to me and grasped my hand. I thought for a moment that he was going to kiss me and backed away. "Thank you, Sir, oh thank you. That was great! Thank you." I was numb. Deep down I was quite certain that he *had* pinched that ring to give to his girlfriend, but the Perry Mason in me had put on a show.

Later the President, who had a slight speech impediment – a short rasping cough in the middle of words – approached me at the bar of the mess. "Young man. I suppose I ought to compli—argh—ment you on a good day's work, even though – argh – you preven—argh—ted me from having a decent lunch." All I could say was: "Thank you Sir".

The result spread quickly and unsurprisingly I was in some demand. Suffice to say that I defended a total of seven courts martial cases, of which two were found not guilty, and was assistant prosecuting officer in one case.

This last one was embarrassing for the Army. A sergeant-major with some 25 years service was tried for selling military furniture and equipment to the Arabs. As we were closing down the Canal Zone in 1956, we had to get rid of all kinds of material. I was fortunate enough to be in charge of transporting horses and mules over to Cyprus where they were housed and used by our regiments on the island. The alternative would have been to put the animals down. But what of all the office furniture and equipment, printers and the like, to say nothing of a number of Jeeps and other vehicles that were "surplus to requirement"? Well, they were taken out to the desert and buried.

Our sergeant-major had provided some Arabs with the detailed map reference of where the "burial ground" could be found. For this he was paid the sum of £500. The buried "treasure" was worth several times that much. The Arabs were caught in the act of digging up the cars and cupboards and our NCO was arrested.

Needless to say, he was found guilty, stripped of his rank and incarcerated in a military jail for a year. As for all the equipment, it was duly reburied in a different part of the desert! I felt sorry for the sergeant-major and must confess to feeling doubly sad that I had not been asked to defend him. I doubt whether I should have got him off but feel that I might have done a better job at defending him than the professional QC who had been flown in for the trial which lasted four days. Perry Mason Izbicki would have dealt a few aces.

The courts martial president had approached me at some stage during my series of cases for another chat – and a proposal. "How would you – argh – like to join the le—argh—gal branch? You'd have a good – argh – life and would get a perma—argh—nent commission. Captain...even perhaps Ma—argh—jor. What d'you say, eh?"

Still at the forefront of my mind was the offer I had from the editor of the *Manchester Evening Chronicle* to contact him for possible employment once my National Service came to an end.

The voice of the editor, John Goulden, played back like some tape recording in my head. "No thank you, Sir. I'm sorely tempted, I must admit, but I have already promised my services to a Manchester newspaper," I said. The president was sorry but there were no ill feelings and we parted on good terms. Of course, I had no idea whether that Manchester newspaper would even remember my name...

I was among the last officers to leave the Canal Zone – and not before time. In the lead-up to the "closure" I had the pleasure of numerous get-togethers with Egyptian contacts, including newspaper editors and senior journalists who taught me the odd "naughty" word in Arabic. We would meet at one of the clubs in Ismailia and even in the restaurants and clubs of Cairo.

I made no secret of my racial background and I was often ribbed mercilessly but always in good fun. "I suppose you're really an Israeli spy," was among the most common "jokes". In seriousness, most of my Arab friends could not grasp how a Jew could be an officer in the British Army and not the Israeli forces. I could explain until I was lost for words that I was not a Zionist and that my loyalty was to Her Majesty and Great Britain alone.

On New Year's Eve, 1955, I had been invited to meet my Egyptian General and the Ismailia Police Chief at the Italian Club for one of our knees-ups. I went there early, arriving at about 10 p.m. and made sure that the reserved table had a few decent bottles of wine and that a couple of bottles of Champagne would be delivered just before midnight. Meanwhile, I sipped a good Claret and listened to the dance music.

About 10.45 p.m. I saw the two of them and a small retinue of other dignitaries come through the door, greeted with bows and salutes by the Maitre D and senior waiters. I stood up and gave a smile and a brief wave in their direction. They walked expressionless towards our table, looking straight through me – and passed on, totally ignoring my mumbled greeting. They disappeared through the crowd and stood at the bar.

It did not need a soothsayer to explain this odd behaviour. It was a clear warning. I called the waiter, paid the wine bill, collected my greatcoat and left the club. I hailed a nearby taxi and ordered the driver to take me back to camp – "at the double". Once there, I joined the few fellow officers still on site in the mess and drank in the New Year. I did not really feel much like celebrating. I felt sick to the stomach. I had never been cold-shouldered by people I considered to be my friends. What could it have meant? I was to find out later – much later.

I had my orders from John Stubbs. He was going back to Blighty before taking on another posting. I was to be posted to Tripoli. I had never been to Libya and was quite looking forward to the change, but it was not as a captain. That was over. I was back to my proper rank: 2/Lt and was to join an RASC company just outside Tripoli.

Saying goodbye to the few remaining people at Moascar was fairly traumatic. But there was one amusing episode that I shall never forget. The Staff Officers' Mess was beautifully kept by a whole series of Arab stewards, all under a rotund, ruddy cheeked man with a bristling moustache, a fez upon his head, and a swagger stick with which, I felt certain, he used to beat his underlings.

This was Abdullah. Had he been a Brit, he would certainly have made a most formidable sergeant-major at a rooky training camp of the Regimental Sgt-Maj Brittan type, for he had a voice that would carry across any parade ground.*

On the last day of the Mess, everything had been neatly packed in crates, ready to be transported to Port Said. The Mess staff had to be paid off and a table was placed on the grass outside the Mess. The Paymaster, a captain, sat behind this table and, standing to his left was Sergeant Crawley, who had been in charge of the Arab staff. He was a fair man but known to be extremely strict, expecting instant obedience. At some distance from the table came the 15 members of staff, all in their best kit. One by one they marched up to the desk, saluted smartly, received their final pay packet, shouted a clipped "THANK YOU SIR!" and performed an efficient about-turn and marched off.

---

* In a debate at The House of Lords on 24th January 2001, Viscount Falkland recalled the remarkable talents of Regtl Sgt-Maj Brittan: "When I was a boy at Wellington, he drilled me, as an officer cadet, to line the route at the funeral of the late King George VI. I measured the commands of Regimental Sergeant-Major Brittan and found that they were audible from a distance of more than 1,000 metres or – to use a measurement that meant more to me in those days – five furlongs. That was, roughly, the distance between Admiralty Arch and Buckingham Palace. That is considerably in excess of what is required to be an opera singer."

Taking up the rear was Abdullah. He must have weighed a good 20 stone. He marched up to the desk, saluted smartly, took his pay, saluted again, shouted "THANK YOU SIR!" and then turned to Sergeant Crawley, gave him the two-fingered salute and shouted: "AND FUCK YOU SERGEANT!". He then did an about-turn and ran off at full speed, looking for all the world like an overweight turkey escaping the axe before Christmas.

The RASC camp at Tripoli was like most camps, fairly austere, with its billets and officer quarters a little more upmarket than the housing for ORs (other ranks). I reported to the Camp Commandant, a tired-looking major called John Timpson. He made me feel welcome at once by pouring me a large scotch and telling me that he was "absolutely chuffed" to have me on his team. He had heard of my various exploits (I suppose John Stubbs must have briefed him) including my performances in both the Moascar theatre and the courts martial and my record programme. "And I believe you also produced a couple of extraordinary progs for the Beeb about our chaps in the Zone. Well done!"

All that was just to butter me up for the bad news. "You're to be Assistant Camp Commandant, ol' boy. Nothin' to it. Piece of fuckin' cake. But I don't mind telling you that I'll be damned glad to get shot of some of my duties. Can't stand these early mornings, what? But you're a young chap. Plenty of vim in you. You won't mind, eh, what?"

And that was that. Not only had I been a National Service Public Relations Officer for the entire Canal Zone of Egypt, I was now to be a National Service Assistant Camp bloody Commandant at an RASC camp.

But the worst was still to come. I was, of course, given a platoon all of my own and made immediate arrangements to meet these men the following morning at 0730.

I walked into the assembly room for the meeting and nearly collapsed. I was looking at the very same men I had been with when we were all rookies at Willems Barracks, Aldershot. What the fuck, I thought to myself. Who had planned this little idiotic joke? I felt myself blushing a deep red. But to my surprise, the entire room of men came to attention and saluted. One of them, who had made it to Lance-Corporal approached me. "Welcome, Sir! We are very pleased to see you and hope you're not too disappointed."

What could I say "Disappointed? Certainly not. Surprised? Very! But pleasantly surprised." And I went round the room, shaking each man's hand and having a little chat about the past 18 months. They were a superb platoon and behaved superbly well. What could have been a most embarrassing and unfortunate episode, turned out to be an unforgettable experience. In retrospect, I suppose they felt some pride, even perhaps responsibility for having "one of their chaps" making it to officer rank and The Big Time.

Shortly after my arrival at Tripoli I "had the runs". They were particularly vicious, so much so that I had to pay a visit to the camp doctor. It did not take him long to diagnose the trouble. "You've got bloody dysentery ol' boy," he said and ordered an ambulance. "What do I need an ambulance for?" I demanded to know. "Dysentry, ol' boy. Can't mess around with that. You're off to hospital."

And so I was. The Military Hospital was a damned sight better than many I've seen in what's called Civvy Street. It was spotlessly clean and the nurses...well, the nurses were sensational! According to military rules, dysentery demands hospitalisation of at least 10 days. My condition was, it seemed, fairly mild and, had I been in a civilian hospital, I should have been discharged after three or at most four days. But here, I *had* to stay for the compulsory ten. By Day Five, I joined the nurses for gins and tonic on the balcony after lights out. By Day Seven, I was having the time of my life in sexual activities. The night nurses were just bored and anything to liven those long hours was welcomed. When the time came for me to return to camp, I tried to persuade one of the younger doctors to write a note saying that I'd suffered a relapse. Nothing doing So I reluctantly kissed the nurses goodbye, organised a date with the fairest of them for the following week, and was driven back to camp in a Land Rover.

Several weeks into my posting, during which time I would think nothing of driving 90 miles just for lunch at a recommended restaurant and of visiting the many fabulous Greco-Roman sites, such as Leptis Magna, one of the finest preserved cities in the world, I received the visit of an Army Major. I had no idea what he wanted; he was not in the RASC and I did not remember him from Egypt. After a fairly lengthy conversation about nothing in particular, I could not resist asking him what I could do for him.

"Oh, nothing really. I simply wanted to meet you. You see, we have a file on you, Mr Izbicki."

"A file? On me? And who's 'we'?" I wanted to know.

"We – I'm with Intelligence. I just wanted to see the man who features third on Nasser's – er – Black List."

I was dumbfounded and for what seemed an eternity I was quite unable to speak. "Is this some kind of practical joke? It's not April the First! What are you talking about? Please do me the favour and explain yourself...Sir." I rapidly added the Sir, realising that I was no longer in Army PR and could not treat everyone as an equal, regardless of rank.

"Well, nothing much to tell really. We got hold of this list of people who feature on Abdel Gamal Nasser's so-called black list. And there you were at Number Three. Funny, isn't it?"

"No, Sir, it's not bloody funny. Not funny in the least. Why am I on such a list at all? It's ridiculous."

"Ah, we asked ourselves that question as well, of course. It's really quite simple. You're of the Jewish faith, are you not?"

"Yes…but…"

"And that's the main reason. At least we think it is. Being Jewish and in the responsible position you were in, makes you an immediate suspect. I understand there were those who believed you to be an Israeli spy." He held up his right hand to stop me from cutting in. "It's all right. We know you're not. But that has not stopped *them* from reaching such a conclusion."

"That explains a lot," I finally said and told him of my ruined New Year's Eve dinner at the Italian Club and how I was cold-shouldered. At last I was able to see the funny side and we both laughed loud and long and went for a slap-up lunch, during which I tried desperately to milk him for more information. I wanted to know who was listed at first and second positions on that list of Nasser's but he was not to be moved.

"Can't tell you that and please don't try to make me. I've already told you far more than I should – and I must ask you to keep that very strictly under your hat."

I think that fifty years further along the line should suffice and I can now let that particular proverbial cat out of the fez.

Tripoli was a doddle compared with Moascar. I had very little to do, other than a weekly inspection of billets and men and the odd disciplinary hearing of some poor sod who had got too drunk and started a fight or of another who had sold a carton of NAAFI fags to some local Tripoli Arab.

Shortly before I was due to be demobbed, at the beginning of October 1956, I visited a synagogue in the city to attend a Succoth service. The Jewish Feast of Tabernacles was always fun and in Berlin, my father would build a Succoth (a small bamboo hut) on our balcony and festoon it with different fruits and flowers to celebrate and give thanks for the harvest.

The synagogue was small but crowded and everyone stared at me in my uniform. Perhaps they had not seen a Jewish officer before. After the service, the rabbi and several other men came over to make me feel welcome. One of them invited me to his home for dinner and the Succoth celebration. I gladly accepted. His home was neat and spotless and his family, a plump wife, two young, nubile daughters and a son of around my age, then nearly 26, made me feel at home. But there was no meal, no prayers, no celebration. Not, that is, until a knock at the door allowed an elderly Arab in full regalia to enter. Everyone shook hands and he solemnly and slowly opened a small parcel of newspapers. From this he produced two perfectly green limes. They were needed for the start of the proceedings.

"Ah, at last. Now we can eat. Come, come let us start," said mine host. We bade the Arab gentleman farewell and I noticed that when the host said *Shalom Aleichem* to him – the Hebrew for *Peace be with you,* the old man responded with *Aleichem Shalom* – using the Hebrew reply for *And to you be Peace* instead of the Arabic *Salaam Aleihum.* After he had left, I expressed my surprise at an Arab speaking Hebrew.

"But that's because he is a Jew." I found it hard to believe. He looked every part the true Libyan Arab. "Just goes to show that appearance isn't everything. There are black Jews and white; oriental Jews and European Jews." It was then that I recalled the famous remark by the versatile actor, singer, dancer, Sammy Davis Junior: "I'm a one-eyed Negro Jew...so you think you've got problems?"

Our conversation over dinner centred on the happenings in Egypt. President Nasser had decided to nationalise the Suez Canal in July that year and at the same time had made two declarations. The first was his plan to throw the Jews out of Israel – a pronouncement that had acted as a dire warning to Jews still living in Egypt. And the second was to remind Great Britain that the agreement allowing troops to be stationed at Suez expired that same year, 1956.

In August, representatives of nations using the Suez Canal which, since its opening in 1869, had stretched a valuable 171 kilometers from Port Said to the Red Sea, met in London to discuss the very obvious consequences. On October 21, Britain's handsome and debonair prime minister, Sir Anthony Eden, met with his counterparts – France's Guy Mollet and Israel's David Ben Gurion – for a round of secret discussions on what could be done to counter Nasser's threats.

Shortly before I was due to return to England, I wrote to John Goulden asking whether the position he had offered me at *The Manchester Evening Chronicle* had remained open.

A week or two later, Sir Anthony Eden went on the air and was relayed by the BBC to us in Tripoli. He explained the sorry tale of Nasser's plans and warned the Egyptian president of possible consequences.

I sat in front of the wireless in silence. Someone later told me that I had an ashen faced appearance. All I could say was: "Well, it looks like I won't be going back home after all. They're bound to want every soldier who can carry a rifle up front. And I thought I had left Egypt. I might be back there after all."

But I had miscalculated the British Army's unflagging resolve to stick to protocol and procedure. My tickets to fly back to London on October 30 were prepared; my seat booked. There was no question of my staying behind. It was in breach of protocol. I had my farewell party in the Officers' Mess and on the prescribed day, was driven to the Military Airport and sent back, whether that was to my liking or not.

The electric storm on the journey notwithstanding, with lightning travelling through the centre of the plane, we limped our way back to Blighty. I went home for a spot of well-earned leave and the joy of my parents was immeasurable.

A letter awaited me in Manchester. It was quite brief but to the point and was signed by Goulden himself: "If you are free, you can start as a graduate trainee in our Newsroom. Please report to Harry Mellor at 9 a.m. on November 5."

To hell with my pips (I left the Army as a full Lieutenant).

I was to be a journalist!

CHAPTER NINE:

REAL WORK BEGINS

November 5, 1956 was the day my demobilisation became official. My National Service had ended and I was a "free man". It also marked the day I started work. Proper work, as I liked to call it. The *Manchester Evening Chronicle* had been as good as its word and had employed me as a "graduate trainee". I had no idea what this meant but expected to have to undergo some fairly rigorous training in journalism.

The first day came and went without anything happening. I was taken round the open plan newsroom and introduced to my colleagues-to-be, a motley mixture of men and women, mostly of what the French would call a "certain age", but they were all cheerful and friendly, welcoming me "to the madhouse". I was taken down to The Swan, a pub frequented by what seemed to be the entire staff and made to down several pints of decent bitter. By the time we returned to the office in dribs and drabs, we were all good mates.

The office was in a drab, grey building which might have been white originally, on the corner of Whithy Grove and Corporation Street, close to Victoria Station, in central Manchester. Its name figured large half way up and was brightly lit at night: KEMSLEY HOUSE. The *Chron* was a Kemsley newspaper and I learned that its owner was a Welshman called Lord Kemsley. Later, I was to learn that his newspaper empire had been built up from virtually nothing. Gomer Berry, born in Merthyr Tydfil in 1883, went to London at the turn of the century determined to make his fortune. He joined his brother William, older by just four years, who had moved to the metropolis in 1898 where he launched a small journal, *Advertising World*. Gomer helped bring in the advertisements and, as he saw the small journal grow stronger and stronger, he decided to start a periodical himself. It was called *My Pet* and dealt with dogs, cats, budgerigars, canaries – even goldfish. Gomer would plod from house to house every morning, knock on the door and, when it was opened, often by a housewife, would say: "Good morning Madam. Do you have a dog or a cat as a pet?" More often than not the answer would be positive. "Then you'll need this weekly magazine." And Gomer would produce – and invariably sell – a copy of *My Pet* and a subscription for it.

Gomer and William Berry went from strength to strength. William founded *Boxing* and a host of other periodicals together with Gomer. In 1937, both were successful enough to divide the business and go their own way. Gomer became the owner of Allied Newspapers – later to be renamed Kemsley Newspapers – which included such titles as the *Daily Sketch* and *Daily Graphic*, the *Sunday Graphic*, the *Sunday Empire News* and the *Sunday Times*. He also bought up some 24 provincial morning and evening papers, including the *Western Mail* in Cardiff, the *Aberdeen Press and Journal*, the *Nottingham Evening Post*, the *Newcastle Journal* – and the *Manchester Evening Chronicle*.

Indeed, Gomer Kemsley became the country's biggest newspaper owner, even though his brother William, who had become the owner of such high-class titles as the *Financial Times* and the *Daily Telegraph*, beat Gomer to a baronetcy by nearly seven years.

William became a Baron in 1929 and Viscount Camrose in 1941, while Gomer became a Baron in 1936 and Viscount Kemsley in 1945. Between them they built one of the finest newspaper empires in the world. A remarkable story.

Little did I know it that November when I joined the *Chron* that, less than a year later, I was to become a loyal collaborator of Lord Kemsley and a close confidant of his wife, the Lady Kemsley.

The *Chron*'s office was just a short walk to Market Street and Lewis's department store where my father and I used to shop on Saturdays during the war. Market Street also housed the Kardomah coffee house where we used to pop in for a tea, coffee or lemonade before returning home. Now, the few non-drinkers and I would visit the Kardomah for a quick cuppa and a slice of their delicious cream cakes.

On my second day I was called in to see the Editor. John Goulden was a short, thin man with horn-rimmed specs, who sat comfortably behind his large mahogany desk and invited me to sit. Despite my having spent two years conversing with high ranking officers, heads of police and the odd Egyptian general, I was nervous.

"Just wanted to welcome you to the staff, Mr – er – Izbicki. Hope you'll enjoy your work with us."

"Thank you, Sir," I stammered. "I'm sure I shall."

"Just one question I have – and I hope you won't mind me asking you. What byline would you want over your stories?"

"Byline? Well, 'By John Izbicki', I suppose," I replied.

"Yes, good, good, yes, of course. By John Izbicki. Now, if you should have more than one story in the paper – and we'd rather not use the same byline twice – what alternative name d'you think you would want to be known by?"

I was taken aback. It was not a question I had expected and I had no idea what he was driving at. But after a moment's hesitation, I said: "Well, my middle name is Howard, so I suppose 'By John Howard' would be acceptable, Sir."

"John Howard, eh? Yes, that's good. Very good. All right, so be it, Mr John Howard Izbicki. Welcome aboard."

And that was that.

Actually, officially I was Howard John. When my parents were naturalized, they considered changing their name and toyed with Isherwood, Ibbotson…but stuck to Izbicki. They didn't have the heart to change it. My mother decided to stick to her first name, Selma; my father decided to exchange Luzer Ber for Leonard; I knew that I would stick to John but could not change Horst to John without doing so by an expensive deed poll. By simply going to the Manchester Food Office armed with our identity cards, we were able to change names free of charge – as long as the initial letter remained the same as the original. Hence, Luzer to Leonard was all right. Horst presented me with a problem but not for long. My parents had received a great deal of friendly advice and help from a Mr Howard who dealt with refugees at Manchester's Society of Friends (the Quakers). He had just died of cancer of the throat and his voice resembled my own hoarseness. In his honour and memory, I decided to call myself Howard and just add the John.

My "training" was handled by the assistant news editor, a chubby bespectacled little man (with a heart of gold) called Harold Mellor. His bark was a great deal worse than his bite. Every morning he would shout an order through the little hatch to his glass-encased office: "Mister Iz-bi-cki!!! Do the calls – and be quick about it!"

Doing the calls was a boring, menial task. It involved telephoning the local cop shop, the fire brigade and the hospitals to seek out anything that might make a story. Any arrests during the night? What crimes had been committed? What fires had the brigade dealt with? And where? Any injured people admitted to hospital? Any other "interesting cases"? I would take notes of anything the police and the others were able to tell me. There was rarely anything really juicy to report.

My next ghastly job was to sift the death notices which had been placed in the *Chron* for that evening. If any of them sounded "interesting" – if the deceased, for instance, was described as company director or chairman of this or that firm – I had to telephone the home number and "get a few lines" for a "story" or a longer obituary.

"Go and visit this one, Mister Iz-bi-cki. He was quite well known in business circles and get a picture!" Mr Mellor would order. In some cases, where the deceased was not well known but had been the victim of a road or other accident, I had to go to the home and "get a picture".

I detested this part of the job. But it taught me humility and a great deal about the composition of Manchester society. The rich tended to regard this young reporter with suspicion and were reluctant to part with any photographs. It was invariably tough going. The poor of Moss Side or Salford or Cheetham Hill were a totally different lot. I would always first apologise for my intrusion in their grief and extend my deepest sympathy and the sympathy of my newspaper (no one had taught me that kind of script). The door would open wide and I would be invited into the kitchen and offered a "nice hot cup of tea". The widow or brother or sister would then talk to me at some length about the deceased. "Isn't it lovely that the *Evening Chronicle* wants to write about him/her. It's so kind of you to come all this way…etc." A photograph was readily available. I would be shown an entire photo album and invited to choose whichever picture I wanted. I always promised to have the picture returned (and *always* made sure that it was). These people were actually grateful and deeply and genuinely moved at the newspaper's willingness to write about their loved one's demise.

Another job was to make up a few letters. "Mister Iz-bi-cki (Harold Mellor always insisted on splitting my surname into three syllables) our letters page is a bit thin today. Why the fuck can't people learn to write a decent letter? Will you do us a couple of short ones? Do one on the bloody fogs we're getting these days. And maybe one on the rotten state of the education system…youngsters leaving school not able to read and write, that sort of thing. And be bloody quick about it!!!"

My letters were quite popular and "Albert Jessop of Oldham Road" (a very long road with little chance of the "writer" being traced) became a regular – as did "Disgusted of Didsbury".

Then came my big chance – and my first bylined story. "Mister Iz-bi-cki!!!

Get round to Belle Vue Circus and interview that acrobat troupe they've got billed. They're fuckin' 'Ungarians. What do they think about the fuckin' Soviets invading their country...that sort of thing."

The October uprising in Hungary and the Suez crisis had virtually coincided. Here was a chance of a local Manchester story about Hungarians who had escaped the Soviet tanks and come to do acrobatics in a Manchester circus. A photographer came with me in a cab and we quickly found the few Hungarian acrobats. But so had other reporters – from the rival *Manchester Evening News* and several morning papers, including the *Manchester Guardian* (as it then still was), the *Daily Express* and the *Daily Mail*. They all managed to get pictures easily enough but the Hungarians didn't speak or understand a word of English.

I drew a young man from the troupe aside. "*Sprechen Sie Deutsch?*" I asked. "*Jawohl,*" came the answer and he called to his mates – all from the same family. "*Dieser Mann spricht Deutsch*" (this man speaks German). I quickly herded four of the seven into their caravan for a detailed interview. This was more like it. This was journalism! They opened their hearts, telling me of those they had left behind (including two toddlers left in the care of grandma outside Budapest), not knowing whether they were still alive or dead. They gave me pictures of the babies. I phoned the story over and rushed back with the pictures. The *Chronicle* had a two editions beat over the *Evening News*. And I had my byline – on Page One!

My "graduate traineeship" had been passed with honours. But it showed me that much of journalism is a matter of luck and being in the right place at the right time. Most Hungarians speak German. Had they been non-English speaking Greeks, I would have been in the same boat as the other reporters. And if one of them had been able to speak Greek, he would have been the one to cash in.

About a week after the Hungarian story, John Goulden called me in. "You're doing well, John. I have a proposition. How would you like to do a weekly column for the paper. We need someone to produce something fairly light, a kind of gossip column, a diary, about the growing number of clubs and pubs in Manchester. D'you think you could handle that?"

Could I handle that? You bet I could! But I just said: "Yes, Sir, thank you Sir. I'll certainly try. When d'you want me to start?"

"Well, go and see the features editor and he'll go into details with you."

And so I began a column called *Getting Around with John Izbicki*. But before I did so, I was called in to see Arthur Saunders, the features editor – tall, lanky with thick grey curly hair and a gruff voice. He picked up a five pound note from the top of his paper-packed desk: "Now John, this is a five pound note," he said and he dangled it before my eyes. "This five pound note is for your expenses. Now you can put it in your pocket and spend it any way you want, or you can bank it. But one thing must be clear. Do NOT, NOT, NOT come to me for any more. If you spend it and then find you need more money to entertain someone at one of those clubs, DO NOT expect this newspaper to provide you with more. This fiver is for one week. You'll get another one in a week's time and another the week after that and so on. Understood?"

"Perfectly," I said and pocketed the fiver. It made a nice addition to my wage packet of £9.15.0 a week. That's a cool £507 gross a year! The additional fiver would turn that into £767 – less tax.

I introduced myself quietly to the city's many pubs and clubs The nearest, just round the corner from the paper, sitting in a quiet cul-de-sac off Market Street, was the Cromford Club, a lively night club which served remarkably decent food and sported a well equipped bar. Arthur Conway, its manager, welcomed me at once in the usual way. In other words, he offered me drink and food without charging me. At first, I smiled and accepted. After all, that fiver would remain safe and saved. But after a while, I worked out that one doesn't get any free lunches in this life. Why, I asked myself, was I being feted?

In those days, gambling was still illegal. I noticed how some customers would sit and drink and then, from time to time, disappear through some doors at the rear of the club. I knew that they were not the toilets. As far as I could work out, they led to the club's kitchens as it was through those same doors that waiters would appear with trays laden with steaming food. What on earth lay in those kitchens?

It didn't take that long to discover that there was a *spieler* back there, a real old-fashioned gambling joint. I was to find it for myself later on: roulette, blackjack, you name it. I didn't let on. It wasn't worth it. Instead, I concentrated on good gossip. Every evening there was a good cabaret act, which always managed to produce the odd paragraph. Matt Busby, the then manager of Manchester United, was a regular with his wife and we used to have long chats. That was, of course, before that dreadful air disaster of 1958 when seven of the team's top players were among 22 passengers killed in a British Airways plane that crashed shortly after take-off from Munich. Busby was among those most seriously hurt.

The Cabaret Club was another of my haunts. Just opposite Manchester's grey and grand circular Central Library and the brightly lit Oxford Street, it also contained a gambling den, also produced good food and drink and a nightly cabaret of leading artists. It was owned by Bill Benny, the all-in professional wrestler, and his wife Enid. They were a strange couple – he, a veritable Man Mountain, big and brawny, bearded; she, a petite blonde with a superb figure. It was almost impossible to imagine Enid being mounted by Bill. But it was an open secret that the lovely Enid was doing all right with a selection of handsome Italian waiters who were more her size. Bill also owned several other clubs on the outskirts of the city – down-to-earth working men's clubs which were well patronised.

Bill met his end in a bizarre manner some years after I had left Manchester and the *Chronicle*. Being his size, he was ever in danger of suffering a heart attack. It came one night while he was enjoying sex with one of his favourite prostitutes. Unfortunately the poor woman could not move him off her. What was even more embarrassing, she could not move him *out* of her and was forced to scream for help. An ambulance was called and the two of them were eventually carried off on a stretcher held by six strong, sweating (and it is said, giggling) ambulance men.

Among the many other clubs on my beat was the Stage and Radio in Princes Street. This was more a drinking joint, small, intimate and friendly and run by Essie Lewis, a peroxide blonde whose heart was as big as her girth. I dubbed her Two Ton Essie (the singer Two Ton Tessie was all the rage at the time) and we remained friends for many years to come. She adored Venice and would go there for her annual holidays, staying at the Belvedere, a small restaurant-hotel on the Grand Canal. It was to become another of my later holiday haunts.

The column went from strength to strength but it did not last as long as I might have hoped because of a sudden call from the editor.

"Ah, John, I've had a call from Denis Hamilton in London (Hamilton was the editorial director of Kemsley Newspapers). It appears that he heard you speak at some meeting or other and has taken to you. Anyway, he wants to know whether you'd be prepared to go to Paris for two or three months."

When I picked myself up from the floor, I said I'd certainly be more than happy to go to Paris. My French was a bit sloppy, but I had taken a summer course at the Sorbonne while I was still at the North Manchester Grammar School, and was able to manage more than what was needed to order a beer.

"You'd better continue with the column for this week and next. We'll find a replacement for you by then. Anyway, this will be a marvelous opportunity for you, so make the most of it. I've already told Hamilton that you are showing great promise."

Another chapter was about to open.

CHAPTER TEN:

PARIS LOVES

My Paris assignment once again proved that a large proportion of a journalist's work depends on luck and being in the right place at the right time.

I had been to Paris on several previous occasions. While still at school I spent summer holidays with one or other of my father's two sisters who had emigrated to France from Poland after he had made his way to Germany. There they married and raised families. Genia, the elder of two sisters, fell madly in love with Oscar Opatowski, a man who had 3,000 volts running through his veins, a workaholic who built up a textile business in the commercial centre of the French capital.

When the Nazis occupied France, he and Genia, together with their children, Charles and Lisette, fled to Vichy, that part of the country that remained unoccupied. They were still forced to hide as Prime Minister Pétain and his government collaborated with the Germans and deported more than 76,000 Jews to Hitler's camps. The Opatowskis – they adopted the name Opa to make it sound less Jewish – escaped detection and returned to Paris after its liberation in 1944. They re-started their business, a shop in the Rue d'Aboukir in the second arrondissement, just off the Grands Boulevards and centre of the French rag trade. They sold wholesale woollens, sweaters, waistcoats, skirts, coats for male and female. It was an instant success.

The other sister, Nacia, and her fiancé, Gabriel Linke, also made their way to Paris and later to Vichy France. They, too, survived and returned to run a tailoring establishment that fed some of the biggest department stores in the city – the Galleries Lafayette and Printemps – as well as some of the smaller, cheaper establishments like Prisunic. Like the Opas, the Linkes worked hard and grew rich. Unlike the Opas, however, they kept their heads in the clouds. They were dreamers and their children, Ettie (also known as Michelle or Mishka) and Yona, became dreamers too. Ettie fancied herself as a great actress (and to tell the truth, she was by no means bad) but could never find work in a proper theatre, although one small ballet company gave her a chance and she spent a while touring the provinces as a dancer. Her parents bought her a theatre – a Yiddish theatre – and she played leading roles in a number of Yiddish plays, including those of Sholem Alleichem. But the theatre attracted only small audiences and, after two years and heavy financial losses, it folded. Yona lived quietly but joblessly, financed by his parents. He later turned to the rabbinate and, although he never made it to Rabbi, played an important part in one of the main synagogues of Paris where he taught Hebrew in Chaida classes.

To these two families I came. I stayed with them while taking the Sorbonne course in *Civilisation Francaise*. Thanks to them and mainly to Ettie and Lisette, my French language improved.

Before my bags had been packed, I paid a visit to 200 Gray's Inn Road, London headquarters of Kemsley Newspapers. There I met the editors and foreign editors of the various newspapers I would be dealing with, and lunched with C.D. (Denis) Hamilton and my immediate boss and line manager, Kemsley's overall foreign editor, Ian Fleming. Both were highly encouraging.

"What we need is someone who will produce stories for all our provincial papers as well as the popular Sundays," Fleming said over the coffee that had followed an amazingly tasty meal in the Kemsley canteen (we were treated to silver service in a separate room away from the main dining hall crammed mainly with printers (the hacks knew better and adjourned to the nearest pub). "We've already got a man covering for the *Sunday Times* but he's reluctant to produce anything for the rest, so they have to depend entirely on agency or freelance copy."

"D'you think you can handle it?" asked Hamilton and answered his own question before I had a chance to do so. "Of course you can. From what I've seen of your work up in Manchester you don't shirk hard graft. And your army career as an officer (I thought he was going to add "and gentleman" but he didn't) adds to my conviction that you're the right man for the job. Anyway, it's only for three months…"

After lunch – and I had to wait until after 3 p.m. when the pubs closed – I went up to the *Sunday Graphic*'s office and was ushered into the editor's large room. I found Gordon Mackenzie stretched out on the carpet surrounded by a mass of glossy pictures. "Just a mo', ol' boy" he called to me and continued "sorting" the photographs. "Yes," he said, tossing one on a pile at his right side; "No," and a picture was thrown onto a second pile on the left; "Yes, Yes, No, Maybe (a third pile for the maybes), No, No, Maybe, Yes...." And so it went on for a good five minutes.

At last he rose and shook me warmly by the hand. "John. Heard all about you. You're going to do great guns in Paris. Lucky chap! Wish I was going. Good luck," and he ushered me to the door, still vigorously shaking my hand.

It wasn't until some weeks later that I found out about the *Sunday Graphic*'s historic libel action. Historic, because it was the highest figure paid out in such an action – more than £40,000 plus costs. It was all due to the owner's wife, Lady Kemsley. She was wont to visit Kemsley House on a Saturday and do the rounds to see the Sundays in preparation. She had already been to the *Sunday Times* and the *Empire News* and was now making her way to the *Sunday Graphic*. There she stumbled into the picture conference and demanded to see what pictures had been chosen for the next day.

Lady Kemsley was a Mauritian and spoke with a strong French accent. She gave a little scream as she picked up one of the pictures. It had been taken the previous day at the Smithfield Market Prize-giving and showed the prize-winning bull. "I will not 'ave a photograph like thees in my newspehper!" she gasped pointing to the bull's prize-winning protrusion. "Very well, Lady Kemsley," the picture editor grunted as she stomped out.

But instead of spiking the picture altogether and replacing it with something more acceptable like a maiden wielding a milk churn, or birdies on a tree, the picture editor decided to have the photograph "doctored". The bull's penis was painted out, thus making the animal neither bull, nor cow and certainly not anything that might have won first prize. Thus the picture appeared the following day. The bull's owner – who had looked forward to selling the beast at a major profit – was furious and contacted his lawyers. It cost the Kemsleys dear. But worse than the costly damages was the humiliation. The laughter spread from Fleet Street pubs all the way to the Gray's Inn Road.

Clearly Gordon Mackenzie was not going to take such a risk again and was carefully picking the pictures himself from that day on.

Instead of creating additional expenses for my employers, I decided to take the ferry. I had packed four sturdy suitcases with clothes and books. They weighed a ton. I was booked into a Left Bank hotel – I chose one that was cheap by my own standards so it must have seemed like slumming to Kemsley's. It was the Hôtel d'Isley in the Rue Jacob. Nothing over-special about it except that Oscar Wilde had slept there just before being taken to jail.

On the ferry from Newhaven to Dieppe (one of my favourite dropping-off points in France) I had little to do other than stand on deck looking down at the rolling waves. A man dressed in a long, brown leather coat and sporting a black trilby stood a few feet away. "Going on holiday?" he enquired. "No, I'm going over to work for a few months. Paris," I replied.

"Lucky you," he said.

"What about you? Are you going on holiday?"

"No. I'm just on a quick trip to attend a christening. Marseilles. I'll be going on by train from Paris. Just two or three days."

"Oh, nice. Boy or girl?" I wanted to know.

"Neither," he replied. "It's a ship. An oil tanker. Though I expect that you'd probably call it a girl. One refers to ships as 'she' doesn't one?"

"An oil tanker!? I didn't know ships could be christened. Do explain, please," I begged.

"Nothing much to explain. It's a bit like any other christening. The ship is named and sprinkled with holy water or champagne. I'm a ship's broker and friend of the ship's owner. What's the work you're going to do?"

I explained that I was going to cover French news for Kemsley papers. He looked a little startled, then laughed. "Maybe I shouldn't have told you about this. But what the hell.

"You really ought to get to know the man who owns this and many other tankers. His name is Getty. Paul Getty. You might find him living at the George V hotel in Paris."

Paul Getty...I'd never heard of him. But it might make a little story. I couldn't think of anything else to do, so two days after I had settled in, I decided to go over to the George V, one of those palatial hotels off the Champs Elysées. I asked for Monsieur Getty at the reception and was glad to see the receptionist picking up the phone and putting me through to the man's room.

A quiet American voice answered and I kicked off by apologising for disturbing him but his ship's broker had suggested I call on him. I'm a journalist for a group of British newspapers...He interrupted me: "Shit, a journalist! What the hell does Bernard think he's doing? He knows I don't speak to the Press for God's sake! Where are you?"

"I'm, I'm down in the lobby of the – the hotel, Sir," I stammered.

"Oh for Christ's sake! You're actually here? Shit! All right, look I'll give you just 10 minutes. Okay? Come on up. Room 501."

I thanked him and met him at his room. A biggish, rotund man just under six foot tall and weighing about 12 stone, with a thin, almost gaunt face and greying hair, burning blue eyes on each side of a long, pointed nose, he shook my hand and invited me to sit down...for just 10 minutes.

He kicked off by cross examining me on my experience and languages. I've no idea whether he was in the least impressed by my lack of journalistic know-how or by my knowledge of French and German, apart from English. He spoke all three fluently plus Italian, Spanish, Arabic, Russian and Greek. He had studied Latin and Ancient Greek. The 10 minutes were long up but Getty didn't seem to notice.

Nearly two hours later, I left him, having been told about his wealth, his women (there had been five marriages and divorces), his love of antique furniture and his passion for collecting works of art including the works of Rubens and Renoir, Degas and Gainsborough, Tintoretto and Matisse. After about half an hour, he asked me if I was hungry but didn't wait for my answer. He picked up the telephone and commanded a plate of smoked salmon sandwiches for two and a pot of tea.

While we both munched away, he explained that he rarely ate fatty foods or big French meals stuffed with cream sauces and garlic. "I eat healthy foods, like salads, fruit and cereals. I walk about two to three miles every single day, rain or shine. And I wash my own socks and pants. Some people think I'm a miser. I'm not but I don't like tipping big. It's not good for the person on the receiving end. In fact, I can't tip big because I never carry more than 25 dollars in notes on me."

Still, he was the sole owner of houses all over the world, to say nothing of major oil companies including Getty Oil and Skelly Oil. "I work around 18 hours a day because I love my business."

I floated back to the office, which was then in the Avenue Gabriel, just by the Rond Point of the Champs Elysées and a short walk from the Place de la Concorde. I had a story – and I thought it a damn good one.

I started off my feature, which I was directing at two of our Sunday papers – the *Graphic* and the *Empire News* – with: "How would you like to be a millionaire – forty times over?" In 850 words it was all there.

When I picked up the papers that Sunday, I found...nothing. Then, finally, there were three paragraphs, including my intro, in the *Empire News*'s Peter Nelson gossip column. I was devastated. Yet those three paragraphs had been noticed, for some three weeks later two American magazines – *Fortune* and *Newsweek* – appeared with the Getty story. *Newsweek*'s cover had a colourful sketch of Getty and the cover-story line: ***The Richest American in the World!***

That same week, I was phoned by Gordon Mackenzie, the *Graphic*'s editor. "Er John, didn't you send me something about that chap Getty?"

"Yes," I almost shouted. "Four weeks ago! It was an exclusive, Gordon!"

"Ah, yes. Don't know what happened to that. Still, d'you still have a copy? If you have would you put it across?"

"But haven't you got my copy?"

"No, ol' boy. As I said, I don't know what happened to it."

So I had to dictate the 850 words all over again. And guess what. Once again, nothing – or almost nothing – appeared. It was the world exclusive that almost got away. A tough lesson but a good lesson nevertheless. As I have since learned (and reluctantly accepted) you win some; you lose some.

My colleague at the office was Stephen Coulter. I rarely saw him for he used to come in only on Thursdays, Fridays and Saturdays to cover for the *Sunday Times*. He spent much of his time at home doing research and working on his excellent biography of Guy de Maupassant.

At the start I asked him about expenses. After all, I really had not the vaguest idea of how much I could spend on stories. In Manchester, I had been given that fiver. "You can put it in your pocket, keep it, save it or spend it – but don't come to me asking for any more..." But this was Paris, not Manchester. Was I able to spend more than a fiver a week?

"How about expenses, Steve" I asked Coulter at our second meeting. "What about expenses?" he responded tetchily.

"Well, what is the permissible amount to spend on stories?"

"Permissible amount!? What the...You spend whatever you spend, damn it. You put in for whatever the story has cost you in fares, entertainment if necessary, research – that sort of thing." And with that, he got on with his sort of thing and left me none the wiser. It was not until later that I came to understand why a journalist's expenses were commonly known as the "Lie Sheet".

I had arrived in Paris at the wrong time as far as the office was concerned. Three weeks after settling into the Avenue Gabriel premises, Kemsley Newspapers decided to move and I had to spend most of my time helping the office manager and circulation director to pack up and then unpack in our new, more airy premises in the wonderful circular Place Vendôme. We were on the first floor of No.20. Most of the floor was taken up by the *Daily Telegraph* and its large staff under its chief correspondent, the rotund and jovial John Wallis. Another large office had been let to the American *Wall Street Journal*. We, who had so many newspapers to cover, occupied a small office, just about big enough for the three of us – Stephen Coulter, myself and Louis Herchenroder. Louis looked after the *Sunday Times* circulation in

France. He was a Mauritian and spoke English with a strong French accent and French with an equally strong English accent. Most peculiar. But he and I got on famously and were to become close friends. Since Coulter was only visible on about three days a week, I often had the office to myself. Bliss.

On the ground floor underneath us was the National Westminster Bank with whom I had opened a sterling account and to whom my salary was sent every month. Most of the other shops in the square were household named jewellers – Cartier, Van Cleef, Boucheron, Chaumet, Arpels and so on. Over on the left was the Ministry of Justice and directly opposite the office stood the Hôtel Ritz.

It was to the Ritz that I was summoned after I had been in my new office a mere three days. The telephone rang and a voice simply said: "Izbicki? Lord Kemsley here. Could you pop over for a moment? It's urgent." Was it a joke, some practical joke played on every newcomer? Perhaps it was Ronnie Payne, one of the *Daily Telegraph*'s correspondents. He had a good sense of humour. I took the few steps along the corridor to the *Telegraph* but Ronnie wasn't there. In fact, no one was. Should I ignore the call? There was a slight Welsh lilt to the otherwise gruff voice. But why would Lord Kemsley ask me to come over. Over where? I telephoned Louis.

"Louis, I've just had the most extraordinary phone call from someone who said he was Lord Kemsley and…"

"Ah, that's good ol' boy. I told 'im about you yesterday and he said he quite wanted to meet you. So you'd better get over there quicklee."

"Over where, Louis?"

"L'Hôtel Ritz! It's straight over ze road…"

I almost ran across the cobblestoned square to the majestic building and suddenly felt totally under-dressed. After all, this is the hotel which has had kings and princes staying in it ever since César Ritz transformed it from a sumptuous private dwelling into a luxury hotel in 1898. Ernest Hemingway and Scott Fitzgerald were frequent residents as were Charlie Chaplin, Greta Garbo and Rudolf Valentino. The clothes designer Coco Chanel, whose workshops were at one end of the square, lived at the Ritz for nigh on 30 years. Now, here I was, stomping in with my threadbare suit and unshined shoes. The receptionist, I thought, looked at me with some suspicion – but then, Paris receptionists have that sort of look on their faces all the time – and said "First Floor, Suite Two".

I took the curved staircase two steps at a time and made my way along a corridor to the Suite. A maid opened the door to my ring of the bell. She smiled and said: "Come in, come in. Lord Kemsley is in the sitting room. He is waiting for you." She opened the door to a room that was almost as big as a tennis court. My feet sank into a thick red and green floral carpet Sitting on a leather settee was Lord Kemsley. He looked up from the newspaper he was reading and signalled to me to sit in an armchair opposite him.

"Good morning, Sir," I managed.

"Hm. Morning Izbicki. Glad you could make it. Won't keep you long. Just to say that what I want you to do is to make sure that all the English morning papers as well as the *Figaro* and *Le Monde* are delivered to this room every day including Sundays, when the only French paper will be *France Dimanche*. It's a rag but quite fun for gossip. These papers are to be charged to the office accounts, is that understood? The office accounts, not the hotel. (I nodded)

"Also, whenever you're in Paris, I want you to telephone Lady Kemsley every morning at 11 a.m. and every evening before you leave the office, just to see whether there is anything she needs. I'm not always here, so I can't do much for her. Of course if you're out of Paris on some assignment, you won't be able to do this, but you must let Herchenroder know so that he can do it. Right?"

I nodded. "Yes, Sir," I said.

"Good. Well, that's all. Nice to have met you."

The interview was over and I was dismissed. As I walked very slowly down that gorgeous staircase, I could not help thinking: "Bloody cheek! That's not the task of a Paris correspondent. What a waste of my time – and what a liberty to charge his bloody papers to the office. He can't be exactly poverty-stricken. Why the hell didn't he ask Coulter? Perhaps he did and I can just imagine what Coulter would have said: buy your own bloody papers through the hotel!"

But, of course, I carried out his orders. After all, I was the new boy.

I filed at least three stories a day and wrote features for the Sundays. But the amount of coverage I managed to get into the papers was abysmally low. The *Graphic* took a double page spread on the Bluebell Girls with pictures taken by Russell Melcher whom I met at a Press conference earlier. He was a photographer for an agency (Black Star), an American with a fabulous sense of humour. He was also a great photographer. I had made an appointment with "Miss Bluebell" (Margaret Kelly, the woman who had formed that group of tall, beautiful women, most of them British, who danced at the Lido nightclub on the Champs Elysées) and provided the Sunday paper with a good background piece just in time for the height of the tourist season.

Russell was to become one of my close friends.

For the first four weeks I continued to stay at the Hôtel d'Isley, occupying Oscar Wilde's former room and using every minute of my spare time (what little there was) in searching for a flat. Flats in those days were tough to secure. The Parisians are a greedy lot and "key money" was all the rage. In other words, to secure an apartment, one would first need to pay a colossal sum of money simply to get "the key". Then one would be required to pay at least three months' rent in advance and obtain references from a bank and an employer (Louis provided this note on official notepaper). I made the mistake of not asking the office – in any case I was under the impression that I would be going back to England within another couple of months. Three months they had said.

So I found a ground floor room in a busy little street in Montparnasse. My landlady, a Madame Dournelle, was the French version of Margaret Rutherford, a woman of a "certain age" (around 60-plus) with a triple chin, cheeks that were constantly rouged and a rotund body that was permanently wrapped in a vividly coloured floral dressing gown. When she spoke, her chins would wobble in tune with the words.

She showed me the room. It was at the back of her spacious apartment and was overpowered by a massive king-sized bed covered by a thick duvet. There seemed to be little else, other than a small table by the window and a large wardrobe. I had the use of the kitchen and was able to eat there as well. It was cheap enough so I couldn't grumble. But the moment I moved in, Mme Dournelle approached me and, wagging a finger, said: "*Alors, Monsieur Eezbeekee, j'ai seulement une commandement: PAS DE FEMMES! Entendu?*" Her one rule was No Women! I had no option but to nod agreement. At the time, it did not apply. I had been too busy to think of sex, although the "flat", for want of a better word, was in the middle of the Left Bank's sex area.

Each evening, when I entered the Rue Bréa and made for Mme Dournelle's apartment, I had to run the gauntlet of women in all kinds of weird dress and undress. "*Alors, chéri, tu voeux?*" "*Viens avec moi.*" "*Je peux te montrer des vrais choses!*" I just smiled at them all and hurried on.

After two days at Mme Dournelle's, she came to me at breakfast. I was just tucking into my croissant, when she said: "*Alors Monsieur Eezbeekee, ce que je vous ai dit au sujet de pas de femmes...bien, si vous avez UNE petite amie, alors je ne dis rien. Vous comprenez?*" I certainly understood. If I had just one girl friend, that would be different and I'd be welcome to bring her "home"...

Strangely enough this was to happen, though not quite in the way she might have supposed. A Tuesday morning at the office, with very little in the line of stories, the phone rang. "Is that John Izbicki?" a woman's voice, clearly nervous, asked. "Ye-es," I replied. "Who's that?"

"Oh, you won't remember me. I think we only met once at the university. My name is Maureen Ryan…"

"Maureen! Well, of course I remember you," I lied. "What are you doing in Paris?"

"Well, I'm working here for a sort of travel agent who arranges student exchanges and au pairs to go to England."

"That's great," I said. "We should meet up. What are you up to this evening? How about a meal?"

"Oh that would be very nice," she said quickly – too quickly I thought. I then suggested a place where we could meet but rapidly changed my mind. I would never recognise her. So I said: "Tell you what Maureen. I've got to finish a story which might just take me a bit longer. I wouldn't want to be late and keep you waiting in the street. D'you think you could find your way to the office? It's in the Place Vendôme…Number 20; first floor, just over the Westminster Bank."

"I know the Place Vendôme. I'll find it. What time?"

"Say 7ish?"

At exactly 7 p.m. the bell rang and I opened the door to Maureen Ryan. I *did* remember her. She was one of the few women I hadn't dated at college and I guess I was one of the few men with whom she would probably not have gone out if I had tried to date her. My reputation in my salad days as a flirt (quite harmless in fact) was well known on the Nottingham campus and Maureen was, as far as I could recall, a *good girl*. She read English and was a practising Roman Catholic. So what brought on this sudden approach to a reprobate like me?

I decided to show her my Left Bank haunts and kicked off with an aperitif at the Deux Magots, patronised by the literati of Paris. We hit it off quickly. She was not only very *nice* but also very attractive and we chatted away for a good hour before moving to one of those little restaurants off the Boulevard St Germain. We ordered something very simple and quite cheap – steak and chips. It was then that I noticed that Maureen tucked into her steak with gusto and had almost finished before I had barely begun. It was then that I realised that she was truly hungry.

"Would you like another?" I ventured.

She turned to me and there was a hint of tears. "Oh yes. Yes, please".

Only then did she confess that she had answered the advertisement for the Paris job not knowing what to expect. In fact, her employer worked her and the other girls extremely hard and refused to pay them a single sou until they had worked a full month. Maureen had taken a room at the Cité Universitaire just past the Jardins des Luxembourg. It was cheap but she had to pay a month's rent up front. It left her almost broke and she had lived on bread and cheese for nearly two weeks.

I had been her last hope. She refused my offer of money. "You've done enough, thank you. You gave me food and were very kind. I can't possibly take your money," she said as we parted.

From then on we met regularly for a drink and a meal – and nothing else.

Our meetings were interrupted by a telephone call from London. This, I thought, was it – my recall. Ian Fleming's secretary called. "Mr Izbicki, could you arrange to fly to London next Thursday for a meeting? Mr Fleming would like a word with you. He'll see you at 3 p.m."

Ah well, I thought, it has been a good experience, even if I didn't have that much to show for it. Nevertheless, I approached Kemsley House with nervousness. I thought I was going to receive some verbal flack for not hitting the headlines more than I had managed.

Kemsley's foreign manager greeted me warmly enough and asked me how I thought I was getting on in Paris. "Very well, Sir," I replied, "although I really don't think I'm getting as much as I would have hoped into the papers. I'm writing enough, I think, but I don't see many results. I'd appreciate it if you could tell me where I'm going wrong."

That is probably a précis of what I actually said at the time. While I was speaking, Ian Fleming was doodling on his blotter. He had not yet become the famous author, creator of James Bond, although he had already published *Casino Royale* in 1953. His fame lay in the work he had done during the war for Naval Intelligence when he worked closely with Admiral John Godfrey, spymaster extraordinary. What was less known about him was that he had already been a spy when, as a journalist with Reuters, he went to Russia to report a spy trial there. In fact, he spent much of his spare time spying for the Foreign Office and was recruited for the intelligence service at the outbreak of war in 1939. Ian Fleming had always envied his then more famous brother, Peter, a journalist and traveller who had excelled at Eton, Oxford and Sandhurst. But Fleming was to catch up and surpass Peter and use his infinite wartime and naval intelligence experience to create James (007) Bond.

After I had finished my diatribe, Fleming looked up. "I don't know what you're grumbling about. We think you're doing fine. Exceptionally fine in fact. I called you over to thank you and let you know that we thought we'd do something about your salary." At this, he turned the blotter round towards me so that I could see what he had been doodling. There on the blotter were some figures: £3,500. I could hardly believe my eyes.

Ian Fleming then produced his second surprise: "I'd like you to stay on, if you agree. You should also take over the *Sunday Times* when Steve's on holiday or sick. D'you think you could handle that?"

My meagre *Manchester Evening Chronicle* wage had been increased to £1,500 a year when I went to Paris. I was now to get a rise of £2,000. I winged my way out of 200 Gray's Inn Road and flew back to Paris in a daze. I simply had to tell Maureen – and it called for a celebration.

Maureen also had something of importance to tell me when we met the following day. She had thrown up her rotten job with the agency. She was virtually penniless and had gone to the British Embassy in the Rue du Faubourg St Honoré to register as a DBS – a distressed British subject.

"I just wanted them to send me back to England and I promised to repay them for the fare once I got a job back home. You thought you were going to be recalled, so I'd have no one over here to talk to and I didn't think it fair to have you take me for meals all the time. But you'll never guess what happened. This woman at the embassy – she was ever so kind and helpful, nothing like the usual civil servant. She asked me how my French was and we chatted a bit in French. I had no idea what she was getting at. Then she asked me whether I'd like a job. A real job – at the embassy.

"The best was still to come. I was taken before a couple of other people in one of the offices and sort of interviewed. They seemed to be impressed with the degree I got in English with a French subsidiary and they offered me a job starting next week." She got a fit of the giggles before being able to tell me what the job was.

"So what is it they want you to do? Clean the loos? Pour their drinks? What?"

"They've put me in charge of the Department for Distressed British Subjects!"

We both collapsed laughing.

That night we decided to go out for a slap-up meal to celebrate our joint good fortune and I reserved a table at the Brasserie Lipp on the Boulevard St Germain, where the *choucroute* is renowned as the finest in Paris. I asked Maureen to come over to my place for a drink beforehand. It was the first time I had invited *une petite amie* to my room. To my decided embarrassment, Madame Dournelle had heard us enter the apartment and toddled out from her private section. I had no option but to make the introduction.

"This is Mademoiselle Ryan, Madame. Maureen, this is Madame Dournelle."

Madame looked Maureen up and down critically. "Enchanté,

Mademoiselle," she said and stretched out a limp hand and while Maureen shook it, asked: "And what do you do, Mademoiselle?"

"I work at the British Embassy, Madame."

The Margaret Rutherford chins wobbled with surprise and sheer pleasure. *"Ah, l'Ambassade britannique!!!"* she exclaimed as if I had introduced her to Her Majesty the Queen. Madame Dournelle, who was an inconvertible snob, almost curtsied and Maureen was readily accepted into the Dournelle household.

Maureen and I had our drink in the seclusion of my bedroom. I sat on the bed, she on the only chair. The temptation was great but dinner beckoned, and we left quietly. As we were some thirty metres down the road, still lined with *les filles*, a multi-decibelled voice called after us. Madame Dournelle had thrown open her window and its shutters and was leaning out to call: *"Monsieur Eezbeeky! Quand vous rentrez avec Mademoiselle, je vous prie PAS DE BRUIT!"* Luckily it was already dark for I believe I blushed. She had demanded that we should not make any noise when we returned. Luckily, Maureen laughed it off. She knew the French better than I.

But we did not live together until many months later. Rus Melcher, my photographer friend had told me about a gorgeous studio at the Porte de Versailles, that could be mine for the asking. The landlord, or rather landlady, was a delightful woman called Annette Wilcox. She was an American and Rus's mother.

Annette had worked at UNESCO for some years – a fairly responsible job – until the right-wing Republican senator for Wisconsin, one Joe McCarthy, had come along in 1950 to claim that the State Department had been infiltrated by Communists. He started a national and international witchhunt. As Mrs Wilcox had never made any secret about her Left-wing politics, she, along with some other UNESCO employees, was sacked and had her American passport confiscated.

Annette took up painting and became a remarkably good painter of landscapes. Her house was divided up into three studios – real studios, not those small rooms that boast the name but are nothing of the kind. She occupied the ground floor apartment and studio; there was another studio on the first floor and a third on the next floor up. I rented the middle one: a huge room with an immense window that allowed the light to flow in and a staircase that led up to a big bathroom. Well, the bathroom was certainly big but the bath itself was one of those sit-up-and-beg baths that abound in many small French flats. The third studio was occupied by another painter, a charming American called Sam Francis. I used to go up for a drink and watch him climb ladders and pour buckets of paint onto a huge canvas that covered an entire wall, then sweep brushes and knives across the canvas to produce trenches in the paint.

I used to stand below, shaking my head sadly. "It'll never sell, Francis. It'll never sell."

That statement must count among the biggest mistakes of my life. Sam Francis's works sell for millions. On a visit to Japan many years later, I visited an art gallery where four salons were filled with Sam's paintings. Had I bought one of his smaller works in the late Fifties, when we shared accommodation in Paris, I'd be a rich man today.

Maureen and I now saw each other regularly. We were very happy in each other's company and interested in each other's work. In fact, her job at the embassy provided me with an excellent story – one which gave me the splash in one of Kemsley's weekly papers, the *Sunday Empire News*. Although it was a broadsheet, it was the kind of story that would today find its way into the tabloids. Through Maureen I became acquainted with numerous other embassy women. All were "locally employed" – that is to say, they were not appointed by the Foreign Office in London and then sent to postings abroad, but hired on the spot, generally for their knowledge of the language.

Whereas the FO-based personnel were provided with handsome salaries – a good basic sum plus an overseas allowance and in many cases additional expenses and, depending on rank, a good housing allocation – the locally employed were paid peanuts. Maureen never complained. She was glad to have fallen on her feet and obtained what she considered to be an "exciting job". But some of her friends were only too ready to "spill the beans" and talk to me about their miserable pay packets. They complained that they could not even afford to buy themselves proper stockings. As one of them, put it: "We're at the bloody embassy. We're supposed to represent Queen and country and should at least look the part."

Two women had taken French lovers because they were rich and would provide them with decent clothes, makeup and perfume. And good food. Many of these young women could not afford to eat properly. I was even told of one who worked as a call girl, a prostitute, on two or three nights a week in order to augment her bank account and live in style.

When the story appeared, the proverbial balloon went up in the Rue du Faubourg St Honoré. The Foreign Office telephoned Paris late Saturday night when they had seen the first editions and dealt with enquiries from rival Sunday papers. At that time, no one had heard of the bylined name. "Who the fuck is this John Izbicki fellow? Ever heard of him?" London demanded of the embassy's press officer, who could only say: "No such feller exists. It must be Sam White writing under a pseudonym."

This was just about the finest compliment I could have been paid. Sam White was the Paris correspondent of the *London Evening Standard* and one of the finest journalists I had ever met. There was nothing of any importance that happened in and around Paris that did not come to Sam's attention. And if it was of real interest, it would find its way into Sam's Friday column. Now, Sam was an alcoholic and a chain smoker with a heart of pure gold. He wrote like a dream and supported the bar at the Crillon, the five-star hotel in the Place de la Concorde and next door to the American Embassy. It was from that bar that he would take out a flimsy little notebook and dictate his column by telephone to his London office. He was a man who was widely respected and feared. To be mistaken for Sam White was not only a great compliment, it also meant that the story was accurate and well written.

The embassy conducted an immediate investigation, interviewing every locally employed person to see who had "leaked" details of pay and conditions. Three FO officials were flown from London to look into the "scandal". When they discovered that John Izbicki actually existed and could be found in the Kemsley Newspaper office on the Place Vendôme, they got one of their press officers to take me to lunch and give me a third-degree grilling. The man was clearly embarrassed. He tried to tell me that my story was an invention and that the allegations of unfair pay were a travesty. When I turned the tables and asked him to call me a liar, he could not bring himself to do so. Nor would he tell me his own salary or the salaries of those locally employed in the press office. In the end, we called truce and downed another bottle of decent claret and promised to meet again "in less formal circumstances".

There was even a follow-up to that splash two weeks later. The foreign office announced that locally employed staff at all British embassies would receive a 10 per cent increase in salaries from Christmas, just a couple of months away. Maureen along with a score of her embassy friends came to my Porte de Versailles studio that weekend, armed with bottles of Champagne, to say thank you and celebrate into the wee small hours.

Shortly after that episode, I asked Maureen to move in with me. There was no doubt about it: we were in love. But making love was another matter. Maureen was a practising Roman Catholic. Intercourse was for marriage. I would have to wait – and she was worth waiting for.

There was, of course, another problem. Marrying "out" is frowned upon by both Jews and Catholics alike. What would my parents and her parents think? What would they say? We were both of age and did not need parental permission to tie the knot but we both loved our parents and would not wish to hurt them in any way. So we decided to spend our next holiday back in the UK and introduce each other to our respective parents.

Maureen's folks ran the post office at Chinley in Derbyshire, a beautiful village that had been tricked by time. Towards the end of the 19th century, planners expected Chinley to develop and grow into another Stockport. This plan misfired. Chinley continued to cling to its rural environs and remained a village. But it was a village with a railway station that could have rivalled King's Cross in grandeur and opulence. It possessed eight platforms that were lit throughout the night and made any passer by believe he was entering Blackpool during its illuminations. Richard Beeching became chairman of British Railways at about this time (1957) and later wielded his great axe over Britain's entire rail network – but even Lord Beeching forgot to close Chinley.

Harry and Nell Ryan lived at the post office, a neat, spotlessly clean house into which I was welcomed, to my surprise and delight, with open arms. Any friend of Maureen's must be all right was, I suppose, their assessment. Nell, a short, plump woman with rosy cheeks and a glorious smile, provided me with an embrace, a smacker of a kiss and a gargantuan tea. The table almost groaned under the weight of great slices of cooked ham, hardboiled eggs, tomatoes, salads and a basket filled with huge slices of bread.

Ham? Luckily, I am not *kosher* so I do not object to eating ham. In fact, I adore it. But the thought did enter my mind that maybe they didn't know I was Jewish. Maureen had probably not told them. Why should she? But they did know (as I later learned). They were simply not aware of the Jewish dietary laws, which only allow one to eat animals that chew the cud and possess cloven hooves, such as sheep and cows but not pigs; only fish that have scales and fins are permitted; shellfish, including prawns, lobsters and crabs are out. I have never really understood the reason other than to believe that prawns and pork in the heat of the Middle East, where these laws were laid down, can be poison and people, including the Prophet Mohammed, have died after eating pork.

So I ate the ham and other goodies and discussed Paris, newspapers, embassies and how expensive French life was. Harry, Maureen's dad, was getting on and didn't speak too much but he smiled a gentle smile at me and didn't need to make much conversation. I felt at home.

Maureen's introduction to Heywood Street, Manchester, and my home at No. 22 was not really very different. My mother loved everyone and my father welcomed everyone into the house. The front room had been prepared (as opposed to the kitchen where one normally ate) for a dinner that only my mother knew how to prepare: lokchen soup – a chicken soup with vermicelli – which is a typically Jewish opener, followed by gorgeous boiled chicken with all the trimmings, including red cabbage.

Mutti fussed over Maureen, saying how attractive she was and what beautiful hands she had. Papa just smiled and spoke loudly about how proud he was of his son who had got a university degree and how proud her parents must also be of her for doing the same. I think that Maureen felt at home just as I had done at Chinley. Heywood Street was then in the middle of Manchester's Jewish area – Cheetham Hill. It housed many synagogues and, as my father was quick to point out, a Roman Catholic church near the ice rink and not far from Strangeways prison. He brought out scrap books to show Maureen the cuttings he had pasted of all my stories. She sounded suitably impressed. I was just embarrassed.

We agreed later that we had both liked our respective parents.

But boyfriend/girlfriend is one thing; marriage is quite another. Would we still be welcomed if we were to get married? I had not yet popped the question, nor had she broached the subject. We just continued to live happily together in the Rue Bréa at the Porte de Versailles.

Meanwhile, I continued to cover events in France and even got to drive a magnificent Rolls Royce. Its owner was an ex-king; not any old ex-king but our own Edward VIII, who abdicated after just 327 days for the love of an American divorcee, Mrs Wallis Simpson. Exiled to France, the Duke and Duchess of Windsor spent much of their lives there. Their splendid house in the Bois de Boulogne was frequently filled with friends and admirers who partied into the early hours. Each year, the Duke and Duchess were guests of honour at the British Embassy party to celebrate the Queen's birthday. It was their only regular bond with the Crown. These parties were attended by just about every major representative of the British community in Paris as well as representatives of the Anglo-American Press Association of which I was to become a committee member.

It was at the Queen's Birthday Party during my first year in Paris that I got talking to a British expat who told me that he had seen a modest classified advert in an English language magazine lying around the British sports club at St Cloud that offered the sale of a Rolls Royce. There was a telephone number, which he gave me quietly and said, almost in a whisper, that he thought he recognised it as the Duke's.

As I was still in my salad days and green in judgment, to cite the Bard, I telephoned the number and introduced myself as John Howard, a British businessman, interested in the sale of the car. The male secretary at the other end arranged for me to come and see it. It was going for $12,000 o.n.o – reasonable even in those days. I immediately arranged for Rus Melcher to accompany me and take pictures. Rus stopped his car near some bushes within sight of the Windsors' mansion and I drove on.

The Roller – a four-door Silver Spirit – was beautiful. I told the flunky who opened the door that I should like to take the motor for a quick test drive. He agreed at once and accompanied me. "Why does the Duke want to sell it," I enquired. "He has another," was all he would say. I wondered whether he suspected me and I hoped my nerves would not betray me. After all, I was then a mere 26 – not the age of a successful businessman, But the Duke of Windsor's secretary or servant remained silent and sat stony faced beside me.

When I reached a point within decent camera range, I stopped the car and said I should like to take a brief look at the engine. He pulled a small lever and the bonnet clicked open. I got out and ambled to the front, knowing that Rus would be busy clicking away. I stooped down to examine the engine and everything else under that fine bonnet. I know very little if anything about the workings of a motor car and could not even pretend to be knowledgeable as my head disappeared into the heart of that Roller. All looked extremely clean, almost polished. So I smiled at my guide and stepped back into the driving seat. I should perhaps remind the reader that I had learned to drive during my National Service – on a ten-ton truck. I was used to a noisy engine, not the soft purr of this Rolls Royce; I was an expert at double-declutching, something that was totally unnecessary with this Silver Spirit. "What's your name?" I asked nonchalantly. "Joseph, Sir," he replied quietly. I had no idea what to say or ask. What a lousy, nerve-racked hack I turned out to be. So I simply took my leave and said I would phone and let him know my decision. "Very good, Sir," he replied and shut the door, leaving me to return to Rus's car and make my way back to the snapper in the bushes.

Rus said he had secured a number of excellent shots of me and the Roller and adored the one of me with my head stuck in the engine. We both laughed all the way back to the office. But the moment I was back at my desk, I began to feel guilty. How on earth could I have been so deceitful? British businessman, indeed! What a load of unadulterated crap. I was appalled at my deception. What the hell for? Was it worth it, for a tuppenny-ha'penny story?

I picked up the telephone and felt myself trembling as I dialled the Duke's number. The secretary answered. I recognised the voice. "Is that Joseph? It's John Izbicki…we met earlier…about the Rolls Royce. I want to apologise…

I – er – did not wish to deceive you or anyone. I must confess that I'm not a businessman at all but a journalist for Kemsley Newspapers – the *Sunday Times* and others. I'm truly sorry. I'm really interested in the car but couldn't possibly afford to buy her. I should quite like to write a little story about the sale – you know, give it some publicity...if that's all right with you and with the Duke of Windsor..." By now I was sweating.

Joseph had let me go on till the end, then said quietly. "I'll have to ask His Royal Highness and phone you back." He hung up and I hung on. I did not expect him to phone. But about half an hour later, he did. "His Royal Highness agrees that you write some short report if you so wish. And Mr Izbicki – " "Yes?" "There was no need for you to play-act your way here. You should have introduced yourself properly and saved yourself and me all this nonsense. All right?"

"Thank you Joseph. You're quite right and I'm very grateful – and very sorry..." But he had already put the phone down.

My three paragraphs appeared under a picture by Rus Melcher in the *Sunday Graphic.*

I vowed there and then never again to try to pull the wool over people's eyes in an attempt to get a story. And throughout more than half a century of journalism, I never did. It's not just that honesty is the best policy, but that honesty is best.

For instance, I bumped into the young Lord Snowdon at the bar of the Ritz Hotel when he was still merely Mr Antony Armstrong-Jones, having just been rejected by Princess Margaret – much against her will and his, but for the sake of the Crown. I introduced myself and said how genuinely sorry I was about the break. We drank a couple of large scotches and I came away with enough to fill a feature.

Work was going well. Apart from the daily news stories on French politics – Algeria was hotting up and there was always plenty to write about – I produced features ranging from fashion to tourism. Shortly before my arrival in Paris, the great Christian Dior died at the ridiculously young age of 52. His very first post-war collection took the world by storm with the introduction of what became known as the New Look. Until that moment, women in occupied France and in the rest of Europe had dressed in "sensible" skirts or trousers and covered their hair with scarves or turbans. The New Look turned women back into *women* emphasising their breasts, nipping in their waists, rounding their shoulders and letting them wear a bell-shaped skirt that showed off their legs. It was a veritable revolution.

His death which was still felt along the boulevards when I arrived was also shrouded in some mystery. His niece, Françoise, had been a fervent Nazi sympathiser during the occupation and after Dior's death, blamed his Jewish manageress for having caused it. She alleged, without a shred of evidence, that the manageress had supplied her uncle not only with medicines and potions but also with young men who were meant to help him relax but only tired him still further. The cloud that Françoise had created fortunately cleared quickly. The niece was recognised for her total anti-Semitic prejudice.

The man who succeeded Dior had started working for him in 1954 – the year I graduated and joined the army for National Service. Yves Saint Laurent, born in Oran, Algeria, was a lad of 18 when Dior appointed him and soon recognised his talent. He quickly rose to take his place on the designing floor and at the great man's death, became the company's haute couture designer. I was privileged to see his first collection in 1958, although I was unable to report anything other than short pieces for the diary pages. The collection hit the world's headlines and was fully covered by our various fashion editors. Yves Saint Laurent went further than his late Master's New Look. He produced what became known as the Trapeze Dress.

Saint Laurent decided to open a boutique called Dior Monsieur a year or so later. Apart from the odd piece in the French press, the venture had not attracted much attention abroad and I felt I might produce a snippet. I phoned Rus and together we stomped off to the store. I asked to see the manager and explained my scheme, which he snapped up with alacrity and asked me to choose any items I wanted to try on. The result was phenomenal. Rus took me outside the shop into the busy street, dressed in a Dior pink silk shirt, a brown leather jacket, black leather trousers and a long woollen scarf. He photographed me as I posed against the heavy traffic. The more people stared at me, the more dramatic my poses became. It brought out the actor in me.

We returned into the store and I reluctantly changed back into my own threadbare gear. I thought the manager might have asked me to keep the creations I was helping to promote but no. Instead, he went up to Rus and quietly whispered to him: "Monsieur, next time please remember that we have some – er – genuine male models. It would be better, non?"

When Rus told me, I felt slightly hurt but instead of moaning about it, we both roared with laughter and retreated to the nearest bistro for a beer.

The pictures were great and made their appearances in both the *Sunday Empire News* and the *Sunday Graphic*, the latter over the headline: *Dior dresses me – and I stop Paris traffic*. The story contained the prices against each article of clothing and totalled a phenomenal £1,948. This might not seem over the top by today's *haute couture* labels, but this was 1955.

CHAPTER ELEVEN:

MY NAKED HEROINE

The good journalist must not sit back and rely on news agency tapes, which every newspaper receives. Journalists need to read papers fromcover to cover – even some of the classified ads. One never knows what might spring up. So it was one day when I was skimming through *Le Monde*, that my eyes fell upon a short paragraph in the French equivalent of our Court Circular. The *Croix de Guerre* was to be awarded to a woman – one Lydia Lova de Korczac Lipski for her work for the French Resistance. I pushed the paper aside but, after some thought, picked it up again. Who was she, this woman who had worked for the Resistance Movement? What did she do? There might be nothing in it, I thought, as so many French resistance workers had been honoured over the years, but I had to find out.

I made inquiries with the award-giving body and discovered that Mademoiselle Lova was a dancer. Not just any old dancer but one who danced in the Folies-Bergère show. In the nude! This, I felt, made her newsworthy.

I met Lydia at the theatre and was invited to see the show (with Maureen). Lydia was a superb ballerina and her acts in the show together with a naked male dancer, were in no way erotic but beautiful ballets that were greeted by thunderous applause from the audience. Lydia's story was sensational. She had already been awarded the Légion d'Honneur and had it pinned upon her fully dressed breast by President de Gaulle himself. It provided me, not only with a three-part serialized story in the *Sunday Graphic* but was later to become the subject of a book – *The Naked Heroine*.

Briefly, Lydia was of aristocratic Polish descent and was brought up by

My Naked Heroine: Lydia Love – nude dancer of the Folies Bergère, who was awarded the Croix de Guerre and Légion d'Honneur by President de Gaulle in recognition for her work in the French Resistance during the German Occupation of France. She died as a result of injections received at Ravensbrück, a Nazi concentration camp.

her parents in pre-war Paris. She went to ballet classes and, by the time she was 14, turned out to be a formidable dancer. When Paris was occupied by the Nazis, she was dancing at a small Pigalle nightclub. It was at that period that she started to work for the underground movement. She was still a teenager of 16 at the time. It was her father, the Prince de Korczac Lipski, who had formed one of the very first resistance groups of the Maquis and for 18 months Lydia worked alongside him and other members of the group. By night she danced before German officers while overhead in upstairs rooms, British airmen who had been shot down over France, lay hidden. By day she spied for the Maquis and helped to repatriate the airmen. But she was betrayed by a woman who was believed to be among the most trusted of resistance fighters – Micheline Carré, whose code name in the Resistance was, appropriately perhaps, *La Chatte* – The Cat. On November 20, 1941, Micheline visited the Lipskis accompanied by one Hugo Bleicher of the Gestapo. She pointed at Monsieur Lipski. "That's him," she told Bleicher. "And that's the girl." Both were arrested. The Cat had caught the Chic in her claws.

Father and daughter ended up in jail and, from there, were moved to one concentration camp after another. At the notorious Ravensbrück, Lydia underwent the most fiendish medical experiments. One of the injections, applied to her right arm by the obnoxious Dr Hans Gerhart in November 1944, was one that would haunt her for the rest of her life.

Gerhart told her: "You'll have no reactions to this little injection. You'll be able to forget all about it for some 25 years. That's when it will activate. So don't worry. You have plenty of time."

After the war and France's Liberation, she joined a number of dance companies, ending up at the Folies-Bergère. In November 1969 – exactly 25 years after Gerhart's injection and prediction – Lydia performed her last dance to rapturous applause. It was a Saturday night and she returned to her apartment feeling unwell. On the Sunday she was rushed to hospital and by Monday evening she was dead.

I wrote the story of *The Naked Heroine* and published the hardback edition in 1963. Of course, Lydia's terrible end never appeared in its pages – nor in the paperback edition, which appeared in 1965. When her death was announced, Neville Spearman, the publisher, contacted me. "I think it's time to publish a sequel, don't you? You've got to include the final chapter and how the Nazi doctors had produced something that would take a quarter of a century to activate." He was astounded when I refused.

"Sorry, Neville. I really cannot cash in on someone's tragic death."

So the full story was never told – until now.

There were, of course, many people, including my colleagues, who refused to believe that anything could be injected for effect 25 years later. I used to tell them that such experiments were not all that unusual. "After all, Hitler promised the German people a 1,000-year Reich. Twenty-five years in such a span is nothing," I would say. And then I told them the story of the soldier who had fallen into the Sweetwater Canal in Egypt. Those effects also took more than 20 years to materialize.

The book had what might be described as moderate success. It was given reasonably friendly reviews, but the title might be blamed for its underwhelming sales. It was too early for such a title. People were still not ready to walk into bookshops and ask for *The Naked Heroine*. Such a demand might have produced a few raised eyebrows. My own suggested title: *The Three Faces of Lydia* was considered too tame by Neville Spearman, although the cover showed my heroine in various poses – as the Folies-Bergère dancer and in uniform being given her *Croix de Guerre* – inside the three colours, red, white and blue, of the French flag.

But the book brought Lydia more than the plaudits of the Folies. A Soho nightclub offered her several thousand pounds to come over and appear for three weeks. The club enlarged the book's cover, designed by Michael Harvey, to engulf half the stage. As the music struck up Édith Piaf's great *Non, je ne regrette rien*, the centre of the cover, showing Lydia in the (almost) nude, became a door. It opened and the real nude Lydia stepped down onto the stage to dance.

The likes of her do not occur often during a lifetime.

During my Paris days, I was often invited to go and speak with Lady Kemsley and have a Dry Martini with her. It seemed to be the only drink she knew. She spoke with a thick French accent acquired in her native Mauritius. She made it clear that she did not really fancy black people or Asians; I'm not sure into which of those two categories she placed Jews but she certainly never implied any form of anti-Semitism. I often felt desperately sorry for her. She was certainly not a well woman, suffering almost constant pain. She had been clumsily operated on in Switzerland where the surgeon had managed to sever a nerve on the left side of her head. This had partially paralysed her as though she had suffered a stroke. Her lips curled down on the left giving her the expression of a woman who was consistently angry and scowling.

But she never treated me as a servant, unlike Gomer, her husband, who treated everyone in his employ as his personal skivvies. But he adored his wife – an adoration that was never returned. He would tiptoe through her bedroom at the Ritz, not wishing to disturb her sleep. But she was rarely asleep. She simply didn't want to see him or speak with him. So she pretended. Eventually he would tiptoe out again.

One day Lord Kemsley was in London lunching with his fellow newspaper mogul, Lord (Max) Beaverbrook, owner of the *Daily Express*. The Beaver was moaning about his paper and his overseas possessions, in particular the house he owned in the Bahamas. It gave Lord K an idea and by the time they were on their vintage port, Gomer had written a cheque for the amount the Beaver wanted for the house. After lunch, they marched into the Beaver's solicitor's office and agreed officially on the sale. The deeds were handed to Kemsley who was driven to Heathrow to catch the next plane to Paris.

He tiptoed into Lady K's room – but this time called her to wake up. She opened a bleary eye. "What?" she enquired curtly. "I have a little present for you," said Gomer and handed her an envelope containing the deeds of the Bahamas house. She just about had the grace to say thank you.

The moment the Kemsleys entered their new possession, Lord Kemsley called in a carpenter whom he ordered to make a new sign. And so, the

Beaver's house in the Bahamas became plain and simple: *Kemsley House*.

But I digress. Lady K confided in me about her illness. "I am very sick *vous savez* Monsieur Izbicki. I see all sorts of doctors and professors and they give me many injections. Nothing helps. Nothing."

I shook my head in sympathy. Where was she leading?

"I wonder if you maybe could 'elp me. You are clever and 'ave your ears to, as you say, the ground. There is I think a man in Paris, I don't know 'is name, a *magnetiseur.* Could you find 'im and bring 'im to me to 'elp?"

I had not a clue but said I would see what I could do. I made enquiries and, sure enough, was told of one such *magnetiseur* who, with the help of a small magnet, had been known to cure people of certain conditions, mainly rheumatic and arthritic pains. I contacted him and he agreed to pay Lady Kemsley a visit at the Ritz that Friday. I telephoned Risa, m'lady's maid, a cheerful petite Austrian, and passed the message to her. Two minutes later she phoned back to say that m'lady was delighted and please would I join her for a Dry Martini when I finished what I still had to do.

Apart from Risa, Lady K had a charming secretary, Elizabeth Fanstone, an Englishwoman with whom I spent many a happy afternoon, when there was nothing much of newsworthy interest happening, gossiping about her boss and Gomer. We met that Friday evening for a drink and she regaled me with the story of an eventful afternoon. The *magnetiseur* had duly arrived at the appointed time of 3 p.m. and was ushered into m'lady's boudoir. She was propped up in bed ready for him.

After establishing what was exactly troubling her, the slightly tubby, ruddy-cheeked man brought out his little magnet and was slowly swinging it to and fro across Lady K's face when the bedroom door burst open and a flushed Risa ran in. She bent down over m'lady's face and whispered into her ladyship's ear: "M'lady – Professeur Levi is here to see you. He says an appointment was definitely made! What shall I do?"

There was no way out of the bedroom other than through the en-suite bathroom and drawing room. The *magnetiseur* seemed to understand at once. He calmly looked round the room, said "*Je vous prie de m'excuser, Madame*", and opened the door of the inbuilt wardrobe. He then stepped inside among m'lady's dresses and pulled the door closed.

Professor Levi, Lady Kemsley's physician and one of the leading Paris neurologists, was then ushered into the room where he sat speaking soothingly to her Ladyship for some twenty minutes before giving her one of the injections she so disliked, and taking his leave. At that point, the wardrobe slowly opened and the *magnetiseur*, sweating profusely, emerged and without a further word, finished his treatment of Lady K with his little magnet. He was, needless to say, well rewarded. But, alas, his magnetism did nothing to cure her.

About a year after this incident, I had a surprising telephone call from Lord Kemsley. "Ah, Izbicki, glad I caught you in. I hear you've been very good to Lady Kemsley (he never referred to his wife in any other way) and I'd like you to be our guest to luncheon (what was wrong with simply lunch?)."

"That's extremely kind of you, Sir, thank you. When and where please?"

"At Maxim's tomorrow. Is that all right? Or are you working on some great story?"

"No, Sir, tomorrow's fine. What time?"

"Oh, at 1 p.m. And will you please reserve the table? Ask them to sit us at a quiet table, away from the crowds, you know what I mean?"

Yes, I knew exactly what he meant. He didn't wish anyone to see poor Lady K – especially anyone who might have known her in past years (she used to be an exceptionally attractive woman but her illness and her paralysis had turned her into a senile old lady for whom one could feel nothing but pity). I phoned Maxim's and was promised a good table at the front of the restaurant where only the most elite were seated and most of these tended to come in for dinner, not lunch. In those days, Maxim's was still considered one of the finest restaurants in France, second perhaps only to the Tour d'Argent.

It turned out to be a very sparse lunch as far as I was concerned. Lady K chose a bouillon to start and a small chicken salad as a main course; Lord K tucked into a dozen oysters followed by a ragout; whatever I ordered brought a curt *Quinze minutes, Monsieur* or even *Vingt minutes, Monsieur* from the *maître d'hotel*. There would not be time for me to tuck into their pheasant stew or roast venison, so I went for the *poulet à la crème*, a dish I could have had at any Paris bistro. Lord K and I shared a half bottle of Côte du Rhone, again a wine that any French greasy spoon would have served in a carafe. Lady K stuck to mineral water. Still, the puds were good and I downed fresh wild strawberries and cream. We dispensed with coffee.

Lord K called for the *addition*, which was presented to him on a silver platter. Then, to my shock-horror, he passed it across to me "There you are Izbicki. Hope you can see to this little bill. I'd like it to go on your expenses." And he added: "If you haven't enough cash on you, I'll lend it to you. You can return it tomorrow." I looked at the bill and inwardly shook with anger. Was this my reward for having been "very good to Lady Kemsley"? Luckily,

I had been to the bank that very morning and drawn sufficient to pay the £60 or £70 (I no longer remember the exact amount but it was high for such a small meal at that period. In today's money, it would be almost three times as much). In those days there was no such thing as a credit card and I did not carry a cheque book on me that day. But I had enough.

What was even more galling was that, as we left, Lord Kemsley handed out a few francs to each of a row of waiters and commissionaires. Each gave a little bow, adding a *merci, melord, merci melady*. I, who had done the paying, obtained no more than an *au revoir, Monsieur*. Ouch. It went into my expenses as: Entertaining the Proprietor and his wife. When the inevitable query came ("What's all this about entertaining the Proprietor, ol' boy?") I told it as it was. There were a few gasps at the other end of the telephone line and I'm sure the story was rapidly spread around 200 Gray's Inn Road. But it was paid back to me.

I had been in Paris almost three years – what a difference from the three months I was originally asked to "do". By now my name was appearing regularly, not only in the two "pop" Sundays, the *Graphic* and the *Empire News*, but also in the *Sunday Times*, whenever its sole correspondent Stephen Coulter was sick or on holiday, and the many provincial newspapers in the Kemsley Group, including of course my own *Manchester Evening Chronicle*. I worked solidly, often seven days a week, either on stories written exclusively for the Sundays or some feature that would be circulated to the Group. And I also produced stories on request from one or another of the provincials – if, for instance, I was asked by the *Newcastle Journal* to cover the official visit of the city's mayor to his Paris counterpart, I would produce the required few paragraphs along with a picture.

The *Sunday Graphic* ran a series of full-page features called *Nothing but the Truth*…comprising a question-answer interview of well known men and women. I used to subscribe to a thing called the *Celebrity Service*, from which I would receive regular weekly lists of who was visiting the French capital, where they were staying and for how long they intended to remain. It helped me seek out some fascinating subjects for this series. Thus it was that I interviewed "sex kitten" Brigitte Bardot (who, incidentally tried, but failed, to get me thoroughly pissed); the surrealist painter Salvador Dali, who insisted on my interviewing him while being driven around Paris in a taxi – a surrealist experience in itself; and my favourite, the Red Hot Momma herself, Sophie Tucker.

I met Sophie at the George V Hotel for tea and we got on like the proverbial house on fire. During our chat, we were approached by an American who was also staying at the hotel. "Sophie Tucker!" he exclaimed. "You are my very favourite entertainer, believe me. Please can I have your autograph?" She readily provided her signature. The man who, like Sophie (and me), was Jewish and introduced himself as a commercial traveller for Hollywood Chewing Gum (clearly a successful one to be able to afford the George V). Sophie immediately showed great interest. "All right, I'll tell you what you can do for me. I'm on my way to Israel to do some charity work and open a children's home. They'd love some chewing gum. Could you let me have a few packets?"

The man excused himself and said he would return in a few minutes. And he did, bringing with him a suitcase filled with Hollywood gum, bars of candy and a "special little gift for yourself, Sophie". He handed her a neat little electric razor for ladies. Far from being in any way insulted, Sophie Tucker accepted the gift gratefully. "And for your friend here – pointing to me – a man's razor...the very latest." I hesitated but Sophie prodded me: "Take it *Schlemiel*. It's not a bribe!"

Following that meeting, Sophie Tucker and I became great friends. Some years later, when I was back in London, she phoned me at home and invited me and my wife to come and see her show at the London Palladium. By now she was well over 70 but was continuing to sing as well as ever, under the excellent direction of her manager who happened to be her brother. I recall seeing one of her last performances, which naturally contained the song that was written for her – *My Yiddishe Momma*. There wasn't a dry eye in the house when she changed one of the lines from "My Yiddishe Momma, so old and so grey…" to "My Yiddishe Momma who has just passed away…" And when she rendered her magnificent *Life Begins at 40*, she added the line "…*and I'm living all over again…*It was a show stopper.

Back in Paris, I thought it about time I got married. Maureen and I had now been living together for nearly three years and I was anxious to consummate our very close and loving relationship. She agreed and, in the Spring of 1959, we set a date: 28th December 1959 for the civil marriage; and 29th December 1959 for the religious ceremony. The British Embassy had kindly agreed to host the civil event with the Consul-General, Harold Braham, tying the knot. The religious ceremony was a different matter, one which I feared as I could not see my parents wanting to see their little boy kneeling down in a Roman Catholic church. Would they even honour us with their presence?

I telephoned home and announced that Maureen and I had agreed to wed.

Maureen – my beautiful first wife pictured before she was struck down with cancer. She died, aged 42, in 1979.

Just married – at the British Embassy in Paris, December 1959

My mother, to whom I spoke first, burst into tears, but said they were tears of happiness. My father was more blunt and to the point. "Are you absolutely certain? Marrying out is not easy. You will be turning your back on not just your religion but tradition." He was not angry, just very deeply concerned. Why could I not have found a nice Jewish girl? Oh, they both agreed that Maureen was a marvellous young woman, beautiful, bright and loving but what would happen if there was a row? Would she not call me terrible names, like "dirty Jew"? I could only assure them that such thoughts were completely, utterly wrong.

Their reaction was understandable and based on bitter experience. Rows among mixed marriage couples in Nazi Germany – even between my Aunty Mary and her husband, Isidor (my mother's brother) – always seemed to end that way. But that was in Nazi Germany where non-Jews were indoctrinated to blame Jews for everything. My parents, I was sure, would eventually come round and accept the situation.

Luckily, I was proved right.

As I disclosed the news to "Papa and Mutti", Maureen also informed her parents by phone. Their reaction was completely different. "About time," her mother intoned and her father wished us both every happiness.

At about the same time, I received a call from the London office to say that Denis Hamilton, Kemsley's editorial director, was flying to Paris and wanted to take me to dinner. Would I please book him a room at the Crillon.

We dined at the Brasserie Lipp on the Boulevard St Germain des Près, which is far superior to Maxim's and certainly less pretentious, despite its age, having been founded in 1880. It is directly opposite those other excellent Boulevard St Germain watering holes, Les Deux Magots and the Café de Flore, which for a considerable time were the centre of the existentialist movement. Jean-Paul Sartre, Camus and Simone de Beauvoir were regulars at both the Flore and Lipp. The night Hamilton and I sat down to study the menu, I recognized François Mitterand and Françoise Sagan at nearby tables. Mitterand was then still an up-and-coming socialist politician and a long way from becoming president of France. The writer Françoise Sagan was certainly far more famous at that time and more heads turned towards her and her male companion than to the politician who was in company of an attractive young woman.

I vividly remember what I had that memorable evening. I kicked off with a Bismarck herring, cool and sharp, followed by Lipp's speciality – the Alsatian Choucroute with its lashings of sauerkraut filling the plate and acting as a bed for a variety of sausages and slices of pork and ham, all washed down with a litre of sparkling beer. My memory of Hamilton's dishes is somewhat vague but I believe his main course was a fine Blanquette de Veau. For dessert I took the profiteroles, and I think he had the deliciously creamy Mille Feuille.

I waited until the coffee to break the news. During the meal we had chatted mainly about politics and the Franco-Algerian problem. He thought I had been doing "extremely well" and the various editors had expressed satisfaction with my work. Hamilton's manner was kind and he had an infectious laugh. He happily told me his own background. I could not help being reminded of Dickie Hull, the general who had torn a strip off me for having panned the Moascar Players' production of *An Inspector Calls*. Perhaps it was because of Hamilton's own distinguished military background. He had come up "through the ranks" as they say, having joined the Middlesbrough's *Evening Gazette* as a reporter in 1937. He moved to the *Evening Chronicle* at Newcastle a year later, again as a reporter, and was there when the Second World War broke out. He saw service with the Durham Light Infantry and, being a highly intelligent young man, was rapidly commissioned and promoted. Towards the end of the war he found himself commanding the 7th Battalion, The Duke of Wellington's Regiment. When the war ended, he was demobbed with the rank of Lieutenant-Colonel and returned to Newcastle to ask for his old job on the *Chron*.

Consternation and red faces all round. How could they offer a Lt-Colonel a reporter's job? It was a ludicrous situation, or so the powers that be at the *Chron* felt it to be. It was not long before Lord Kemsley, owner of the paper, heard of the dilemma and took immediate action.

"If this young man is good enough to have been made a Colonel, then he's bloody well good enough to be my PA," Gomer Kemsley is reported to have said.

And so it was that Charles Denis Hamilton stepped into Kemsley House in 1946 as an editorial assistant to Lord Kemsley. After four years in this role, promotion came once more and he was given the mantle of Kemsley Newspapers' editorial director, a position he held with distinction until 1961 when he doubled up as editorial director of the group as well as editor of the *Sunday Times*.

But at our Brasserie Lipp dinner, he was still "only" editorial director of the Kemsley empire – a good and useful man to know – so it was with more than simple pride that I produced my "news".

"Apart from my parents, I should like you to be the first to know that I am getting married…"

If ever a jaw was actually seen to drop, then this was it. His jaw cascaded towards the tablecloth and his face grew taut. "Married?" he repeated in a monotone. And then again: "Married?"

"That's right," I said quietly, almost in a whisper. I had no idea how to interpret his totally inexplicable change in facial expression and attitude. "Probably later this year."

"You're quite sure about this, are you Izbicki? You see, I have always felt that our foreign correspondents should remain single. It makes it so much easier to move them around the world. For you I had so many plans, so many plans. I was, in fact, going to ask you tonight how you felt about becoming our Washington correspondent..."

"Washington?" I gasped. "Yes, well, of course, I should like that very much..."

"Yes, but now...if you're to be married..." his voice dwindled away, like water disappearing down a plughole. Then he suddenly straightened himself up, reached across the table and shook my hand. "Many congratulations, John. Many congratulations. We'll talk about this again." And he called for the bill, paid and made for the door with me at his side. Outside, he hailed a taxi and we parted on good but puzzling terms.

It was not the last I heard from Denis Hamilton – but his proposal to send me to Washington was never raised again.

He called me one day to ask a favour. "Two of my sons are doing French at school and I've arranged for them to spend a few weeks in France with a French family," he began. "I was wondering whether you could meet them at the airport and drive them down to the family I've arranged for them. I'll give you the full address and all that of course, if you can do it."

I naturally agreed at once. I duly met both lads and escorted them to their holiday address, a farm, where a very nice, elderly lady greeted us warmly and immediately offered us all refreshments. The boys appeared to like their room and the surroundings, although there seemed very little for adventurous lads to do. Still, they would have a decent rest on their public school holidays.

A week or so later, their landlady telephoned me in some distress. "Ah, Monsieur, I am so sorry to disturb you," she said and I was immediately alerted. "What has happened, Madame? Are the boys injured?" "*Mais non, pas du tout Monsieur*," she said and explained that the matter was "somewhat embarrassing".

"Please tell me, Madame, whatever is the matter?" "Ah, Monsieur, you see, I am just a silly old woman perhaps but I was brought up always to be polite to my elders. But these two, *mon Dieu*, do not know what it is to be polite. They have told me that my food is terrible; they do not like this, they do not like that. And they never ever say thank you or please but order me as if I was a servant, Monsieur. I am really so very sorry to trouble you with this matter, but do you think you could perhaps have a word with them?"

I naturally promised to speak with them at once. "I shall come down to see them." My diary was clear for a day or two, so I travelled down the following day and took the boys for a few lemonades at the nearby village bistro. Clearly, they didn't like it at their holiday home; they were "bored" and would rather be at home. I explained that it would be nice if they would at least be polite to their landlady who was elderly and not used to bad manners. "If I get any more complaints from her, I shall have to let your father know," I told them as gently as I could.

"Do what you bloody like," replied one (I don't recall which) and there was no alternative but for me to take them back to the farm and return to Paris.

A few days later, another call from Madame to tell me that the Hamilton lads were "*pire que jamais*" (worse than ever) and that she would rather refund the money and send them home. I had to let Denis Hamilton know – and did so in a brief and I hope diplomatically worded confidential memo.

It was a mistake on my part. Probably one that would not be forgotten in a hurry.

I was asked to escort the boys back to the airport and put them on a plane to Heathrow. They (the boys) were delighted and thanked me profusely for helping them escape from their "boring, boring, boring holiday in Frogland".

Ouch!

Dates for the wedding were fixed but I had first to undergo a "course". I had no idea what this would entail. I feared some kind of indoctrination by a Catholic priest and I went to meet Father Martin at St Joseph's, just a stone's throw from the Arc de Triomphe, with more than a little fear. Fr Martin turned out to be a jolly fellow, small of stature, grey hair topping a triangular face with ruddy cheeks, suggesting either a bad heart or (more likely) a taste for French wines. His eyes were the giveaway. They radiated warmth and kindness and were in perpetual smile-mode. Despite his name, he turned out to be Irish and when he spoke, the lilt brought with it the flow of the Liffey.

"So you're John, are ye?" he said with a little laugh and shook my hand. It was a firm grip that made me feel completely at ease. The "course" was no more than a chat about marriage and the Catholic views on contraception, birth and children. "And will ye be makin' sure that your children will be brought up in The Faith?" he asked, still smiling.

"Hey, Father, not so fast, I'm not married yet...but, yes, I suppose the answer has to be yes," I said a little lamely.

"You're Jewish I believe, John, is that right?"

"Yes, Father."

"Well, Our Lord was a Jew, too, of course. I'm just tellin' you what it is we believe and not what we want you to believe, d'you understand my meaning?"

"Yes, Father. You make it very clear, thank you."

"Well now, that's all right then, and I look forward to seeing you and the lovely Maureen on the 29th December, is that right? "

"Yes, Father,"

He rose and shook my hand warmly once again. "Then I can just wish you both a very happy Christmas and may you both enjoy every happiness."

The "course" had ended. My fears of indoctrination were completely dispelled and I returned to my Place Vendome office with a spring in the step and lightness of heart.

Some three Saturdays before the wedding, I had to return to St Joseph's to report another wedding. Stella Jebb, daughter of Sir Gladwyn (later Lord) Jebb, Britain's ambassador to France, was to marry Joel de Rosnay, the writer and a member of one of the most Catholic of French families. Stella, on the other hand, was Anglican. Did she have to meet Fr Martin for one of his little courses?

The media was well represented in front of the church. Television cameras, radio, my fellow hacks and the usual throng of paparazzi stood there, ready to go into action as soon as the happy pair stepped outside. I could not understand why they were not inside the church. I went in and stood at the back. St Joseph's was packed. And the bride and groom were there, kneeling in front of the altar. I could not believe it. Fr Martin was officiating and was giving the couple the full works – a nuptial mass. I had been under the impression that a mixed marriage could only be performed at a side altar and could only have a shortened service.

When Joel and Stella became man and wife and made their joyous journey from the church, accompanied by the crescendo of the organ's rendition of the Wedding March by Mendelssohn (another Jewish boy...), I stayed behind to have a little chat to the priest.

"Ah, 'tis you John, welcome. Did ye enjoy it?" he asked, as he grasped my hand.

"Yes, Father, I did. But I was a little surprised. Was it not a full nuptial mass you performed?"

"Och, sure it was that. D'ye see, I feel that once a dispensation has been given, there's no reason why I shouldn't provide them with a proper Mass."

"Well, now Father," I said. "As you know, I have been given dispensation too and..."

"And you, too, shall have a nuptial mass, me boyo. But first I shall have to air the church. Otherwoise it'll stink of mink for weeks."

Maureen will be delighted, I thought. So will her mother and aunt, both of whom had planned to come. But first, I had to get back to the office and file my story for the *Sunday Graphic*. A picture of the couple outside the church was already on its way.

My piece was factual, spelling out the wedding in some detail and quoting Fr Martin's comment about the many fur coats present. Not many minutes after I had dictated the story to one of the many copytakers at Kemsley House, the phone rang. It was the news desk. "Got your piece, John. Nice colour. We're thinking of splashing the back page with it." "Thanks," I said. "Tell me though, John, you're not a Roman Catholic are you?" "No," I replied. "Why d'you ask?" "Well, you've got them as having had a full nuptial mass. And that's impossible." "But that's what it was," I countered. "I was there in the church and saw it from start to finish. And anyway, I'm going to have one at the same church in three weeks from today. The priest also confirmed that it was…"

"I know, I know. But if we run this story as it stands, there'll be a helluva row. I can hear the readers phoning in already…"

I suppose a certain libel action involving the obliterated penis of a prize bull might have crossed the news editor's mind at the time. I could do no more than protest that my story was 100 per cent correct and I would stand by it. We left it like that.

The next day, the story alongside a beautiful picture of the event, did indeed lead the back page (the *Sunday Graphic* did not report its sports coverage on the back in those days) and under my byline were the words: "Stella Jebb, the British ambassador's Anglican daughter, and Joel de Rosnay, prominent French author and a Roman Catholic, were married at a side altar of St Joseph's church in Paris yesterday…" There followed a brief explanation why it had to be a side altar and not a nuptial mass before returning to the story as I had written it.

I was furious and immediately phoned London. No one would be in the Sunday paper's office until Tuesday, but I dictated a brief note, marked "URGENT" to await the *Graphic's* editor, John Anstey. "It is with regret that I have to inform you of my resignation with immediate effect. Today's story on the back page of the paper was re-written and made factually incorrect despite my assurance to the News Desk that the couple had undergone a full nuptial mass before the main altar. The least that should have been done is to have removed my byline."

Needless to say, I received a phone call that evening from Fr Martin who wanted to know why I had written such an inaccurate report. When I explained what I had done, he immediately sympathized. "Oh, John my boy, you shouldn't throw in the towel just for that. Your news desk is the one to look foolish, not you. I'll write your editor a letter to back you and tell them what I think of them…"

My resignation was reported to Ian Fleming who in turn phoned Lord Kemsley. Gomer Kemsley contacted me on the Wednesday and asked me to come over to the Ritz. He told me not to be such a "bloody young fool" and said that Denis Hamilton had "already rapped the knuckles of that news editor very soundly."

Admittedly, I had calmed down considerably, thanks mainly to the backing of Fr Martin and Maureen's sound advice to put this mistake on the part of the paper behind me. There was the usual reminder that today's newspaper wraps up tomorrow's fish and chips!

The wedding at the British Embassy was amazing. Despite the date – 28 December – the sun decided to shine throughout, allowing the Champagne and canapés to be served on the lawn. Speeches were brief and the wedding party comprising some 30 close friends retreated to my favorite lunchtime bistro in the rue Castiglione, which was closed for this special party. The guests included Nell, my mother in law, and May, her sister, as well as Louis Herchenroder, my best man, Steve Coulter, my colleague, Sam White of the London Evening Standard, who I considered one of the finest columnists in the business, Peter Stephens of the Daily Mirror, Rus Melcher, my photographer, Annette Wilcox, his mother and my landlady, Sam Francis, the painter from the studio above mine, Geoffrey Myers, Ronnie Payne and John Wallis, all three of the *Daily Telegraph* office. John gave Maureen away in place of her dad who couldn't make it.

I had arranged for Nell and May to sleep in Sam Francis's studio; Sam was kipping down at Annette's – and as for me and Maureen…well, we'd sleep in mine "officially" for the first time.

"Oh no you won't!" Nell exclaimed as I told her of the sleeping arrangements.

"Won't? What d'you mean, Mum?" I had decided to call her 'Mum' from the moment Maureen and I had got engaged. That in itself was a strange event. Maureen had become sick in Paris with terrible pains in her lower abdomen. The local French doctor ordered a blood test and the results showed appendicitis. There was no doubt about it. Maureen decided to go home to have the operation on the NHS and phoned her GP in Chinley. He wasn't much help. "I don't do diagnoses over the telephone. You'll have to come home and have an x-ray," he said. "But I've had a blood test and they said it was conclusive," she argued. He wouldn't listen. "Blood tests, fooey. An x-ray is what you need."

So she went back to Chinley and was sent to Stockport for x-rays in the plural as none of them showed anything. The pains were getting worse and she was admitted into Stockport General for an "exploratory op". What they discovered was a highly inflamed appendix on the point of bursting but for the bodily fat in which it had miraculously been wrapped. The appendix was duly removed. And, as she came round from the anaesthetic, there in a bed of the general ward, I held her hand – and proposed. She was probably too dozy to have said anything but yes, so that was it.

But back in Paris, after the wedding and slap-up lunch…"Won't? What d'you mean, Mum?"

"I mean that you're not married – not yet and not in the eyes of God," Nell said quietly but very firmly. "Your proper marriage isn't until tomorrow in church!" So there.

Nell and May – and Maureen – slept in my studio while I climbed slowly, dejectedly up the stairs to Sam Francis's paint-filled pad to spend the night alone.

The St Joseph's wedding was, indeed, a full nuptial mass, conducted by an unsteadily tottering, flaming-cheeked priest. No, he wasn't drunk. Poor Fr Martin had a bad bout of the 'flu and was running a high temperature. He performed the ceremony as though in a dream and, following his offering the bride a holy communion wafer and a sip from the goblet of wine, was about to terminate the mass and the ceremony. He was stopped from doing so by John Wallis who rushed to the altar and tugged Martin's sleeve. "You can't end it yet, Father. Just look around you: there are people requiring communion!"

Fr Martin looked and, sure enough, Nell and May had come down to the edge of the altar to receive Communion. They were kneeling and waiting for the blessing to be brought to them. Martin, who had already locked away the remaining wafers and drunk the rest of the wine, had to perform a virtual playback. He came down eventually to pronounce the traditional "Body of Christ" for the two elderly women before him.

This time, the party, which had expanded to about 70 people, returned to the rue Olivier de Serre for nosh washed down by Champagne and a collection of wines. Annette's own large studio had been cleared to accommodate the horde. We cut the huge cake produced by a Porte de Versailles patisserie and danced to records by the two Frankies, favourites of the period: Frankie Laine and Frank Sinatra.

And at last, we could wave everyone goodbye, step into a taxi and be rushed to Le Bourget (as Charles de Gaulle airport was then still called) and fly off on our honeymoon – to Marrakesh.

CHAPTER TWELVE:

TAKEOVER

Maureen and I settled into our Paris home – still the studio at the Porte de Versailles – with remarkable ease. We entertained our friends to some home cooking produced in our tiny kitchen or hurriedly imported from the array of excellent charcuteries that abounded in the area. Maureen was happily working at the British Embassy and I was getting an increasing number of good stories and feature articles into the many papers for whom I covered.

Lord Kemsley called me across to the Ritz early in 1959. He looked pale and weary.

"Sit down, Izbicki," he said quietly. His voice was tired. I thought at once that something terrible had happened but sat and said nothing. "You've been very good to Lady Kemsley and me these past two or three years and both she and I were wondering whether there's anything we might do for you in the way of thanks."

"Oh, no, Sir, there's no need…" I stammered. "Whatever I have managed to do to be of some help was done with pleasure."

"Oh, I know that. I know that. Anyway, I want you to know that we are thinking of giving you something and if there's nothing you can think of, well then, we shall have to think of something for you. That's all then, Izbicki, thank you."

The dismissal on that occasion took me by surprise. I was deeply moved yet had no idea why. I half expected him to say he'd give me something and please would I put it on my expenses…but this time, there was nothing approaching such a request. Whatever it was, it had to be serious and I went slowly down the sweeping Ritz staircase in something of a daze.

About a week later, Louis Herchenroder phoned me. Would I come and have lunch with him at the Crillon at 12.30. The Crillon! It was one of the best hotels in central Paris, standing as it does next to the American Embassy in the Place de la Concorde. Louis and I used to lunch fairly regularly and Maureen and I would have him to dinner. He was Lady Kemsley's nephew and, like her, spoke English with a Mauritius-based French accent and French with an English accent. But this was the first time that he had chosen such a swanky place to treat me to lunch.

"You must keep thees under your 'at, all right?"

"What on earth is it, Louis? Of course I'll keep it under my hat, whatever it is…"

"Gomer is selling Kemsley Newspapers. The whole bloody lot. To a bloody Yank. Well, a Canadian. 'Ave you ever 'eard of a man called Roy Thomson?"

"Good God!" I could hardly believe it. "Thomson? Doesn't he own *The Scotsman?*"

"You've got it," said Louis. "And we've 'ad it," he added with a laugh, a bit of *Galgenhumor.*

He went on to describe the entire deal in some detail. Thomson had his eye particularly on the *Sunday Times* but had agreed to swallow up the entire Kemsley empire. When was all this to become public? I wanted to know between mouthfuls of a delicious *gigot à l'ail.* "It is being settled as we speak. It should be in the papers before the end of the week if all goes according to Gomer's plan. And before you ask me, I've no idea how much Thomson is paying."

Kemsley was a thorough businessman and, despite his niggling demands for me to add a few daily newspapers and a Maxim lunch to my expenses, he was not a mean man. Just careful and very precise. And he was by no means stupid. As editor-in-chief of his four national newspapers and a long chain of more than 20 provincial ones, he knew exactly the value of each. In his office desk at 200 Gray's Inn Road, he kept a thick file of accounts, each dealing with one or other of his papers and showing their circulation figures, their income from advertising, their expenses and their gains and losses. Although he sometimes tended to give an impression of being ignorant of what was going on in offices outside the *Sunday Times*, favourite of his "babies", he knew every editor by name, whether he was in distant Newcastle or in Cardiff. He was, after all, owner of the largest newspaper empire in Britain – an empire he had built from scratch, carefully nurtured and developed, turning it into a rich and, above all, influential empire that was at once feared and respected by whichever government was in power. He fully deserved to become First Viscount Kemsley and when he died at the age of 85 in 1968, it was the last of the true self-made newspaper barons who was buried.

Roy Thomson was completely different. He was a go-getter who had started life as a ruthless salesman who fought his way through the Great Depression by bargaining and sometimes conning. But he became a successful businessman who thought more about making money than spending it. When he bought commercial television in Scotland he said that it was tantamount to getting your own printing press to churn out dollars and pounds. He knew more about the newspaper industry than anyone else in the business, having launched the first colour supplement and acquiring *The Times* to add to his long list. He also invested in the lucrative North Sea Oil drilling fields of Piper and Claymore. His thick-lensed glasses reflected his poor eyesight, yet he was anything but blind and could see money-making enterprises a mile off. Unlike Kemsley, he gave his editors complete freedom and would never have allowed his wife to interfere with a picture editor's choice, let alone have her order the emasculation of a bull. Thomson made it to first Baron Thomson of Fleet and was honoured with a plaque in the crypt of St Paul's Cathedral. He was born in Toronto, Canada, 11 years after Kemsley came to the world at Merthyr Tydfil and died in 1976, eight years after Lord K, aged 82, just three years younger than Gomer.

So what was it that my lord and master wanted to give me? He never told me, but Elizabeth Fanstone, Lady Kemsley's faithful PA and companion, revealed it to me in confidence. The Kemsleys wanted to leave me their car, a lovely old Rover. And I, like a fool, didn't want it. What did I need with a car, especially of that size, in Paris? To park was virtually impossible and to garage it would have cost a bomb. I was totally naïve and should have accepted it gracefully – and sold it later. But I could never sell a gift. Liz Fanstone clearly passed on my decision for the car was never mentioned.

But shortly before the Kemsleys left France, a note was brought to me, signed by Gomer himself. It simply said: "Just a little thank-you from Lady Kemsley and me."

Attached was a personal cheque for £1,500. I was flabbergasted. Much better than the old Rover!

My three-and-a-half-year stint in Paris for Kemsley's was at an end. I really couldn't complain. After all, I was originally asked to cover for three months and I had certainly enjoyed my stay. It had, to say the very least, changed my life. Not only had I found the woman I loved and married; I had also developed my career. I was no longer a "graduate trainee" but a fully-fledged foreign correspondent with cuttings of every description and bylines that appeared in more than 20 different newspapers.

But what of the future? I was given a choice back in London – the *Sunday Graphic* or the *Empire News*. Hold on, what about the *Sunday Times*, I wanted to know. There wasn't a vacancy, I was informed. I could hardly believe it but swallowed my disappointment and chose the *Empire News*, where I was welcomed with open arms.

Peter Cattle, the features editor, was a jovial man with a round, bronzed face who knew exactly what stories he wanted – and would dictate the headline and opening paragraph before one even left the office to chase the story. And if one returned with anything that didn't meet with his expectations, it was likely to be spiked. Jack Fishman, the news editor, was a realist and gave his reporters proper briefings before they left the office. And he was a stickler for his staff producing their expenses every Thursday, come rain or shine. I had only started on the Tuesday and, by Thursday, had managed to deliver one brief story of three paragraphs that had cost me one solitary bus fare and one telephone call.

"Where are your exes, John?" Fishman called across to me in the newsroom where I was placed. "Not worth a sheet of paper, Jack," I called back. "Do them. Now!" he commanded sternly and a few minutes later I handed Hilary, his secretary, the result: it came to 2s 9d (that's just a little less than 14p in current money).

There was suddenly a shrill shout from the newsdesk: "John IZBICKI!! Come HERE!!" It was Jack Fishman's high-pitched command. What on earth had I done? I took a few rapid strides to the desk and stood there like a naughty schoolboy. "What's up, Jack?"

"What's up? What's up? This is what's fuckin' up." And he waved my expense sheet at me "What the fuck is this you've given me? Do you really expect me to sign this? Well, the answer is no. N. O. No fuckin' no!" And he tore the sheet into several pieces and threw them in the bin at the side of the desk.

"I don't understand. You asked me for my expenses – and that's them."

"Well, they're no fuckin' good. Listen, if you think you can come here from gay Paree and undercut my staff with some twopenny-ha'penny rubbish, then you can just go back there. Now," and his voice became calmer and he continued in a gentler manner: "Now, go away and do them again. I don't ever want to see any reporter's expenses that are less than twenty quid. Is that understood, John?"

At last I had learned what the so-called "Lie Sheet" was all about. Take a bus and charge a taxi fare. Never produce a story without having taken the subject or subjects of the tale out for a few drinks or dinner – as long as you could produce a proper bill. When some eight or nine of us reporters gathered after a Press conference and took ourselves for lunch or dinner, one colleague, who shall remain nameless for obvious reasons, used to call the waiter at the end of the meal. If the total bill came to, say £72.50, he would ask the waiter to bring us eight bills – either each for that amount or blank. These would be handed round to one and all. Another colleague once showed me some of his expense sheets. His expenses came to more than my salary (and possibly even his).

Today, I hasten to add, that kind of thing is no longer possible. Economy measures have erased the last of the hack's greatest benefits. I remember, many years after my "inauguration" at the *Empire News*, getting out of a taxi in front of the *Daily Telegraph* in Fleet Street and paying the driver when a hand suddenly gripped my shoulder. When I turned round, I was staring into the eyes of Peter Eastwood, the *Telegraph*'s much-feared and oft-hated managing editor. On that occasion he smiled as he said: "And I suppose you'll be charging a bus fare for that, eh?"

The dear old *Empire News* came to a sudden and sad end less than a year after my arrival. The announcement of its closure was not totally unexpected. In fact, the paper announced it the week before, saying that the following Sunday would be the last time the paper would appear and thanking readers for their loyalty and support over the past 43 years when its title was first launched (it had been known as *The Umpire* before that and was based in Manchester). It had lasted just about a year under the ownership of Roy Thomson for whom it was clearly not bringing in enough profit. The *Sunday Graphic* was also discarded by him.

It was more than just a sad time for the staff. Jack Fishman was perhaps less anxious than many of the others. He had his music to fall back on. Although he could not read or write a musical score, he managed to dream up music for pop songs and whistle them to a professional who transcribed the whistle to the page. Jack would then write the lyrics and sell the result. He had a lovely house on Hampstead Lane to which I was often invited. I recall being most impressed with his underfloor heating. Property in London was already expensive and in Hampstead it was extortionately so. When I asked him how much he had paid for it, Jack laughed and replied: "Oh, I bought it for a song." And he meant it. But it was a "pop" song that had entered the charts. He was full of brilliant ideas, so for instance, when *Dr Who* was launched on BBC TV, Jack immediately saw the possibilities and purchased the copyright of the Daleks, those incredible dustbin-shaped robots that have remained *Dr Who*'s most infamous – and most popular – enemies. The result was the world-wide sale of Dalek toys. Jack was one of the best news editors and entrepreneurs I have ever met. He did not need another job following the death of the paper in October 1960.

But other members of staff were not as fortunate. Some, like David Roxan, was taken on by the *News of the World*, which had also offered me a job and I, perhaps stupidly, politely declined the offer. I fully expected to be taken on by the *Sunday Times*. I had, after all, already written for it whenever Steve Coulter was on vacation or ill – or taking time off to write his excellent biography of Guy de Maupassant.

So when I was called for an interview with C D Hamilton, I thought that my future would be sealed. How wrong I was. Denis Hamilton had not forgiven me for having passed on the criticisms of his sons by their French landlady – another lesson I was to learn: never criticise, however true, the offspring of your superiors. What I had not expected was his curt advice:

"Well, John, I'm afraid I have nothing to offer you, although you will be given very generous compensation. My advice, quite frankly, is that you should seek something outside journalism. It's not your world, is it?"

I could not believe my ears. "But I *am* a journalist and have never had any complaints from editors. Even Ian Fleming has always praised my work. I don't understand how you can now tell me I should get out of journalism."

"Quite. But there's no use going into long discussions about this now and I have many others still to see. A cheque will be in the post. Meanwhile, I wish you the very best of luck," and he held out his hand which I, still in a daze, shook. And left.

Troubles, it is often said, comes in threes. At the same time as the *Empire News* vanished, two other newspapers hit the proverbial dust. The *News Chronicle*, launched in 1856 as a weekly and becoming *The Daily Chronicle and Clerkenwell News* in 1869, shocked the political world when it was shut without warning on 17th October 1960. Lloyd George, together with a syndicate of fellow Liberals, had purchased it in 1918 and it became the *News Chronicle* in 1930. It was a great newspaper and the voice of British Liberalism, selling nearly two million copies a day. It belonged to the Cadbury family and was sold to Associated Newspapers and "merged" with the *Daily Mail*, a paper which was anything but Liberal. First-class writers, including James Cameron and Richie Calder, lost their jobs.

At the same time, the *London Evening Star*, also in the Cadbury stable, went with the *News Chronicle* to Associated Newspapers and became a subtitle of the *London Evening News*.

I was not the only one "on the street" as it were. Many other journalists and clerical staff, lots of them with far greater experience than I, were also made jobless that fateful October. Granada Television published a notice in *World Press News*, a trade paper read by many hacks, to the effect that all journalists who had lost jobs due to the closure of the *News Chronicle*, *Empire News* and *Star*, would be given "top priority" for vacancies with Granada. Naturally, I applied – as did hundreds of others. I learned later that none of us had been given a job with the Manchester-based television company (which had once offered me the post of its first newscaster from the North). It was simply an advertising gimmick.

At least Maureen managed to find a decent job and become the breadwinner. She had answered an advertisement in the *Times Educational Supplement* for an English teacher at a girls' secondary school in North London. She was called for an interview and travelled from Avenue Road in Highgate where we had rented a small furnished ground floor flat opening onto a lovely garden, to Holloway Road. This is the A1 and one of the busiest roads in London. Just opposite North London Polytechnic (which was many years later to play a major part in my life) was the vastly misnamed Paradise Row. And at the end of this dusty street stood Our Lady of Sion, a Roman Catholic grammar school.

Later that evening Maureen told me about her interview. "I was asked to sit in a small waiting room outside the Headmistress's office. It was strange, for all around the walls were posters saying things like: '*Always remember Our Lord was a Jew!*' and '*Jesus was Jewish*'. I didn't know what to make of it.

"Anyway, I was finally summoned and met the head – an elderly, smiling nun. She turned out to be Mother Superior. She offered me tea before starting on the interview proper. She asked me what experience of teaching I had had and I had to admit that I hadn't really had any experience, other than teaching English to a few French friends in Paris...So then we talked about Paris for a while and she even broke into a quite reasonable French.

"Now wait till you hear this," Maureen said as she poured me another glass of red wine. "She wanted to know whether I was Catholic and when I told her yes, she said that, although it didn't really matter, it was nevertheless good as most of the girls were Catholics. Then she said: 'And your husband? Is he also a Catholic?' I became quite worried because I thought that this would be the end of the interview – and, in a way, it was. I told her you were Jewish at which she threw her hands up in the air and said 'that's wonderful! Wonderful!' and she offered me the job!"

At this, Maureen burst into tears of joy. "I've got a job, so you needn't worry, darling."

"I don't quite understand," I said, genuinely flabbergasted. "What has my being Jewish got to do with you getting a teaching job at a Roman Catholic school?"

"The Mother Superior explained it all, because I was as surprised, possibly even more surprised than you. She told me that Our Lady of Sion was an Order of nuns founded by two rich French Jews – they were brothers, called Ratisbon. It's an amazing story. It appears they were on holiday in Italy when one of them went off on his own and got lost. His brother searched for him for three days and finally, the lost one was seen stumbling out of a small church and mumbling 'I've seen her…I've seen her'. Who have you seen, his brother demanded to know. 'Her,' he replied pointing to a small medallion he had bought at the church. It bore the face of the Virgin Mary. 'Her! I've seen her!' the young Ratisbon insisted.

"Once he had calmed down he said that the Virgin had told him to build a church and perform loving acts. Anyway, the Ratisbon Brothers founded this Order of Sion whose headquarters are in Jerusalem and whose purpose is the conversion of Jews."

She saw my face and rapidly added: "Don't look so worried, darling. No one is going to convert you. The Order apparently no longer keeps to this rule. Instead, they promote friendship and goodwill towards Jews. But the real surprise is that the Mother Superior as well as all the other nuns at the school are former Jews who converted to Catholicism."

We poured some more wine to celebrate Maureen's good fortune and toasted the Ratisbon Brothers and Our Lady of Sion.

A year or so later, after Maureen had become a fully accepted member of the school, I received an invitation from Mother Superior to come to dinner at the convent in Knightsbridge, in the posher part of West London. I always thought that men could not eat at the same table as nuns and, in fact, as it turned out, I didn't. Both Maureen and I were served by a whole gaggle of nuns who stood gloating over us, watching each mouthful with thorough enjoyment. They had prepared a totally kosher dinner and, had it not been for their veils and habits, I should have thought I had fallen into the midst of a group of proper Yiddishe Mommas. This was especially so when they heaped still more fish and vegetables on my plate and ordered me to: "Eat, eat and enjoy!"

I remained out of work for nearly three months. It was the only period of my life when I was jobless.

I wrote more applications for jobs during those three months than many others might do in a lifetime. Some of the replies I received astounded me. The news editor of *The Times* told me in a curt note that I was "clearly over-qualified". Over-qualified for a general reporter's job? Should I perhaps have written him a poorly spelled, ungrammatical letter of application?

But there were a number of interviews. Only one of these do I recall most vividly. I had written to the *Liverpool Post* which was after a theatre critic, a job I truly fancied, having always loved the theatre. I had eagerly devoured every volume of the *Ego* autobiography James Agate had penned, so I thought I should certainly succeed at this interview. The London editor of the paper interviewed me in his remarkably tidy room overlooking Fleet Street and, after the normal run of questions ("Why do you want this position? What do you think you could give us that few other people might? How often do you go to the theatre? How often did you visit the theatre when you were in Paris?") came the one that killed my chances:

"You are visiting the premiere of a play here in the West End. What would you write about it?"

A fairly innocent question, one might have thought and I rammed in with: "I'd say what I thought of the cast, the direction, the set, the this and the that and whether I had liked or disliked it and why…"

The *Liverpool Post* London editor stared at me. "And is that all you'd say? Now think, what's the first thing you might say?"

I was stuck. He helped me: "Look," he said kindly but firmly, "you are writing for people up in Liverpool and the city's surrounding area – people who rarely, if ever, get down to London and rarely, if ever get to see a play in the West End. They couldn't give a toss about the direction or the set. They'll want to know what the bloody play's about, man. You'd have to tell them a brief but clear outline of the story before you even bother to mention Laurence Olivier or Ralph Richardson or your own likes and dislikes. Always try to remember that young man."

He was absolutely right and it's a lesson I never forgot.

My first return to meaningful employment was with United Press International, an American news agency in Bouverie Street, just off Fleet Street. After a few weeks in their features department, which I thoroughly enjoyed, I was called down to the main news desk and offered the job of Europe Editor.

Wow! Europe Editor! What a title. It was nights but what the hell: Europe Editor! And in "The Slot" to boot!

It turned out to be just about the most boring job one could imagine. Being in The Slot meant standing inside a claustrophobic little square with a chair and a desk and being surrounded by teleprinters, each of which would be vomiting printed stories from every corner of the world. The Europe Editor's task was to tear off each story, read it and mark it up and hand it over to teleprinter operators just a few feet away so they could regurgitate it to other parts of the globe. Marking the top of the page "1 1 1" meant the story should go to the United States; "2 2 2" would mean sending it to Italy and Spain; "3 3 3" to Frankfurt and the north and so on.

Being an automaton did not suit me at all. I could not just tear off a story and re-direct it after just a glance. I would take an interest in each page, decide that the lead was ridiculous and should be rewritten before being sent on. Of course, by the time I had read and considered two stories, I was confronted with two miles of other stories spouting from the printers.

There was no rest – not, that is, until I had managed to travel back to Highgate, arriving there at about 8.15 in the morning, just as Maureen was leaving for school. We would quickly kiss on the doorstep, then not see each other until 4 or 5 p.m. After a fairly hurried meal, I'd be off again back to UPI and another night of doldrums.

Still, the summer proved great. I would drag a camp bed out onto the patio and go to sleep in the blazing sunshine. People thought I was on a constant holiday, judging by my bronzed appearance.

When a friend telephoned me to ask whether I would be interested in joining a new news magazine, I jumped at it. Interested? You betcha!

And so I joined *Topic*, a newsmagazine edited by the great Morley Richards of *Daily Express* fame as its foreign editor. Launching a weekly news magazine is tougher than giving birth to a daily newspaper. In fact, it's probably tougher than giving birth. It certainly comes with hefty pains and a load of aggro. The mag came out on a Thursday and a poster stretched across the newsroom at its offices in Charterhouse Square, very close to Smithfield Market, that read: ***"What can I tell readers on Thursday that they've not read in the Sunday papers*?"** A good question. In other words, just about every item had to be exclusive or a comment on a major story of the week.

I collected together a vast number of foreign correspondents who were paid only if their pieces were used. The owner was a man called Norman

Maskell, whose "other business" was rearing pigs. He was a wide boy, putting money from farming into *Topic*, but failing to make a profit. So he pitched losses against tax. He was selling shares in his animals, mostly to old age pensioners who looked forward to making a few pounds once "their" pig was grown fat and slaughtered. Visitors from the Ministry of Agriculture discovered that Maskell's pigs did not just have the one shareholder's number tattooed in their ear, but the numbers of four, five or even six shareholders – in each ear.

Topic was going bust – and Maskell ended up in jail.

By strange fate, I was offered a job as features editor of an as yet unpublished English language magazine – in Italy. Maureen was already happily packing bags in readiness for a new adventure. Neither of us had expected *Topic* to be saved at the last moment by two men who walked in one day at the height of summer 1961 and called the staff together. "This magazine will not close and you can all get back to work."

None of us could understand this turn of events. Our typewriters and desks were already plastered with sticky labels stuck down by the official receivers.

The two men were Clive Labovitch, a young Jewish lad with black curly hair and thick hornrimmed spectacles, and Michael Heseltine, a tall and handsome blue-eyed fellow with a mane of unkempt blonde hair. I had never heard of either but immediately approached them to say: "I'm terribly sorry, but I have just been offered a job in Italy and have more or less accepted it, so I'm afraid I shall be unable to stay on."

Heseltine received the news and turned up his eyes in some consternation. He was the first to respond. "That's a shame A real shame. You see, you and two others were the only people we really wanted to keep on. Isn't that so Clive?"

"Absolutely," Clive Labovitch retorted. "Give us a couple of minutes, will you please, John?"

I left the room and returned to my receiver-labelled desk. A few minutes later I was recalled. "We are prepared to meet any salary you've been offered in Italy, if you say you'll stay," Michael Heseltine cooed.

I was delighted. I liked the news magazine and took pride in the work my colleagues and I had performed. I readily accepted the generous offer but had to take Maureen out for a decent meal to make good her disappointment. We had always adored Italy and had looked forward to starting a new life in Milan, where the proposed magazine was to be based.

So *Topic* continued under the Heseltine-Labovitch direction. But not for long. Shortly before the Christmas of 1962, Maureen and I drove up to

Manchester to see my parents and spend a few days with them. My mother produced her usual super meal of lockchen soup followed by roast chicken with all the trimmings and ice cream and we tucked into it all with gusto.

In the middle of the ice cream the phone rang. Dad answered and handed the receiver to me. On the other end of the line was Lesley, my faithful secretary. She was in tears. "Calm down, Lesley, and tell me what has happened," I said as gently as I could. This made her cry even more. Between sobs she told me: "It's terrible...terrible. Oh, John, I don't...know...how to tell you... (more loud sobbing)... *Topic* is CLOSED. It's no more...!"

"What?" I blurted. "Tell me all that again but this time tell me how it happened."

She then calmed down a little and gave me a blow-by-blow account of the day's events. First, they were told by Heseltine that they should stop whatever it was they were doing until further notice. Then, after lunch, which everyone had spent in the pub, they sat around and waited. At last, around 5 p.m. both Heseltine and Labovitch gathered the staff around them and announced that *Topic* had lost too much money and would be closed.

"When's the closure, Lesley?"

"Now. Immediately. As of today," she blurted and started to cry bitterly again. Later she told me that she didn't really care all that much about whether it folded or not. She wept because she knew the news would upset me and she hated doing that.

Maureen and I decided to drive back to London at once. My parents were upset and worried that we might have an accident on the way.

Although there was no accident, the journey was horrendous. A thick blanket of fog had descended and visibility was down to about thirty yards – about 27 metres in modern parlance. With it had come freezing cold and driving was cut to a snail's pace It took us around eight hours to reach our flat in Cecile Park, Crouch End, but we did it in one piece. We had shared the driving and kept ourselves awake by telling each other a string of jokes. My own collection of Jewish stories had grown and was to serve me well at future after-dinner functions and cabarets.

It was foolish to have made that journey, not so much because of the danger but because of its total uselessness. Heseltine and Labovitch allowed us all to continue using the office until we had found alternative employment and they continued paying our salaries. I was on a two-year contract, so my own salary was safeguarded and I did remarkably well out of it in the end.

I made the odd telephone call to other papers and magazines but no one wanted to employ anyone at Christmas. It was the wrong time of year. When,

I should like to know, is it ever the right time of year?

So we sat back and took things easy for a few weeks, enjoying Christmas to the full and returning once more to the North. We spent Christmas Eve and Day with Maureen's parents at Chinley, breathing in the fresh country air, eating ourselves silly and walking it all off by taking the dog, a rather snappy Corgi, across the beautiful hills of the Peak District.

Boxing Day, and it was off to Manchester and Heywood Street to stay with my parents, breathing in the fumes of Cheetham Hill, eating ourselves silly and walking it off by taking ourselves to nearby Heaton Park. Manchester then was not as extensively developed as it is today. Cheetham Hill was still a mixed area, mainly Jewish but synagogues snuggled close to Roman Catholic churches. Today it has become almost exclusively Asian and, I suppose, is more colourful now than it was 45 years ago.

One of my *Topic* colleagues was an elderly journalist called Edwin Rees. Eddie telephoned me while I was still "resting" and asked whether I'd like a job. "What kind of job, Eddie?" I asked and added: "Do you have one?"

"Yep, I've joined a new medical magazine called *Abbottempo*. I think you might find it interesting."

"Abbo–what? It sounds like some dance mag. What's the job?

"Well, you'll probably be surprised to hear that I'm the executive editor of this 'dance mag'. I'm offering you a job as my deputy. What d'you say?"

I was taken aback. Medical journalism? I knew nothing about medicine. "Sorry, Eddie, but I shall need to know a bit more about it before I come to any decision. But, hey, I'm very grateful. It's very good of you to have thought of me…"

"You're the linguist, that's why I think you could be very useful – in fact, ideal for the job."

"Tell me more…"

"Well, *Abbottempo* is an American publication for Abbotts, a big pharmaceutical company in North Chicago – hence the name. It's being published every quarter in seven languages and…"

"SEVEN languages!" I interrupted. "What languages? I don't speak seven languages…"

"Well, I'll tell you. They are separate editions, and are to be very well illustrated in full colour, and each edition will be in its own language: English English, American English – that's two languages for a start – then there's French, German, Italian, Spanish – oh, and Turkish."

"Ye gods, Eddie, that sounds like a very ambitious project. Will the articles be written in English or in these other languages? And if they're in English, who'll translate them. I suppose they will be translated?"

"Oh yes, of course. I'm already arranging to meet with some expert translators."

And so I joined *Abbottempo* as Assistant Executive Editor, a highfaluting title which I held in a freelance capacity, so as not to lose out on my regular monthly salary from the defunct *Topic*. It was a superb publication, printed on web-fed presses by a Dutch company called Smeets at Weert near Eindhoven. Eddie and I had to traipse over there regularly prior to it going to print to make sure all was well. The Dutch were true professionals and nothing ever went wrong. While we were putting finishing touches to proof pages, we were brought regular cups of strong coffee. Dutch coffee is second only to Italian coffee. Weert is a small, very neat town, clean enough to allow one to eat off the pavements and the hotel where we were put up served the most gargantuan breakfasts I have ever come across.

Our translators had a variety of permanent jobs at the BBC, the Spanish, French and Turkish departments of Bush House, and there was also Amelia Nathan, a splendid Italian woman who took on the translation of the Italian edition. A Paris-based doctor, Alain-Yves Dubourg, was the editor. His English resembled that of Peter Sellers' Inspector Clouseau. He would say things like "Let's go for launch" meaning lunch. At least it meant we could go to Paris for our monthly editorial meetings. Once, just for a change, we decided to spend a few days in St Raphael in the south of France, where we ate the most gourmet meals. On one occasion, we dined at a restaurant situated on rocks out to sea. I made a real pig of myself, downing a dozen oysters followed by an entire sea bass. I thought one of the oysters tasted "a bit funny" but I didn't want to disgrace myself by spitting it out, so I swallowed and washed it down with a couple of gulps of a cold Chablis.

That night I spent running to and from the lavatory with bouts of acute diarrhoea. We flew back to London the following day and I was still having to make regular trips to the toilet.

My period on *Abbottempo* was a happy one, mainly because I had good relations with the rest of the staff and with Andre Carus, who presided over Abbotts of North Chicago. My knowledge of languages also helped and I decided to meet the various translators and local editors and distributors of the magazine. This meant travelling to the United States and having a few days with the Carus family in Chicago; to Italy, Spain and Turkey, finishing off in Paris before returning home.

Just before I left the hotel in Istanbul, I telephoned Maureen. "Why not come and join me in Paris?" I said and added: "I've already booked a room at the Pays des Galles (one of the best hotels in the city and right next door to the George V). We'll have some fun. Anyway, I think you deserve a break after having been left alone all this time." I had been away more than a fortnight. "But I've got school. I can't just up and go…can I?"

But she did. She phoned Our Lady of Sion to say she was sick.

We had dinner with Alain-Yves Dubourg at Fouquet's on the Champs Elysées. A huge lobster and an entire *plateau des fruits de mer* was devoured. I didn't know that lobster was an aphrodisiac. That night, Maureen and I made love as never before.

And that night, our baby was conceived.

Her playing truant from school – the only time she had ever done such a thing – rebounded. A couple of nuns from the school decided to visit their poor sick friend on the Friday afternoon but had no reply to their ringing and knocking. Maureen had to pile on another lie and say she had gone to a friend's to be looked after.

But we decided never again to skip school – and never ever to give poor health as an excuse. Somehow being "sick" often turns out to be true. It wasn't long before morning sickness took hold of Maureen.

Not many weeks after my return to *Abbottempo*'s Fleet Street office, I received a call to meet the publishers of another magazine – *World Medicine*. It had still to be launched and I was offered the deputy editorship with a considerably enhanced salary. It was being published by Haymarket Press. I was back with Michael Heseltine and Clive Labovitch.

The editor was a pukka doctor, Donald Gould, who had come from *Medical News*, where he had been deputy editor. Like *Abbottempo*, *World Medicine* was a freebie and went out to every general practitioner in the country as well as every university library and heads of medical schools. It was glossy and, also like *Abbottempo,* had close American connections – a magazine called *Medical World*. We swapped articles and, wherever there was one worth publishing, it was published.

Donald Gould was probably the first real medical journalist. He pulled no punches and hated the establishment. Copy had to be slick but not "tabloid". As he kept telling us: "We're talking to doctors, not quacks, so don't talk down to them. And call a spade a spade. If you're talking about pricks, then call them penises, but don't go overboard and mamby-pamby."

Donald, small of stature – and a slight stoop made him appear still smaller – with unkempt sandy hair and ruddy cheeks, had a great sense of humour. He chain-smoked and joined "the lads" in the pub for a noggin or four. Before taking up medical journalism, he had been an academic. He qualified at

St Thomas's Hospital, whose patients he regarded as "ignorant peasants" but he actually meant it kindly. He spent nearly 15 years in the Far East as professor of physiology at the University of Singapore, then taught physiology at Barts (St Bartholomew's) in London for three years.

He detested stuffiness and refused to kowtow to the pharmaceutical companies that paid for our bread and butter. "I will not recommend this or that fucking product just because its company takes out a page or two of crappy advertising," he would say.

Although I enjoyed my time with *World Medicine*, medical journalism was having a dreadful effect on me. I found myself turning into a thorough hypochondriac. Every illness we were featuring in the magazine passed on its symptoms to me. My desktop displayed an array of little bottles and phials of medicines. One day, a Monday morning, this phenomenon had gone too far. We were running a well-illustrated feature on venereal disease, which was making a disturbing come-back in the UK. The magazine's cover showed a close-up of a left hand with a little circle of nasty red blisters. This was syphilis of the left hand.

I was making a few corrections to the cover's layout when I spotted my own left hand. The palm clearly showed some red blisters. A chill wind swept along my spine and cold sweat covered my forehead. I sat back in my chair, trembling with shock and fear. "How could this have happened?" I thought. I hadn't "been" with anyone other than Maureen and surely she couldn't...I dismissed that thought instantly. I didn't believe in "catching" VD off a lavatory seat, so how and why? Why me?

I plucked up some courage and slowly looked at the palm of my left hand again. Sure enough, there were some blisters. But on closer examination, there were only three small ones and they were not in a circle as on the cover photograph. Once again I pondered the problem. What was so different about this day? It was a Monday morning and I had spent the weekend digging our garden. The blisters must have been caused by the rough handle of the spade. Thank God, I thought.

Thank God – but that's the end of my phase of medical journalism. It was time to get the hell out. Had Denis Hamilton been correct? Should I leave journalism altogether and try something else? I pooh-poohed the idea. Mr Denis-bloody-Hamilton was wrong! I would not be hounded out by the likes of him!

I needed to get back to daily newspaper journalism. And so I sat down and made a list of just about every paper I could think of and drafted a letter to each seeking employment. My CV, after all, was not bad: good at languages

(French, German both fairly fluent), experienced in evening paper reporting (*Manchester Evening Chronicle*, for which I had not only written reports but also features and a good gossip column), experienced as a foreign correspondent (Paris covering for the *Sunday Times, Sunday Graphic* and many provincial Kemsley papers), and medical journalism (*Abbottempo*; *World Medicine*). Surely somebody would take me on...

CHAPTER THIRTEEN:

THE TORYGRAPH

Newspaper editors are reluctant to employ people who work on magazines. They believe that magazine hacks know nothing about deadlines, so rarely keep to them, and are too laid back to think in terms of hard news. I sent off letters of application to news editors, feature editors and even editors of papers from *The Times* to the *Daily Mirror*. My CV must have appeared faultless and I emphasized the work I had done in France, stressing my fluency in French and German. The letters of rejection poured back. Most of them were outrageously brief. One (from the *Daily Express*) actually said curtly: "Sorry, we have no vacancy for a foreign editor". An amazing piece of misunderstanding since I had never applied for such an august position.

Then one day, an envelope bearing the logo of the *Daily Telegraph* tumbled through the letterbox. I threw it onto the kitchen table. "It'll be another bloody No!" I grumbled and waited until I had finished my breakfast before venturing to read its contents. It was a brief letter from someone called Jack Hill, News Editor, and said:

"Dear John Izbicki –

I have your letter of application in front of me. If you are interested in returning to general reporting, please ask my secretary for a suitable date to see me."

Bloody hell, I thought, the Torygraph! "The Torygraph has come up trumps!" I shouted to Maureen and we fell around each other's necks.

As deputy editor of *World Medicine*, I was being paid the princely sum of

£2,950 a year, not at all bad for 1964. My interview with Jack Hill went well. A tall, slim man of fair complexion, bright blue eyes and grey hair, he spoke in crisp, clipped words and said that there was a vacancy for a general reporter ten days away. As far as salary was concerned, I'd have to see Mr Pawley, the Managing Editor.

I was wheeled into "Pop" Pawley's spacious room and asked to sit down. Whereas Jack Hill was so tall and thin that he walked with a slight stoop, Pawley was squat and rotund with white hair framing a ruddy face that rarely seemed to smile. "Mr Hill tells me you're going to take over the newsroom, Izbicki, is that right?"

"Er – no Sir, I just want to be a reporter…"

"No, no, I know that. I mean is my pronunciation of Izbicki right."

"Yes, Mr Pawley. Absolutely correct."

"Where does it come from, your name?"

"My father, Sir. He was born in a part of Poland which had been annexed to Russia. Izbicki is a Russo-Polish name."

"I see. Russo-Polish eh? D'you speak Polish or Russian?"

"No, I'm afraid not, apart from the odd word…mainly swear words."

"Ha. But you say you speak French and German. Is that correct?"

"Yes, Sir, it is. I was born in Berlin and I have been working in Paris until fairly recently."

"I know you've been working in Paris, Izbicki. I didn't know you were born in Germany. Are you Jewish?"

"Yes, I am."

"Hm. All right. Now look here, your current salary you say is £2,950. There, I'm afraid, is the rub as you might say. We couldn't possibly meet you on that figure. The salary I'm offering you – and I don't expect you to accept it – is £1,950. All right? Now don't give me an answer straight away. Go away and think it over. Let me know in a day or two. All right?"

I got up dumbstruck and took my leave. I descended the wide marble stairs to the front hall of the building and made my exit through the revolving doors into Fleet Street. The time on the familiar *Telegraph* clock hanging above the entrance was 11.20 a.m. I had been there for just over half an hour. It felt like a lot longer.

I discussed the offer with Maureen that evening. "It means taking a cut of £1,000! That's a third of my present pay. That's one hell of a drop. We'll have to tighten our belts if I accept. The guy I saw, the managing editor fellow, said he didn't expect me to accept his offer. I got the feeling that my face didn't fit."

"What makes you think that?"

"Oh, it was just his whole attitude to my name and when he heard I was born in Berlin and that I was Jewish, well I don't know…I just got that feeling."

"Oh, John, I wish you'd get rid of that chip on your shoulder. As for the money, who cares? Remember when I had nothing at all and went to the embassy for help? They gave me help all right. Put me in charge of the helpless Brits and paid me for it. It wasn't much as salaries go but I was happy and we were together."

I decided there and then to write a letter to Jack Hill, thanking him for his kindness in offering me the job. "If Mr Pawley agrees and is not too disappointed, I shall be happy to accept the salary he offered. After all, the *Daily Telegraph* is worth a cut."

While waiting to start my new job, I read every word of the *Telegraph* from cover to cover every single day. I also made sure to read its main competitors, the *Manchester Guardian* and *The Times*. I certainly considered it the best of the three papers for it contained more news to the column-inch than the other two. *The Times* was too erudite; the *Guardian* was good but, frankly, boring. I had already been a regular reader of these papers during my time in Paris. I had shared the large apartment in the Place Vendôme with The *Daily Telegraph*, so I was certainly familiar with it. But its foreign news coverage and that of the other papers, particularly the *Daily Mail* and the *Daily Mirror*, had interested me more at that time. By the time I started in Fleet Street, my first true entry into this, one of the most famous streets in London, I had familiarised myself with its style and its policy.

There was no question as to which side of the political fence the paper stood. It was Tory to its paper clips. But I also noticed that, although its editorial comments and features were firmly entrenched in Conservatism with a very capital C, and its headlines tended to betray a Tory line, the news stories were generally objective, putting forward both sides of any controversial case. Its journalists followed the orthodox principles of writing in the shape of an inverted pyramid and giving the "Five W's and an H" in the first paragraph or two: Who did What to Whom, Where, When and How. The rest of the pyramid would be taken up with quotes, descriptions and explanations. All the virtues of a great newspaper.

During my frenzy of letter writing for jobs outside the medical field, I had responded to an advertisement seeking someone who could run a school of journalism – in Berlin. English was the principal language demanded; an experienced journalist would be "an advantage". It certainly appealed to me and I had applied at once. But I received neither a reply nor even an acknowledgment and by the time the *Telegraph* came onto my scene, I had quite forgotten all about it.

Just about two weeks after I had started in Fleet Street, a letter arrived from the *Internationales Institut für Journalismus in Entwicklungsländer* (the International Institute of Journalism in Developing Countries) thanking me for my application and asking me to attend an interview at the Connaught Hotel at 11 a.m. on the following Tuesday. What on earth was I to do? I had only just started in my job and felt I did not stand a hope in hell of getting this very responsible position in the city of my birth. Nevertheless, I decided to take an early lunch break and go.

Two men greeted me warmly. The older of the two was one Robert Lochner, an American German who, it transpired, had founded and headed the RIAS radio station (it stands for Radio in the American Sector) and who now was the chairman of the Institute. It was Lochner who taught John F. Kennedy to say and pronounce those immortal words when the American president visited Berlin and made a speech close to the Wall: "*Ich bin ein Berliner*" Much as he tried, Kennedy could not pronounce the "ch" and it came out as "Ik". But the Berliners adored him and what he said – particularly the "Ik" for the Berlin dialect also pronounces "ich" as "ik". So *Ik bin ein Berliner* was perfect Berlin street-speak.

The other man was Horst Scheffold, a German with a decidedly American accent, who was the Institute's director. Both men were in search of a general manager who would take charge of running the day-to-day activities of the college, whose students were all fairly senior journalists in their home countries – a mixture of men and women from Asia, the Middle and Far East and the Pacific. Their common language was English and all of them had won three-month scholarships from the Berlin Senate which sponsored the Institute. The idea was to give each one a course in advanced journalism, the type of journalism conducted in European countries. At the same time, the students would be given a "Good Time" in Berlin and taken on trips to East Berlin, so they could compare both types of democracy. They would then write articles to their papers and magazines extolling the beauty of West Berlin…It was an excellent piece of propaganda and it worked.

Horst Scheffold, Robert Lochner and I somehow hit it off from the word go. We chatted over numerous cups of coffee and biscuits about Germany and my origins, about Paris and my experiences there and about my knowledge of languages. Only at the end of the interview did I realise that I had been "cross-examined" for more than two hours. When I left, four other young men were sitting in an ante chamber, glaring at me and waiting for their call.

Three days later, a Friday, a letter popped through my letter box, offering me the job. The salary was to be £10,000 a year plus a furnished apartment in West Berlin, plus expenses and two annual free return trips to the UK.

The day I started at the *Telegraph*, I was handed a memorandum from Mr Pawley offering me a £50 increase in salary, bringing the total to £2,000 a year – a drop of only £950 to what I had earned at *World Medicine* – and £8,000 less than the Berlin job offered. The year was 1964 – when £10,000 a year plus a rented apartment was a small fortune.

So why didn't I accept? Could it have been something to do with it being "German" and my having to return to a city that had driven me and my parents out?

No. Nothing like that even occurred to me. It was simply that I had only just joined the *Telegraph* and I could not reject their kindness in taking me on without at least giving them a couple of years of my time. Maureen agreed with me in principle. She, too, felt reluctant to give up her job at Our Lady of Sion and, as she explained, she knew not a word of German and might have felt very much alone in a strange land.

And so I wrote back to Robert Lochner that I was truly sorry but that I could not accept the very generous offer without insulting my very new employer. However, I added a codicil: "I would be more than happy to come to you as a lecturer in journalism…" And so it came about. I was invited to Berlin as a well paid Dozent (lecturer) and managed to get away for the weekly sessions as much as twice a year.

That arrangement lasted for more than 15 years. My time with the *Telegraph* lasted 23.

The news room was on the first floor of the *Telegraph*'s large white stone building and overlooked Fleet Street. A balcony ran the length of the 50-metre room so that one was able to step outside to watch whatever went on below. Usually, this simply meant the general bustle of buses, taxis and other noisy traffic but over the years there were also equally noisy demonstrations or parades that ranged from the Lord Mayor's annual colourful passage to Winston Churchill's funeral. Whenever demonstrators marched past our building, they would give the Nazi salute and shout obscene slogans such as "Fuck the Torygraph" and "Out – Out – Fucking Tories Out – Out – Out!" Such shouts were completely unjustified. The paper was certainly Tory; there was no question about that and it never pretended to be anything else. But it was in no way Fascist, let alone Nazi. It abhorred the activities of outfits such as the National Front or the British National Party, the true Nazis inside postwar Britain. It remained right-wing but never overstepped the mark and any members of the Conservative party who rubbed shoulders with real Fascists were met with fierce criticism in the paper's leader columns.

When I arrived, the news room was furnished with a series of long wooden tables behind which sat the reporters. Each faced a telephone and his or her typewriter, mostly old machines – Olivettis or Remingtons. One soon became used to the cacophony of telephones ringing, voices conducting phoned interviews and the regular trundling of a large trolley bearing urns of tea, coffee and biscuits. The room had its own smell, a mixture of smoke and sweat. Everyone seemed to smoke and, come high noon, the room would almost empty as reporters scurried out for lunch. This was mostly taken at close-by hostelries – the King and Keys next door, the Falstaff opposite, the Bells down the road towards Ludgate Circus, and the Cheshire Cheese, one of London's oldest and consequently frequented by American tourists. For the more senior members of staff, there were the Wig and Pen, towards the Aldwych and opposite the impressive Assize Courts, and El Vino's, which stood about 100 metres diagonally across from the *Telegraph*.

El Vino's often pretended to be a club and for years barred women from standing at its bar. With the approach of the women's liberation movement, this crazy rule met with increasing opposition. Many men, including myself, sided with the women and threatened to boycott the pub. It had no effect on the management who decided to stick to tradition. Women who, in defiance, stood at the bar were totally ignored and never served. It was one of the *Telegraph*'s ace reporters, Gerda Paul, who took the campaign the whole way and issued an injunction against El Vino's. The matter came to court and Gerda and her large entourage of women supporters won the day. It was a great victory in the history of Fleet Street.

Some years later, I myself had a run-in with El Vino's. I was meant to join a party of my colleagues for drinks there on a Friday night. My son, Paul, who was then about 20 years old, had just returned from America where he was studying as part of his degree course at York. He looked great, tall, bronzed and athletic in his open-neck shirt. We entered El Vino's only to be stopped. "Sorry Sir," I was told, "the gentleman in your company is not wearing a tie and cannot be admitted."

"You must be joking. He's a young man. He's my son and we are joining a group of friends and colleagues over there…" Sure enough, everyone was waiting for us and pointed to the chairs kept for our arrival. "Sorry Sir, rules is rules…but I'll happily lend your son a tie for the duration of your visit."

"No thank you," I retorted in a huff. "I'm not going to drink in a pub that pretends to be a club. Come on, Paul, we'll take our custom elsewhere."

I went to my friends to explain – and they, too, got up, leaving half emptyglasses behind. We all stormed out. That night, El Vino's lost the custom of around ten people. I, for one, never returned.

When I started my new job, I was seated at a table at the very rear of the newsroom, stuck between two other reporters. On my right sat the Estate's Correspondent, John Armstrong; on my left, a small bespectacled reporter by name of Paddy Travers. I later realised that I had been placed there deliberately for the two of them never ceased to argue. Sometimes the rows became so fierce that I thought they would end in blows, with me getting some of the "shrapnel". John Armstrong was an amazing man. He had been seriously wounded during WW2. He was blind in one eye and both his arms had to be amputated. He wore a harness from which his artificial arms hung. At their ends were two pointed "fingers" with which he typed his reports. I don't think I ever saw anyone type faster or more accurately than John. His name, Armstrong, was a piece of incredible irony. As for Paddy Travers, there was nothing wrong with him other than a vicious Irish temper which he let fly at Armstrong. And yet, it never did come to blows and I even got the feeling that there was a kind of devotion to each other.

Many reporters came to greet me and invited me to join them at the King and Keys. One of them, a tall, heavily bearded man called Michael Morden, who looked for all the world like a youngish King George V, sidled up to me one day, held out his hand and said: "Welcome to the madhouse, John…" He continued, bending a little closer to my ear, "Just a little warning. There are quite a few queers in this office, so please take good care of yourself, won't you…" I was shocked. "Thanks, Mike, but can you please point them out to me? Where are they?" He smiled: "Gimme a kiss and I'll tell you!" It was all great fun and Michael Morden, who later left the *Telegraph* to join the *Brighton Argus*, was as heterosexual as they come. He used to call all women pussycats and was among the most popular guys in the building.

After a restful two or three weeks (they liked a new reporter to become slowly acclimatised), I was given a few stories to do – and did them well. They appeared in the paper but not with a byline, only "By Daily Telegraph Reporter". But, hell, it was a good job and the men at the top were obviously waiting to see what I was really made of.

We had moved from our Highgate flat to unfurnished accommodation in a block, Cecile Court, in Cecile Park, Crouch End, still in North London. We felt that we should at least get our own furniture and prepare ourselves for raising a family. Maureen was pregnant, though it was not yet too evident. The flat was comfortable (two bedrooms, sitting room, bathroom and kitchen all on the first floor of the building) and at the corner of the road was the Mountview Theatre Club, which I had joined prior to my *Telegraph* appointment. I had a number of decent parts, the best of which was the Magistrate in *Lysistrata* by Aristophanes, which must rank as the very earliest Women's Lib play and a great example of the 'Sixties slogan "Make Love, Not War". The Mountview's director, Peter Coxhead, somehow managed to recruit many professional actors to take part in his productions while they were "resting" from their paid employment. He also ran a fine theatre school on the premises. Later, I was unable to commit myself to any further productions as the *Telegraph* took up every spare minute of my time. I always regretted this for acting was something I loved and, had I really taken C D Hamilton's strange advice, I should have gone into the theatre.

Shortly after we had moved to Cecile Park, a letter arrived from my uncle Asher in Israel. It was he who had saved the family's skins by acting as guarantor for my father, mother and me to be given entry to England. Admittedly, he withdrew the £1,000 once we were safely ensconced in London, but his action had saved our lives and we were always indebted to him. His letter told us that his son, Jacob, my cousin, was coming to London to study a building course and English. He would be grateful if we could find him a place where he could live.

Of course, there was no question as to such a venue. He could stay with us. Jacob, whom Maureen and I had already met on a brief holiday in Israel, was a nice young lad, but his English left a lot to be desired. He learned quickly and settled into Cecile Park with ease. One day, Maureen and I were invited to a party thrown by one of our best Irish friends, Grainne O'Sullivan. We asked Jacob if he'd like to come. He didn't appear to be too enthusiastic. "Will they all be as old as you?" he asked (Israelis are fairly direct to say the least). Anyway, he decided to come despite his doubts. Lucky that he did for he met Liz Jones at the party and they hit it off immediately, and were married a year or so later. What is more, they have remained married ever since and have two beautiful children and three gorgeous grandchildren to adore.

Jacob gave up his building course and decided to go into business by himself. He went to Israel and bought a collection of semi-precious stones, such as the Eilat jewels, brought them back to the UK and had them mounted. He hawked them round the big London department stores and, lo and behold, they were snapped up like the proverbial hot cakes. He then started importing more and so on, moving on to precious stones. In short, he moved from strength to strength, opening a small jewellery factory in Covent Garden and today has boutiques in Harrods, and many other top department stores in London, Manchester, Leeds and Dublin.

I have always been very proud of his achievements and only wish that his father had lived to share in his son's success.

Meanwhile, Maureen's pregnancy was progressing and we felt it was time to make another move. The Cecile Park flat was not good enough for a growing family. We wanted to live in a proper house with a garden of our own and with neighbours we could relate to. Although many people lived at Cecile Court, we knew no one. It was fairly typical of an inner London block of flats where no one knows anyone else and doesn't want to know anyone else either.

We began the search in the Highgate area but, frankly, couldn't afford anything we saw. We moved further and further out. I wanted to stay somewhere reasonably close to the M1 to simplify journeys to and from our respective parents. So eventually we ended up in Cockfosters – a pretty suburb at the end of the Piccadilly Line, making the tube journey into Central London a little less complicated. The ability to fall asleep during the homeward journey and wake up at the terminus was a real luxury.

It was there that we found a suitable semi-detached corner house in a delightful street called Belmont Avenue, which had beds of sweet smelling flowers planted all along the edges of the pavements. It was a lovely house with a 40-metre garden, which was in desperate need of tidying – a job I intended to tackle on Saturdays and whatever Sundays I had free. Being a daily paper, we had to follow a roster and we found ourselves working on every second or third Sunday. Sundays were usually quiet and so we were constantly urged to produce stories on a Thursday or Friday marked: SET & KEEP, SUNDAY FOR MONDAY (+ the date). Monday's *Telegraph*s were often stuffed with such set-and-keep stories – although they never appeared on Page 1.

There were several shifts: 9 a.m. until 5 p.m.; 3.30 p.m. until 11 p.m. and 7.30p.m. until 2 a.m. This last shift was best known for mopping up stories and picking up reports from the first editions of other newspapers, particularly our main rivals, *The Times, Guardian, Daily Mail* and *Daily Express*. An elderly man was employed to cycle round the offices of these papers every night at about 10 p.m. to pick up copies of their first editions, which he would then race back to the *Telegraph*. The night porter would then take over and deliver them to the Night News Desk as well as the Chief Sub's desk. The Night News Editor was a man called Peter Eastwood. He would scour each paper from cover to cover and never missed a thing. Once he found a story that was worth "following up", he would call for one of the reporters, cut out the story and hand it to him or her (oh, yes, we had several women working the late evening shifts), demanding to know the answers to many questions not treated in the original story. The reporter then had to discover the source of the story and telephone whoever might be able to answer those questions. I hated having to make such calls as on many occasions, the source was already in bed or hosting a dinner with friends and many bottles of wine and port.

Strangely enough, although a few would slam down the receiver in anger, most would be willing to stand and speak to the caller. Of course, they didn't give a damn for the caller but were thrilled to be woken up or brought away from the dinner table by the *Daily Telegraph*. If *The Times* or one of the others had a hot exclusive with which they were to lead their paper, they would hold it over to their second edition, thus making it more difficult for rivals to follow. Our elderly cyclist was also paid to collect second editions around 11.30 p.m. and we had to go through the same routine, this time, more often than not getting the source out of bed. Once the story "stood up" and a couple of additional questions were answered, we would then have to get going and produce a decent piece, typing away like crazy and, frankly, "lifting" whole chunks, slightly rewritten, from the original. There was no time to produce a masterpiece for our third and final editions.

The first edition would be transported to the airport, bundled onto planes and flown to the four corners of the earth. The second and third editions would go by trains to the provinces and the final would be reserved for Central and Greater London. We had a separate office and printworks in Manchester and stories would be exchanged between both. The Manchester editions would go to northern towns and cities by train and van as well as to Scotland and Northern Ireland.

Peter Eastwood was a short, stout man with spectacles that emphasized his pink, high cheekbones and white hair. He ruled the roost and was *always right*. One night he called me to his desk and had the copy of a story I had written in front of him.

"You can't say that," he said quietly (his voice was always very quiet and I rarely heard him shout).

"What can't I say?" I enquired.

"This," he said, circling a phrase I had written. It said that something or other was not as good "compared to" something else. "You went to university didn't you? Then you should know that it should be 'compared with'. Not 'to'. Now remember that and don't do it again." I was waved away.

I went straight down to the library and asked for a copy of Fowler's *Modern English Usage* and looked up "compare". Eastwood, of course, had been right. But so was I. It was (and I cannot now recall the exact sentence) one of those cases where 'to' was interchangeable with 'with'.

I returned to see Eastwood and slapped Fowler in front of him. He read it, but still argued that the version he had chosen was better.

On another occasion he called me in and handed me a cutting from one of the rival papers. "Have a look at this one, will you. I think you'll find that something very similar happened in 1951. I think it was February 1951. Might have been the 14th or 15th."

I went to the library and asked for cuttings relating to the reported incident. He was wrong! But he was nearly right. It was the 16th February. What a memory the guy had. One could only admire him.

When I was on the late shift – the one that dragged on until 2 a.m. – I often found myself on what was called the "Grand Piano". It was nothing of the kind but just a simple desk that dealt with late obituary notices. The *Telegraph* obits were often regarded as superior to those in *The Times*. An entire department looked after the dead. As soon as one of the royals is born and as soon as someone becomes a celebrity (great singer, jazz player, conductor, actor and so on) their obituary is written and filed. As they continue to make news, so their obits are updated. And when they become seriously ill, it is further updated and filed. Every obit, whether of the living or dead, begin (they still begin this way): "Charles Bloggs, who has died aged___, was among the..."

Whenever I was on the late shift, people used to die like flies. I imagined them on their death beds, asking their loved ones: "Who's doing the obits on the *Telegraph* tonight? Izbicki? Oh, good..." cue last breath. I often had a dozen deaths to deal with and had to get the cuttings out and write what was known as a "nugget" – five or six lines relating to the person's demise. These would appear alongside the long, pre-prepared obits, as a little column. Anyone famous would get such a nugget on Page 1 or 2, with a longer follow-up notice the following day.

During the day shifts I was being given increasingly good stories to cover, and many of them obtained what is known in the business as good shows – either page leads or decent Page 1 coverage. But, although many other reporters were given bylines, I continued to be nothing more than "By Daily Telegraph Reporter". After I had been with the paper about two months, I received a summons from the Managing Editor, "Pop" Pawley. His office was next door to the news room so I was able to answer his call within a matter of seconds.

"Ah, Izbicki, do sit down," he began jovially and continued: "I just wanted to tell you that we think you've been doing a good job. Yes, a pretty good job. Very satisfactory. In fact, we're increasing your salary by another £100. Happy?"

"Well, yes, thank you very much (goodness, I thought, that's £150 more than I had been offered only a couple of months ago – but I thought I'd just ask one question). May I ask, if you are so satisfied with my work, why I am still only DTR and have never been given a proper byline?"

Pawley looked slightly startled and his smile disappeared. "Ah, a byline. I see. Well, you see, Izbicki, if we were to give you a byline, we'd have so many readers writing in to ask us why we were employing so many – er – foreigners, people like Loshak and Guy Rais."

He could have added: Aneliese Schultz, Peter Schmidt and several other *real* foreigners who covered news for the paper abroad. The difference was that David Loshak, who was to become one of my closest friends, and Guy Rais were, like me, Jewish. The others were not.

I decided to tell him the story of what happened at the start of my first job with the *Manchester Evening Chronicle*, when I was asked what I might choose as a second byline if this was necessary. I had chosen my middle name, Howard.

"John Howard, eh?" Pawley mused. "And did you write under that name?"

"As a matter of fact, this was never considered necessary and I continued to write under John Izbicki."

"Oh, well, jolly good, jolly good," he said. The interview was clearly terminated and I returned to the news room. But my step was light. A hundred extra quid was most welcome.

My reporting assignments grew and grew and I was sent to various parts of the country.

The day I was asked to take myself off to Birmingham to cover a strike by the Austin Motors plant, was to have another curious effect on the question of bylines. I filed the story which turned out to be exclusive and was actually better than the one I was originally expected to do. I returned to my hotel in the centre of the city, lay down on my bed and read a book, waiting for the phone to ring to let me have a dozen queries. The desk was good at queries.

Sure enough, the phone rang. "John? Harry Winslade..." (Harry Winslade was by then the Night News Editor following the promotion of Peter Eastwood to Managing Editor. Harry was a dapper little bespectacled man who rarely walked but always strode along in a great hurry). "...We've just read your story..."

"Oh, what's the matter with it, Harry?" I was immediately on the defensive as I knew there was nothing wrong with it. In fact I thought it was a good piece.

"Nothing old boy, nothing at all. In fact it's a jolly good piece. So good, in fact, that we're splashing with it."

"Great, Harry. That's really great. Thanks for letting me know." I was truly chuffed. But I added a rider: "Just one thing Harry. If it's good enough for a splash, is it also good enough for my byline?"

There was a little humming and hahing at the other end of the line. "Don't know about that old boy…"

"Well, Harry…" and I told him the same story I had told Pop Pawley. "So, Harry, if it's going to be a case of my going through life as "Daily Telegraph Reporter" or as John Howard, then I'll accept John Howard."

"Like I said, John, I don't know but I'll certainly look into it old boy. Leave it with me."

He hung up and I poured myself a stiff scotch from the mini bar. I felt I deserved it.

Twenty minutes later, just as I was about to go down to the hotel restaurant for dinner, the phone rang again. It was Harry.

"John, is that Howard with an 'a' or Howerd with an 'e'?"

For the next year or so my stories were written **By John Howard**.

Then, in December 1965 at a pre-New Year's party at friends in Enfield, not far from our Cockfosters home, I was called to the phone. "It's your office John! Tell 'em to get stuffed!" There weren't mobiles in those days but it was the duty of reporters to leave a number where they could be reached, even on a day off .

It was the night news desk. "Sorry old boy, but there's been an escape from Dartmoor and we'd like you to get down there a.s.a.p. to cover it. I guess we can leave it to you to book yourself a hotel and get yourself down there all right…" And he added with a light laugh: "You'll like this one. The prisoner is Mad Mitch…Frank Mitchell, the Mad Axeman. You'd better take care but an interview with him would be appreciated…"

"Ha, bloody ha," was all I could find to say before he hung up.

There was no question about whether I had already had my fill of drink. That didn't seem to matter then. Nor were cars fitted with seat belts. No one had bothered asking me whether I knew the way to Dartmoor. It was up to reporters to find that kind of thing out themselves. It was nearly 11 p.m. when I wished everyone good night, kissed Maureen a fond farewell, shaking off her offer to come with me "at least to map read", and asked a friend to drive her home later. I drove home quickly and consulted the AA book, looking up Dartmoor. There was a Dartmoor Hotel in Princetown, home of the prison. Now there, I thought, was a bit of luck. I phoned the number and was answered by a woman who sounded well and truly pissed. I booked a room, jumped into the car and drove off into the foggy, foggy dew.

Luckily I had plenty of fuel as all petrol stations appeared to be closed and I drove fast but carefully all the way to Dartmoor, arriving at the hotel at around 6.30 a.m. The place looked dreadful and when, finally, someone came to the door, it also smelled terrible. The landlady, nursing a beauty of a hangover, signed me in and showed me to the room. I was horrified. The room stank of a mixture of booze, vomit and urine, although there had been some attempt to clean it. The wardrobe door was hanging precariously from one solitary hinge and the pillow on the bed was stained with what I could only imagine was some form of brylcreem.

I desperately needed some sleep but did not fancy lying down on that bed.

"Have you come to visit one of the inmates, dear?" the landlady enquired.

"Er – no," I said and introduced myself properly. "*The Daily Telegraph*!" she said with wonderment and awe. "Well, I never!"

No self-respecting newspaperman had ever stayed there at that time, I thought. "Who normally stays here, then?" I asked. "Mostly wives and sweethearts or mothers coming to see their little no-good boy," she replied and added: "You should have come last night. We all had a lovely time, dear. There aren't many here today and they're still asleep but they'll be getting up soon for breakfast and visiting time…You must be starving. D'you want breakfast?"

"No thanks. I think I'll have a look at the prison and get a bit of local colour but I'll probably come back later this morning." She was right. I was starving but I felt slightly nauseous and just wanted some fresh air. Besides, I was growing increasingly suspicious that I was in the wrong place. Although the famous prison was just a matter of a few metres away, something very important was missing.

Surely, I thought, I could not possibly be the only hack to be covering this story. I drove through Princetown and couldn't see any activity, not even a single policeman hanging around.

I looked at the map and saw that I wasn't far from Tavistock. I had never been in this area and had no idea which might be the best place to go but Tavistock was in bold on the map so it must be a bit bigger than this godforsaken place.

I stopped outside the Tavistock Hotel. What a glorious difference to the place I had just left. I went in and there they all were – hacks galore, all tucking into eggs and bacon and gallons of hot tea. I went to the desk.

"I'd like a room please," I said, keeping my fingers firmly crossed.

The young receptionist looked at the register, tut-tutted for a moment, but her eyes lit up: "You're in luck, Sir. Just one room left. It's turned out a busy day. How long will you be staying?"

"I'm sorry, I've no idea but it's bound to be several days."

I joined the others and soon made friends with Roger Mount, the Man from *The Times*. We got on like the proverbial house on fire. His great advantage was that he had brought with him a somewhat large short-wave radio and when the others had left to check with their offices or visit the police station just across the road, my new friend switched on his machine and tuned it to the police wavelength. We sat in the lounge listening to the latest sightings and as soon as these reports sounded sufficiently reliable, we would get up and rush to the spot to join the police. In exchange for Roger's radio help, I would drive the two of us to the spot. Soon we managed to get to know some of the policemen in the hunt for Mitchell.

We returned to the hotel for drinks and lunch, keeping an ear on the police messages. What we were doing was quite illegal but it kept us happily occupied at the hotel. I had to return to the Dartmoor Hotel and make some damn good excuse to get out of my booking. Roger helped me out and telephoned the hotel asking to speak to me. "Sorry, he's not here. Haven't seen him practically all day," the landlady said. "Shall I give him a message, Sir?"

"Very good of you, yes. When he comes in will you tell him that I called? It's the News Editor of the *Daily Telegraph*. He's urgently required to return to London. Have you got that?"

"Oh yes, Sir, I'll tell him the moment I clap eyes on him."

And she did. I felt sorry for her but she was very happy to have spoken to so august a person as the *Telegraph*'s news editor. I offered her one day's rent and she was more than happy.

Each day we would telephone some copy about the hunt. It kept the office happy and we had a restful time that lasted nearly three weeks.

Later we found out that Mitchell's escape had been orchestrated by the Kray twins and they moved him to a flat in the Barking Road in London's East End. But he was too impatient to remain hidden and became increasingly violent. Once again he was moved but this time it has been alleged, he was shot dead. His body was never recovered but it is believed that it had been thrown into one of the massive shafts supporting the Hammersmith Flyover which was then being built. These pillars had to be filled with concrete, making the retrieval of any body thrown into the wet cement an impossibility.

The Kray twins were later tried for his murder but in the absence of a body and of proof, they were acquitted.

We never did get much of a story out of the Mad Axeman's dramatic escape, but Roger and I both managed to obtain some good material out of the police. The station was in a building resembling a small castle and we would climb the steps in the late evening to share a few beers with the coppers. They spent much of the time complaining about the lack of proper pay and the appalling state of their uniforms. They had not been provided with waterproof boots or jackets and were really angry at having to run around in search for some "bloody madman" when he was "probably many miles away". They were of course right.

The police did start smelling a rat when Roger and I kept turning up at places indicated on their radio – sometimes even well before they managed to get there themselves. But they never made a fuss about this and didn't even bother to broach the subject. We never got in their way and, if anything, proved quite helpful – especially in providing the odd crate of beer in the evenings…

My few reports from Tavistock continued to be bylined John Howard. I could do nothing other than sigh and enjoy the comradeship of the news room. No one ever asked me whether I was Jewish or even where I was born although quite a few were interested in the origin of the name and were satisfied with my usual answer.

CHAPTER FOURTEEN:
THE TORYGRAPH (2)

Fellow hacks in the newsroom found it exceedingly strange that the man they knew as Izbicki was being bylined Howard. When I told them the reason, they found it even stranger. "Why on earth did you ever agree to change your name?" one man wanted to know. He believed that I would have to remain Howard for the rest of my life on the paper. "And if you decided to join another paper, whether it was the *Daily Mail* or the *Express* next door, you'd have to continue writing as Howard because that's the name they'd all know your work by," he felt. This kind of comment didn't make me feel any better.

On one occasion when I was up in Birmingham for a story, I bumped into David Hopkinson, another old friend and colleague from the *Manchester Evening Chronicle*. He had certainly fallen on lucrative ground, having been appointed editor of the *Birmingham Post*, a lively paper with a big circulation. We went for a drink and I told him about my byline history. He was genuinely shocked.

"They're bonkers to have done that to you. I'll tell you this: I should be happy and proud to have someone called Izbicki on my staff. It might be a little difficult for folks to read and remember at first – but by Christ, they'd remember it once they'd seen it two or three times. Whereas Howard – well, they'd forget it as soon as they'd read it. Not that there's anything wrong with the name Howard. Don't get me wrong. But there's nothing unusual about it. Izbicki is memorable. They're crazy to have changed it."

I shall always remain grateful to David Hopkinson for that observation.

It bucked up my morale. But it also increased my anger against the *Telegraph*'s decision to force me to change my name.

Meanwhile, Maureen's pregnancy was nearing its conclusion and it looked like she might deliver at any moment. The baby was making it very clear that he or she was getting fed up with waiting inside and was kicking to get out. We had no idea what sex "it" was going to be and, frankly, could not care less. As Maureen said: "As long as it has two arms, two legs, all its fingers and toes, that'll be good enough for me." I shared her opinion.

On the 24th November 1964, she felt that the time had come and I drove her to the Whittington Hospital at Archway, where a bed had already been reserved for her. I was determined to stay with her and be with her when our child was born. Her waters broke the moment we arrived at the Whittington and she was taken to the Labour Ward. We waited. And waited. And waited. She was transferred to a private room, and I was able to sit with her and wait. And we waited. And waited. Night fell and Maureen's contractions came in shorter intervals. By 2 a.m. the contractions were about one minute apart and I kept running into the corridor to seek a nurse to report my timings of those wretched contractions. I was still doing these hectic reports at 3 a.m. The nurses were getting fed up with me. But they were also becoming impatient with the time Maureen was taking. And a little concerned. A doctor was called to examine her and I was asked to wait outside.

At 3.45 a.m. the ward sister came to me: "Mr Izbicki, why don't you go home? You're not doing your wife or yourself much good, getting all worried and stressed. Go home and I promise faithfully that we'll phone you the moment there's any real development."

I told her that I wanted to be with my wife for the delivery. The sister considered this briefly, then said: "Yes, dear, I know you'd like that but I think this might be a bit difficult. The doctor has been to see her and it seems that the baby has turned its head and is slightly stuck behind the pubic bone. Nothing at all to worry about but it looks like it'll be a forceps delivery. Honest, it'll be okay, so please don't worry and get a bit of sleep. Go home!"

I have always been one to obey authority, whether the police or a doctor or a nursing sister. So I reluctantly did as I was told and drove home to lie on my bed for a quick snooze.

Just a little after 6 a.m. on the 25th November the phone rang. "Mr Izbicki? It's a boy. Congratulations. Yes, you can come at any time to see him and your wife. She has been very good!"

I raced back to the Whittington, breaking every speed limit and stopping only at red lights. A boy! Wow! But what did they mean by saying that Maureen had been very good? Why the hell didn't I ask for an explanation? What did it mean? Had there been difficulties? How were they both doing? I hadn't been told. Or at least I think I wasn't told. Perhaps I hadn't listened properly.

I rushed up to the Labour ward and was taken to the operating theatre. "I'm sorry, Mr Izbicki, but we've only just finished cleaning the baby up. It has been a long and complicated delivery. That's why they're still in there, sleeping it off," the sister said and added: "Don't worry. They're both doing fine now. A consultant will come to see you in a few minutes and explain things to you…"

Fear gripped me as I entered the operating theatre. What had they done? Then I saw the cot in the middle of the room and, a little further away, Maureen stretched out and fast asleep on an operating table. I went to her first. My God, how beautiful she was and how very peaceful. I mustn't disturb her, I thought, although I wanted to take her in my arms and kiss her.

The silence of that room could be heard. There was no sound of any description. Why wasn't the baby crying, I thought. I tiptoed my way to the cot and looked down at its occupant. A pair of radiantly blue eyes looked straight up at me and to my utter amazement, followed my every move as I slowly circled the cot.

It was an eerie, quite creepy experience.

I then noticed two remarkable things. The boy, for whom there was still no name, already had curly blonde hair. I had always expected newly born babies to be bald or have only slight, straight hair. But here were curls of fairly thick blonde hair, The second thing I saw filled me with horror. A hole, a distinct hole, appeared just above the nostrils, forming a sort of tunnel from one side of the nose to the other.

What did this mean? What could have caused this dreadful injury?

But, regardless of the hole, the child was beautiful, simply beautiful, and a deep love surged through me. I had always believed that all newly born babies are ugly, appearing like ruddy wrinkled prunes. This child's skin was fair and smooth and those eyes that continued to stare at me were clear and blue. Later, I saw his hands, so tiny, with shiny, tiny nails. When I placed a finger to one of his hands, the finger was gripped tightly. Oh, what utter bliss. Welcome to the world!

The consultant surgeon came to see me. "I am so very sorry, Mr Izbicki, that you've had to wait such a long time for the delivery of your son. Such a lovely little boy. He put up quite a fight and I had to use forceps and also had to cut your wife a little. His head had got stuck behind the pubic bone and I suppose I should have done it by Caesarian section. I can certainly promise you that the next baby your wife has will definitely be done by Caesar. She won't need to go through this kind of trouble a second time, not if I have anything to do with it. Both she and the baby will have to stay in hospital for a few days longer, I'm afraid. You might have noticed a little hole in the child's nose. This was, alas, caused by the forceps, but should heal in a day or two."

On another occasion when we went to see him, he admitted that the birth had been more difficult and dangerous than he had first described. He had faced the dilemma of losing not only the baby but the mother as well but had managed to save both, thank God.

The following day, when I came to the hospital bearing a huge bouquet of flowers, Maureen was still sleeping. The birth had completely exhausted her and the cuts she had had to endure were still raw and painful. The baby, on the other hand, was well awake and crying lustily. And the hole in the nose had not only healed, but there was no sign of it having ever been there. The nose was clear of any blemish.

When Maureen eventually woke and looked at me, she appeared startled. "How's the baby?" was her first agonising question. "Oh my darling, he is fine, absolutely fine and very beautiful," I said through my own tears. "He?" she said. "Is it a boy?" I nodded. "And has he two arms and hands and eyes and is everything all right?" she enquired. "Oh, yes, my darling, yes." She sighed with satisfaction and a smile, then closed her eyes and returned to sleep.

Both sets of parents, now grandparents, were overjoyed and arrangements were made for their visits to London. I made them promise to wait until mother and child were at home again. Nell had a mass said in thanks for the life of her daughter and the wellbeing of her grandchild.

We decided to call the baby Paul Howard Izbicki. Had it been a girl, she would have been Pascale. After all, it was Easter when Paul was conceived in France. The name was French and was related to Easter – the Pascal Lamb.

As Paul was a boy, I needed to deal with another problem. Jews have their boys circumcised within the first week of their birth. To honour my parents and tradition, I had to do the same for Paul. Circumcision, the removal of the foreskin of the penis, is said to make boys grow up stronger and, in general, healthier than those who have not been circumcised. It is also a religious ceremony, performed by a rabbi who specialises in circumcision. I needed to find such a man, a *Mohel*, and had no idea what a struggle I would have to face.

I bought a copy of the *Jewish Chronicle* and found several advertisements for *Mohels*. I picked the first one that came to hand, a reverend gentleman called Rabbi Mendelbaum and telephoned him.

"Hello," an elderly voice said.

"Is that Rabbi Mendelbaum? Hello, my name is John Izbicki and I'd like you to perform the circumcision please…"

"Yes. Vere is de child?"

"At Highgate, in the Whittington Hospital…when could you do it?"

"Yes, I know the Vittington Hospital…" Then: "Vot did you say vos your name?"

"John Izbicki…"

"Izbitzki? Izbitzki? Vere have I heard dis name already?"

I thought, he couldn't have read it in the paper, where it was still Howard, but I asked him what newspapers he read.

"Newspapers? Sometimes the *Jewish Chronicle*, but I don't read newspapers… But I know ziss name. From vere is comink your fahder?"

"My father was born in a small Polish town called Lenczyca…"

"Ah so, dat's from vere I know ziss name. Lenczyz! Of course. Your grandfahder, he vos a baker?"

"Why, yes. Did you know him?"

"Yes, of course! Very good!"

Very good indeed, I thought. Any problems I might have expected are over!

"Your wife, she is Jewish?" he asked.

I could not tell a lie. "No, she is a Christian, a Catholic. Why?"

"Oy, I am so sorry but I cannot do this for you. I coult lose my licenz von de Beth Din. I am so very sorry."

"But a friend of mine who is not Jewish and her husband who is also not Jewish managed to get their son circumcised without any trouble."

"Dat's right. If both parents are Christian, there is no problem, but if the mother is not Jewish, I cannot."

He was sorry. I was sorry, too. I tried several other *Mohels* and the answer was the same each time. Then someone advised me to telephone Rabbi X (I do not wish to publish his name for obvious reasons). I gave him my name, the hospital's name, the baby's name and we made a date. He would come three days later at 10.30 a.m. He had not asked me about Maureen at all. I simply asked him how much he would charge. "Fifteen Pounds," he said and added: "But I've never gone to court over money…ha-ha"

Had I heard correctly? Perhaps he had said Fifty Pounds? Why the little quip about going to court over money?

Came the day and I met Rabbi X at the Maternity Ward of the Whittington. He put on his skull cap and a tallit, picked up his little bag and said: "So, where is the child?" Maureen was still too weak to attend the ceremony but several nurses were standing by to watch and learn.

Just as we were going into the little room set aside for the event, he turned to me and said: "Oh, by the way, the mother is Jewish?" I froze. Do I lie? I just couldn't, not for something as solemn as this. "No," I almost whispered, "I'm afraid she isn't."

"Ah," he said and stopped dead in his tracks, took off his skull cap and tallit and placed them in a little bag. I was almost in tears. Then he said: "Right, so where is the child?"

He performed the circumcision quickly and cleanly and in thanks, Paul peed all over him. He just laughed and wiped himself and Paul dry. "He's a lovely little boy. May he bring you lots of Naches (luck)." I handed him the envelope containing £15 and hoped for the best. He seemed satisfied and we shook hands. Later one of the nurses told me that he had slipped them a £5 note for the nurses' Christmas box.

I have always remembered Rabbi X with admiration.

Not long after the Dartmoor episode, I was approached by one of the *Telegraph*'s many eminent specialists. Blake Baker, a tall, bespectacled man with a slight stoop and a Geordie accent, was the paper's industrial correspondent. He told me that he had admired my work and would I consider joining him as his deputy. I readily accepted.

Blake Baker had a tragic story. He used to be the *Telegraph*'s correspondent in Vienna and prior to that, in Berlin, and spoke German fluently. He had married a German woman and they had a son on whom Blake doted. The boy died in a dreadful road accident. It nearly killed Blake. He never really managed to get over it and, although he continued writing for the *Telegraph*, his normal punch had gone out of his reports.*

---

* In what is nowadays called "a blog", Kate Connolly, the Berlin correspondent for the *Telegraph* in the earlier part of the 21st century, came across a pile of fascinating old documents dating back to 1949. She, or rather the *Telegraph*, was in the process of killing the Berlin office. The documents, which she was binning, related to the Baker epoch and showed the man's character long before the tragic death of his son. For instance, there was a note he sent to E H Marsh, the foreign editor – known to one and all as Ricky Marsh – about his car, an Opel Kapitän. "After all," the note said, "the *Times, Express* and *FT* provide their correspondents

When I joined him it was clear that he was still ill and pining for his son and the boy's memory. His work certainly suffered and he passed many of the good stories to me. Unlike some specialists he did not put his name on the stories I wrote. Frankly, there were times when I should not have minded such a slight of hand. I liked Blake. He was a Catholic yet almost rebelled against his religion following his son's death. He returned to the Catholic fold once his priest told him that his son was now an angel sitting at the side of Christ.

Industrial reporting was no picnic. It often meant doorstepping at the TUC and Number 10. Strike meetings and salary negotiations often dragged on late into the night and on one occasion I recall standing outside Number 10 waiting for Barbara Castle, then Secretary of State for Employment and Productivity under Harold Wilson's premiership. That meeting kept us hacks waiting for many hours and she didn't emerge until well after 2 a.m. Now one might have thought that this would be too late to catch any newspaper's print run. But there was always a little space left for the 4 a.m. edition – the one that sold in the West End and immediate suburbs of London.

I remembered Barbara from my days at the *Manchester Evening Chronicle*. At the age of 35 she was elected Labour MP for Blackburn. I interviewed her quite early on when I had a weekly column called *Getting Around with John Izbicki*. I was a comparative youngster to journalism whereas she had had loads of journalistic experience, having edited a magazine called *Town and County Councillor* and been the housing correspondent for the *Daily Mirror*. Amazingly, she remembered me and the piece I wrote as a result of that interview some ten years earlier.

Blake Baker was responsible for giving me my name back. He wrote a terse memorandum to Peter Eastwood who – it will be remembered – had by then been promoted from Night Editor to Managing Editor, replacing "Pop" Pawley who had retired. Eastwood became more feared as managing editor than he used to be while sitting among the subs at the night desk. He was protective of *his* patch and *his* reporters and lauded it over every column inch of news. Baker's memorandum was brief and to the point: "It is nothing short of embarrassing to have Izbicki meet senior TUC officials and political leaders

---

with Mercedes…" Another note on the same topic, this time sent to H J C Stephens, the *Telegraph*'s company secretary – 'Mr Moneybags'— declared: "There is no doubt that in Germany much representational value is attached to the kind of car one runs"… Kate Connolly went on to recount another of Blake's complaints. When the new *Times* correspondent arrived in Berlin from his last post, Tokyo, Baker wrote: "He came complete with Japanese chauffeur-houseboy…"

as John Izbicki, then appear in the paper the next day as John Howard," it said. Had Eastwood been the man to decide the John Howard byline, he might well have torn that memo up. But the man responsible for that decision was Pop Pawley.

So a memorandum was circulated to just about every responsible person in the building, from Editor, Foreign Editor, Picture Editor and Chief Sub-Editor to News Editor and Librarian, this time penned by Eastwood. It read:

Subject: John Izbicki

John Izbicki, who has been bylined John Howard, will in future be bylined John Izbicki, Industrial Staff, whenever the occasion so demands.

Signed: Managing Editor

A memorandum from Peter Eastwood was equivalent to the Ten Commandments brought down Mount Sinai by Moses. Each morning a sheet of paper bearing Eastwood's green stamp would list a number of "wanted points". It would often start with five little words: "Can we get back to..." There would follow five or six stories he had read in the paper that had omitted some little detail or other. It meant that the author of the original piece would have to "get back to" the story again that day and it would have to appear in the following morning's paper. If the wanted point did not "stand up" – in other words, if the reporter could not have that particular point or points confirmed – it did not matter. The story would still have to appear even if it kicked off with: "It was denied yesterday that"...followed by the required point(s).

The News Editor or his assistants who had to pass on the daily variety of Eastwood wanted points could be heard to groan loudly every morning. Those close enough in the newsroom to hear the groans knew exactly what was meant and prayed that whatever it was would not be passed on to them.

My period with Blake Baker proved hectic but mentally stimulating. There seemed to be strikes of one kind or another erupting on a daily basis. My doorstepping at the Ministry of Labour and unions became a regular occurrence and my face became known at the TUC, where I got to know George Woodcock, its general secretary, reasonably well. The son of a Lancashire cotton weaver, Woodcock started his working life in a cotton mill while he was still at Brownedge Roman Catholic Elementary School. He once told me that his eternal regret was that poor health had prevented him from becoming a professional footballer. He had wanted to play for Preston North End. "It wasn't to be, I'm afraid. I was struck down by this ghastly illness," he told me. I could only suppose that the dust of the cotton mill caused it. As a lad he was already active within the Labour movement and he later won a TUC scholarship to New College, Oxford, the first member of the Woodcock family to go to university.

He obtained a first class honours degree in Philosophy, Politics and Economics and, after a comparatively short period working for the civil service, he joined the TUC staff and soon headed its research and economics department. In 1947, at the age of 43, he became the TUC's assistant general secretary. He stayed 13 years in the wings before taking over the post of general secretary from Vincent Tewson.

He never gave me the impression of being a member of the "working class", unlike Vic Feather, who replaced him as assistant general secretary in 1960, when Woodcock moved up and became general secretary in 1969 on Tewson's retirement. George Woodcock was soft spoken, always immaculately dressed and looked distinguished with wavy grey hair. Vic Feather, on the other hand, was a brusque Yorkshireman, Bradford-born and bred, he left school at 15 and worked at a Co-op grocery store. He tended to look unkempt but had a brilliant mind and a wicked sense of humour. Press conferences taken by Woodcock were informative but solemn affairs; those with Feather were equally informative but in a lighter vein and constructed with ready-made headlines. And whereas Woodcock declined the honour of a peerage when it was offered to him in 1970 (but he was made a CBE as early as 1953 and became a member of the Privy Council in 1963), Vic Feather gladly accepted his life peerage in 1974. Feather also accepted a string of honorary doctorates (from the universities of Bradford, Manchester and the Open). It was Feather who led a TUC delegation to argue with the Labour government against proposals that would draw union teeth. It resulted in the withdrawal of the Wilson government's plans to introduce anti-union legislation.

The Industrial department of the *Telegraph* had a team of three: Blake Baker, myself as his deputy, and Robert Bedlow as the "Number Three". Bob and I got on remarkably well, even though I had been appointed above him – not the first time this was to happen to me on the paper. But after about a year, Bob applied for the Shipping job which had become vacant and was successful. This meant that another space needed to be filled. In those days the *Telegraph* along with the other "heavies", was able to afford large departments so that important stories could be covered by two, even three people at a time. Blake and I would go tandem to such annual conferences as the TUC, the TGWU (the Transport and General Workers Union was then the biggest of all TUC-affiliated unions) and the NUR (National Union of Railwaymen).

The man who stood out above many others in Fleet Street was a 27-year-old redhead called John Richards. Blake and I picked him without unnecessary debate. He was working as industrial reporter on the *Daily Mail* and had been prior to that London industrial correspondent of the *Scotsman*. He was earnest and meticulous in his concentration to detail. He ate, drank and breathed industrial relations but had a tendency to criticise Blake behind his back. John and I shared an office, so I got the brunt of these digs and found myself defending Baker virtually daily.

"He's fucking lazy, John. He should be going out doing the big stories but he's content to leave them to you and me. It's bloody silly," he would say.

I told him about Blake's tragic loss and how he still grieved. "Come on John, he knows his stuff and anyway, there's nothing wrong in delegating."

"Yes, I know he's still in a state of mourning. But how long should this sort of thing last? He has a duty to the paper. You and I are getting more in these pages in a day than he does in a week."

I just hoped that he would confine his views to our little office and not go around the pubs or the news room spreading them. In any case, there was no real need as the gap in productivity was easily noticed by anyone reading the paper – and that included Peter Eastwood. Now, whatever slings and arrows one might aim at Eastwood, one has to admit that he did possess a heart – as I was to find out in a very personal way some years later. He knew that Blake was not pulling his weight but he also knew that Blake was still deeply affected by the death of his son. As long as the work was done by Blake's team, Eastwood would not interfere. What he did do was to call Blake down to his office a few times and hand him some cutting from one of the rival papers on an industrial subject with the gentle command (oh, he could even be gentle): "Here Blake, take a look at this. It's a damn good piece there but it leaves a lot of questions to be answered. Now, I want *you* to do this one, d'you understand?" Blake could not pass it on to me or to John but he would shut himself in his office to research the story – and write it.

When Blake eventually retired in 1969, I was offered his job – and refused. I shall return to that episode later. So John Richards got it and, of course, was brilliant. His second-in-command was Maurice Weaver, taken from the news room, and Bob Bedlow was also used as a backup. John did all the things he had criticised Blake for not doing. He would make a round-trip of the major union headquarters at least once a month, thereby managing to grab one exclusive after another. He was an ardent union man himself and became

Father of the *Daily* and *Sunday Telegraph* Chapel.* He was also elected to the National Union of Journalists' national executive.

Richards was a Westcountryman and was educated at Brockley Grammar School – but went north for his higher education, getting a degree in Psychology, Philosophy and English at Manchester University. And whereas I had started my career on the *Manchester Evening Chronicle*, he began his under the great Harry Evans on the the *Manchester Evening News*, the *Chronicle*'s main rival.

He stuck it out on the *Telegraph* for three years – the same time I had devoted to the Industrial department. Frankly, such a period suffices in a job that drains the truly efficient reporter of all energy and skill. After a couple of years I used to say: "All this has happened before. There's been no change, just a carbon copy of last year's. How can one use fresh words for so old a story?"

John left to take up the post of public relations chief at the Commission for Industrial Relations and the British Institute of Management. Amazingly perhaps, he upped and left PR to return to the *Telegraph* in 1980 – again as industrial correspondent – just in time for the miners' disastrous strike during the reign of the Iron Lady, Margaret Thatcher, and the move to Wapping of Rupert Murdoch's *Times* and the defeat of the printing unions. Richards was probably the last of the mighty industrial correspondents, for soon after the *Telegraph* quit its historic home in Fleet Street to move to Docklands, he led a 24-hour disruptive strike, then relinquished his badge of FoC and resigned. By now, most other papers had given up labour and industrial reporting.

He was just 66 years old when he died on May 9, 2006.

When Blake Baker told me that he was stepping down and that I was going to be offered his job, I thought long and hard. Although I never disliked the job and had obtained a good reputation among colleagues and rivals alike, it was draining me of my energy and, frankly, my home life. I never knew when I would be able to get home and give Paul who was growing fast, some father-time, to say nothing of giving Maureen the love and care she so richly deserved. We always had to wait for some proper holidays when we could get

---

* The word FoC – father of the chapel – originated in the Middle Ages. Even before printing was invented, every monastery had a team of monks who would produce illuminated manuscripts and beautifully illustrated books. These would be put together in one of the smaller chapels. The monk who was in charge of this production line would be called the Father of the Chapel.

away together. I could not risk having to put in still more hours, more door-stepping, more conferences.

But two other events had appeared to help me make up my mind. The year was 1968. May of that year saw the start of *les événements* in France and I was called to see Ricky Marsh, the foreign editor. Ricky was a small, restless man who was constantly busy and alert to everything that was going on around the world. He smiled a greeting and asked me to sit.

"John, I'd like you to go over to France for me to take a look at what's going on there. You've been before, haven't you? You were there for the *Sunday Times*, weren't you?"

"Well, yes – er – Kemsley Newspapers, Ricky – the *Sunday Graphic* and *Empire News* and all the provincials as well. Steve Coulter covered for the *Sunday Times*."

"Yes, yes," said Ricky impatiently. "Well, how would you like to go over there for us – just till these troubles are over?"

"But what about Blake Baker and industrial reporting?"

"I've cleared it with Peter Eastwood and the Editor and I've had a word with Blake as well. Blake said that John Richards would be able to cover during your absence and Blake might even take on a bit more as well…"

So I packed my bags, took my passport and kissed Maureen and Paul goodbye. I thought this would be just a bit of an extra holiday and was looking forward to being back in dear old Paris.

I received a call from another old friend – Ronnie Payne of the *Sunday Telegraph* was also going over and wondered if I'd like to come with him. He was taking his car over, and this might be of some help. We had heard that planes and trains were being seriously delayed. He had booked one of those quick crossings from Lydd to Le Touquet, a flight of about 25 minutes. As it turned out, we had the plane to ourselves. Well, almost to ourselves. There were two rather gorgeous stewardesses – or hostesses as they were then called.

We ordered large scotches and the four of us had a boozy party lasting just a little over 20 minutes. We landed and, as we prepared to walk down the plane's little steps, we found ourselves staring at a group of 15 or so workmen ready to help unload. I stood at the top of the steps, held my arms high above my head in a V and called in a voice which I hoped resembled that of their president, the General de Gaulle: *Je vous ai compris*! It was something he had said a few days earlier when he claimed to have understood the students who were creating all this trouble. I received a round of good humoured applause.

We drove to Paris and I settled myself into my old billet – the Hôtel d'Isley in the Rue Jacob and hoped I might once again be given Oscar Wilde's room.

Les événements proved to take longer to subside than we had anticipated – much longer. This time I was at a desk in the *Telegraph*'s sumptuous Paris office, the same as I knew from Kemsley days, above the Westminster Bank and across the road from the Ritz in the Place Vendôme. I was made to feel most welcome. After all, I was considered additional to the team of regular Paris correspondents.

Every day I was in the midst of the trouble, mostly alongside the students tearing up the pavement slabs and throwing stones at the advancing police. It did not take me long to become addicted to the tear gas that was shot at the students. My reports were given good shows in the paper and I found myself getting the "splash" every other day. Amazingly there was no jealousy at the Paris office only congratulations. "Izbicki's done it again! Well jolly good ol' boy; jolly good. I think you can buy the drinks tonight – if you've got the time that is," John Wallis (the man who gave Maureen away, remember?) would say. "But in case you won't have the time, which is more than likely, have one now..." he would add, pulling a bottle of whisky from a drawer and pouring me a stiff one.

On one occasion I found myself inside the Sorbonne, the Paris university off the Boulevard St Michel, interviewing the leader of the Anarchist group. We were sitting in the beautiful library of the Sorbonne at around 11 a.m. and I was asking him to give me reasons for the rioting. He explained that there simply wasn't enough room in the lecture theatres for all the students and many had to miss lectures as a result. So the riots had nothing really to do with a protest against the war in Vietnam. It was a purely educational protest.

Towards the end of the interview, when I had run out of questions, I asked him something that I immediately regretted. "You're an anarchist, you say. And yet here you are in this library and you haven't destroyed anything, not a single book..."

He looked at me and then at the thousands of books, many of them priceless and medieval, behind floor-to-ceiling glass doors, all of which remained intact. I could see his brain in action. What should he do? Indeed, what should I do? It had been a totally irresponsible question on my part and I tried to make amends. I slapped him good naturedly on the shoulders. "I was only joking, *mon vieux*, only joking," I said and was relieved to see the clear relief on his face. "*Ah oui*," he said with a lame smile. I left, feeling cold sweat trickle down my back. I hoped he would not decide that this English journalist was right to question the principles of anarchy. I gladly report that he was a civilised human after all. The Sorbonne's library remained safe.

Every night I filed copy from wherever I could. On one occasion I was invited to a party on the eighth floor of an apartment building. I thought I'd have just one drink and ask the people there for their opinions of the events. The apartment overlooked the Rue St Jacques which runs parallel with the Boulevard St Michel. Suddenly we heard the sound of a major riot down below and the firing of tear gas and rubber bullets. I stood on the balcony with the apartment's telephone in my hand and dictated a colourful piece to the copytakers in London. Cars below me were burning brightly and one petrol tank exploded, sending flames high into the air.

The copytaker at the other end was even more excited than I was. "My God John, are you all right? For Christ's sake, I can hear the shooting. Oh, fuck. This is super stuff John…hold on while I let this page go. It should make the early edition"

It made the splash. Again.

Some years earlier, in 1961, Walter Ulbricht the dictator of East Germany, had ordered the building of a Wall that would imprison the population of his country and stop them from escaping to the West.

Shortly after I had joined the *Daily Telegraph* I suggested a visit to East Germany to report in feature form what life was like behind the Wall. Both Pop Pawley and Ricky Marsh agreed that it was a good idea. I could speak German and might be able to get more out of the people there than was being done from correspondents stuck in West Berlin. So, with the *Telegraph*'s support, I applied for a visa. The East German wheels ground slowly. Very slowly. In mid-1968, I received a letter telling me I could come and collect my visa and make other necessary arrangements. But it was not collectable from the GDR Embassy in London. It would require a trip to Berlin to "make other necessary arrangements".

I coupled this visit with one of my week-long series of lectures at the Berlin Institute of Journalism in Developing Countries. I had already made several good friends there including Robert Lochner, director and founder of Berlin's RIAS radio station. Among my other friends at the Institute was Peter Prüfert, who had been appointed to run the place when I declined the offer of the job. Peter was perfect – young and capable and, above all, well liked by the students.

The two women secretaries at the Institute were also friendly and very efficient in proper German style: Lieselotte Mühlen, whose English was faultless, and Waltraut Höft who later married Peter Prüfert. Among the other lecturers who became lifelong friends were Jim Fraser, the photographer who taught photography and make-up; Stefan Gänsicke, deputy editor of the

Berliner Morgenpost, one of Springer's Berlin newspapers, whose English was perfect, who taught news editing; and Monika Gruber, who taught the students some day-to-day German. She taught English at a Berlin "Gymnasium" – grammar school – and her English, too, was faultless. I taught news gathering and writing as well as "the art of the interview".

No sooner had I returned to London following *Les événements* in France, than I flew to Tegel in Berlin to do another week's stint at the Institute – and collect my visa to the East. I crossed to East Berlin and visited a small office in a back street off the Friedrichstrasse. It was the *Auslandsdienst*, a service for foreign journalists wishing to visit the DDR (*Deutsche Demokratische Republik*). A grey-suited, grey-haired, grey man with a small moustache greeted me without a smile and demanded to see my passport. The uniformed immigration people at Checkpoint Charlie had already studied my passport and charged me 15 Marks for the one-day visa to enter East Berlin. Now here was this ghastly little man pretending to be God Almighty.

For a dreadful moment my mind whisked me back to my childhood and Nazi Germany. He reminded me of the Nazis; probably was one at the time.

"Why do you want to visit my country?" he demanded to know in German.

"My newspaper is very interested in your country and so am I," I replied – also in German.

"I see from your passport that you were born here in Berlin. When did you leave to go to Great Britain (there was a touch of sarcasm in his pronunciation of *Grossbritannien*)?"

"On September 1, 1939," I answered quietly.

His eyes shot up and stared into mine. "So you were just in time!" he exclaimed.

"Yes," I responded and added: "Luckily the British were more friendly in receiving my parents and me than the Germans were at throwing us out."

For the first time he looked just a little embarrassed. After all, even if he had been a Nazi in those bygone days, he was probably an equally loyal Communist now.

"Well," he said after a pause that seemed to stretch for more than a minute, "well, you shall have your visa, but you will have to pay for it, of course."

"Of course," I echoed.

"And also you will need a chauffeur driven car, which will cost you another thousand Marks a week. How long are you proposing to stay here?"

"I suppose I shall be able to see most of your interesting places within three weeks."

"Three weeks? What exactly interests you?"

"Oh, you know, Berlin, of course, then other places, such as Dresden, Leipzig, Weimar, and I should like to speak to people – ordinary people, perhaps in their homes and in the pubs or dance halls, if there are any…"

"What do you mean, 'if' there are any? You think we do not have dance halls here? Our people know how to enjoy themselves probably better than they do in the West, even perhaps in your Great Britain (again the sarcasm)."

I realised that I might have gone too far. "Of course, of course. I simply meant that…"

"I know what you meant, young man. You don't have to explain."

I was grateful for this interjection, especially as I had no idea how I could get round my little gaffe.

"So then three weeks. I will give you a visa for four weeks and the chauffeur-driven car. And then also you will need an interpreter (*ein Dolmetscher*)…"

As we had been speaking fluent German throughout the interview, I found this suggestion baffling. "Do you really think I need an interpreter?" I asked with a light laugh – the first bit of humour to have entered that room during my visit.

He looked startled as he realised that we had both been able to understand each other without any problem. But he recovered quickly. "Oh, yes, not of course to translate the words but to make it easier for you to see people…to help open doors that otherwise might not be so easy."

I arranged my visit for November. This gave my office time to rustle together the required money and forward it to the East German bank. It also gave me time for an altogether different trip.

On 21st October 1968 the Russians invaded Czechoslovakia. That evening my phone rang. It was the Foreign Desk.

"Hello John, Ricky Marsh. Is your passport up to date? We'd like you to pop over to Belgrade and cover the Czech invasion from there. I've arranged for you to have a desk at the AFP (the Agence France-Presse) office. They cover for us normally but I imagine they'll have quite enough on their hands. You did a good job in France and we think you'll do us proud again over there. We've arranged for you to pick up your ticket at Heathrow tomorrow morning. It's a BEA flight. Business class. Our man out there, Serge Stoicjovic will fill you in and he'll arrange your hotel. All right? Well, good luck ol' boy. Good luck."

I kissed Maureen and Paul goodbye yet again and packed my bag. It's no fun being married to a hack.

Belgrade proved more newsworthy than I had imagined. The invasion had caught many Czechoslovaks away from home. Thousands had been on holiday. Being in a Soviet satellite country, they could only get permission to travel to other satellite countries – Poland, East Germany, Bulgaria, Yugoslavia. Most of them – or so it seemed – were on their way back home through Yugoslavia and my first day in Belgrade was spent visiting a huge refugee camp the Serbs had opened for their Czech comrades.

Here I found families cooking meals on primus stoves; women and children weeping, men anxiously discussing the situation – and all of them more than ready to speak to a British journalist. I was able to make use of both English and German and the first story I filed made a page lead in the *Telegraph*. The next night, the Czechs marched in their thousands to their embassy and stood there solemnly, and with tears streaming from their eyes, singing their national anthem.

They marched on – this time to the Soviet embassy. There they howled their rage and threw stones, breaking several windows. It made another page lead – this time on the front page.

It went on like this for some two weeks. One afternoon, I was sitting in the AFP office when a young woman walked in to speak to Serge, the office boss. She spoke earnestly for about ten minutes while Serge shook his head and made disparaging clucking noises. I had no idea what they were talking about as my knowledge of Serbo-Croat is just about zero. When she left, Serge explained that she had come to tell him that Alex, the young man who did the night shift on the wire, typing stories destined for all over the world, was unable to come because he had been called up.

When I heard this, I put my skates on and rushed out of the office, taking two steps at a time down the stairs and into the street. It did not take me long to catch up with her. She was a very attractive young woman and stood out from the others milling about the street.

"Do you speak English," I asked as I grabbed her arm

"Yes, I do…a leetel," she said with a puzzled smile on her face.

"I am from the AFP office and I saw you up there just now," I explained.

"Yes, I did saw you zere. Is anysing wrong?"

"Can you please tell me why Alex cannot come to work today? Perhaps you could explain over a coffee…"

We sat down at a nearby café and talked. "Alexander is a soldier…a how you say—reserve? Zis morning he got call to report to ze army. We don't understant why zis order is comink."

"When must he go to the army? When should he report?"

"He has gone alreddi. I don't know ven I vill see him again – or if I vill see him again." Tears sprang to her eyes. As we drank our coffees, I could hear the rumbling of heavy trucks. Four army lorries, packed tightly with soldiers passed down the road in an easterly direction.

I added two and two and perhaps made six. I did not dare ask Serge to telephone the Ministry of Defence to check on troop movements. They wouldn't have provided him with any useable answer and if they had done, I would not have wanted him to flash the news round the agency wires.

I took the risk and disclosed that Tito had mobilised the Yugoslav army and sent it to the border with Rumania. It was a precaution – in case Russia decided to send more Warsaw Pact tanks in Yugoslavia's direction. Tito was no friend of the Soviets and had made no secret of his disdain for what Russia had done to Czechoslovakia.

My story made the "splash". The foreign desk telephoned me at my hotel to let me know. It was now my turn to sweat. I had taken a big risk and I fully expected Tito's police to knock on my room door during the night and whisk me away for breaking some top secret event. I read a novel most of the night – but no knock came. My story had been picked up by most other British newspapers and the next day it was announced officially in Belgrade. The word "scoop" is not often used these days. One tends to speak more in terms of "exclusive". But Ricky Marsh used it and cabled me a brief: "Thanks for scoop. Congratulations. Marsh."

I did not spend a great deal of time at my hotel. There was too much to do – and I managed to get more Belgrade-dateline reports in the paper about the Czechoslovak crisis than my poor colleague in Prague. He found it difficult to telephone or cable stories, thanks to an almost total communications clampdown.

Every night I came to the hotel, one of the porters would approach me to ask if there was anything I wanted, anything I needed. "Ah, Mr Izbitzki," he would say, using the correct pronunciation, "I have something very special for you this evening. A beautiful young blonde lady. Very lovely. Would you not like her to keep you company?"

"No thank you. Very kind, but no thank you," I would respond with a smile. No point in being angry with the man.

On other occasions he would offer a brunette, a redhead, a dark-haired girl with big breasts. And each time I would smile sweetly and thank him – but no thank you.

Then one evening he came up to me and said: "Mr Izbitzki, please let me apologise to you."

"Apologise? What for?"

"I have made suggestions to you for young women and you did not wish them to keep you company. I am very foolish man. Please forgive me."

"Well, of course you are forgiven. Don't even think about it," I said magnanimously.

"Yes, Sir, but tonight I have for you something very, very special: a young boy...just 18 years old..."

This time I did display some anger. "I am not interested. Do understand that and don't give me any more suggestions. I don't wish to have any company." And I left him standing there, looking quite forlorn.

I had heard of these "offers". Nine times out of ten, these hotel porters were working for the secret police and the prostitutes, male or female, they were "offering" were being employed for later blackmail purposes. When Ronnie Payne, my friend and colleague, found himself on a reporting job in Poland, he entered his hotel room late one night to find one of these beautiful, curvaceous blondes in his bed. Ronnie had his wits about him, apologised and left the room. He returned to the reception desk and complained: "There's a woman in my room. I don't know how the hell she got in there but she has obviously gone to the wrong room. Please see that she leaves immediately."

Had he succumbed, a photographer would have interrupted proceedings as they reached a climax and he would have been threatened later with having the pictures sent to his editor or his wife...unless he agreed to write stories for them and be generously paid for them. Maureen and I had discussed such a possibility and I said that if some pictures of such a situation were presented to me, I would say: "Oh, I'll have one of these – and two of these, enlarged please!"

But it never happened.

I returned home just in time to pack my bags again and fly to Berlin, cross Checkpoint Charlie into the Soviet Sector where the guards already knew about me once they had inspected my passport. A big black Volga limousine (by East German standards) complete with chauffeur awaited me. The driver, whose name turned out to be Helmut Schwantze, drove me to the Linden Hotel, close to Friedrichstrasse S-Bahn (overhead railway) station and diagonally across from the Unter den Linden, where, as a child, I used to watch many a Nazi parade with wide-eyed admiration. I even used to give the Nazi salute as did the many hundreds of Berliners who thronged the wide pavements. The day I arrived at the hotel, all was quiet and the streets were almost deserted. No loud marching music; no goose-stepping; no cheers of *Heil Hitler*.

Although the hotel gave an impression of grandeur from the outside, inside it was gloomy to a point of grimness. A porter silently and ungraciously carried my bags to my room on the second floor. I followed him along a narrow, dimly lit corridor that seemed to go for ever, with doors on each side. At last we reached room 264. Like the rest of the place, it was dark even with all the lights on. I handed the porter a couple of (East German) Marks which he took with a scowl.

"Don't you have any West German Marks or American dollars?" he said without a thank you or a please. I did have both as well as some British pounds, but I shook my head. "Don't you want your own country's good money?" I asked him grimly. He must have thought I was a true Communist, so he immediately excused himself. "So sorry, mein Herr, of course this is very good. Thank you. I meant no harm." And he was gone.

This, I thought, was going to be an interesting trip.

I did not meet up with my "interpreter" until the following morning, so I left the hotel to make an important visit. My mother's youngest brother, Georg, had gone out with a pretty German girl who was, according to my mother, madly in love with him. She wasn't Jewish but wanted to marry him. But Georg turned her down – not because he did not love her but because he knew that to marry her would mean trouble and possible death for her.

In 1938, about a year before our own departure from Berlin, he packed a couple of bags, jumped on his motorbike (he had always been a keen biker) and raced off to Holland, waving a visa he had just obtained. Once there, he met and married a Jewish doctor. Together they had a child, a little girl whom they named Beatrix, after the eldest daughter of Queen Juliana. Beatrix was about the same age as the child who was to become Queen of the Netherlands when her mother abdicated many years later.

Georg thought he was safe. But when the Nazis marched into Holland, he, his wife and their lovely child were rounded up together with other Jews and sent to Auschwitz. We never saw them again.

I had to go and pay a visit to his beloved Lonni who was alive and well and living just off the Frankfurter Allee, one of East Berlin's "show" avenues. She had married Otto Liese, whom I was to meet for the first time that day.

I grabbed a taxi and gave him the name of the street where they lived but was careful not to give the number of the house in which they had a small apartment. I made sure that the taxi had disappeared and that I was not followed before I approached the house and rang their bell. It was an emotional meeting. Lonni had only seen me as a little boy and immediately burst into tears. "Oh my God, you look so much like Georg. And I can see your mother in you." And she hugged me.

Lonni was elderly. Otto had only one leg. Over coffee (a weak version of Nescafé) he told me that he had lost his leg in the war and had now retired from work. He used to punch tickets at the U-Bahn (East Berlin's underground trains). Lonni used to work for a baker's from dawn until late afternoon, seeing loaves from the ovens onto the shelves.

From her I obtained my first story – a story which was to get me banned from any future visits to East Germany while it was still the DDR.

Lonni's mother and the rest of her family of brothers and sisters lived in West Berlin. They had not seen one another for seven years, not since the Wall went up in 1961. The West Berlin house where they lived was a matter of four kilometres from the East Berlin apartment. One could have walked the distance but the Wall was in the way.

Her mother became dangerously ill and Lonni asked permission of the authorities to go and visit her. She was ordered to go and see a doctor who examined her to make sure her health was reasonable and her head was not falling off her shoulders. Permission to see her mother was rejected.

Three months later, her mother died. Lonni again asked permission to attend the funeral. This time, she was visited by a *Volkspolizistin* (a policewoman) who spent nearly two hours at the apartment explaining why Lonni should not really want to go to the funeral. Had she been over 60 and retired or if the doctor had found her to be too ill to work, permission would have been readily given.

But Otto, who was over 65 and fully retired, was allowed to go in her place. It was like the Queen sending Philip to represent her at some dignitary's funeral.

Lonni then said: "*Hier ist das einzige Land der Welt, wo man sich freut alt zu werden!*" It struck me like poetry and translated as: "This is the only country in the world where one looks forward to growing old!" In other words, if you are too old to work, then you can leave this godforsaken place and not before.

It was that one sentence put into the mouth of an anonymous woman that brought me the ban, to which I shall return.

Günter Schnabel, my interpreter, collected me from the hotel the next morning. His English was excellent – a young man who had not long left college and whose spectacles kept sliding down his little nose. He was amusing and was most anxious to be helpful. Yet I distrusted him from the start. He had to be a member of the Stasi, the secret police, who would make sure that I did not trespass into any high security places.

One day as we were travelling along the Autobahn to Karl Marx Stadt, an entire convoy of tanks and armoured cars were rolling along the lanes going in the opposite direction. It was clear to me that here were vehicles from the Warsaw Pact which had been active in or around Czechoslovakia. I sat up and focused my camera at the convoy.

At this, Günter grew almost wild, tearing the camera from my hands and shouting: "What are you here for, Herr Izbicki? You are not here to look at these things. They are of no interest to you – or are they?"

I felt myself turning red. "What the hell?" I said. "Listen, if I was driving along one of our motorways and saw a whole lot of tanks passing on the other side, I would stop the car, get out and take as many fucking pictures as I'd want! This is not bloody spying, you idiot, this is pure human interest!"

I have always found with Germans that the louder you shout at them, the greater the effect. Even as a student, I would shout at customs officers who were trying to confiscate a food parcel my mother had sent me. I shouted back louder – and it worked. I was allowed to go with the parcel and was never shouted at again. So it was also with Günter. He immediately apologised and explained that he could not allow me to take photographs of such delicate things as military movements.

The driver meanwhile took no notice but continued to drive us to our destination.

Günter accompanied me everywhere. He was a real charmer, forever smiling and desperate to be helpful – so much so that I was now really convinced he was a member of the dreaded Stasi. I had to watch my step and be economical with my criticisms of what I saw and heard. Helmut, the driver, avoided anything that was remotely connected with the East German military. Only once could I see an army camp at the other end of a long road along which we were travelling. Helmut stopped the car at once, apologised for having taken the wrong way, turned round and went another, much longer way to reach our destination.

Slogans such as *Kämpft für den Frieden* (Fight for Peace) appeared at regular intervals and every town was equipped with loudspeakers attached to the lamp posts of squares and main shopping streets. Music, mostly marches, blared from them and from time to time, announcements were made concerning important meetings or concerts.

At Karl Marx Stadt, I was introduced to the mayor, a buxom lady who shook my hand so hard that I thought it would surely fracture. She showed me round the new part of town, including a block of apartments. "Our workpeople live in such apartments for a very small rent," she told me in excellent English (she was an English teacher when she wasn't doing her civic duties). The flats were unquestionably comfortable. All of them were furnished with exactly the same sofas, beds, cupboards, tables, chairs and so on and painted in exactly the same colours. I supposed our own council flats might be similar if they were ever furnished by the councils.

As we left the block, I asked her about the television aerials that protruded from each roof. "All these apartments have television sets," I said. "Most of them do, yes, but we do not supply these. They are bought by the tenants."

"The aerials look quite good. I suppose they would pick up all kinds of channels, wouldn't they?"

She understood immediately what I meant to imply. She looked at me, smiled broadly and said: "Oh yes, they can see the programmes from the West. But I think most of them don't bother. Western television is such rubbish."

What little I managed to see of East German television was certainly rubbish and much of it had some kind of political message.

One night, Günter and I went to a "night club". It wasn't really a night club as we understand it but a dance hall with a reasonably decent little band playing "normal" dance music (nothing even remotely like rock and roll). Snack food was on sale (sausages, cheese sandwiches, that sort of thing). We shared a little table with a young couple and I engaged them immediately in conversation. I bought a bottle of wine and filled four glasses (they were only able to afford soft drinks, some sort of lemonade). He was a plumber; she was an assistant in a local haberdashers. They had one child, a little girl of six who had just started school and was being looked after that evening by his mother who lived with them. They were happy, but would have liked a bigger apartment. Their daughter was sharing their room and grandma was in the second bedroom.

"The rent is not high, but if we moved to something bigger – if we could get a bigger apartment, which not everyone can – it would cost more in rent of course," the woman, a slim blonde with shapely breasts and good legs, told me. We discussed their everyday lives – even the food they ate. "We can only afford the ersatz coffee. Hans (the husband) loves proper coffee but that's just impossible except for very special occasions, like birthdays and Christmas."

Günter, who had been ogling the young woman, plucked up the courage and asked her to come and dance. Hans just smiled his consent, so off they went. I felt in my back pocket and took out a West German 10 DM note. I knew that if Günter or for that matter anyone from the police saw what I was about to do, I would be in serious trouble. I spoke quietly to Hans. "Listen, I'd like to give you a little present so that you can get yourself some real coffee and perhaps a little something for your daughter. But please you must say absolutely nothing to the person who is accompanying me and who is dancing with your wife. Please don't even thank me. No one else should see or hear anything. Is that all right?"

Hans looked around him and over to the dance floor where his wife and Günter seemed to be enjoying their dance, then back to me. The light was quite dim but I could see him blushing. He was clearly embarrassed, but just nodded his head as I slipped him the note. He pulled a handkerchief from his pocket, blew his nose and replaced it together with the note in his pocket. Cleverly done.

Half an hour or so after the dancers returned, we left. Günter would have liked to have stayed on and danced some more with the blonde, but I said I was tired and wanted to turn in. We had a couple of busy days ahead of us. I felt I had done my good deed for the day and the warmth with which Hans shook my hand as we said goodbye was thanks enough.

Our next stop was Weimar. This remarkably beautiful little town has always been famed for the expansion of German culture. It became the home of such literary giants as Goethe and Schiller, the poet and preacher Herder, the philosopher Nietzsche, the genius composer Johann Sebastian Bach and even the Hungarian musician Franz Liszt who moved to Weimar to direct its opera and orchestra. The gifted architects of the Bauhaus school were also settled in the town. Indeed, so great was its reputation that it even became the seat of Germany's government following World War One.

Rooms at the *Hotel Elephant*, one of the finest in that part of the country were reserved for us and the Saturday evening meal was certainly among the best I ate throughout my three-week stay in East Germany. We had arrived there on a Saturday and shops were closed in the afternoon but I noticed the churches and admired the architecture – and concocted a little plan which I hoped to execute the following day.

On the Sunday I awoke at dawn, quietly showered, shaved and dressed and left the hotel before 7 a.m. in the knowledge that, on a Sunday, my accompanists were unlikely to be awake before eight. For once I thought I'd lose them.

I had noted the times of church services and by 7.30 had entered Saints Peter and Paul, the Protestant church – or the Herderkirche as it is better known in honour of the poet who was its pastor for some 30 years. There were not many people in the congregation. They stared at me, a stranger in their midst, but left me alone in the otherwise empty pew. It was a very ordinary service, lasting not more than half an hour, including two hymns sung halfheartedly. The 10-minute sermon praised goodness and hard work. It was boring.

The Roman Catholic church was a matter of 400 meters of brisk walk from the Protestant and the service had already started by the time I walked in at about 8.20. It was packed and I joined those standing at the back. It was mainly in Latin and, as I had often joined Maureen at church before the mass started to be celebrated in the language of the country, I was able to follow it with ease. Hymns were sung in German. The sermon, too, was in German and lasted a good 20 minutes. And what a sermon it was! The priest took as his theme: "Give unto God what is God's and unto Caesar what is Caesar's". He pulled no punches, decrying the demands of the State to ignore or even to defy God and the Church. He was careful not to become too political but made his message very clear.

After the mass had ended and the church was emptying of its flock, I approached the priest and complimented him on his excellent sermon. It pleased him to hear such praise. It was apparently rare. "But you are not one of my parishioners, are you, my son?" he said.

"No father..." and I introduced myself by saying that I had that morning "escaped" from the people who accompanied me round the DDR. "They will show me only the things that they want me to see."

The priest touched my arm gently and said: "My son, when you invite someone into your home, you do not show them the untidy rooms."

It was a quote that has stuck with me ever since.

Naturally, both Günter and Helmut were furious when I did not turn up for breakfast. One or other had gone to bang on my door and even asked for it to be opened. My absence from the hotel was a sign of their failure and when I returned, I was cross-examined in no uncertain terms.

"Herr Izbicki," said Günter, "you must surely know that to go out on your own without letting me or Helmut know where you are going, is not, repeat not acceptable."

He had learned to call me John so his use of the formal address reflected his fury. But I was not to be bullied.

"Come, come, Günter, why are you being so ridiculously afraid? Do you think I had gone off to photograph some stupid military installation? I thought I'd let you sleep in for a bit. It's Sunday, damn it. Sunday. A day of rest. Anyway, I just went to church. Surely there's nothing wrong with that!"

Günter even managed to look crestfallen. "Ach, why did you not tell us you wanted to go to church, John? We could have taken you..."

"That's just plain ridiculous. I'm a grown man, not a little boy who might get lost between the hotel and the church. I can get there and back by myself and don't need a nanny to take me by the hand. And now, if you have no objections, I shall sit down and order a coffee."

I knew that we did not have any plan until after lunch. Then we would take a journey of just five kilometres from the hotel.

At 2 p.m. Helmut drove us those five kilometres into a dense and beautiful forest of tall beech trees. It was heavenly and resounded to a melodious chorus of birdsong.

A little way through the forest was a sudden clearing overshadowed by a huge memorial commemorating a camp that opened up before us. It was Buchenwald, one of Hitler's most notorious death camps, where many thousands of Jews were murdered.

We walked through its barracks in silence. Only later did we realise that there was nothing but silence throughout this concentration camp. Nothing lived there – no birds sang, no rabbits ran around its grassy banks, not even a worm could be seen in the soil. Only the ghosts of those who had been imprisoned for no other reason than that they were Jews or homosexuals or gypsies, people whose homes and whose identities had been torn from them.

That evening I excused myself. I could not face a dinner at the *Elephant*. That night I had a nightmare. People surrounded me with their hands outstretched, begging for food and I had nothing to give them. They were dying in front of me and there was nothing I could do to help them survive. I awoke in a cold sweat.

For two hours I lay awake and thought of the schizophrenia that was Nazi Germany, where Beethoven and Buchenwald, Brahms and Belsen, Schiller, Schopenhauer and Auschwitz go hand in hand across the pages of history.

What was I doing in such a land?

Some days later we were visiting a farm and I was shown how cows were artificially inseminated. We were all standing inside a large barn facing a row of cows on the other side of a desk on which stood a microscope and a variety of instruments.

"Here, take a look at this in the microscope," the farmer said and beckoned me to come closer.

"Thank you," I said and turned to give my notebook to Helmut to hold while I freed myself to look at the fascinating slide and the sperm upon it. It really was interesting. "You should also look at this, Günter," I said and turned round to speak to him. To my amazement and I have to admit, my horror, I saw Helmut flicking through the pages of my notebook.

Now Helmut was the driver who could not speak or understand a single word of English. Normally, everyone, no matter in what country, be it Japan or France or Russia or Germany – everyone is able to conjure up the odd word of English, if only "hello" or "Manchester United". But Helmut could not even say "goodbye". Yet here he was studying what I had written – in English.

I had been wrong all along. Helmut was the man from the Stasi, not Günter.

This became even clearer when we were all back in East Berlin and I was ready to return through Checkpoint Charlie to the West. Günter came up to me, threw his arms about me and said: "Oh, John, I wish you had just a little corner in your suitcase to take me with you!"

Back home at long last – just in time for Paul's fourth birthday on November 25 and Christmas a month later. It had been a vintage year, what with the riots and strikes of France and the tear gas of Paris, the invasion of Czechoslovakia by Soviet and Warsaw Pact tanks and the watch from Belgrade, and finally my 3,000-kilometre tour of the so-called German Democratic Republic where people looked forward to growing old.

As my father always said: "You can go East; you can go West; but in the end, Home is best". We were a family again. Paul had grown at least two more inches since I had been away. One evening, we were all sitting and cuddling together when Paul suddenly excused himself, ran out of the room and returned clutching a box of chocolates that was almost as big as he was. Someone, it appears, had bought him, toddler that he was, a box of chocs. He struggled to open it and at last came over to me, holding it open:

"Have a choc'lit, John" (he always called me John…because "that's what everyone calls you!").

"Ah, thank you very much darling, but ladies first," I said pointing to Maureen.

"No," he replied earnestly. "You first. You're the visitor."

Oh, my God. It's time to change jobs for something a little quieter, I thought.

CHAPTER FIFTEEN:

ON TO EDUCATION

Many a true word comes from the mouths of infants. Paul's three little words: "You're the visitor", stabbed me close to the heart. I really could not neglect my family any more. I could certainly not step into Blake Baker's shoes when he retired. I really could not burn the candle at both ends in Industrial, door stepping at Number 10 until four in the morning and being back there again just a few hours later. There had to be something better. Something easier.

If there was one job I should really have loved to do more than any other it was to be theatre critic. There was a vacancy for a Number Two and I went down to the First Floor and knocked on Colin Welch's door. Colin was deputy editor and spoke the clearest English but sounded as though he had plums in his mouth. He also possessed a great sense of humour. It was Welch who invented the Peter Simple column, a daily piece of hilarious satire.

Colin Welch was probably the most natural off-the-cuff ad-libber I have ever met. He would shock without any intentions at deliberate nastiness. For instance, when he was told that John Lennon of The Beatles had been shot dead in New York in 1980, he said: "One down, three to go."

Peter Simple was born on 18th October 1955 and, although it always went under the title *Way of the World*, it was signed Peter Simple and readers actually thought he was a real person and would write to "Dear Mr Simple". When Colin Welch became deputy editor in 1964, he handed the column over to a newcomer, Michael Wharton, who was already 44 when he joined the *Telegraph*. Michael was the son of an unsuccessful businessman of

German-Jewish origin and possessed the *chayn* and *chutzpah* of Yiddish humour which he injected into Peter Simple from New Year's Day, 1957 until just before his death 50 years later.

I knocked and entered. "Ah, John Izbicki. I suppose you've come to see me about a raise in salary…"

"No…Good God, no. Worse. I've come to see you about a possible job change."

"My turn: good God, why? You seem to be doing more than quite well with Baker and could well be trying on his shoes soon…"

"I know. That's why. I don't think I'd want to spend the rest of my days here in Industrial and wondered if I might be able to try something else."

"Something else, eh. Well, what else were you contemplating John? You don't want to replace poor old Michael Wharton, do you?"

"Certainly not, Colin. Michael is doing a superb job and I'd never ever be able to approach his wit."

"So what did you have in mind?"

I swallowed hard and said: "I'd like to join the Arts Page and do some theatre reviews, please."

He sat back in his swivel chair sucking in air and drumming his fingers on his polished desk. At last he looked at me and said: "Right. So go away and let me have your CV showing me that you know what you might be taking on – if, that is, you take it on."

The interview was over and I went back to my office to type out the CV he wanted. I told him about my acting and directing experience, from the time Dame Sybil Thorndike offered to propose me for a RADA scholarship while I was still at school, to my various acting parts and my translating and directing of the Franz Wedekind play at university (Colin Welch spoke fluent German and I thought that might impress him), to my reviews in the Canal Zone of Egypt and my acting in *Reluctant Heroes* there, and my various acting parts at the Mountview Theatre Club in Crouch End. I did not spare any details and the account dragged on for four pages.

Two days later, I received Colin's reply. It consisted of seven words: "Have you tried selling the film rights?" It was to the point and, although I felt disappointed, I had to laugh.

But not all was lost. It was obvious that Colin had spoken to Jack Hill, the News Editor and must have mentioned my reluctance to stay in Industrial, for Jack called me down to see him. Jack sat at the head of a busy, noisy newsroom on the first floor of the building.

He came to the point at once. "I hear you're not happy in Industrial, John.

How would you fancy Education?"

I was completely taken by surprise. Education? I had never for one solitary moment even considered Education. I had to catch my breath. "Er – Education, Jack? I don't quite understand. There are already two people doing it. What's happening to Jim Dawson and David Fletcher?" James Dawson, who looked for all the world like the headmaster of a public school, was always well dressed in a three-piece suit, a sober tie and highly polished shoes, and always sat earnest and upright as if to attention at his desk in the newsroom, typing methodically away at some story or other. Opposite him was his number two – David Fletcher, an equally earnest young man, who produced some excellent stories in the paper.

Jack Hill said quietly: "Dawson is about to retire and we thought you might take over as education correspondent, if you think that would suit."

"But what about David Fletcher? You surely can't just appoint me over his head. He'll be furious – and I wouldn't blame him."

Jack just looked at me and eventually said quietly – but then he always spoke quietly, even if there was a news crisis – "Don't worry about David. Let me worry about that.

Anyway, you don't need to decide straight away. Take a couple of days to think it over. Let me know by Monday. All right?"

Education? I started sifting the paper for every education story that was published over the past two or three months. I had always been interested in schools and had even toyed with the idea of teaching. Indeed, I did teach for some weeks at a secondary school in Manchester, just before I moved to Göttingen to study at its university for a year as part of my Nottingham University degree course. I had thoroughly enjoyed it. Would I also enjoy writing about education day in day out?

Of one thing I was certain: I would not be required to do a great deal of doorstepping as with Industrial. I would have lots of free time and be able to spend it at home with Maureen and Paul. Ah, bliss! I might even be able to return to the Mountview for some juicy parts on the boards. Education? It'll be like a rest cure!

How wrong, how very wrong I was to have such thoughts.

Luckily, David Fletcher and I got on well. It could have all gone pear-shaped, with me being appointed over his head as it were. Although David could not have been happy about the situation, he was professional enough to accept it and realize that it was none of my doing. Between us, we covered the vast subject of education and filled more square column inches than the correspondents of any other paper.

No sooner had I settled in the education correspondent's seat in April 1969, than all hell was let loose, first at the London School of Economics. Robin Blackburn, a lecturer, had been suspended in a row over the pay and conditions of technical staffs, and lecturers signed petitions demanding the resignation of Lord Robbins, chairman of the LSE governors and its director Dr Walter Adams. Onto the stage pranced Clive Jenkins, leader of the Association of Scientific, Technical and Managerial Staffs (ASTMS) to defend Blackburn at his tribunal and support the rest of the LSE staffs. The entire matter was later to be referred to Barbara Castle, Secretary for Employment and Productivity. I also already knew Clive Jenkins from my years in Industrial, when I had dubbed him the "troubleshooter supreme" when he handled the peace negotiations of a BOAC pilots' strike.

Close at heel came a bitterly fought dispute in Durham where 63 teachers had been suspended for "working to rule". Their union, the National Association of Schoolmasters (NAS) was fighting to reinstate them on full back pay or there would be an all-out strike by the city's 42,000 NAS members. Then, London teachers marched through the city's streets to Parliament demanding an increase in their London Allowance pay. The National Union of Teachers (NUT, biggest of the teaching unions) as well as the NAS gave the teachers their full support.

This industrial action meant that my inauguration into Education turned out to be an action replay of the position I had played in Industrial. That football refused to be kicked out of the arena. My dream of coming home early to spend more time with Maureen and Paul was resoundingly dashed.

Aubrey Jones who chaired the National Board for Prices and Incomes, was another leading character who straddled both the industrial and educational fields, having tried to impose strict income ceilings, not only for BOAC pilots, bank employees and ICI workers but also university teachers.

I recall one Transport Workers' delegate at a TUC conference speaking vehemently against the board's incomes policy: "Brothers," he declared into the microphone, "always remember that three-and-a-half percent on top of nothing is bugger all!"

I, for one, have always remembered it.

Even the usually taciturn National Association of Head Teachers (NAHT) broached the topic of strikes, demanding the introduction of smaller class sizes – or else. The call came at the NAHT's annual conference of 1969, a conference held during Whit Week each year. Heads also complained against the "abysmal" quality of new teachers entering the profession.

This was all new to me – and it was to be repeated year in, year out for the 18 years I spent as head of the *Telegraph*'s Education department.

The first Secretary of State for Education during my time in education was Edward Short. Much to my regret, I had just missed Patrick Gordon-Walker who preceded Short. I had the greatest respect for Gordon-Walker, not because I considered him an effective politician or even a good socialist, but because I remembered hearing him speak regularly on the radio in the early, dangerous days we spent in England. His voice gave my parents and me the courage to continue smiling throughout the Blitz when Nazi bombs cascaded down on London, destroying all in their path. He spoke in fluent German on the BBC's German Service. Strangely, I couldn't remember any of the themes of his talks and still can't.

Ted Short was 26 when World War Two started. He joined the Durham Light Infantry and served the war as a Captain. After the war he decided to teach and by 1947 had made it to headmaster of a secondary modern school – the Princess Louise County Secondary School at Blyth, Northumberland. It was clear from the start that he knew education, not as a politician but as a practitioner. Yet he made mistakes, not the least of which was to describe the publication of the first batch of *Black Papers* as "one of the blackest days for education in the last 100 years".

That terse and quite unjust description turned *Black Paper I* into a best seller. I doubt if this or its subsequent editions would ever have found the notoriety they did had Short ignored it altogether. The first two were edited by Brian Cox, a Professor of English at Manchester University, and Antony Dyson, a lecturer at the University of East Anglia who later resigned, took the cloth and lived on as a popular vicar.

In brief, the *Black Papers* were an attack on the way comprehensive schools were being run, on "discovery methods" of teaching, on egalitarianism, on expansion in higher education and so on.

One needed only to look at some of the chapter headings and their authors to understand what these papers were all about: *The Egalitarian Threat* by Angus Maude; *The Mental Differences between Children* by Cyril Burt*; *Undotheboys Hall* by Robert Conquest; *Pernicious Participation* by Kingsley Amis; *Student Problems in Edinburgh and Beyond* by Michael Swann and others.

---

* This one created a major row following Burt's death in 1971 when it was revealed that he had fabricated research figures to suit his thesis, rejecting the effect of the environment on children's mental capabilities.

One of the contributors was the headmaster of a successful London comprehensive school – a Dr Rhodes Boyson. Boyson was to edit the fourth and final edition of *Black Papers* prior to resigning his headship and entering Parliament as a Tory MP for Brent North. He eventually became a Minister of Education under Margaret Thatcher's premiership.

Anything remotely connected with the *Black Papers* or any of its authors was resoundingly attacked by the Left as reactionary, even fascist. Yet by 1976, when James Callaghan took up the reigns of the Labour government, he paraphrased many of the criticisms contained in those books – that taxpayers' money was being resoundingly wasted on educational claptrap, that standards in schools and universities were too low and that children were being deprived of their rights to basic literacy and numeracy. He ordered his Secretary of State for Education, Shirley Williams, to run a national debate on education.

Rhodes Boyson and Brian Cox, in their final introduction to the *Black Papers*, recalled Ted Short's original "blackest days" description of the *Papers*. Yet the *Times Educational Supplement*, in reporting Callaghan's speech at Ruskin College, said: "He has gathered his *Black Paper* cloak around him".

The Boyson-Cox intro then explained the reason, as they saw it, for the strange "change of heart" and wrote: "In 1969, the contributors to the *Black Papers* were treated with abuse and contempt, but their stand gave heart to many teachers who knew from their own experience that informal methods were not working. As the years passed by, the evidence that standards were declining became overwhelming."

Much later on still, when a so-called New Labour prime minister came onto the scene, the outpourings of the *Black Paper* Tories became almost gospel. Tony Blair's mantra *"Education, Education, Education"* prompted one education secretary after another to introduce legislation echoing the once-abused pronouncements of the *Black Papers*. Indeed, things changed rapidly. The *Black Papers* disappeared, swallowed up by the mists of time, and were rarely mentioned. My own postscript to them came in 1998 when I was invited to address an adult audience in Camden on *"Education – Yesterday, Today and Tomorrow"*. It was a full house and I spoke of the way that education had changed over the years. I naturally included in some detail the publication of the *Black Papers* and the turmoil they had caused and how things had changed since those stormy days.

During question time, a black lady towards the back of the audience stood up to have a go at me. "How do you think I felt sitting back here to hear you going on about black papers. You should be ashamed of yourself using these terms…"

She went on in this vein for a while. Clearly, she had understood nothing other than that the word "black" had been used and that it was somehow detrimental.

"Madam," I countered once I was able to get a word in. "Madam, *Black Papers* was the title of a series of books dealing with education. I am not prepared to change the title of a published work simply because you object to the word black…" She walked out to applause. Political correctness had entered the scene and would help to muddy the waters.

But I have digressed…

Apart from the second edition of the *Black Papers*, the coverage of one particular story brought me to the point of resignation – and I hadn't even been in my new job more than a few months. It involved a series of sex education film strips produced by the BBC and aimed at children aged eight and nine. A preview of the films was shown to education correspondents at Broadcasting House and the general view was positive. The strips comprised colorful drawings of birth from little lambs being born to a man and a woman making love. Both were lying in a bed with the sheets drawn up to their chins, the man on top of the woman. A voice over gently explained what was going on, while another picture showed diagrams of what was happening to the man's sperm and the woman's egg. Straightforward drawings of a naked man and woman showing in graphic form the journey of the sperm to the ovaries formed another picture.

Two people objected strongly. The first was Mrs Mary Whitehouse, whom I admired a great deal. She was secretary of the National Viewers and Listeners' Association, a watchdog body she had created to keep tabs on what was being performed on television and radio. I always sided with her objections to violence, thoroughly agreeing that too much of it would simply dull our minds to such an extent that we would eventually be unable to differentiate between fact (such as the horrors of war, the torture of prisoners, Africans starving as a result of drought and so on) and fiction (such as vicious fights and killings). I could not go along with her on her constant objections to virtually anything dealing with sex. In the case of the film strips, Mrs Whitehouse saw red because the woman in bed with the man had her left arm dangling from the bed – and there was no wedding ring upon her finger.

The other objection came from a Dr Louise Eickhoff, a Birmingham child psychiatrist. She protested against the series on the grounds that sex education delivered in schools had a "poisoning effect on children's lives". She demanded that the series and all forms of sex education in schools should be banned by law.

The story was given the "splash" treatment, leading the paper's front page. But, whereas I had downplayed both Mary Whitehouse's and Dr Eickhoff's protests, the sub-editors had brought them to the top of the story, blowing both up out of all proportions. It was a typical piece of *Telegraph* editing and I was furious when I read it the following morning. As soon as I arrived at the office, I typed out my resignation and sent it down to Peter Eastwood. I was called down to see him almost immediately.

"Come, come, John, aren't you over-reacting about this?" he began.

"I really don't think so. If anyone over-reacted, it was Mary Whitehouse, Louise Eickhoff and whoever subbed my copy. I firmly believe that I placed their objections in the right place, somewhere near the end of the story. Many parents were shown the strip – as I also rightly pointed out in the piece – and were perfectly happy for it to be shown to their children."

"All, right, all right, I hear you, but that's still no reason to resign just when you're doing so well. Look, I want you to get back to the story tonight and tell readers what you yourself think about this film or whatever it is. Now run along and don't let me hear any more about resignations."

The matter, as far as the managing editor was concerned, was closed. I did get back to the story and got in a line saying that the film was extremely delicately handled, that Mrs Whitehouse and Dr Eickhoff had both clearly over-reacted and that I should have no objections to my own child, then still aged under five, seeing the film.

The story was published without a single alteration (clearly by order of Eastwood).

In those days, teacher salaries were fixed by the Burnham Committee – another echo of my industrial reporting days of doorstepping and running from one side to the other to hear as many arguments as possible. The Burnham management committee was made up of representatives from the various local authority associations whereas the teachers were represented by their various unions. The bigger the union, the bigger the number of representatives. So the National Union of Teachers (NUT) which had a membership of some 232,000 in-service teachers, held the biggest number of votes on the teachers' side of Burnham with 16 members; the second biggest of the unions, the National Association of Schoolmasters, who later amalgamated with the Union of Women Teachers, had more than 100,000 members and, therefore, the second highest say-so in Burnham, having just six votes.

Then there were the also-rans – the Assistant Masters Association which was shortly to join up with the Association of Assistant Mistresses, and had four votes; the National Association of Head Teachers, representing about two-thirds of all primary and secondary schools, had more than 19,000 members and two votes.

The NUT and the NAS/UWT were always at daggers drawn and it was clear that, whichever way the NUT voted within Burnham, none of the others could drum up enough votes to beat them. It was considered quite unfair that the NUT, whose membership was only 2.4 times as big as its NAS/UWT rivals, should have 5.3 times as many members on Burnham as its rivals.

What is more, the NUT had one additional ally – the National Association of Teachers in Further and Higher Education (NATFHE), which even had their offices at the same headquarters as the NUT – Hamilton House, near Euston Station. NATFHE represented some 40,000 lecturers in further education colleges, not schools, but still had a couple of votes to themselves. Naturally, they would always throw in those votes whenever the NUT needed them.

As for the Management Panel, it held a total of 27 votes, made up as follows: the Association of County Councils (13); the Association of Metropolitan Authorities (10); the Welsh local authorities (2) and, of course, the Department of Education and Science (DES) representing the government (2).

My introduction to the Burnham proceedings found me facing a massive strike by the teaching profession. It not only reminded me of those tough Industrial days (and nights) but also of my National Service time in Egypt and the bargaining that went on in the markets of Ismailia. There, the seller would ask for a price the buyer always considered far too high. A counter-offer would be made which the seller rejected as derisory. Only after the buyer walked away in disgust (his version of a strike) would the seller make a better offer.

The teachers had rejected as derisory an interim pay offer of £50 a year. They, in turn, had demanded an increase of £135 a year. To readers in the 21st century, this demand might seem more than reasonable. But in November 1969, it was considered crippling. At that time, some 35,000 teachers were earning less than £1,000 a year. After three years' training for a teaching qualification, the starting salary was a measly £860 a year. These teachers would have to wait two and a half years to reach a pay packet that would bring them £975. At the higher end of the scales, about 100 – mostly the head teachers of large comprehensive schools would earn a princely £4,000 a year.

These were the main reasons for all the haggling and the constant rejection by the local authorities – behind whom stood the Labour government and its representative, Ted Short, himself a former headmaster.

So the strikes went ahead in London, the Home Counties and eventually, throughout the land, hitting hundreds of schools and many thousands of children.

I continue to be convinced that those strikes, the first of their kind since the Depression of the early 1930s, were the major cause of widespread indiscipline in British classrooms. It was the first time that pupils were made aware what "Miss" and "Sir" were earning and that they were just like other workers, no different from the dockers, the miners and the transport workers. Youngsters suddenly realized that their own bigger brothers or sisters were earning more than the teachers they had always respected, whether or not they wielded a cane. Yet here they were demanding more money via their trade unions.

Why, not even the great Jarrow March of October 1936 – which had brought miners and shipbuilders walking from Durham to London to hammer home the case for the unemployed in the Great Depression – not even that great march had been joined by teachers. They were the only profession that remained at their desks – not for the money they continued earning, but for the sake of their pupils. That action blighted the profession's reputation as "scabs" in the North East for many decades to come.

On January 6, 1970, a feature titled *Why teachers are militant* began:

Militancy, a word that has rarely soiled the lips of the teaching profession, has within the past few months become common usage in the vocabulary of Britain's teachers. More than seven million children returning to school this week after their Christmas holidays will be wondering whether they are included in the next forced 'vacation' starting on Monday.

With the Burnham pre-Christmas offer (a teacher) could earn £1,255 a year and in London enjoy a further £85 'weighting'. A total of £1,340 a year does not sound bad for a beginner. But a man with a good honours degree has sweated through his university course for three years and then done a further 12 months' teacher training. It is not surprising that he may think twice before going into teaching when there are more tempting jobs available in industry. That is why there is a desperate shortage of science and maths teachers. Only one in every eight secondary schools enjoys the luxury of a graduate chemistry teacher.

For the *Daily Telegraph* to come out in support of teachers was almost revolutionary. The cynical amongst our more knowledgeable readers were beginning to mutter: "Well, of course, you realise that Izbicki's wife is a teacher. I suppose he daren't say anything different." But the teaching unions knew that they had found an ally within the Tory Press.

As far as I was concerned, neither party had got it right. Maureen never tried to influence my thinking, although she was a great source of factual information. Nor were the unions correct in their theory. I was certainly never their enemy. Yet I would criticize teachers and union leaders when I considered there was something to criticize and praise them when I considered them praiseworthy.

The crippling strikes were not settled until the following March, a struggle by 335,000 teachers that had lasted four months. It took nine hours of a heated row within the Burnham Committee and two personal interventions by Ted Short to ring a peace bell. The teachers had asked for £135 as an interim increase in salaries, based on the rise in the cost of living since July 1967. They eventually got £120 – just £10 a month or half a crown a week extra in their pay packets.

The delightful Ronnie Gould (Sir Ronald Gould, the retiring general secretary of the NUT) put the reaction succinctly: "It is just about acceptable, but it's not good enough for us to throw our hats up in the air."

Not everything David Fletcher and I reported involved school strikes. There were moments of blissful change. Towards the middle of January 1970, I received a phone call inviting me to come to a private showing of an American television show that was being shown to youngsters of five and six. It was being shown in a small studio in Wardour Street, home of movies, on a Saturday morning. I took Paul along with me. He had his fifth birthday on November 25, so was the right age for the movie.

It was called *Sesame Street* and Paul sat throughout almost mesmerized. I, too, enjoyed every one of the 58 minutes' duration. Here, I felt, was an educational show that deserved a British audience. If ever I am asked to name three events in my working life of which I feel proud, *Sesame Street* is certainly one of them.

I wrote an exclusive report about it, illustrated with cartoon stills from the show, and explained how it helped pre-school children to recognize letters. Indeed, many of the 6,000,000 American children who watched it were later able to start their first schools already able to read.

The programme was clearly based on commercials. The one Paul and I was shown had a short cartoon in the middle of which a voice boomed out: "This programme comes to you by courtesy of the letter W". The cartoon then continued by showing various things dealing with the letter W. It told the story of **W**anda the **W**itch who **W**ashed her **W**ig in the **W**ell on a **W**ednesday in **W**inter.

The show was born at a Los Angeles supermarket one Saturday, when a film cameraman took his three young children shopping. He was amazed when two of them, who were still too young for school and could not read, recognized and named certain branded goods, having seen them on TV commercials. It gave him the idea that, if one can sell cornflakes and beans, why not 'sell' literacy and numeracy the same way.

Monica Sims, then director of Children's Television and Kenneth Fawdrey, head of BBC Schools Broadcasts were all set to discuss the programme with David Connell, *Sesame Street*'s executive producer. Connell told me at the time that he had the greatest respect for the BBC's children's programmes, particularly *Play School*, *Blue Peter* and *Jackanory*. But Kenneth Fawdrey had his doubts. "Pre-school education is something very new indeed. I doubt whether we could put on a show of this kind for an hour a day," he said.

I persevered and kept reporting the reluctance of Auntie Beeb. Among the objections were that the show was "too American". Children would be baffled by the use of such words as "trash can" (for dustbin) and "cookie" (biscuit). Despite my telling them that my five-year-old son had understood every word perfectly and that children were able to recognize Americanisms because the BBC was showing lots of American movies watched by youngsters, Auntie stuck to her guns.

It looked as if the Izbicki campaign within the *Telegraph*'s pages was going to fail. This failure was underlined almost a year later – on November 25, Paul's sixth birthday – when I had to report that the BBC had rejected America's top-rated children's television programme. I quoted the Beeb's spokesman as saying: "Our schools television experts agree it [*Sesame Street*] is highly entertaining, but feel it is designed for an American audience. The social situation is different here. They are also not happy with the show from an educational point of view and don't like the constant music and fast pace."

The BBC was totally mistaken, even foolish to reject an undoubted winner. I did not give up my own attempts to bring this kiddies' laugh-in to Britain. I had to wait until the Spring of 1971 to be able to report that where the BBC had failed, ITV had won. *Sesame Street* had been shown experimentally each day for two weeks during April by Harlech Television. Mums in South Wales and the West Country sat down daily with their toddlers aged from three years to watch the hour-long show. The result saw many hundreds of letters pouring into the Independent Television Authority offices from parents and infant teachers unanimously praising the show and demanding more.

Most mothers expressed their total surprise that the programme had managed to hold the attention of their youngsters for such a long period of time. It was found that toddlers had managed to count to ten and recognized letters and entire words after only two weeks of viewing.

A confidential report, which the ITA sent to me, said that the programme showed that, as well as being of special value with immigrant groups and with children with deprived home backgrounds, it was also followed by children from other homes. Mothers and teachers found it "educationally excellent".

Sesame Street did not look back and the BBC must have blushed with composite shame to see this American gem hit the heights of TV charts not only in the UK but also in virtually every country in Europe. I later saw the programme in France, Spain, Italy and Germany, excellently translated and transcribed.

No sooner had the series of teacher strikes come to an end, when students started another round of militancy. It wasn't a repetition of the student riots of 1968, which swept through America and Europe, nor was the reason for it in any way similar. Just after the Christmas vacation of 1969, students claimed that universities were keeping "secret files" containing information about their political affiliations.

Warwick University held a two-week sit-in to protest against confidential files allegedly being kept by the vice-chancellor's office giving details of the politics followed by students and staff. Manchester University followed and more than 1,000 undergraduates invaded the administrative building. Sussex, Aston, Sheffield, Glasgow and Edinburgh also joined in the battle. Even Oxford undergraduates saw fit to occupy a room in the Clarendon building.

I travelled down to Oxford to see the action for myself. To my surprise I discovered Hilda Bullock, wife of Alan Bullock, Oxford's vice-chancellor, sitting on a stool outside the padlocked gates of the Clarendon. She was busily reading Sir Kenneth Clarke's beautiful work *Civilisation*. She told me with a glint in her eye: "I'm speaking for the moderates who never come forward to say anything. The moderates have taken so much from these wreckers. They just want to destroy society!"

Later, students at the University of Kent at Canterbury were presented with a £2,800 bill for damages caused during their sit-in and my own *alma mater*, Nottingham University, where 5,000 students had invaded the administrative block, took disciplinary action against the union for breaking and entering, theft, burglary and causing actual bodily harm (an assault on one of the stewards).

But after five months of this form of campus unrest, the moderates that Mrs Bullock had accused of never speaking out, cried "enough". A so-called third force movement calling itself "Put Education First" was formed by a group of twelve students, led by Tony Blake, president of Birkbeck College students union and vice-president elect of the National Union of Students. Support came from campuses throughout the country. "Students," said Blake, "should have a voice. But they should not use it only to destroy. Students have so much of value to give to the community."

My education portfolio at the *Telegraph* was getting heavier and heavier. The powers that be must have recognized this as they gave education an office of its own. It was fairly small, was stuck towards the back of the second floor and looked out onto and into the "well" of the building. But there was room for three desks, ample shelves and two big filing cabinets. And most luxurious of all, David Fletcher and I were to be given a secretary of our own – a veritable PA.

I interviewed several young women for the job and one not so young lady who was already working at the *Telegraph* – for Kenneth Rose, who wrote a weekly diary column for the *Sunday Telegraph*. It did not take me long to appoint Ettie Duncan, a Scot with a gentle Edinburgh accent. Ettie was, as the French say, "of a certain age". She was already a grandmother and was married to Denis Duncan, a minister of the kirk who used to edit a weekly newspaper north of the border. Ettie and I took to each other immediately and she acted, not only as a very efficient secretary but also as a kind of mother to David and me.

When she broke the news of a move to Kenneth Rose, he tried to make her change her mind. But her mind was perfectly made up. "In that case," exploded Rose, "you can bugger off!" She later confided in me: "He was not a very nice man."

Ettie was to stay with me for a little more than ten years.

David, on the other hand, did not stay and who could blame him? He decided to apply for the *Telegraph*'s Health and Social Services correspondent's job – and got it. It was a title he built up over the years with great distinction and, I am happy to say, remained my friend well into our respective retirements.

CHAPTER SIXTEEN:
THE THATCHER YEARS

The year was 1970. A general election brought a Tory government into power. Harold Wilson, with whom I had become reasonably acquainted during my time in industrial and labour relations, had to vacate 10 Downing Street along with his poetess wife, Mary, and make way for Edward Heath, who remained single and aloof.

Heath appointed a woman to be his Secretary of State for Education and Science. She had already been well groomed while in opposition, having been spokesman – or perhaps one should say spokeswoman – on Pensions and National Insurance in 1961; on Housing in 1965; the Treasury in 1966; Fuel and Power in 1967; Transport in 1968; and Education in 1969.

It was as Opposition spokes*person* on Education that I first got to know her – rather well. In May of that year, the National Association of Head Teachers invited Mrs Margaret Thatcher to be the guest of honour and speaker at its annual dinner. The association's conference was, as usual, during Whit Week, on this occasion at Scarborough, a town I have always found attractive. The dinner was at the St Nicholas Hotel on the night of Monday, May 25. Dress was formal *de rigeur* – dinner jackets and, for the ladies, long evening gowns. It was tradition to follow the dinner with dancing.

The Press, always well represented on these occasions, had already filed two stories: first, a report on the conference proceedings, when the 480 delegates representing the NAHT's 15,000 members had given a verbal caning to the country's education colleges for failing to teach teachers properly; and the second, a report of the speech the fairly new Shadow education secretary was delivering at the dinner. As usual, the media received copies in advance so that they may prepare their stories, with the proviso that they "check against (the speech's) delivery".

The association, led by its general secretary, David Hart, made two mistakes that evening. The first was to provide the Press with a large round table of its own instead of mixing reporters among the delegates, with whom they could speak, make new contacts and possibly even reap a few extra stories. Putting hacks together with waiters constantly fetching more bottles of wine and refilling their glasses was simply asking for trouble.

The second mistake was to have a long line of speakers getting their ten cents' worth in before coming to the highlight of the evening – the speech by the guest of honour. So we had the Mayor of Scarborough welcoming everyone to the town and giving us a 25-minute description of the many things one can do there in one's spare time. Then, the assistant president had his say. Then it was the turn of some MP or other. Then the president introduced the main speaker of the evening – and did so at some considerable length. By the time Margaret Thatcher stood up, it had gone 11 p.m. and people were beginning to stifle yawns.

As for the Press table, we had managed to keep ourselves amused by ordering more bottles of wine, having already had large doubles of cognac and cigars. At last we were able to take out our notebooks – and the Thatcher speech to "check against delivery".

It was a good speech – attacking militant students who put university buildings out of order with their sit-ins and general strikes; Tories, she said, would tip the law in favour of the moderates and law-abiding. She said that a Conservative government would go all out to enrich the life of the individual, make sure that there would be sufficient supplies of skilled people to enrich each community; that it would train people to lead responsible lives in society and "advance the frontiers of knowledge".

It was also clear that this new face in education was a skilled politician and knew that her prepared speech was too long to deliver to an audience who was already half asleep. So she cut out a number of pages which she considered worthy of temporary destruction. They included three pages dealing with the importance of teaching children to read. Parents, she had written, should encourage their young to read whatever they liked – even comics, such as *Beano* and *Dandy*.

And she added a couple of sentences which were not in her prepared text. A Conservative government would pay a great deal of attention to law and order so that no one, no child, no pensioner, should ever be afraid to go out into our streets at night.

She received warm applause from the diners. At the Press table, however, one colleague went purple with rage. It was Bruce Kemble, who had imbibed a little more than was necessary. Bruce was the education correspondent of the *Daily Express*. I did not wait to find out why he was so furious as I had taken a note of those last few sentences and rushed out of the hotel to one of the telephone boxes in the square to phone the London office and dictate a brief "Page One cross-reference" (to the report of her speech on an inside page) about the pledge to attend to law and order and safety in our neighbourhoods.

When I returned to the St Nicholas, a strange sight greeted me. There in the lobby stood the guest of honour, surrounded by a group of hacks. And there was Bruce Kemble, jabbing his finger at the advance copy of her speech, and shouting: "You didn't say any of this...not a single word. Are you saying that what's written here should not have been written here? Or what?"

Mrs Thatcher stood there in fear and trembling – literally so. I saw that the long gown she was wearing was actually shaking, which meant only one thing: her legs were trembling. I'm no Tory and never have been but I suddenly felt desperately sorry for this poor woman. She waved her hand and said quietly to Bruce: "Of course what was in my original speech stands. I mean every word of it, but I had to cut it down because of the time..."

"So, if I used that part of your speech, you will not deny having said it?"

"No. Rest assured. I have no intention of denying it."

But Bruce continued to badger her and I stretched out my arm and tapped her gently on the shoulder. She turned her head towards me. "D'you dance?" I asked.

"Oh yes," she said. "Yes, I'd love to."

And to the amused amazement of my colleagues,I led her into the ballroom and onto the dance floor for a slow foxtrot. I'm no ballroom dancer by any means – nor was she. But I had saved her from the media jungle and she was grateful.

I did not stop at just a dance. I knew that if I let her loose, she would have to undergo further inquisition. So I made small talk and then said: "Have you been to Scarborough before?" It was, I suppose, the equivalent to "do you come here often?" "No," she said. "This is my very first visit. Of course, I've seen nothing of the town. Is it nice?"

"Oh, Mrs Thatcher, you must come and have a look at the sea from up here. It's a wonderful view..."

And when the foxtrot ended, I boldly marched her out of the ballroom and out of the hotel. We crossed the square towards the Grand Hotel, which has sadly lost much of its original glamour as a major vantage point high above the beach, and took her to the wall bordering the chine. There was a full moon and not a cloud in the sky. The sea far below was still, almost like a lake. Mrs T. looked across to the horizon and, filled with admiration, declared: "Oh, this is absolutely heavenly. Thank you so much for showing me this, John. I may call you John?"

At this point, one of the NAHT executive officials came running up to us. "Oh, Mrs Thatcher, so sorry to interrupt. Your presence is requested in the ballroom. You are meant to draw the raffle tickets!"

Together they almost ran back to the hotel. By the next day, the rumours were rife. The man from the *Daily Telegraph* had kidnapped Mrs Thatcher, their guest of honour, and taken her for a moonlight walk! Would you credit it!

I have often been asked whether I had actually made a pass at Mrs T. I can say with all honesty that my action was taken simply out of sympathy with a woman under high pressure. It was her first major speech as Shadow Secretary of State. At no time did I ever consider her in any sexual way whatsoever, nor, I'm equally certain, did she so consider me. Would I have had a similar urge to "rescue" her had she been a man? I doubt it very much.

As Secretary for Education and Science under Heath, Margaret Hilda Thatcher became one of the most controversial figures in government and among the most misunderstood women within education.

The moment she took over Ted Short's office at the Department of Education, then still housed in Curzon Street, Mayfair, she called a "non-attributable" meeting with education correspondents on June 23, 1970. It showed her impatience and keenness to get on with the job, but it was a major blunder.

Non-attributable gatherings do not mean they are "off the record". They mean that the information gathered at them can be used but must on no account be attributed to the informant. Politicians, particularly those of Cabinet rank, are eager to use such meetings as public sounding boards. Instead of saying that "Such and such a Minister said..." or "Mr Bloggs, Minister for thingy, said...", the recipient of information will write: "It is understood that..." or "I understand that the Minister for thingy will do such and such...". If what "is understood" happens to be something controversial and there is a public outcry against it, the Minister concerned will drop it and even say that he or she knew nothing about such a ridiculous idea...

Ted Short often called such non-attributable meetings and was never quoted directly by any journalist. In her non-attributable get-together with the most senior of education correspondents, she decided to lay out her policy in full.

Her first act was to withdraw Circular 10/65 – sent in 1965 to all local authorities by Anthony Crosland, the Labour education secretary, directing them to reorganise their secondary schools and turn them into all-in comprehensives. This advance information was dynamite. But she wasn't finished. She would also tell those local authority leaders who were planning to withdraw grants and places from direct grant schools to allow the brightest children to continue to be accepted at those schools. She also wanted to develop nursery education for all children from the age of three.

There were several other plans – such as the expansion of the polytechnics, an inquiry into teacher training, and a go-ahead for the Open University with an attached warning that it would be carefully watched. She would not consider the abolition of corporal punishment.

All this information would have to be presented in the formula explained above and every newspaper followed it – bar one. The *Daily Express* went to town with this great story by Bruce Kemble. Instead of using the "I understand" rule, he unblushingly stated that: "Margaret Thatcher, the new education chief, told me last night that…" It was an unforgivable breach of journalistic etiquette.

I have always admired Bruce Kemble and we have been close friends and colleagues. He was an honest and highly experienced journalist, whose book *Give Your Child a Chance* was an excellent handbook for teachers and mothers alike. Whether he was still sulking from the Scarborough NAHT conference and Thatcher's editing of his speech, was never made clear. But he certainly managed to blot his copybook with Margaret.

It created a stink in the House of Commons, when Ted Short rose and accused the Secretary of State for Education of "holding secret tea parties with education journalists". The unions were unhappy as well and complained that Mrs Thatcher was seeing education correspondents before meeting teacher union leaders. And worse, she was telling things to the Press before discussing them with Parliament.

Her own anger was made crystal clear to me a week or so later when I obtained the first official interview with her. We shook hands warmly and, as she poured me a large gin and tonic, she said: "One thing is certain, John, that man Kemble will never be invited to another meeting with me, whether on or off the record. I've never been so badly let down by a journalist."

Now, I've never gone along with any form of censorship and had no wish to see any colleague barred from a Press conference, so I said: "President de

Gaulle only ever allowed one journalist to have a *tête à tête* interview with him."

"Oh, yes? Was it you?"

"No, Margaret. It was the man from *L'Humanité* (the Communist party newspaper). He knew that he needed to befriend the enemy before he befriended the friend."

She was silent for a moment, sipped her drink, then said: "Well, let's get on with it shall we?"

The interview began. And I believe my lesson in psychology had worked. For Bruce Kemble continued to be invited to all her Press conferences.

Margaret Thatcher proved that she rarely if ever changed her mind many years before she delivered that memorable speech to a Tory conference at Brighton on October 10, 1980, in which she told delegates:

"To those waiting with bated breath for that favourite media catchphrase, the U-turn, I have only one thing to say: You turn if you want to. The lady's not for turning!"

She had told education correspondents at that controversial "non-attributable" conference on June 23, 1970 that she was going to withdraw Circular 10/65. A few weeks later, on July 13, she met a ten-man deputation from the NUT who tried for more than two hours to change her mind. She remained adamant. "I shall leave the question of secondary school reorganisation to local authorities." A few days earlier she had sent her own circular to every local education authority in England and Wales and made her position clear: it would be left up to them to do as they considered best for their own areas.

Ted Britton, the teachers' general secretary, looked crestfallen on the delegation's departure from Mrs Thatcher's office. "Her policy has put the clock back 26 years," he said. "It is a return to the 1944 Education Act where selection was according to age, ability and aptitude. It will mean chaos… absolute chaos."

For Britton, the Thatcher put-down had come as a veritable slap in the face. More than that: it was a loss of face. When he was elected general secretary the previous year, many teachers and quite a number of union executive members felt that he was not the man for so exacting a job. He had followed Sir Ronald Gould, a man who had a towering presence, a quick wit and who was an orator able to memorise speeches without difficulty. I remember his swan song when he stood before the NUT conference and delivered a magnificent one-hour long farewell address without once referring to his notes. Ted Britton could hardly follow that.

Ted used to be a teacher and worked his way up to head teacher at Warlingham County Secondary School in 1951 – a headship that lasted ten years. It was there that he learned that selection following an 11-plus examination was not enough to show what a child could achieve by the time he or she was 16. He became an ardent union man but he was never an orator in the Gould category. Nevertheless, he became NUT president in 1956 and three years later applied for and got the general secretaryship of the ATTI – the Association of Teachers in Technical Institutions.

Britton was no Left-winger, even though the ATTI had shown him just how far to the Left further education technical teachers could be. His later elevation to the leadership of the NUT brought him many would-be back-stabbers who considered him not just of the Left but a Lefty. Britton, a thorough Socialist of the middle-of-the-road Labour party school, wanted to take the union into the TUC. Many teachers, even Labour followers, considered this a dreadful mistake. They had no wish to be treated like transport workers, dockers or miners. But Britton pointed out the many advantages and, in the end, got his way.

His "defeat" at the hands of Margaret Thatcher proved that he still had a long way to go before he could persuade the union membership that he was the right leader for the task. I always found Ted a most kind and amiable man who would tell it to you straight.

What surprised Mrs Thatcher most was how many teachers had sided with her and against their own general secretary. Far from being "of the Left", most teachers are middle-of-the road and many are completely a-political. The very idea of forcing teachers to "go comprehensive" was abhorrent to those at the chalkface. The NUT's journal *The Teacher* found itself inundated with letters attacking Britton's stand. Labour's circular compelling local authorities to go comprehensive had been "almost entirely on party lines," one letter complained.

Another said that the educational case for comprehensives had scarcely been mentioned and the debate had done "educational harm" because it "placed the comprehensive issue in the political arena."

Ted Britton found himself forced to defend his argument. His article appeared opposite the many published letters. "The NUT," he explained, "was merely following conference policy. As long ago as 1943, conference passed a resolution favouring multi-lateral schools."

I found it strange to learn that in the middle of a world war, teachers had still found time to gather in conference to debate and vote on the kind of schools they would want to see. How strange, too, to find that Harold Wilson had sent both his sons to an independent fee-paying school "at a time when there were comprehensives to go to."

This appeared in a letter from Mr B. V. Slater, senior classics master at Bradford Grammar School, who claimed that "nearly all headmasters of comprehensive schools I know prefer to send their offspring to direct grant or independent schools."

Another correspondent, a Mr H Wheaton of Bristol, said that "enforced comprehensive education smacks of dictatorship."

Not only *The Teacher* found itself in the forefront of the NUT/Government row. The Inner London Teachers' Association – all NUT members and fervent Left-wingers – lobbied their MPs at the House of Commons, handing out leaflets demanding that they oppose "Mrs Thatcher's sabotage of the comprehensive system".

One Tory MP, Anthony Buck (Colchester) put his marker into the debate by announcing that he had received 56 letters from teachers in North-East Essex supporting Mrs Thatcher's move.

The same day as the Britton-Thatcher kerfuffle erupted, the *Telegraph* published a feature by me entitled quite simply *Understanding Mrs Thatcher*.

This is what I said on July 17, 1970:

"Rarely has one woman been misunderstood by so many in so short a time as Margaret Hilda Thatcher, Britain's new Secretary of State for Education. Even Ted Britton, sincere and honest leader of the country's biggest teachers' union, shook his head sadly the other day after a two-hour session with her and said: 'She has put the clock back 26 years.'"

Shortly before Mr Britton and his NUT delegation left the Curzon Street Ministry, an attractive young girl reporter described Mrs Thatcher as a woman who "sounds as though she is always wearing a hat".

That was quite true. Mrs Thatcher looked and sounded "upper middle class". She had a habit of stressing every third word of each sentence she uttered. In order to improve her voice and her image, she secretly took a series of elocution lessons and, by the time she had done her education job for a year, her speaking improved immensely – but she still sounded "upper middle class". Yet in a one-to-one relationship, as during our interview, she spoke completely normally.

Margaret Thatcher might as easily have grown up a Labour supporter as a Tory. She was born Margaret Roberts in the small Lincolnshire town of Grantham on October 13, 1925. Her parents depended on their modest grocery shop and she lived in a house that had neither a bath nor even any hot water. Alfred Roberts, her father, had left school at 14, lacking the money to go on to any further education and realise his ambition to become a teacher. He was totally self-educated and consequently, self-made.

"There wasn't any television in those days and we didn't even have a radio at home," she told me at that interview. "We didn't have a bathroom but we had plenty of books. My parents encouraged me inside and outside the home." She went through a fairly normal education, attending a local state-maintained grammar school – Kesteven and Grantham Girls' School. "When I found out that I needed Latin to get a university place, my father raided his savings to provide me with a tutor." When she reminisced about her childhood, the sting went completely out of her voice. It took her just eight weeks to reach the School Certificate credit required in Latin – equivalent of O-level or a GCSE at Grade C.

Her childhood did not resemble today's. There were no children's parties, no dances, no boyfriends. "I grew up in the Thirties. It was a time of depression, and politics played a big part in my life from the very start." Politics grew increasingly attractive to her. "I preferred the company of adults and talked politics with my father's friends whenever they came to the house. My interest in a political career grew and grew. But I knew that I couldn't afford to go in for politics without some profession to back me up. That's why I went to university," she said.

She won a scholarship to Somerville College, Oxford, and read chemistry because she realised that there was a great future in plastics and wanted to join that field before it became overcrowded. She gained a Second Class Honours degree and became a research chemist, but she wanted more and started work at the Revenue Bar to become a qualified barrister, which she did in 1954.

"When I was up at Oxford, there was Edward Boyle, Wedgwood Benn, Ludovic Kennedy, Kenneth Tynan…it was talk, talk, talk."

She became violently anti-Fascist and read books about Nazi Germany with horror. Later she met and befriended a young Jewish woman who had been saved from Auschwitz extermination camp. That episode in her life probably explains why the woman who in October 1959 became Conservative MP for Finchley, a predominantly Jewish constituency, became known as the "Finchley Nightingale". It also explains why she rarely declined invitations to speak at local Jewish women's meetings.

She met the man who was to become her husband in 1949 when she was standing as Conservative candidate for Dartford and he was working for a chemical company in Erith. Denis Thatcher offered her a lift into London. But the question of marriage did not arise until three years and two unsuccessful elections later.

In August 1953 she gave birth to twins – Carol and Mark.

This then was the woman who had been so viciously attacked by Ted Short a week before I interviewed her. He called her "the feminine version of the Selsdon Man".

And when I asked her whether she enjoyed such a political scrap, she replied without a smile: "I don't care for rough political fights when they are about something so serious as a child's education."

I have always taken a keen interest in the reading skills of young children and consistently campaigned for an emphasis by teachers on "The Three Rs", but with particular concentration on the first of them – reading. Perhaps it was because I was able to learn English only through reading. Comics, such as the *Dandy* and *Beano* were my very first "aids" to the English language. The colourful illustrations and antics of Desperate Dan, Korky the Cat, Lord Snooty and the Gang, all helped me to understand this strange and beautiful language.

By the time we had lived in Llandudno a couple of years, I had become a fairly confident reader and, although comics continued to hold my attention for quite a while longer, I had graduated to the world of books. Among my favourites were the *Just William* series by Richmal Crompton and the *Biggles* series by W. E. Johns. I borrowed each of them from the public library and devoured them one by one.

By the time I was married and on the *Telegraph* and Paul was born, television had become the altar of every home. Although books still played a major part of my own household and I enjoyed telling Paul bedtime stories from the time he was nowt but a toddler, I could only encourage him to read when the time for this pastime came. Far too many other children worshipped the TV screen and abandoned both comics and books.

Around this time, I was shown a new gadget – the *Talking Page*, which had been invented by Richard Kobler, an American educationist, and was being distributed in Britain by Rank REC. By the time I first saw it in action, 44 out of the 163 local education authorities in England and Wales had introduced it to their primary schools. This machine not only helped children to read, but improved their reading ages.

The way it worked was simple. It was really nothing more than a glorified record player, with the record being synchronised to reading material. From start to finish, it is controlled by the child using it. Excellently illustrated and colourful reading books are placed on a desk-like surface of the machine and the record is slipped into the back. Along the side of the book's pages are little black markers and a lever, operated by the child, moves a pointer along the page from marker to marker. At each "stop" the record is set in motion and a voice either reads what is printed alongside the marker, describes a picture on the page, or asks the child to read and describe.

The child can repeat the same line as often as he or she likes, simply by lifting and stopping the lever at the same marker. At the end of the page, the voice says: "Now please turn to the next page…" and so on.

I took Paul up to the Rank REC offices and he took to the *Talking Page* with gusto. He was then just five and a half years old. He followed to the letter what "the man in the box" instructed him to do and say but got very upset at one stage when he was trying out a simple mathematics course. "Now," said the voice, "for this next page you will need your counters. Have you got your counters ready?"

Consternation. No counters had been provided. Paul jumped from his chair and tore off his earphones. "Where are the counters?" he yelled. "The gentleman told me I need to have counters ready. Where are they?" He was close to tears. Once counters were provided, peace returned and he happily followed instructions.

I felt totally satisfied that this machine would revolutionise reading methods and help solve our literacy problems. I saw it in action in one classroom of a large inner London primary school where the average age of the boys and girls was seven-plus – and the reading age was one year behind. After two terms with this gadget, the reading age had soared to eight-plus.

I was determined to persuade Margaret Thatcher to see this machine for herself. She very readily accepted my invitation to take her to Ranks – and, of course, Ranks were more than delighted to welcome her. Not only did she go along. She also brought in tow her Chief Inspector of Schools, her PPS, her head of Public Relations and one or two others from the Curzon Street offices of the Department of Education and Science. Together with one of the Rank chiefs, I showed her how to use it – and she loved it. She made each of her retinue sit down and try it out for themselves.

Then she turned to the Chief Inspector and said: "I want you to send your chaps round the schools that are already using it and ask the teachers what they think of the machine."

It was her greatest mistake to date.

When the inspectors reported back, they said that teachers were of the opinion that no machine could possibly take the place of a human teacher. Of course they would say that. They had to protect their jobs.

As a result, the massive order Ranks expected to obtain, never materialised and eventually the *Talking Page* was removed from the market. Britain could have beaten literacy problems with a mere £100 a year per machine. A primary school would have needed about five of them. Instead, the first of the Three Rs remained paralysed and reading methods are still being debated by ministers, teachers and educationists to this day. Only pupils with special needs have been able to enjoy later versions of the *Talking Page*, such as *Talking Books*.

Polytechnics came next on Mrs Thatcher's list of "things to do". She always considered the polys "cheap and cheerful" and admired their emphasis on the vocational and technical. As far as she was concerned, they formed a suitable bridge between further and higher education. So she decided to increase their number from 23 to 26. She planned to approve a further four at a later date. The three were the North-East London, the South Bank and Thames Polytechnics, which, together with the City of London and Central London, would complete the capital's quota of five. She signed all the letters of designation.

Nearly a quarter of a century later, the country's polytechnics would become fully fledged universities – a translation in which I played a fairly major part.

What Margaret Thatcher could not have foreseen was the riots by students over the appointment of one poly director. The governors of two institutions – the Northern and the North Western polytechnics, which were to merge to form the Polytechnic of North London – appointed a 53-year-old professor called Terence Miller as overall director. Prof. Miller had been principal of the University College of Rhodesia.

No sooner was the news of his appointment released, than a 36-page booklet was published with the title: *Terence Miller – a Conscientious Objector*. Its author, Tim Matthews, aged 22, was a history student at the college until he was expelled from Rhodesia for his Left-wing views. He enrolled as a student at the London School of Oriental and African Studies and spread the news that Miller was an incompetent fascist racist. More than 1,000 polytechnic students immediately demonstrated against the appointment and threatened to ruin the new poly's designation.

Miller appeared before the students at a packed meeting in a Highbury Grove hall, just opposite the main poly building on Holloway Road, one of London's noisiest and dirtiest thoroughfares (the A1). "I was not expecting to appear here as a prisoner in the dock," he declared to jeers and boos. "My past seems to have aggravated a lot of people. I don't object to being challenged on that past but I do object to being accused of being inefficient and incompetent," he added.

He called the document about him "nothing but a pack of lies and distortions of the truth." He also explained that in July 1969 he had gone to Rhodesia from England, where he had been Professor of Geography at Reading University. "I went to Rhodesia to support the African side of the affair – but if I had said that, I would have been given a ticket straight back to the UK."

I later discovered that he was telling the truth and that, once he had become principal of University College, he made black students welcome. It was the only college in the country that permitted integration.

This, of course, did not interest the militant students. The extreme Left was determined to make a fight of it and disrupt the lives of other students as well as staff. Some 500 occupied the gymnasium at the North Western Polytechnic at Kentish Town to decide on further occupation plans. They also took about an hour debating whether or not to allow the Press in to witness their proceedings. Each journalist who wanted to enter had first to identify themselves. When it came to John Izbicki of the *Daily Telegraph*, there was uproar and a chorus of "OUT! OUT! OUT!" Many objected to my presence on the grounds that a recent *Telegraph* leader had been considered "unfair and anti-student".

A number of students rose to defend the *Telegraph* and freedom of speech. This in itself had no effect on the minds of the militants. But a note sent up to the young man who appeared to act as chairman did have an effect. It was a hastily scribbled note from the journalists present saying that if a single one of them was refused entry, they would all leave. The vote taken at that point was hugely in favour of us staying.

It was the first of many sit-ins and riotous occupations of this polytechnic. Miller continued to reign with a rod of iron. He often presented himself like some medieval knight on a white stallion who would slay any dragon in his path. The Polytechnic of North London (PNL) struggled on and on.

Chairman of PNL governors was Brian Roberts, who happened to be the editor of the *Sunday Telegraph*. Although he had his own education correspondent, the excellent Nicholas Bagnall, he would often call me to his office. Roberts was a man small of stature but big of intellect. "Ah, Izbicki," he would say as I walked in. "You might like to know that the governors are meeting at PNL tonight. We're expecting a bit of trouble from the students. You might like to look in…"

It always turned out to be a good story. The meetings were usually in the middle of the week and my only explanation of his decision to pick on me to cover the events rather than Bagnall was that it would clearly not wait until Sunday publication.

The very first governors' meeting of PNL was invaded by some 50 slogan-shouting students. Afterwards, Roberts said he very much regretted the scenes that had so disrupted the proceedings. "I have been governor of the Northern Polytechnic for 25 years and chairman for the past 15. There have always been good relations with the students here."

On another occasion, when again I had been tipped off by Brian Roberts, I took a photographer with me. He was a man of about 5ft 3ins whose name was Robert Hope (Bob Hope to everyone). The front hall of the poly was completely crowded with howling students. Those in front of this wave of militants were banging their fists upon the heavy oak doors of the council chamber. I was later told that the governors inside could not hear a word of their own meeting.

I beckoned to Bob to follow me with his camera while I pushed my way through the crowd and managed to reach the front just as the council room doors opened and Terence Miller stepped out. "Please be quiet," he shouted at the top of his teacher's voice. He was howled down. There followed one of the most embarrassing scenes I have ever witnessed. Terence Povey, student union president and by no means the worst of the militants, stepped forward to argue the toss with Miller, but Miller would not listen. Instead, the director grabbed hold of Povey by both shoulders and pushed. Povey naturally pushed back. A struggle ensued and both fell to the floor, rolling over and over, hitting out at each other. Noses bled and eyes would be black by morning.

What a great totally exclusive picture!

I looked round for Bob. He was nowhere to be seen. At last I saw the little man struggling through the crowd, arriving at my side just as the protagonists rose and dusted themselves down. Miller disappeared back into the council chamber.

"Where the fuck were you, Bob?" I shouted.

"Christ John, it was hell trying to clamber through that bloody lot," he replied sheepishly.

I would just have to try and describe the whole thing in words alone. They say that a picture tells a story far better than 1,000 words. How very true.

Not everything in a journalist's day-to-day life is a bed of roses. One has to face plenty of brickbats. *Daily Telegraph* representatives in particular have to ward off verbal attacks from the Left who consider the paper a Tory mouthpiece. *"Daily Torygraph"* is the least nasty of the insults hurled at it. One example, which continues to amuse me to this day, was recounted to me by Maureen.

By now she was working at Southgate School, a large mixed comprehensive in the London borough of Enfield. She was a teacher of English and became one of the most popular teachers there. One day she came home and said:

"The head of physics came up to me in the staff room and asked me if I was married to you. When I admitted it, he said: 'Ah, do please tell your husband that I read his stories in the *Telegraph* every day without fail and I cut each one of them out.' Oh, I said, do you collect them? 'No, not really. I stick each one on the board in the physics room, then stand back and throw darts at them.' I was quite annoyed but he seemed to think it funny."

I thought it funny too and we both laughed about it for quite some time. Maureen and I often had good laughs together and when we went out as a family with Paul, we'd run around a park just laughing. We just had great fun.

When the brickbats come from the direction of one's enemies (that is to say, the enemies of the *Telegraph*) one can sit back and smile, even laugh. One's skin gets tighter by the day and one becomes used to verbal canings. But when the attack comes from those one considers one's friends, it hurts.

One such incident, which still upsets my memory, happened at Cheltenham on May 31, 1971. The date is etched on my mind. I was covering the annual conference of the National Association of Head Teachers (NAHT). This was always a pleasurable conference to cover. David Hart, its general secretary and a lawyer by profession, had quickly become a genuine friend, as had Roy Nash, the association's public relations officer, who held the distinction of having been the nation's very first education correspondent.*

---

* Roy Nash was a reporter on the late, lamented *News Chronicle* and was sent to do a "write up" of a teacher union meeting. It happened to be the annual conference of the NUT and took place at the Odeon Cinema in Croydon. The Press was never invited in those early days and Roy, a young man then, walked through the cinema's doors and made himself comfortable in a circle seat. Before conference opened, the Grand Wurlitzer organ lifted itself up in front of the stage and the organist entertained delegates to a sing song. Then the curtains opened, revealing the executive sitting behind a long table. The lights were lowered and Conference began. Roy, his notebook on his lap, took shorthand notes. Teachers were surprised to find their debates reported in detail in the following day's *News Chron*. The story was bylined Roy Nash, Education Correspondent. That's how it all began…

The following day, my report spoke of a "bitter attack" launched by the head teachers against local authorities who interfered in their, the heads', actions. An emergency resolution was passed that deplored a series of recent "misguided interventions". Among the authorities named were Croydon and the Inner London Education Authority (ILEA). Croydon had, it was said, reversed a head's decision to suspend a boy who had refused to be caned for writing a flippant essay. Ashley Bramall, the ILEA leader, had criticised the dismissal of Christopher Searle, a teacher who had published poems written by his pupils, contrary to governors' instructions.

The following morning as I entered the conference, a colleague came up to me. "Take care, John. The bastards are after your neck. I overheard a conversation at breakfast and some of them are about to crucify you," he said. I thought he was joking, but he assured me it wasn't a joke.

It was apparently something in my story. I wracked my brain and re-read what I had written a couple of times. There was nothing wrong with it as far as I could see and I sat at the Press table, prepared for the worst.

The President, one Jim Rudden, opened the conference with the usual (and very silly) traditional: "Good morning boys and girls" to be replied by delegates with "Good morning Sir". No sooner had Rudden sat down when one delegate, a William Barnett of Birmingham (the alliteration has stuck with me – Barnett of Birmingham) stood up, exclaiming: "Point of Order Mr President!"

"Yes Mr Barnett, what is your point of order?"

"Have you read today's newspapers, Mr President?"

"Yes I have, Mr Barnett. Why do you ask?"

"Have you read the *Daily Telegraph*'s report on this conference?"

"Yes, I have it before me now, Mr Barnett."

"Do you recall anyone criticising the ILEA in this chamber?"

"Can't say that I do, Mr Barnett. I note that the article was written by John Izbicki, whom I recognise sitting at the Press table below us."

"I must say, Mr President, that one must demand an immediate correction and apology from this journalist."

"I shall ask him, Mr Barnett." Then, looking straight at me, by now shaking in my boots, said: "Will you correct this article at once, Mr Izbicki? Can you give me that assurance?"

I was seething with anger and embarrassment. "No, Mr President, I cannot give you such an assurance," I shouted back.

This time, Jim Rudden looked embarrassed. All he could bring himself to say was: "A fair question – and, ahem, a fair answer. Next business…"

I had given up smoking three weeks before this deplorable incident. I immediately turned to Roy Nash, who was at my side. "Have you a cigarette, Roy?" I stammered. He didn't but he went and got me one. "Stupid, stupid buggers," he said as I lit up (in those days one still could smoke). "Don't let them get you down, John, for God's sake". I was convinced that what I had written was accurate – although the ILEA criticism might, in retrospect, have been made outside conference. Ashley Bramall, who attended that Cheltenham conference, certainly never complained to me or anyone else.

Rudden had issued an invitation to the Press to join him at tea that evening. Bruce Kemble of the *Express*, John Scott (the best education correspondent the Press Association ever had) and one or two others, signed a terse note, saying that they "regretted" being unable to accept his invitation to tea and demanding an apology for his "crucifixion" of a good colleague.

It was so obviously stage-managed.

David Hart rushed up to me afterwards, threw his arms about me and apologised for what had happened.

I had a queue of delegates, all wanting to pat me on the back and say how sorry they were. One woman delegate, whom I had never met before, came up to me and declared: "Oh, Mr Izbicki, I wept for you earlier on today," with which words, she tugged a tissue from her handbag and wept again. They were real tears.

I made more friends among the country's head teachers that day than I could ever have hoped.

What is more, on the following day, Jim Rudden publicly apologised for his "unfair treatment of John Izbicki".

If Margaret Thatcher is remembered as the Iron Lady (Khrushchev's description of her) and "The Lady's Not for Turning", she is also remembered as "Thatcher, Thatcher, Milk Snatcher". It is true that she stopped free milk from being served to primary school children every day. It was a public relations mistake on her part and the PR machine played it totally wrong.

Under the 1944 Education Act, local authorities were duty bound to provide all children with a third of a pint of free milk each day. This provision continued unabated until 1968 when the then Education Secretary, Edward Short, decided to withdraw it from all secondary school children. He had the blessing of the Prime Minister of the day, Harold Wilson, who had asked for some radical economy measures to be imposed. Primary schools continued to receive their third-of-a-pint until September 1971, when Mrs Thatcher, again as an economy measure, withdrew it from junior schools. Children aged from three until seven (in infants' classes of primary schools) continued to enjoy the daily injection of fresh milk. In juniors' classes, children aged seven to 11, continued to get these small bottles of milk if a medical examination found them in need of it.

The cut brought the Tory government a saving of £9 million a year – and an invaluable amount of poor publicity.

The country's 163 local education authorities were up in arms and demanded the right to decide for themselves whether or not children in primary schools needed milk. They demanded that Mrs Thatcher should allow them to pay for the milk out of their rates. At a meeting of the Association of Education Committees, "Thatcher, the Milk Snatcher" was attacked for her "magnanimous suggestion" that only children requiring milk on medical grounds should continue to get it. "The health of all children depends on their intake of milk," one delegate cried.

It wasn't just a matter of milk alone. Town halls were angry and frustrated at the Big Brother attitude of the government. They saw their power ebbing away under the constant interference of Whitehall.

The verb "to spin" had not yet entered the vocabulary of the civil service. Otherwise the media could have been told that the £9 million was a mere bagatelle and that milk had been but a mere pawn in the real battle that Mrs Thatcher had fought with the Treasury over funding for education. In return for the saving, she had won £12 million of new money for better school equipment and £135 million for school buildings. This was not something released by the PR machines of government but gleaned by investigative reporters, including myself. We never reveal our sources – at least we *should* never reveal them – but I can reveal, as they say, that the information came to me from the most reliable source – the Milk Snatcher herself.

The annual teacher union conferences meant that Easter and Whitsun could never be spent with loved ones at home. Hiding Easter eggs for Paul was not abandoned, but simply brought forward by a week or so. Paul always managed to find them and, once found, would offer them round to family and friends. He was a generous lad. But at Easter, it was off to the National Union of Teachers conference which would be held at one or other of the seaside resorts – Blackpool, Brighton, Scarborough, Harrogate or (rarely) Llandudno. The NUT would kick off with a Press conference on Good Friday, giving us all the chance of filing a decent story for the Saturday papers, which were generally thinner than normal, due to the reduction of advertising. Full conferences would be held on the Saturday (a day off for me, as the *Sunday*

Telegraph would send its own Nicholas Bagnall, to cover for them), Sunday and Monday. Conference would close on Tuesday – just as the National Association of Schoolmasters/Union of Women Teachers (NASUWT) would start its annual meeting, usually also in a seaside resort but as far from the NUT as possible. So if the NUT was at Blackpool, NASUWT would be at Brighton.

Many of the correspondents would disappear on the Monday night to attend the "other conference". I was lucky in this respect. I had no need to rush away as I could send one of my deputies to cover NASUWT. I had two: Michael Durham, a fine reporter who I had managed to recruit from the *Times Educational Supplement*, and Margot Norman, a strikingly beautiful young woman whom I had managed to pinch from the *Peterborough* column, the *Telegraph*'s daily diary. Margot had first come to the *Telegraph* as assistant to Peter Utley, our blind leader writer. Peter was genuinely blind, but I always had my doubts because every single assistant he had employed was more beautiful than the last. There was nothing wrong with his hearing and, I suppose, he must have recognised beauty by touch. The assistant would have to read every paper, every article to him each morning, then type his leader to his dictation as he paced up and down his small office. The carpet was seriously worn along the path of his pacing. An amazing man with a photographic memory and the brain of a genius.

Margot could touch-type and she knew her shorthand. What is more, she wrote like a dream. Her greatest failing was time. She simply could not keep to deadlines and I often had to stand over her and threaten: "You have just five minutes, Margot, not fifteen or eight, but FIVE. Finish it now or it'll be spiked." Her features, for which she could take longer, were always brilliant. Anyway, either she or Mike Durham, who never needed to be reminded of deadlines, would cover NASUWT.

Then at Whitsun (another week wrecked by the godless who abolished those wonderful Whit-week Walks in Manchester) it would be the turn of the National Association of Head Teachers (NAHT) at another of the seaside resorts. And there was still the Assistant Masters Association (AMA) as well as the Assistant Mistresses. Luckily, the two amalgamated into AMMA, which we liked to call the Assistant Masters and their Mistresses. And there was the Secondary Heads Association (SHA).

And away from schoolteachers, there were those covering higher education: the Association of University Teachers (AUT) and the National Association of Teachers in Further and Higher Education (NATFHE), the former concentrating, as the name suggests, on university professors, readers and lecturers, while the latter dealt mainly with the staffs of further education colleges (both also amalgamated some years after my retirement).

One other union sprang into life during my time. Indeed, I was closely involved in its formation. In 1970, at the time when teachers were downing chalk and coming out into the streets to shout for better pay and conditions, I received a letter from a teacher called Peter Dawson (no relation to the Peter Dawson who was general secretary of NATFHE at about the same time) who told me that he and a large number of other teachers were thoroughly disgruntled with the militancy among so many of their colleagues – mostly members of the NUT and NASUWT. They were thinking of founding an association "with a difference" – one which would concentrate purely on teaching children and their education. Members would need to take a pledge never to strike, whatever the provocation, as strikes could only cause serious hurt to children.

I wrote back and suggested that this should be written for publication. It was and the letter appeared in the *Telegraph*.

Thus, the Professional Association of Teachers (PAT) was born. It immediately became the most unpopular "union" on the face of the earth as far as all other unions were concerned. They were dubbed "a load of Tory shits" and other, even less complimentary descriptions. But the association rapidly became like Topsy and "growed and growed", although it would never match the strengths of the NUT with more than 235,000 in-service (actually teaching) members, NASUWT with some 100,000, the NAHT with around 19,000 and NATFHE, closely associated with the NUT, with a membership of around 40,000. But PAT's membership soared from a mere handful to nearly 12,000 – an envy-making figure for such an infant.

At that time nine unions and associations existed for teachers. Eight of them were represented on the Burnham Committee, which negotiates teachers' salaries. Only the PAT was the exception and was kept out of the committee. It nevertheless shared in the pay rises finally agreed after many nights of oft vicious arguments between the unions and their employers – the Association of County Councils and the Association of Metropolitan Authorities as well, of course, as the Department of Education and Science, a Government department which kept on changing its name across the years.

Salaries and conditions naturally took up large chunks of conference time, no matter which of the unions and associations were in session. The NASUWT tended also to concentrate on the question of discipline – not how to punish pupils but how to stop pupils assaulting teachers. There were "good stories" to be had along these lines each and every year. The NUT, on the other hand, was often divided along political lines. The union's delegates were mainly Left-of-centre. Very few were Tories and those who were, would be reluctant to admit it in public. But a fairly large proportion was made up of "the Trots" – adherents of the Socialist Workers Party, Workers Revolutionary Party, Revolutionary Socialist League and Militant. Communist Party members were veritable Conservatives compared with that lot. Max Morris, who was on the NUT executive and actually became the union's president, was a Communist and hated the guts of the Trots. He resigned from the CP executive at the time of the invasion of Czechoslovakia but Margaret, his wife, remained on the Communists' executive, thus allowing Max to continue seeing party papers. He became a good socialist to the Left of the old Labour party.

The NUT always invited the Press to a special dinner on the Monday night of conference. It was served at the main conference hotel and the wines flowed freely. In my second year as education correspondent, I felt that we could not just accept such generous treatment without giving our hosts something in return. Big, expensive dinners are all very well and I was sure the union did not intend them as some kind of bribe but as a thank-you to us hacks for reporting their debates fairly. And yet I felt that it was our job to report conference fairly, so something in return should at least be considered. But what?

I discussed the matter with Bruce Kemble. Like me, the *Daily Express* man was an extrovert, and we agreed that we might be able to drum up a short cabaret and put it on at the end of the dinner. Most of our colleagues could, we thought, think up a party turn.

Our first "show" at Easter, 1972, lasted not more than 20 minutes. What we had not anticipated at that time was that the "Education Correspondents' Cabaret" would become a regular feature of these dinners, and our last – or at least, the last I took part in – was in 1985 and lasted a little over 90 minutes! Within four or five years, news of the "show" we put on for the NUT had spread throughout the teacher union world and we were invited to produce it for almost everyone else, including the NASUWT, the NAHT, SHA, and the Local Authorities conference.

We tried to vary it from year to year, but the teachers wanted to see many acts repeated again and again. Bruce Kemble, who worshipped at the shrine of Max Miller, delivered some fairly risqué jokes in the Miller tone and idiom; I put on a number of mimes, such as The Lady Takes a Bath, in which I "stripped" prior to stepping into the very hot water, cooling it down, and gingerly letting myself down with great relief at the end, and From Cradle to

Grave, a more serious mime which I had unashamedly stolen from Marcel Marceau, portraying an embryo gradually growing into manhood and into age and old age before returning to embryonic shape in death. Tudor David, who edited a magazine called *Education**, produced an "opera" with topical lyrics set to a series of popular folk or pop songs – as a Welshman he had the gift of bringing together a choir of Welsh delegates and making them sing like angels; then there was Charles Lyte of the *Daily Mirror* who came out with some slick patter while setting up a tower of books on which he balanced six wine glasses half filled with water, covered with the top of a square biscuit tin on which were six matchbox lids, each balancing precariously six fresh raw eggs. All this took a while and, as the tension mounted, Charles would stand back, holding a boot with which he gave the tin lid a resounding smack. The result was (usually) incredible. The tin lid would crash into the audience with a loud clatter and each egg would drop into the centre of the wine glasses of water. It would bring roars of long applause. Charles later became the gardening and, would you believe, poetry correspondent of the *Mirror*.

There was one other memorable performance on another occasion. In lovely Scarborough I was walking to the conference hall with John Clare, then of the BBC and remonstrated with him: "John, you've never done anything for the cabaret. Surely, you must be able to concoct some small thing!" He thought for a moment, then said: "Yes, all right, I'll do something for you. It's tonight, isn't it?" He would not go into any detail and so I introduced him that evening after the dinner as "Your own, your VERY OWN MISTER JOHN CLARE!"

John came onto the stage we always had erected by the hotel staff earlier in the day, carrying a tape recorder (the one from the BBC) on his shoulder. He was a tall man and had to bend down slightly to speak into our mike. His voice smouldered and everyone was glued to their seats awaiting his surprise contribution.

"Ladies and gentlemen," he began. "I should like to play you a recording of an interview I had last week with Sir Keith Joseph (the then Secretary of State for Education). I intend to play it in full." There were audible groans from the audience, but John held his tape recorder close to the microphone and switched it on. He asked the first question: "Sir Keith, are teachers being paid enough?"

It was a brilliant question and a hush fell on the NUT executive. What

---

* *Education* was later killed by Longman's, but rescued by one of its regular columnists, Demitri Coryton, and re-launched as the monthly *Education Journal*.

would Sir Keith answer? Sir Keith suffered from an infection that troubled his throat and meant that he often had to clear his voice He cleared his voice very audibly….and after a brief silence, cleared it again….and again….and yet again. This throat clearing to the accompaniment of silence went on for nearly two minutes – an age on radio. Then, after yet another throat clearance, Sir Keith calmly said: "Would you repeat the question?" The audience collapsed. John Clare almost stole the show that night.

I understand that he was severely reprimanded by his bosses at the Beeb a couple of days later, for his "revelation" found its way into the *Daily Mail* diary.

Sir Keith Joseph was among the most honest politicians I had met. He was dubbed the "Mad Monk" simply because, if he was asked an awkward question, he would stare wildly into space for a long time before answering. On one of the many occasions we lunched together, I asked him whether he really wanted to privatise the whole of education. It was a naughty question and I didn't really expect much more than a laugh in reply. We were sitting in the Royal Festival Hall restaurant and he stared out of the window and across the Thames which flowed below. I was beginning to wonder whether he would perhaps fall asleep when the answer came: a crisp "Yes, I would."

But of the various Ministers of Education I got to know, Margaret Thatcher will continue to stand out as the best. Her support of the Open University, her approval of the polytechnics (as the cheap and cheerful colleges of higher education), her raising of the school leaving age (ROSLA) to 16, her insistence on the teaching profession being open only to graduates, her prescription that teachers should concentrate on literacy and numeracy and her many fights with the Treasury to obtain more new money for education, will keep her up there in lights while many another minister will have disappeared into oblivion.

I regard it only as a great pity that she lost the soul she possessed as Secretary of State when she entered Number 10 Downing Street as Prime Minister.

But there were some others who will continue to have their page in the educational history books: Shirley Williams, for one, will be remembered for her personality and her determination to uphold educational standards – even if it meant following Mrs Thatcher's earlier policies. She will also be remembered for organising an almost farcical round-Britain discussion about education which became known as The Great Debate.

This wasn't exactly Shirley's doing but must be blamed on her boss, Farmer Jim. James Callaghan, then Prime Minister, had decided to tread on his education secretary's toes by delivering a speech at Ruskin College, Oxford that was entirely educational in tone and intention. It was he who would order Mrs Williams to meet with parents, local education authority chiefs and the leaders of industry, teacher and lecturer unions, students and so-called education experts from one end of the country to the other to see whether she could discover the answer to all problems faced by schools and universities.

Callaghan attacked "discovery methods" in very much the same way as they had been attacked by the Right-wing *Black Paper* authors. They produced good results while in well-qualified hands but failed completely when doled out by inexperienced teachers. He wanted a fresh look at the country's examination system insisted that "profane hands" should not touch education inside or outside the classroom. He demanded a proper monitoring service to uphold national standards of performance.

Shirley Williams had to traipse round Britain, chairing these "debates" to the best of her marvellous ability. But it turned out to be a circus. Everywhere she and her entourage went, they were met by the same clones, all singing from their respective hymn sheets. In October 1976, when she launched the Great Debate, she said that education had undergone "tremendous changes" over the past 20 years, including many new methods of teaching in a variety of subjects including modern languages, mathematics and science. Child-centred teaching was more commonly found, particularly in primary schools, she said. As for secondary reorganisation – that is, turning the tripartite grammar, secondary modern and technical school models into all-in comprehensives – it saw 76 per cent of all pupils in this age group in the comprehensive sector, compared with a mere 8.5 per cent just ten years earlier and 32 per cent in 1970.

Shirley Williams, like Maggie Thatcher, found herself with a fight on her hands. The unions were not the enemy; nor was it the local authorities. The enemy was within the Department of Education and Science itself. The civil servants insisted on ruling the roost. Viewers who followed *Yes Minister* and *Yes, Prime Minister* on television might have thought it an exaggeration of reality. Far from it. It reflected perfectly the tug-of-war that existed more or less permanently between Ministers and their civil service "advisers". The DES classified many documents as secret and papers that should have been open to the scrutiny of those involved in the Great Debate, remained hidden on the dust-laden shelves of Elizabeth House.

Whereas Thatcher battled on against the Treasury and the DES and flattened her opponents with one blow of her sharp tongue, Williams remained peaceful and unsuccessful in her office. However, she did insist on dealing with every item of correspondence herself. As a result, letters had to wait many weeks before they were answered. Shirley was dubbed a charming slowcoach.

She did, however, make a very decided mark. She merged the O-levels and Certificate of Secondary Education (the oft-maligned CSE) into one, giving birth to the GCSE.

Her growing frustration with education, the DES and the squabbling within the Cabinet at its Thursday morning meetings made her look to pastures new. She started to become increasingly fed up with the direction the Labour party was moving. It seemed that things were becoming so Leftist that it was almost turning towards a form of Trotskyism. She sounded off about this, possibly too often, and at the 1979 election, lost the seat she had held at Hitchin since 1964. In 1981 she blew the proverbial whistle, resigned from the Labour party's national executive committee – a position she had held for 11 years – and resigned from the Labour party after a loyal 35-year membership. She then joined the "Gang of Four" to found the Social Democratic Party and become the SDP MP for Crosby. Her later life peerage and move to the House of Lords as Leader of the Lib-Dems brought her political career to its climax.

Unlike Lady Thatcher, who had remained tied to Denis for life (although it was really he who was tied to her), Baroness Williams had found romance and marriage twice in her life. Both husbands were academics – Bernard Williams, was Professor of Moral Philosophy and Fellow of Corpus Christi College, Oxford (their marriage was dissolved in 1974 when he met another) and Professor Richard Neustadt, an American political scientist.

My own professional life was constantly entwined with education ministers. There was, for example, the stormy story of the Open University. Peter Eastwood, managing editor of the *Daily Telegraph* – the man the staff loved to hate – took an immediate dislike to its formation, not so much because it represented a new piece of academe on the horizon but because it was the brainchild of Labour party apparatchiks. True, the original University of the Air was dreamed up by Harold Wilson but it was his Minister of the Arts, the fabulous Jennie Lee, who gave flesh to the bones and brought about the Royal Charter it obtained in 1969. But Eastwood wanted it strangled at birth.

He called me into his office in the summer of 1971. "John, this wretched University of the Air...I'd like you to write a really scathing piece about it. I hear that it's not altogether popular with Government (then Tory) ministers. It'll be a total waste of taxpayers' money..."

I was personally in favour of the idea of a university that would teach its courses by radio and television and give people who had lost out the first time round in education another chance to do well. But "orders is orders", as they say and, yes, it was true that some ministers were critical. On August 31 that year, a piece stretching across four columns appeared on Page 1 of the *Telegraph*, headlined: **Parliamentary Pressures for Abandoming £6.5 million-a-year Project**. A strapline, heavily underlined, reported: Open University runs into difficulties. Under my byline the story opened with the following sentence:

> *The Open University will have to fight for its life during the next academic year.* It continued: *Unless it can prove that its courses by radio, television and correspondence are paying dividends, it faces moves in Parliamentary circles to close it.*

I had done my job well, for I had discovered that Iain Macleod, the Chancellor, had told the Prime Minister and others at a Cabinet meeting that the new university would cost far too much money. According to my story Mrs Thatcher was not among those to oppose the OU's opening but was coming under increasing pressure to join the ranks of its enemies at the Treasury. I then drew up a list of "teething problems" facing the institution. Its computers had "expelled" 600 students for failing to pay a £10 course fee. A month later, another mistake when 2,500 students – half the social science faculty – were awarded A-grades, although they were worthy of only Grades B or C. A postal strike earlier that year had cut off an entire batch of 24,000 students as well as many more applicants through no fault of the university. The list was impressively long. I was not particularly proud of a story which was accurate in every detail but mischievous in its intent.

Eastwood sent me a two-word note (an unusual act on his part). "Well done" it said.

I angrily tore it up.

The piece had immediate repercussions. I was interviewed by the BBC's morning news programme as well as the Open University's own radio news service. Did I consider the Government would order the university's closure? Did I agree with the views I had heard from Government sources? And so on. I did my best to explain that these were all "simply teething troubles". Every new organisation suffered such problems...and admittedly, the OU had suffered more than most etc etc.

Looming in my diary was a visit to Keele University which was hosting the OU's very first summer school. This had been scheduled some months earlier and certainly well before my report had appeared. An annual summer school was part of the Open's degree course – about the only time that its students would live on a campus for a week of intensive lectures and seminars.

I was going to join some of those lectures and that evening was due to deliver a talk on "Politics and the Media".

I was petrified at the prospect. I fully expected to be lynched.

But the students were not long-haired passion-filled youngsters. They were all mature men and women – some of them very mature indeed and well into their sixties and seventies. I particularly remember one social science class where a student put a particular question to the lecturer. It involved a very recent complicated change in a rule. The slightly embarrassed lecturer had to admit that he did not know the answer. But one of the students did know it and gave a splendid explanation. She had worked in her local social security offices for years and knew more about the subject than the much younger man in front of the class.

That was what was so exciting about the OU. People learned not only from books and from tutors but from each other as well.

When the time came for my own lecture, I was taken to the university's biggest lecture theatre. It was absolutely packed. I kicked off by saying: "I have been asked to speak to you about Politics and the Media and I shall, of course, do exactly that…for not more (I promise) than ten minutes. After that, I shall expect you to ask me the questions I'm sure you have already prepared and I shall do my very best to answer them."

I was right. The questions came thick and fast. This was *their* university. It was a university they all loved and did not want to see closed. So what could they do to stop the Government from closing it? My answers were brief but very much to the point:

"You know who the Prime Minister is and where he lives. Write to him and tell him how you feel. You know who the Secretary of State for Education is and where she lives." (I used the chalk and scrawled on the blackboard: The Rt Hon Mrs Margaret Thatcher MP, Curzon Street…) "Write to her and tell her how you feel. You know – or should know – the name of your own MP. Write to him or her and say how you feel. And write to your friends, your relations, your fellow students elsewhere and ask them to write to Mr Heath and Mrs Thatcher and their MPs. Don't forget to do it!"

The discussions between students and myself went on until 11.30 p.m. after which we withdrew to the bar and continued discussing the matter over some welcome pints of beer.

I was not lynched. In fact, I made some good friends that night.

Some three weeks later I was to have lunch with William Van Straubenzee, one of Mrs Thatcher's junior ministers. Bill was a plump little man, balding and ruddy of complexion who was coming to meet me at a restaurant quite near to the Curzon Street education offices. He bounced in, some ten minutes late, fairly breathless but grinning from ear to ear. One always knew when he was telling the truth or when he was lying, for Van Straubenzee had a strange twitch that would move his left cheek, part of his nose and an eye whenever he told a lie. As soon as he had sat down and gulped at the gin and tonic placed before him, he said: "Maggie has asked me to give you a message. She hopes you are well and wants you to know that the Open University won't close. It is to remain open and receive our help."

He was not twitching. I knew it was true.

Apparently, the Prime Minister, the Secretary of State and scores of MPs had received sackloads of letters from Open University students throughout the country. It was the biggest postbag on any single subject they had ever received.

On October 5, not many days more than a month since the original article had appeared, a single-column story, again by me, was simply headlined **Open University to Stay** announced: *The Government is to continue its support of the Open University despite a Parliamentary lobby which wants to see it closed.*

I had also managed to include quotes from some of the Tory MPs who had been lobbied by students. Julian Ridsdale, MP for Harwich, said: "I am all in favour of helping the Open University to keep going and see what it can achieve." And another, Sir David Renton, MP for Huntington, said: "I appreciate the value of the Open University especially since its students do not take drugs and don't have campuses on which to bellyache."

I did not receive a note from Peter Eastwood.

This story has an interesting postscript. Some years later when Harold Wilson was back at Number 10, he decided to stage his very first visit to the OU. Although the university did not have its own campus, its administrative offices were at Bletchley, not far from Milton Keynes. He had never set foot in those buildings so his visit was considered something of a Press event and he had agreed to deliver a speech that evening. We hacks took our seats at a long table at the foot of the platform where Harold appeared.

Following the usual niceties, the Prime Minister said: "I am glad to be here particularly as this occasion might never have happened. The Tories wanted to close the Open before it even opened. But luckily it was saved from closure and the man who was responsible for saving it is sitting right here beneath me: John Izbicki."

There was applause in which Wilson joined. My own embarrassment made my cheeks burn and suddenly I realised that there were tears streaming from my eyes.

Sometimes, even hardened journalists can cry.

CHAPTER SEVENTEEN:

SADNESS AND LIGHT

L ife was not all work. Although many might not have believed it, I did have a home life – and a very happy one it was. Maureen and I took holidays both with Paul and without him. There were times we would leave him with his Nanny – Maureen's mum, Nell, who had gone to live at Cleveleys, near Blackpool, after she was widowed. Paul adored going there because it was near the sea and he and our wonderful dog, Striker, a cross between an Alsatian and a Labrador who was as soft as they come, could run along the beach and play in and out of the sea. Nell was a bit like Striker – she had a frightening bark but was an old softy with a heart of gold and a good sense of humour.

Every morning she would have the *Daily Telegraph* delivered and take it up to bed along with a hot mug of tea. She would carefully cover the top sheet with a towel before putting the *Telegraph* down. In those days, the printers' ink would still come off and stain any white sheet. "Dreadful, your paper," she would tell me. "It dirties my hands every time I touch it. Ugh!" But she would continue reading it and take pride in telling neighbours that "John, my son-in-law, has a nice piece in the *Telegraph* today…"

Maureen and I would take ourselves off to Ireland and travel from one end to the other; or we would go on one of several cruises to which I had been officially invited, so that I could write about them in my column, which by now had become a weekly "must read" in educational circles.

The little anecdote on how the column came about in the first place is worth the telling. I had heard that the *Guardian* was planning to launch a weekly supplement to be called *Education Guardian*. This was clearly meant to compete with the *Times Educational Supplement*, which was the money-spinner for Times Newspapers, best known for its many pages of classified adverts for teachers' and head teachers' jobs. Naturally, the *Guardian* wanted desperately to cash in on this pot of gold. Why, I thought, shouldn't we on the *Telegraph* have such a brilliant scheme? I thought I would tackle the editor, then a loveable elderly gentleman with a stoop. I knocked timidly at his oak door and heard a muffled "Come". I hadn't been on the staff that long and was still a little nervous.

I went into the vast carpeted room and wound my way through the thick cigarette smoke. Maurice Green was sitting at his desk, bent over sheets of white paper on which he was writing – with a pen. A cigarette clung to his lips, its long stick of ash hanging down and about to drop. Green continued laboriously to write, while I just stood there. At last, while still writing and smoking and looking down at the paper on which he formed his words, came a queried "Yes?"

"I was just wondering, Sir," I stammered. "The *Guardian* newspaper is going to publish a weekly *Education Guardian* and I thought maybe we should perhaps do something similar…" My words trailed off, while Maurice Green continued to write. Then he said: "Ah, you were wondering whether we could do something similar, eh?" "Yes, Sir," I mumbled.

He thought for a full moment, then put down his pen, lit another cigarette from the dimp in his mouth, and puffed out a cloud of smoke. "Well. Izbicki, when we are as much in need of advertising as the *Guardian*, we'll think about it." And he picked up his pen, stooped over his desk and continued to write. I shuffled for a few seconds, just in case further words of wisdom were to come my way and, when they didn't, turned and walked out.

I have always considered this as one of the worst errors of judgment throughout my years at the *Telegraph*. He was, of course, right at the time. Companies were queuing up to purchase space in the paper – and very expensive space it was too. Compared with us, the *Guardian* was poverty-stricken.

But back to our beautiful holidays. One of the cruise ships was the *SS Uganda,* which was then best known as an educational cruise ship. It would transport thousands of secondary school children half way round the world. On board they would get daily lessons in their usual timetabled subjects from their own teachers; then they would have additional lectures by specialists in aspects of the cruise. So, if we were sailing to the Greek Islands, the boys and girls would be told something of the history and the mythology surrounding

A Happy Marriage with a tragic ending:
Maureen and me on an education cruise, 1975

each island about to be visited. The specialists would then accompany the pupils to the various historic sites and describe everything in more detail. It was a wonderful idea. The *Uganda* was an old ship and was eventually "retired" – but later brought back as a troop carrier during the Falklands War and praised for its sturdy durability by Mrs Thatcher.

Maureen and I joined two *Uganda* cruises and on one of them we were accompanied by Paul who thoroughly enjoyed the lessons alongside children from a totally different school to the one he attended.

The other cruises were also educational – but directed at adults and run by the Swan Hellenic company on a smaller cruise ship, the *Orpheus*, which was flying the Greek flag. Again, experts accompanied these splendid cruises and lectured both on board and on shore, standing alongside the ancient sites of Troy, or Ephesus or Rhodes. Luckily, each cruise was also accompanied by a doctor for on one of the *Orpheus* expeditions, Maureen was taken ill with sharp pains when urinating. It was diagnosed as cystitis, an inflammation of the urinary bladder and prescribed antibiotics.

Although the drug did manage to appease the pain after some days, it did not go away entirely. Back home she went to her GP who also concluded that it was cystitis. As the pains grew sharper, I insisted that she should see a specialist. Thanks to the *Telegraph*, the family was fully covered by BUPA, so Maureen took herself to the nearby Nuffield Hospital for a proper check-up. Later that day I was telephoned by the doctor who asked me to come along "for a chat". I was surprised and a little frightened when he would not tell me if there was anything wrong on the phone.

When I entered his room a little later I was further perplexed not to find Maureen there. Again, I demanded to know what was wrong.

"Please sit down Mr Izbicki," he said with a little smile. I sat.

"I've had a good look at your wife – internally. I'm afraid I discovered a small tumour."

I felt myself turning pale. "Tumour? What kind of tumour?"

"I'm afraid I've no idea, but I've sent off for a biopsy so I should know later today. I should tell you that not every lump one sees these days turns out to be malignant, so I shouldn't get too anxious…"

"And if it is malignant?"

"Oh, let's cross that bridge when we come to it, shall we? But there are all kinds of very effective treatments, so I should tend to look on the bright side rather than get all stressed unnecessarily, Mr Izbicki."

"Does Maureen know? And where is she, doctor?"

"Oh, she's fine. We've put her to bed for a little rest and she can stay the night. Yes, she does know. I've had a chat with her and she's not the kind of woman over whose eyes one can pull the proverbial wool, so I put her in the picture. I think you'll find her in reasonable spirits…"

He was right Maureen would not have accepted some cock and bull story. She was already fairly certain that it wasn't cystitis as previously diagnosed. I found her, just as the doctor had forecast, in good spirits, smiling broadly, kissing me fondly and telling me at once *not to worry*! She knew me well since I am a worrier. And if I have nothing to worry about, I'll worry about not worrying, so she actually put *me* at my ease. She was in a big, bright room, fully equipped with a television set, a bowl of fruit, a bell that would bring a nurse scurrying in within seconds, a good view over the extensive grounds and an en suite bathroom. In fact, a typical Nuffield/BUPA private apartment and obviously extremely expensive. But it was all paid for.

The tumour turned out to be malignant but Maureen continued to be optimistic. Her parents and mine, on the other hand, were understandably distressed. Nell, Maureen's Mum, and May, her aunt (Nell's sister) immediately rushed to the priest and ordered a special Mass. They prayed solemnly and daily. My parents also prayed. And cried. Paul was simply told that Mummy was unwell and he accepted it stoically. He was not quite 13 and had many friends both locally and at school, which kept him going.

As for me, I had my work to keep me busy during those early days but accompanied Maureen to every treatment she was given. We went to the North

Middlesex Hospital for her radiotherapy. As it happened, we had an excellent friend who was a doctor there. Indeed, Maurice Sutton was even a radiology consultant at that very hospital. But we were seen by a colleague of his, a Dr Victor Levison, and didn't insist on seeing Maurice. We felt it might not have been quite the thing to do. I have always regretted this and have since felt that, if there are any strings one can pull then bloody well pull them!

There was something else I have always regretted. Maureen was advised almost immediately to give up smoking. Both of us smoked fairly heavily, certainly 20 a day – each. Cancer of the bladder – for that is what she had contracted – was more seriously affected by cigarette smoke inhalation than cancer of the lung. She accepted the advice and gave up smoking immediately. It turned out to be the only pleasure left to her and I always felt that this one pleasure should have been left alone.

Victor Levison had Maureen's notes and studied them carefully while we both sat in his room awaiting his words of wisdom. "Right," he said at last. He addressed Maureen. "You'll need a course of radiotherapy. It'll mean coming here twice a week to begin with." He then turned to me. "Do you want this done privately or on the National Health?" he asked.

"What's the difference?" I wanted to know.

"Well, if you have it done privately, I shall perform it myself."

I looked at Maureen. She smiled at me. I turned to the doctor. "We'll have it done privately, of course," I said It simply *had* to be better to have the top man performing whatever radiotherapy was, I thought. No matter what the cost.

Only later, when Maurice Sutton heard of the decision, he told me, not so much in anger as in regret: "Why didn't you come to me, John? I'd have done it and I certainly wouldn't have charged you. The NHS would have been no different and certainly no worse."

Maureen stood the treatment valiantly. It made her tired but she continued to teach until the end of the term. She said it took her mind off it. She said she had no pain.

Three months later, she was examined. The tumour had gone. All was clear and we had a great celebration with family and friends. Several bottles of champagne were consumed and several chickens devoured. We danced into the early hours and the bloody man next door banged on the wall for silence.

It was all a false hope. The cancer returned with a vengeance and we were referred to "the best man in the country" for this kind of carcinoma. His name was Richard Turner-Warwick, the senior surgeon and urologist at the Middlesex Hospital in London's West End since 1961. We made an appointment and were amazed at the speed with which he saw us.

Turner-Warwick was a small, thin man with bright blue, piercing eyes and a mop of brown curly hair. He sat with his hands folded in his lap and used them to make a particular point. His fingers were long and slender, clearly the fingers of a surgeon or a violinist. He discussed the case at some length, making us both feel totally at ease.

"I shall perform this operation myself," he said and I immediately thought: "Here we go again…he'll no doubt ask a small fortune…" I was wrong, for he said with a finger pointing at nothing in particular:

"I shall tell you now that I shall not be doing this privately but only on the National Health. If I did it privately, you might just as well sell your car and your house now and then still be unable to meet the costs, for I shall require a large team around me during surgery and an equally large team around Maureen for a few weeks after it."

He was right. The operation lasted some nine hours and he had to cut away large sections of the colon.

It was the first of numerous operations.

After one such surgical session, I met Turner-Warwick on the stairs of the Middlesex and he told me that things had gone reasonably well. "What's the next step?" I wanted to know.

He looked at me solemnly and replied: "Well, you might try saying a little prayer."

This, I thought, coming from an eminent surgeon, a scientist, whose belief in a deity was not generally considered to be terribly serious, must reflect the true seriousness of the situation. I took myself off to a corner, sat down and wept.

I do not wish to give a blow-by-blow account of Maureen's long and painful stay at the Middlesex. The memory of those two-and-a-half years – almost three – is still too upsetting. Suffice to say that she had to be fed intravenously for nearly a year (so unusual that a paper appeared in *The Lancet* about it); that she had the bladder removed and had to wear both a colostomy and an ileostomy to replace the colon and the bladder; that these two bags, twisted around two stomas constantly leaked or split, gushing out urine and shit; that she lost all her hair and had to wear a (remarkably good) NHS wig; that she had to have her entire blood changed following a massive bleed and that she almost died three times during her ordeal.

Often I wished that she would have died if only to release her from these many agonies.

I used to commute between home and hospital every morning, spend half an hour with her, then go on to Fleet Street to the office, see what's on the diary for the day, dish out jobs to my wonderful colleagues, Margot Norman, Sarah Thompson and Mike Durham and continue to write my weekly columns and take on any of the major stories and conferences. On one occasion, while I was in Brighton covering the annual conference of the National Association of Head Teachers (NAHT) I received an SOS from the hospital. Would I please hurry back to London to see Maureen who was "very ill". I raced back, thinking that I might probably be too late.

But on arrival, totally breathless, I was met by broadly smiling nurses. "She's fine, John, she's fine. She was very poorly and had to have a few pints of blood pumped into her, but she made a remarkable recovery. Quite remarkable!"

Maureen met me with a weary smile and a weak hug.

She once recovered sufficiently for the hospital to give her a little holiday and I drove her home as slowly and as carefully as it was possible to do in my old Ford Escort. We had a daily, a Mrs Baldry, who did the washing and ironing and cleaned for me and Paul during Maureen's hospitalisation. When we opened the front door, there were two immediate reactions: Mrs Baldry gave a piercing scream and fell around Maureen's shoulders, almost flattening her to the ground, and Striker yelped with joy and jumped up at her, trying to lick her face. Paul hadn't yet returned from school but when he did, he, too, fell around his Mum's neck, hugging and kissing her many times. Maureen and I were in tears but they, too, were tears of happiness.

The joy was not to last before she was back at the Middlesex and I returned to my commuting from home to hospital, to office and back to hospital, arriving home around 9 p.m. every night. Fish and chips was a fairly regular meal before slumping into bed. Paul also lived off junk food most of the time.

Our mothers and May, Maureen's aunt, would take it in turns to come down to us from their homes in Blackpool, Cleveleys and Manchester. They would cook nice meals and also do the washing, ironing and cleaning, giving Mrs Baldry some time of her own. In their absence, and if it wasn't a quick purchase from the Greek-owned chippie round the corner, I would have to do the cooking on arriving home. It meant another long day but my culinary skills improved to some extent as a result. Some weekends I would take Paul for a professionally cooked meal at one or other restaurant in the area but he was often out on a Saturday night, seeing his friends – or they would come to the house and play games in the cellar, which had been converted for his use. Friends, like the Goldings or the Blocks, would also invite Paul and me for meals. In times like this, one knows who one's friends are.

Paul's school – King Alfred's at Golders Green – was extremely understanding and the head, the marvellous Nikki Archer and her staff held a meeting to decide whether they should withdraw Paul from the O-level exams in view of the fact that he was not really able to concentrate on his work properly and was likely to get some poor results. But they decided against such a proposal. According to Nikki, "banning the poor lad from the exams would be worse than letting him do his best and not do as well as he might otherwise do." She was, of course, right. He didn't do too well but didn't have to resit either. He left King Alfred's to do his A-levels at Southgate Technical College. Techs make youngsters feel more like adults and, as many students fall into the "mature" category, the mix is almost perfect.

Maureen's cancer was showing no signs of improvement and I started to clutch at straws of hope. My humorous experience in Paris with Lady Kemsley and the Magnetiseur suddenly took on the prospect of a possible treatment, even cure. I didn't really search hard for a magnetiseur, but I threw myself into an almost frenzied hunt for a faith healer. I bought copies of *Psychic News* to help me in my research for The Answer. After all, I had once seen a friend's eyesight restored through the intervention of a psychic "doctor".

While I worked on *Topic* magazine, Joe Bernard Hutton became one of my contributors. He was an expert on Soviet affairs and throughout the five or six years that I knew him, he wore thick lensed-glasses. Even then he had to hold a paper or letter a matter of a few centimetres from his eyes to read it. Then, one day, he walked into my office – by now I was deputy editor of *World Medicine* – and demanded that I should hand him something – "anything" – to read. I handed him a galley of type and was astounded to see him holding at arm's length and read it perfectly without the help of his spectacles. He told me the story of how he had visited a Dr Lang in Aylesbury. Dr Lang, it turned out, was a medium who worked with the help of a deceased ophthalmic surgeon from Moorfield's Hospital. Lang greeted Hutton with his eyes firmly closed, speaking with the voice of an old man. He then "operated" on my friend's eyes, asking "nurses" to hand him various instruments. The "operation" was some centimetres above the eyes and Hutton could feel nothing except a slight tingling sensation. When his wife drove him back to their home in Worthing, he suffered a headache and found the street lighting to be "too glaring". Some days later, he could read his morning newspaper in a normal position. His wife nearly dropped the tray of coffee and biscuits she was bringing him when she saw this "miracle".

Although I found the entire episode strange, I had to believe that it had happened. Joe Bernard Hutton would never have walked around for years wearing thick-lenses glasses simply in order to play such a confidence trick. I later edited his book *Out of this World* – and wrote its foreword – so years later, when I was seeking help for my poor darling Maureen, the Hutton episode played back like a video in my mind.

I telephoned a faith healer, picked at random from *Psychic News*. He sounded friendly enough on the phone and invited me to one of his sessions held every week at his home in Reading. It was a Thursday evening and it took me some time to find the address. It was a very simple terraced house in a fairly run-down area of the city. A small, white-haired woman opened the door to me and pointed up the uncarpeted staircase. Upstairs, I could hear voices coming from one of the rooms – obviously a bedroom – and, as the door was slightly ajar, I entered to find it full of people, men and women, all sitting and murmuring in almost total darkness. I realised that what I was hearing was prayers, appealing to God and Christ for help.

One upright wooden chair was free so I sat down and tried to get my eyes used to the murkiness. I was able to see the outline of a more comfortable armchair in the middle of the room. This I was to discover was where the healer performed his miracles. I found myself silently praying for help to be sent to Maureen.

The healer came in at last and stood in the middle of the room. There was sudden silence. Although my eyes had by now become accustomed to the gloom, I still could not make out details of faces. The healer himself appeared to be a man of medium height, not more than five foot six or seven inches, wearing long trousers and a shirt with its sleeves rolled up.

The session started with the healer walking over to a buxom woman sitting on one of the hard wooden chairs. He whispered something to her and she rose and went to the middle of the room with him. There he proceeded to place one hand on her head while the other hand gently stroked her back. The process lasted no more than a couple of minutes. The woman, by now in tears, thanked him and left the room, still praying between sobs. Another woman was chosen and a similar activity took place again for about two minutes. She went away, seemingly happy.

Most of those undergoing some form of healing treatment seemed to have trouble with their backs. When it came to me, I was gently led to the middle of the room and the healer whispered: "I can see that you have pain in your back." I agreed quietly that my back had given me trouble for some years but added that I was not there for me. "I know. I know. You have come to me about your wife, haven't you?" he said very quietly. I was surprised.

"How did you know that?" I asked.

"Oh, there are many things that I know. You don't need to tell me. She is, I think, in hospital and in great distress. Please tell her not to worry. I shall visit her in her sleeping state and I hope we can do something for her. But now, let me see to your back."

And he laid his hand upon my head, squeezing gently, while the other hand moved to the bottom of my back and let it rest there for a minute or so. There was no pressure but I felt a distinct warmth pervading my flesh as though his hand were a hot water bottle.

"Thank you for coming to see me," he said very quietly and moved to the next person awaiting his attention.

I went downstairs in a daze. My back still felt warm and I was convinced that I would probably find Maureen in better condition, too. The elderly lady met me in the hall and I asked how much I owed.

"Oh, nothing, Sir. Anything you give is purely voluntary. I hope he'll have helped you."

I slipped £10 into a little tin on the table near the front door. Later I thought that a tenner must be considered extremely mean. If he could heal Maureen, I could not even afford the money he deserved.

When I visited Maureen the next morning, she was smiling and assured me that she was feeling "quite well". I told her of my experience and she laughed. It was so good to hear her laugh. I had not heard her laugh for such a long time. But all we could do was to embrace each other. The nurses and the sister were all delighted. I used to spend a great deal of time in their room at the end of the ward, drinking tea and chain smoking cigarettes while Maureen was undergoing treatment, like having her drips and her bags changed.

Unfortunately, the healer's brilliance was only very temporary. By the weekend, Maureen had taken a turn for the worse again. There was no laughter.

I was given the run of the Middlesex Hospital and was able to use their kitchens. Maureen was unable to keep any of the hospital food down. Whatever she managed to eat, she would vomit back. She had lost so much weight and was no more than a pale shadow of the woman I had known and loved. I used to buy fillet steak and fry it in olive oil, then cut it into very small pieces and take it to her on a plate garnished with a little tomato and one small potato. I would then sit on the side of the bed and feed it to her, little by little. She told me that she enjoyed it but I was never quite sure whether she had enjoyed my food or my feeding it to her.

Another little holiday had been promised to her and I was told that I would be able to take her home for a long weekend. I made use of this time by searching out a medical hypnotist not far from the hospital. An appointment was made and I drove Maureen to see him. I had already explained to him about her constant sickness. He sat Maureen down in his consulting room and told me to take a walk. "We'll be about an hour," he said as he ushered me out of the front door.

I walked and walked, consulting my watch every five minutes. I passed a small café and decided to treat myself to a cup of tea and a bun, still continuing to look at my watch. I was back to collect Maureen on the dot and made her comfortable in the car. Seat belts had already been introduced but it was painful for her to have one. When one is nothing but skin and bones, the pressure of a belt of that kind can do more harm than good. I decided instead to drive very slowly and carefully back to Barnet.

We spoke of the treatment the hypnotist had given her. I knew that she was a superb subject for hypnosis. While in France, I did a story about a hypnotist who had turned a simple postman who liked painting but could not produce anything other than chocolate box-type flowers and cats, into an impressionist of great talent. He would put the postman into a trance in front of an easel and a pallet of different oil paints and would then suggest that he was standing on a beach in Tahiti, with its palm trees, bathing beauties and a blue sky. Throughout these descriptive interludes, the postman would attack the canvas with brushes and pallet knives, producing within a matter of seconds excellent paintings of the scenes as described, but in the style of impressionism.

At one of these sessions, the hypnotist put Maureen into a trance – from behind! She was standing looking at the postman's canvas, when the hypnotist standing two metres behind her, simply put his hands in the air and beckoned her towards him, murmuring some words at the same time. Slowly, Maureen grew taut and fell backwards into his arms. Those who witnessed this spectacle, including myself, applauded wildly. She was quickly brought round again and knew nothing of what had happened. That is how I learned what a good subject for this type of hypnosis she was.

About halfway back to Barnet, Maureen suddenly said: "D'you know what I really fancy, darling?"

"No, what d'you fancy? Just name it," I replied.

"You'll think it silly but I really fancy a nice glass of sherry."

My hands shook on the steering wheel and my foot pressed down a little on the accelerator. It was the first time in at least two years that she had asked for an alcoholic drink. We always used to drink wine with our meals and have a digestif afterwards. Her request almost made me cry with pleasure. Had the hypnosis worked? And why had no one thought of hypnosis before?

As soon as we were back home, I poured her a schooner of La Fina, her favourite sherry – and watched her sip it. I poured myself a stiff scotch and together we sat drinking. It was like the old days. It was just like the old days.

I cooked her some fillet steak, potato, tomato and one vegetable (cauliflower, I think) and watched her eating it by herself.

I then waited and prayed. But amazingly, what she had consumed was retained. There was no sickness. That night she slept well. The next day was also reasonably good and we phoned the two Mums in Cleveleys and Manchester and Auntie May in Blackpool, just to share our happiness.

I shall never forget those two happy days.

Maureen's church had been of great help throughout the illness. She worshipped at Christ the King Roman Catholic Church at nearby Oakwood. Many, if not all the priests were Dutch and many of them would visit Maureen either at home or at hospital. I cannot praise them enough for their regular visits, when they would pray with her and, possibly more important, speak to her.

Only once did I lose my temper with the visiting clergy. It was on one of those days when Maureen was home and was propped up in a comfortable armchair in one of the downstairs sitting rooms. One of the Christ the King clerics had brought with him an earnest young priest who said he would be able to do something positive for Maureen. I was delighted. "Anything you can do for her, Father, would be most appreciated," I exclaimed and left the two of them, Maureen and the priest, alone, while I took the other priest into the kitchen for a drink and a chat.

Nearly an hour later I heard a plaintive cry coming from the sitting room. It was unmistakably Maureen's voice and I rushed to find out if anything was wrong. I found her in a torrent of tears, clearly extremely distressed.

"What on earth is the matter?" I demanded.

Between sobs she told me: "Please ask the Father to leave. Please, please, I don't want to let him do this…"

"What has he done to you?" I shouted and, turning to the priest, I shouted even louder: "What have you done to her? You bastard! Get out. Get the hell out of here!" And I struck out but was held back by the other priest who said: "Calm down, my son, calm down. Let's find out what has happened, shall we?"

After a long discussion between the two priests and my equally long talk with Maureen, I discovered what had happened. The priest had spent more than half an hour praying with Maureen…but then started telling her that her illness was caused by an evil spirit within her and he needed to get rid of it. Then everything would be all right again. He was performing an exorcism. The poor girl was terrified.

I threw the priest from the house. "Take your fucking exorcism with you, you bastard," I shouted after him before returning to the room to comfort the poor girl.

There was one other clergyman who was a constant and very welcome visitor. That was Denis Duncan, my Ettie's husband. Denis was no Catholic but a minister of the Kirk of Scotland. He was brilliant throughout, visiting Maureen in hospital at least once a week and sitting with her for an hour at a time, just speaking quietly, giving her encouragement and praying with and for her. Both he and Ettie were consistently kind and generous with their time and sympathy. Ettie often held the fort for me, taking copious notes for me from contacts, while I was at the hospital. The powers that be at the *Telegraph* encouraged me to spend "as much time as you want" at the Middlesex. Peter Eastwood asked for my bulletins of Maureen's progress and when things were not going well, would tell me off in the gentlest of ways (so unlike the Eastwood everyone seemed to detest). "Go and spend more time with her, John. You have a good and loyal staff. They'll keep your office ticking over. You really needn't worry on that score," he would say.

Between the Church and the *Telegraph*, I was getting all the help and encouragement I needed. But Maureen was not getting any better and one of those few occasions when I managed to bring her home for "a little holiday from the Ward" and provide her with a little precious time with Paul, we had another crisis. One of her bags, the colostomy one containing her faeces, burst.

Paul screamed when he saw the excreta cascading from the bed onto the floor. "Daddy, daddy, daddy!" he shouted (he only called me daddy when he was in serious trouble; otherwise he would always call me John – because "that's what everyone calls you"). I abandoned my cooking and rushed from the kitchen to the front room where we had placed Maureen's bed. "Daddy, there's shit everywhere. *Do* something!" I asked him to leave the room while I would "do something".

Before he left the room screaming, he shouted hysterically at Maureen: "You're always ill! Why are you always fucking ill?" He ran to the kitchen and fell to the floor, continuing to scream and sob while banging his fists on the floor. He was almost 15 years old.

I turned to Maureen who had also started to cry. "For once, darling," I said quietly but felt myself shaking, "for once I think he needs me more than you do. I'll be back as soon as I can…" Maureen looked up at me and between sobs, said: "Yes, yes, do please go and see to him…and tell him I'm sorry."

I found Paul prostrate, the tears flowing in waves down his chin and snot pouring from his nose. I knelt beside him and took him into my arms.

"Shush, shush, darling. Mummy wants you to know that she's very sorry – but she can't help it, sweetheart. She is very ill and we can do nothing except try our best to help her and show her our love. I know these past years have been awful for you and both Mummy and I have not been able to be with you as much as we should have liked to. I'm so sorry that I've not been the father I should have been to you and that I've been spending so much time at the hospital. You've been such a good boy and I know you've been working hard at school. Nikki Archer speaks very highly of you.

"I know also that you really love your Mum. You love her very much and she loves you more than her life…"

At this, his hands grasped me hard and both he and I sobbed our hearts out together, there, down on the kitchen floor.

What neither of us had noticed was that Striker, our faithful dog had come in and had draped himself close to both of us. We heard his whimpering. He was quietly crying in sympathy.

We were rescued by a nasty smell of burning. "Oh, my God, the food. I forgot the bloody food," I exclaimed as I jumped up and Paul jumped up and Striker jumped up. I rushed to turn off the gas and rescue the pans.

Then we both simultaneously started to laugh.

"I'll go get a takeaway," I said and we laughed some more and Striker wagged his tail and ran into Maureen's room, followed by me and Paul. We tried to ignore the shit. We all held onto each other.

I cleaned Maureen up, changed her clothes and bedding. I went to soak all the soiled sheets and nightdress in the bath. They would later go into the washing machine. And I changed the wretched bag before washing myself thoroughly and leaving to fetch that blessed takeaway.

It had been a traumatic but valuable evening for the four of us – and that included Striker.

If the Church wasn't able to help Maureen directly, some indirect intervention might have still been possible. I discussed the possibility of a trip to Lourdes with Father Gregory at Christ the King Church. Everything would be arranged and a specially designed ambulance would be sent to take Maureen along with others to fly to Lourdes for a miracle.

Maureen looked forward to the experience and prayed solemnly together with two nuns who were regular visitors from her old Our Lady of Sion

School, for God to give her the strength to be able to endure the journey, particularly the flight.

I was in two minds about this trip. I knew Lourdes from the time I was working for Kemsley Newspapers in Paris. I had gone down there to write a long feature for the *Sunday Empire News* and, frankly, although I had witnessed the odd "miracle" – mostly people who had waded through the waters of Saint Bernadette with bad backs or ulcers, or terrible rheumatism or arthritis – there were none whose life-threatening illnesses like cancer – were cured. Many sick people came away with serene happiness printed across their faces, huge smiles, happy hymns and laughter.

What upset me most was the dreadful commercialism of the whole scene. Lourdes had developed from a peaceful and holy shrine into a big, noisy business. Shopkeepers and stallholders would shout their wares to the crowds of believers. It was all rather reminiscent of scenes from Chaucer or the sales of indulgences that made Luther lose his temper, rant against Rome and hammer his bulls to the Cathedral doors. I could not help feeling that, if the good Bernadette could really come back to earth and witness this circus, she would shed bitter tears.

But Maureen had set her heart on going. She was, after all, a true believer. Who was I to deny her? Lourdes was yet another straw, probably the final one, at which to clutch for a cure by miracle.

It was not to be. She was back at the Middlesex with yet another relapse and doctors pronounced her too weak to make such a stressful journey.

One night I was sitting at her bedside when her drip failed and a doctor had to be called to get a new one working. I had not met this young houseman before. He could not long have qualified. His smooth adolescent features peered down at Maureen, whose breathing was shallow. "Hello," he said cheerfully. "How you keeping?" "Fine, just fine," replied Maureen with the tiniest of smiles. "Good," said he, "then we'll soon fix you up…" What an ass, I thought. He had no idea what she was suffering or for how long she had suffered it. One of the hospital sisters who suddenly appeared to lend a hand, put him wise. She pulled him gently away and explained, then said aloud: "This is Maureen, doctor, one of our very favourite patients. She's just about the bravest woman I've met during all the years I've been here."

The young man unwrapped the brand new drip and long tube from its box and fitted another bottle of the expensive serum to its stand, entering the feeder needle through the top of the bottle. He then tried putting the needle into Maureen's thin right arm. The poor girl was nowt but skin and bone and I stood there thinking how beautiful she had been. Here was a woman who always knew exactly how to dress and what makeup to put on. Her favourite perfumes were *Madame Rochas* and *Femme* and I used to bring them back through duty-free whenever I had to go abroad on stories. She had such a good figure and beautiful auburn hair. Men would lust after her and when I was asked why I was never jealous, I would reply: "On the contrary. I'm proud. If I think her fantastic, why shouldn't others think the same?"

Now here she was – her hair gone, wearing a NHS wig, her face pale and sunken and her body eaten away by a disease that knows no compassion. But her eyes – her eyes still had some of her old magic; they would often shine at me and at her many regular visitors. Her eyes would never die.

The doctor could not find a vein into which to stick his needle. He tried one position after another, repeating "Sorry" each time. Had she not suffered enough pain?

On his fourth and this time successful attempt, Maureen looked up at him, smiled and said: "If I were a horse, you'd shoot me, wouldn't you?"

The poor man didn't know what to say or where to look. He just bowed and said: "I hope that'll stay in…good night." And he made an embarrassed exit.

There were times when we discussed euthanasia. She wanted me to take a pillow and suffocate her. She had read of such a mercy-killing in the *Telegraph* and other papers, where the husband had killed his wife to save her from suffering an incurable illness, then given himself up and been put on trial for murder. We both felt great sympathy with the man. But, although I knew it made a lot of sense, I lacked the guts, the sheer courage to kill. And Maureen, being a good Catholic, did not really believe in suicide. I knew she was suffering not only immense physical pain, eased only through shots of morphine, but also excruciating mental agony, caused by the demoralisation of a woman whose attractions and whose love of life had been cruelly expunged. Yet her life was not mine to take. So she continued to live and I to love.

One day she apologised to me. Apologised? To me? "What on earth for?" I asked her. "I just want to say sorry for not having been able to give you another child. I know how much you love children and I'd have so wanted to give you another but…"

I interrupted her. "I'm perfectly happy with Paul. You have given me all I ever wanted. And you will always be in him."

And then she said: "You must get yourself another woman you can love. I don't just mean after I've gone but now. I won't mind. You deserve some physical love and I cannot, I'm just not able…"

"Please don't speak like that. I don't fancy anyone else – and I'm still convinced that there'll soon be a cure that will treat your cancer and make you well again."

"How can it? Come on John…" and there was bitterness, even anger in her tone, "I no longer have a bladder; I no longer possess a bowel; they've taken away my womb, for God's sake. They didn't even seek my permission but gave me an entire hysterectomy during one of those bloody operations. They even removed my fallopian tubes…"

We did a great deal of crying at the Middlesex.

Among Maureen's many visitors, was one man whom we had met just once at a party. John Love turned out to be a buyer for the supermarket Sainsbury's and whenever he appeared at the Middlesex ward, he would carry a huge bouquet of flowers in one hand and, precariously perched on his other hand, a large wooden tray of fresh fruit. Poor Maureen loved the flowers but could not eat any of the fruit. But the nurses were invited to help themselves and all apples, pears, bananas, grapes and peaches would disappear within an hour or so.

Nurses didn't get much in the way of salaries but were often left to eat up sandwiches that patients had left (or which were quite often ordered for empty beds). John Love's fruit as well as chocolates, biscuits and the like that were brought in by other visitors for other patients were always gratefully received and devoured in Sister's room among clouds of cigarette smoke.

When patients died, the curtains were drawn around the bed while nurses went to work, carefully washing them before quietly wheeling them out of the ward, away to the mortuary. Often one would hear close relations, sons and daughters who had come to visit their sick mother or sister, wailing over the body. And no matter how long some of the nurses had treated this or that patient, they would be deeply affected by their death. Many a nurse would seek momentary refuge in Sister's room while I was sitting there and burst into tears.

"Whatever's the matter?" I would sometimes seek to know.

Back would come a tiny voice: "It's Mrs Jenkins (or whoever). She's gone. She was a nice woman and I'll miss her." And the tears would gush again.

On the 11th December 1979, I was stopped by Sister as I arrived at the ward. "Hello John…She's not so good today. In fact, I think you should prepare yourself for the worst. Go on along to see her. I'll bring you a cup of tea." And she pressed my arm. "The two sisters are there with her already," she added.

I rushed to Maureen's bedside, nodded to the two nuns who were to sit in vigil at the bedside until the end. She lay there seemingly asleep. Her breathing was deep and wheezy. I sat down and gently touched her arm. She half opened her eyes and I thought I saw a little smile about her lips. "Don't try to talk, my darling. Have a good rest. I'll be here when you wake up," I whispered. As if to comply with this advice, her eyes closed and she fell into a deep sleep. The nuns prayed.

I spent that night and the next sleeping at the hospital. A room had been prepared for me a couple of floors up. I was told that someone would call me immediately whenever it was necessary. I contacted Nell, May and my mother as well as Maureen's cousin, Margaret, and they all came down to London by trains from Blackpool (her Mum and Aunt May), Manchester (my Mum) and Chesterfield (Margaret, May's daughter). They stayed at the hospital on the night of the 12th.

The 13th was a bleak day. I was woken with a cup of tea at 6.15. To this day I cannot recall whether or not I shaved and showered, probably not. I just threw on my clothes and ran down two flights of stairs to the ward. The curtains had been drawn around her bed. I asked the duty nurse to go to the family room and tell them to come. Strangely enough, they didn't. I just sat at the bedside, stroking her hand and waiting. The nuns were there – they had probably sat there throughout the night – praying.

At about 10 a.m. I thought I could feel her fingers squeezing mine, ever so softly. So softly. Her breathing had started breaking up. It had lost its rhythm. I knew she was going and I suddenly buried my face into her pillow and sobbed quietly. I could hear one of the nuns whispering to the other: "Look at John…she must be gone. *Dominus vobiscum…*" Both nuns prayed a little louder. A priest had already performed the last rites two days previously. It was then that I heard that last of all breaths, the one known as the death rattle, for that is exactly what it is, a rasping rattle within the throat. "Goodnight, my darling one," was all I could say.

As I looked at her for the last time, I noticed that the worry lines on her face had disappeared. There seemed to be the faintest of smiles about her lips. Her agonies had evaporated and she looked truly beautiful. For her, death was a release.

I continued to sit and weep. I could not say the Kaddish, the Jewish prayer for the dead since she was not Jewish. But I said it inside my head. I didn't think God would mind.

She was 42. Had she lived another fortnight, we would have "celebrated" 20 years of a happy marriage.

The Church at Cockfosters was packed for the funeral. Teachers, a mixture of nuns from Our Lady of Sion, former colleagues from Southgate School, including the head and great friend, Peter Targett, his wife, Val, and teachers from her last school – Queen's School at Bushey, and its head, Stanley Bunnell as well as his wife and our close friend, Brigitte, filled a number of pews, along with some doctors and nurses who had looked after Maureen for the best part of three years.

Then there was a small crowd of very tearful pupils, many of whom had been regular visitors at the hospital. And, of course, all our dearest friends, most of them Jewish, along with many of my colleagues as well as Ettie, my faithful PA, and Peter Eastwood who represented the *Daily Telegraph*. The family was there in force including my wonderful cousin, Jacob Izbicki and his wife, Liz. Frankly, I was worried about bringing Paul along. I thought he'd be too upset. But he wanted to go and, indeed, he showed a brave face throughout the Requiem Mass performed by four Roman Catholic priests – and, to give it an ecumenical touch, by the Rev. Dr Denis Duncan, Ettie's husband.

It was Denis's eulogy that really hit home. Not only did he extend his condolences to the family but he also included in that family, Striker, our loving dog.

The burial took place at Southgate Cemetery. On her gravestone I borrowed a line from a Shakespeare sonnet:

So long as men can breathe, or eyes can see,
So long lives this, and this gives life to thee.

One short *post scriptum* to this chapter: Paul rarely shed a tear over his mother's death and this worried me. It's not something a child should keep wrapped up inside. After the funeral, I took him on a holiday – skiing in Switzerland. We stayed at Aiglon, that fabulous international Round Square school of which I had become "A Friend", and had a splendid time, him on the slopes, me on the "*après ski*". But tears were there none. But some years later, when Paul was 19 and Striker, aged 16, had become seriously ill and sadly had to be put down, the floodgates opened and Paul cried his heart out. I was content for I knew that, at long last, he was crying not only for Striker but also for Maureen.

CHAPTER EIGHTEEN:

BACK TO PARIS

After Maureen's death, I threw myself into work. I was always a workaholic but now I would appear at the office earlier than usual and, if necessary, stay later. Paul seemed happy in the midst of his mates but it didn't stop me from feeling a surge of guilt every now and then, that I wasn't showing him the amount of attention a father should be showing his son. It is something that has haunted me and remained with me ever since.

But there was our little holiday at Aiglon College, which, to a certain extent, helped both of us relax a little. Philip Parsons, the head, and his lovely German wife, Inge, made both of us feel thoroughly at home. They, too, missed Maureen, whom they had met on several occasions, both in London and at Chesières-Villars, where Aiglon was housed.

Even then I could not forget work and managed to write a couple of stories about the school. The first disclosed that only 34 out of the 240 boys and girls enrolled in this British International School were actually British. Philip Parsons was unhappy that so few British parents had opted to send their children to what was, after all, one of the most exclusive independent schools in Europe. In order to increase their number, Parsons set up a scholarship scheme for the children of parents who could not afford the fees, which at that time ranged from just under £6,000 to £7,430 a year. It would give bursaries of up to 10,000 Swiss francs (about £3,000) to 20 additional British youngsters a year, giving them the opportunity of coming to Aiglon.

The other story appeared in the *Peterborough* column, the *Telegraph*'s daily diary, an up-market gossip column, and told of the two septuagenarian sisters who had flown into Switzerland and made their way through the heavy snow to Aiglon, where they unveiled the bust of their late brother, John Corlette, who founded the school.

Corlette was a disciple of Kurt Hahn, the German Jewish educationist who was responsible for the establishment of a group of so-called "round square schools".

The expression evolved from one of Hahn's foundations – Gordonstoun School at Elgin in Scotland, which has educated thousands of youngsters, including Prince Philip, the Duke of Edinburgh and Prince Charles, Prince of Wales. Hahn first built Salem, his masterly school in Germany, in 1933, but later fled from Hitler and the Nazis. His philosophy was to educate the whole person (*"plus est en vous"* was his and Gordonstoun's motto). It was all a question of brain competing with brawn, so children would be taught normal lessons in the morning and, come the afternoon, would go out to climb, sail, ski, make music and theatre.

Gordonstoun contained buildings that circled a square. The story goes that the devil chased a rider across the fields and woodlands until the rider reached the school and entered the circular square. Here, the devil could not touch him. The Round Square Schools, of which there are about a dozen throughout the world, all follow Hahn's philosophy. And I became one of their humble friends and followers.

On the night the sisters unveiled John Corlette's bust, the school served a banquet. I asked to be sat among the pupils and was placed with a group of sixth formers, boys and girls. The first course was a Minestrone soup. On downing the first spoonful or two, I said: "Hmm…it's good. The very best that Knorr could produce." Everyone around me exploded with guffaws of laughter. I didn't think what I had said quite that funny so I asked what the joke was. The girls opposite me pointed to the nubile young woman on my right. It turned out that she was the daughter of Mr Knorr himself and heiress to the Knorr empire.

When Paul and I returned home from Aiglon, I had to go straight to bed. The carton of Benson & Hedges cigarettes I had bought in the duty free shop had to wait. I had caught the flu.

Four days I lay there. Once again, Paul had to look after himself. Mrs Baldry came daily to make me soups and ply me with water and fruit juices. On the fifth day, I rose and took myself unsteadily down the stairs to the bathroom. I opened that golden carton and reached for a cigarette. At the same time I looked at myself in the mirror. Horror! My eyes had sunk somewhere behind my cheekbones and I had grown a reasonably sized beard. But the hairs of that beard were not black to match those on my head but a mixture of grey, white and red. Red? Me? Ridiculous!

I stuck the cigarette between my lips but did not light it. The tobacco somehow didn't taste right. I removed the cigarette, looked at myself in the mirror and said: "Let's see how long you can keep this up." It was a personal challenge.

I have not smoked since (except for the odd annual cigar at Christmas, but after about four years of this ritual, it, too, was abandoned).

By now, the education scene had changed once again and I asked the question: Why do politicians all treat our young people like so many footballs to kick from one end of the wretched field to the other? And why are so many youngsters not only unemployed but virtually unemployable? Mark Carlisle was by now in the chair at what was then still called the DES (Department of Education and Science). I found him thoroughly affable. As a politician, he was remarkably honest, trying always to tell the truth and often succeeding. He was in the throes of introducing yet another new examination, getting rid of the CSE and the higher-level O-levels and replacing them with the GCSE.

At this I thought it best to leave the country once again – and I went to my beloved France where I visited an old disused macaroni factory to take a look at children who could not pass such conventional tests in academic ability. Many of them had been dropouts from their "normal" schools. The pasta factory on the outskirts of Paris had been transformed into a very special school by ORT (the Organisation for Rehabilitation through Training) – which was founded towards the end of the nineteenth century in Russia to train poor Jewish youths – many of whom were dropouts from "normal schools" in which they found great difficulty in passing conventional academic tests – for artisan and agricultural occupations.

In France, ORT had opened eight such schools throughout the country. Up to 1,000 young people aged 14 – 18 as well as about 1,000 adults aged up to the age of 45 were being taught some 30 different trades during the day and at evening classes. On admission, the youngsters would first be allowed to 'taste' one of several trades they might fancy during their first semester. By the end of that period, they would choose the trade they most liked to follow, anything from bricklaying or plumbing, to carpentry, tailoring or telecommunications.

They would be taught the normal curriculum but would spend a strong proportion of the day on the vocational aspects of their school. I saw many youngsters who had kicked off by trying to be secretaries but ended up going in for tailoring. It seemed fairly natural that many Jewish boys and girls would opt for the *schmatte* trade, but in the secretarial section, I saw scores of young men and women hammering away at typewriters (the age of the computer had still to hit schools in a big way).

After three years, the students would sit the *Brevet d'Etudes Professionelles* (a Certificate of Vocational Aptitude) but some "late starters" would successfully go in for the higher Baccalauréat in electronics and electronical engineering. The school produced an annual quota of telephone engineers who were guaranteed jobs with France Telecom. The beauty of the scheme was that the final vocational examinations passed by the students counted as their apprenticeships. Companies that employed these young men and women were assured of getting properly trained professionals.

I felt that this form of education, aimed at those who could not cope with the rigours of formal academic schooling, was just what was needed in Britain. I went on to speak about it at some length with Sir Keith Joseph, the Secretary of State for Education whose response to a question on teachers' pay had inadvertently had such a starring role in the NUT conference cabaret.

Sir Keith was always willing to listen and on this occasion immediately wanted to go and see the place for himself. "I shall certainly discuss this with Margaret," he said. "I'm sure she'll be most interested. It's the kind of thing that's needed over here – and I don't suppose it'll have to be Jewish."

Sir Keith went on to send Alan Hazlehurst, a member of his central policy committee, to take a look and he was not the only one. Margaret Jackson, while she was Under-Secretary of Education in a Labour government, also paid ORT a visit. Even John Tomlinson, when he was chairman of the Schools Council, and Ken Cooper, chief executive of the Training Services Agency, both went along to "see for themselves". And when Dr Rhodes Boyson became Minister for Higher Education in Margaret Thatcher's government and told me of a trip he was making to the French capital, I pleaded with him to go and visit my macaroni factory.

Dr Boyson used to be the headteacher of the Robert Montefiore Secondary School, a Jewish secondary modern in Stepney before he went on to become the head of the Highbury Grove Boys School, which became a comprehensive. Boyson ruled the school as a benevolent despot. He always assured me that he never used the cane on any of the boys and yet some of the school's old boys contradicted that assurance.

The first time I visited Highbury Grove, he showed me round. Coming down the stairs from one of the upper floors, he pulled me up at a window. "Look down, look down, what d'you see?" I looked, searching for something unusual but saw only the school gardens and paths. "What am I supposed to be looking for?" "What d'you see, man, what d'you see?"

I shrugged my shoulders. "Grass, a couple of paths, some garden benches…"

"Do you see any litter? Any rubbish lying about?"

"Well, no. Nothing like that…" I muttered.

"That's what I wanted to hear. Go to any other school and you'd see plenty of rubbish, I can assure you."

Boyson was from oop t'north and his rubbish was still "roobish". He then presented me with one of the best lessons anyone ever gave me. "If you want to know what a school is like, d'you know what you should do?" he asked and gave me the answer immediately: "You should demand to see the lavatories!" With that he took me to the nearest lot of toilets, storming in and opening every cubicle. A couple of boys were having a pee but they soon scarpered. "There, take a look. Any graffiti? No. If there were, there'd be a full and immediate enquiry and someone would be in for the high jump," Rhodes Boyson said.

Boyson was an amazing man. His first real entry into politics was through education and he took over the co-editorship of the *Black Papers* with Brian Cox after the original co-editor, A E (Tony) Dyson, resigned from the University of East Anglia to take the cloth and become a priest. Boyson was a Tory through and through and was genuinely concerned about standards in education and scared that the lack of discipline and the "permissive 'Sixties" would do untold damage to teaching and learning alike. *Education: Threatened Standards*, which he edited in 1972, was ample proof of that; the series of *Black Papers on Education* (1969-1977) produced the ultimate evidence. He stood as Conservative candidate for Brent North and got in. After that, he went from strength to strength, being picked as a junior minister by Margaret Thatcher.

Privately, Boyson was a lovely man. In 1971, he invited Maureen and me to dinner at his home. There were just the four of us, Rhodes, his wife, Violet, Maureen and I. We had an absolutely delightful evening with good wine and food and conversation that rarely touched on papers, politics or education. The following day we sent Violet a bouquet of flowers and a thank-you card.

About three or four months later, I went to a school charity lunch organised by Rhodes. After all the speeches, I was approached by an attractive lady who said: "Hello, you're John Izbicki, aren't you? I thought I should introduce myself. Florette. Florette Boyson." She saw my puzzled expression. "I'm Rhodes's wife."

"Ah, of course, of course. I'm so very pleased to meet you," I said and we chatted for a few moments. As soon as I could, I sidled up to Rhodes. "I – er – I've just met your wife – er – Florette…"

"Ah, good, good. Yes, she said she'd like to meet you…"

"Yes, but Rhodes, if Florette is your wife, who was the lady we had dinner with recently?"

"Ah yes," he answered with a chuckle. "That was Violet, my wife. That was the last evening we were together. The marriage was dissolved the next day. We thought we simply wanted to spend one last evening in good company and have a civilised meal. Your flowers arrived just as she was getting into the taxi with the luggage. She took them with her. She was very pleased, John, very pleased indeed. Very thoughtful of Maureen and you…"

As for my suggestion for him to visit ORT, he did and told me how very impressed he had been. He even organised the opening of a similar experiment in Salford.

At the time, I wrote in my column: "We are still so busy fiddling around with an examination system for the top 20 per cent of our children that we are tending to ignore the needs of the majority – and the requirements of industry and commerce." And I quoted Peter Gorb of the London Business School who had told me: "We should be concentrating on teaching people to run the factories we have got instead of teaching them to run empires we haven't got."

Sadly the ORT system was never properly adopted in Britain and British ORT now concentrates on fund raising to help open schools in Russia, Israel – just about everywhere, except here.

It is by no means unusual that when a woman is widowed, she often remains uninvited to dinner parties. I suppose too many women think she might run off with their husbands. On the other hand, when a man becomes a widower, people seem to fall over themselves to invite him into their homes. I was invited twice or three times a week to drinks, dinner, long chats. Many of my friends also invited other "lone" women along in the hope of finding a match for me.

I didn't want any "matches". I didn't even care much for the women to whom I was introduced. A favourite ploy seemed to be that the female guest would appear without any transport, having come by taxi or having been brought by a neighbour. When it was time to leave, I'd be told: "Oh John, you won't mind taking Miriam/Alexandra/Pauline/Josephine home…" And, of course, I would oblige – but resisted "coming in for a coffee".

I grieved for a long time. I suppose I never really stopped grieving.

But time is a great healer. One day, my good friend and colleague David Loshak and his wife, Molly, asked me to dinner at their home in distant Dulwich – a long drive from Barnet, where I still lived. It was, after all, "South of the River" and I was well to the north of it.

Molly sat me at one end of the long table. The other guests, some of them colleagues from the *Telegraph*, were evenly distributed, but I noticed that the husband of the woman on my left was sat right at the other end. I noticed it but did not question it, even to myself. The woman was introduced to me as June Gordon-Walker. Her husband, Robin Gordon-Walker was also a journalist but worked at the Foreign Office as a Press officer. He also happened to be the son of Patrick Gordon-Walker who had long been a loyal supporter of Hugh Gaitskell and became shadow foreign secretary. In the Wilson government, he was briefly Foreign Secretary, then Cabinet minister without portfolio in 1966 and Secretary of State for Education and Science from 1967-8. He was made a life peer in 1974 and was elected Member of the European Parliament a year later. His son was sitting at the other end of the table that night.

All I remember of Robin was that he wore large spectacles and had an infectious laugh that pierced the air. His wife and I formed an almost immediate rapport and chatted throughout the excellent meal, washed down with numerous glasses of fine claret.

Molly, I discovered later, had deliberately placed June and me together. She and June had met at a health club and she knew that June's marriage was all but completely over. So she felt that "no harm could be done" if she, Molly, engineered a "relationship".

Molly was right. Even June assured me after a few reasonably harmless dates that her marriage was over and that she had already filed for divorce. Our relationship grew more intense.

One day in my office, the phone rang. Ettie covered the mouthpiece with one hand and whispered across the room: "It's Robin Gordon-Walker for you, John." She was well aware of June's existence and was warning me that Robin might be on the proverbial warpath. I picked up my extension nervously. "Hello, Robin..." I said.

He sounded pretty angry and wanted to know what my intentions were towards June. I'm not sure if I were able to provide him with the kind of answer he might have wanted to hear, nor was I sure that I might have been able to say what could be considered satisfactory. I mumbled something about my intentions being perfectly honourable. I hadn't even considered the relationship that has formed between us – at least not until that moment.

Luckily perhaps, the line went dead and I was shaken. It was then that I realised that I had fallen in love.

June, a keen tennis and squash player, snapped her tendon playing squash and was rushed to hospital to have it repaired. The poor girl lay at King's College, miserable and in pain. I visited her; so did David Loshak – her two admirers. As for her husband, Robin, there was no sign. June was clearly in pain, with her leg strapped and hoisted by a contraption of pulleys. I was naturally reminded of the dreadful time that Maureen had to suffer in hospital, but there was nothing life-threatening about June's torn tendon, thank goodness. And there was something about the whole hospital atmosphere that filled me with sorrow and fear. And there was something else, something very strange that started my emotions racing. I could not understand this first, but I realised that it was love. Quite simply love!

June was a teacher. I suppose it wasn't strange that I came into almost constant contact with teachers but it did seem strange that the only truly meaningful relationships of my life were with teachers. Like Maureen, June had taught English but had then developed her professional talents and specialised in special education, bringing hope and often success to many a child in whom all others had lost hope.

And she had two children by Robin – a beautiful little girl, Anna, and a very handsome but sometimes quite naughty little boy, Patrick, named after his grandfather. Anna turned out to be studious and clever. She was a little over six years old when I came onto the scene; Patrick was two years older. Both were clearly disturbed at the breakup of their Mum's marriage and yet they and I managed to form a loving relationship. Patrick would often lose his cool and I admit that I was becoming increasingly worried about him. But I needn't have been. It was normal that he should have been in some mental turmoil. Like his father, he was passionate about sport – anything involving a ball, whether cricket, football, rugby, tennis, hockey, golf or snooker, got him going and he developed into a very good tennis player and could more than hold his own on a golf course.

June had bought herself a little semi in the Herne Hill area of south-east London. It was directly opposite the beautiful Brockwell Park, which at weekends was alive with every kind of activity from jogging to tennis, family picnics, singers, gymnasts and fairs. It was a pleasure to walk and chat over a cup of tea at its well-stocked café. I would stay some nights at June's house and was surprised and deeply moved one morning at breakfast when gorgeous little Annie suddenly blurted: "It's nice when you're here." The only reply I could find was, "I think it's nice too."

June had the use of a delightful cottage tucked away in the Cotswolds where we would spend the odd weekend. Paul also came along and June played tennis with him and helped him prepare for his English and other exams. We were slowly but surely turning into a family unit.

People were beginning to think that I held shares in BP, considering my constant commuting between Barnet and Herne Hill, a round trip of more than 30 miles – and petrol wasn't getting any cheaper. So it was with the greatest regret that I decided to sell my Park Road house, which I had grown to love, and buy something "south of the river".

Park Road sold quickly to a musician who immediately transformed the extensive cellar into recording studios. It was a cellar that had seen many a party hosted by Paul and his noisy but otherwise well-behaved pals. I never paid much attention to what was going on down there, although one night a girl had stumbled upstairs into the house, was violently sick and passed out. An ambulance had to be called and she was whisked away to the Barnet General. I believe she had drunk a great deal and probably smoked too much pot. Drugs at the house were a rare (I hoped very rare) occurrence and I thanked God Paul had never entered that sleazy, dangerous world, although he did take up smoking cigarettes. Couldn't blame him for that, as I had smoked far too much until after Maureen's death.

The house I bought was detached and on a main bus route in East Dulwich and stood next door to one of the country's better independent schools – James Allen's Girls School on East Dulwich Grove. It backed onto a tennis club and was just round the corner from North Dulwich railway station. There was a large garden and an extensive lounge-diner with huge windows framing the entire L-shaped room. The kitchen, too, was big and upstairs were five bedrooms and two bathrooms. Five bedrooms? Just for me and Paul? Oh, and Striker? Or was it some sub-conscious expression on my part that it might soon be occupied by another woman and two more children? It was also a lot closer to Fleet Street and I could sleep in that little bit longer before rushing off to catch a train. And Paul was soon to leave me – for university – leaving me all alone (alongside Striker) in a great big house. I was certainly able to see more of June, whose *decree nisi* had been made absolute.

My next-door neighbours were marvellous and by the sheerest coincidence turned out to be Jewish. Tony Jaffé sang in the choir of his *shul* (synagogue). He and his wife, Joy, were strict vegetarians and in typical Jewish fashion would constantly invite me round for a meal, and me, an orthodox carnivore!

I had hardly been at 152 East Dulwich Grove for more than three weeks when I returned from work to find the place in a mess. But it was only when

I spied a half empty bottle of scotch on one of the armchairs that I realised I had been burgled. My video recorder, a radio and various other bits and pieces had gone and the main bedroom had been ransacked. The only stolen item that switched on my fury and made me weep was a pair of golden cufflinks. They were not very valuable. They were not even very attractive and I never actually wore them. But they had been my father's and had come with him from Germany. I would have gladly given the thief the rest of the furniture and every bottle of whisky and cognac in the cupboard, if I could have had those little cufflinks returned.

When I had calmed down, I called the police. About half an hour later, a weary constable, looking for all the world like Jack Warner's portrayal of PC George Dixon of Dock Green, appeared and took some notes, licking the tip of his pencil every now and then. "Strange thing is that I only moved in about three weeks ago. These burglars don't waste their time, do they?"

"No, that they don't, Sir," said PC Plod. "And where did you move from, Sir?"

"I lived in Barnet, just a few steps from Cockfosters, end of the Piccadilly Line…"

"You moved 'ere from Barnet?"

"Well, yes…"

"Well, Sir, if you don't mind me sayin' so, you needs your 'ead examinin'…"

He explained that this was not the easiest place from a security point of view. "You're sandwiched between Brixton over to the west and Peckham to the east. They're not what you'd call crime-free places." He didn't say that they were "black" ghettos. Brixton had its troubles, to say the least, but I always found it an attractive and colourful (in every way) part of London. Peckham was less attractive and has certainly had more than its share of violent crimes.

PC Plod gave me a crime number, accepted a cup of tea, and left. He was one of the last "on the beat" coppers that I saw during the 15 years I lived in Dulwich. The burglary was the first of six suffered during that period.

I continued to cover education for the *Telegraph*. The education scene never seemed to change. After 18 years heading the department I was beginning to get just a little bored. Education ministers came and went and I continued to interview them with monotonous regularity. Kenneth Baker's stint as Secretary of State for Education coincided with this spate of boredom on my part and when I walked into his sumptuous office at Elizabeth House, overlooking Waterloo Station, an office I had visited so often to interview his predecessors, I opened our conversation with: "You are the eighth Education Secretary I've had to interview…"

He guffawed and struck up with: "I'm 'Enery the Eighth I am, 'Enery the Eighth I am, I am…"

I immediately offered him a part in the Education Correspondents' Group cabaret –and we got on like the proverbial house on fire. But the boredom remained. At that time, senior officials of the various teacher unions used to ask me for advice. That I considered to be the beginning of the end. I needed a change of air, a change of job. I sent a memorandum to the then editor, Bill Deedes. "Eighteen years in education is, I think, enough for any self-respecting journalist. Any ideas?"

Bill called me in. He always leaned right back in his swivel chair, his hands nestling behind his head. "Shit down, John, shit down." He had that rather curious speech defect that pronounced an 's' as 'sh' – as in "shome mishtake, shurely…" a phrase immortalised in *Private Eye*. "Now, what'sh all thish?" He waved the memo at me. "You're doing a shplendid job. Explain. Ish it money?"

"No, certainly not. I'm quite happy with what I'm getting. It's just that I'm getting a little fed up of covering the same old ground day in, day out."

We chatted on for a while and, as it was nearing lunchtime, went out to his favourite restaurant – *Paradiso e Inferno*, an Italian on the Strand, where he had a regular table (and which today bears a plaque: "This Was The Late Lord (Bill) Deedes Usual Table For Over 30 Years"). It ended with Bill explaining that he was not at all happy to go through the job of finding someone to replace me, but that he would think about it. "How about joining the leader writers? Jusht an idea, Ishbicki, jusht an idea."

At that time, neither of us knew that his own days and the days of the *Telegraph* were numbered. In 1985 the paper was on the skids and Lord Hartwell was on the brink of calling in the Receivers. It was losing millions of pounds. But a Canadian with pots of money was on the horizon and because the paper was in such dire straits, Conrad Black managed to snap up the *Daily* and *Sunday Telegraphs* for a song. And at the same time he appointed a lanky, bespectacled young man with long dark hair as editor. Bill Deedes, who had edited the paper with kid gloves and great sympathy for the staff since 1974 was sacked by the new regime. In 1986 he was replaced by Max Hastings, who had managed to brown-nose Black by sharing a mutual interest in war. Hastings had notched up a few positive points when he had covered the Falklands debacle for the *London Evening Standard* and had boasted that he had been the first to land on the islands and help liberate it. Black was passionately interested in naval battles and Napoleon and appointed Max after an hour's gossip at his Ottawa offices during which Max confessed to being a left-of-centre Tory (Black was much further to the right and considered Hastings a bit of a "pinko").

Hastings immediately changed the paper to his own liking, introducing an "Op-Ed" page – a page of up-to-the-minute features opposite the leader page. There were sackings and shiftings and new appointments, including new Features Editor and Assistant Editor, Veronica Wadley. Ricky Marsh, who had been foreign editor for many years, was "promoted" to Managing Editor, the position that had been held by Peter Eastwood, the man dreaded, even hated, by many. As it was, word spread that Ricky had become "Managing Editor in charge of postage stamps", a position he held until his retirement.

Replacing Ricky as Foreign Editor was Nigel Wade, recalled from Peking as it was still called in those days, where he had been the paper's China correspondent. This was a strange move. Some months after Maureen's death, I had gone to China along with a number of other education correspondents and spent three fascinating weeks looking at schools and universities. While in Peking I naturally contacted Nigel and we had dinner together. He was in a terribly shaky state at the time and kept telling me that he was sure he was going to be given the push. I pooh-poohed this vehemently.

"You're doing a great job, Nigel. Why on earth d'you think they're going to sack you?" He could not tell me other than to say that he feared the worst. His wife, who ran a small nursery school for the young children of other Brits in that area, a large, enclosed block of apartments specifically for foreign subjects, asked me whether I could get her a few children's books. She gave me a list and I did, indeed, manage to purchase all of them soon after my return to London. I sent them by special parcel post to Peking.

Nigel's return to London at first looked like he had been right in his crystal gazing. But instead of being sacked, he was being appointed as Foreign Editor. And instead of becoming a friend, he was eventually to turn into my *bête noir*.

Max Hastings telephoned me at home fairly late on a Tuesday night. "I hear that you are a bit fed up of education. Is that true?"

I thought at first that he was going to follow up that question with something like: "Then you might as well fuck off out of the paper…" He was known for his choice use of language.

But instead, he said: "I also hear that you like Paris. Is that true?"

"Well, yes, that's certainly true," I said carefully.

"Then come and see me in the morning – say 9.30. Alright?" And before I could answer, the line went dead.

The interview was quick and informal. Ettie, who had been poached from me some years before to become Bill Deedes' PA, was kept on by Max when he was swept to power, kissed me on both cheeks when I entered the ante-chamber, then opened the door to the inner sanctum where Max, in shirtsleeves, was sitting in what I still considered to be Bill's swivel chair.

"Ah, come in, come in John. You've been to Paris before, haven't you?"

"Yes, I covered the May '68 troubles..."

"But you were there some years before that, weren't you? Was it not for Kemsleys? "

"Goodness, you are well informed. That was in the late Fifties. I spent some three years there."

"Yes, that's right. I was quite impressed with a piece you wrote a few weeks ago when you were in France...about Brittany Ferries..."

"Oh, that... Thank you. I enjoyed doing that." (I had gone to Brittany with June and produced a feature about Brittany Ferries floating on a sea of artichokes because I found out that, for every ton of artichokes grown and sold by Brittany farmers, ten francs would go to Brittany Ferries. Indeed, the company had been financed entirely by farmers and I even managed to attend several auctions of produce from the co-operative farms of the area. It did make an entertaining piece. And, what is more, it made a welcome change from education).

"Well, this is what I suggest. We'll be sorry to lose you from education, but if that's what you want...I'll send you to Paris as head of the office and our man in France. How'll that suit you?"

I was flabbergasted. But all I could say at the time was: "It'll suit me fine. Thanks!"

I floated out of the office to be given a great big hug by Ettie. She, of course, had already known about it. Ettie always knew everything that was going on at the *Telegraph*. She was happy for me, for she knew how much I loved Paris. After all, it was there that I met Maureen; it was there that I married her and it was there that Paul was conceived.

Now I had another love and I could not wait to break the news to her. I hoped that she would let me sweep her off to Paris.

But when I told her my news she did not appear all that happy. "What about the children? They'll have to leave all their friends behind, and the school to go to a place where they won't understand or speak the language. And I would have to give up my job, lose all hope of further promotion. Then there's the house I've not long bought it. What the hell do I do with it if we were all to simply pack our bags and go with you to France?"

Married for the second time to the lovely June Gordon-Walker at a Lambeth register office.
This picture was taken by Anthony Marshall, one of the Daily Telegraph's ace photographers

Her argument was a fair one and one I had not fully contemplated.

"What if we got married?" I blurted out.

There was a brief silence. "Are you proposing to me?"

"Well, yes, I suppose I am…Will you? Will you marry me and come with me to France? I agree the children won't find it easy to part with friends and they'll have a tough time at a French school for a while. But they'll learn French fast and make many new friends. You'll see."

And so June and I were married – on the 18th October 1986, we stepped into the Camberwell Register Office, along with a host of friends and relations that included Paul, Anna and Patrick as well as June's brother Bruce and his sons and Jacob and Liz. Tony Marshall, one of the *Telegraph*'s best photographers, was "on parade" and shot June and me swinging round a rather splendid lamppost outside the Registry. The party, well sprayed with champagnes and wines that washed down sufficient food to keep an army going, was held back at East Dulwich Grove. An outside caterer was worth every penny.

The honeymoon, if it can be described as such, was spent in Manchester of all places…Unfortunately, my mother had been rushed to hospital on our wedding day to have a hip replacement. She had managed to jump off a moving bus because she suddenly remembered she had forgotten to buy a Polish loaf of rye bread – one I particularly liked. I was expected on a visit and she had not waited for the bus to stop. Because she was due to have an operation – and because I had no idea how she might receive the news of my then impending marriage to yet another *Shiksa*, I thought it best not to tell her until it was safe to do so. So it was up to Prestwich that June and I drove, staying in Mum's house and visiting her at the Crumpsal Hospital.

We took her flowers and the usual bunch of grapes. She looked tired but well and so I gently broke the news to her and kept fingers and toes firmly crossed.

She broke down in tears – but they were tears of happiness and she kissed June and me and wished us *Mazeltov* (good luck). She was genuinely delighted that her little boy had found renewed happiness and did not appear to mind having missed the actual ceremony. After all, she had also missed the wedding ceremony in Paris 27 years earlier – although I fear that she might not have been as happy to see her little boy married with full nuptial mass at the altar of a Roman Catholic church instead of under the traditional *chuppa* in a synagogue.

I flew to Paris for a brief reconnaissance of the office and the situation. I was greeted with a hint of suspicion but amiably by Michael Field, who had been the *Telegraph*'s man ever since John Wallis's retirement many years earlier. It was Wallis who had "given away" Maureen at our wedding, an event of which Michael Field was unaware. Michael and his Spanish wife, Juliana, lived just round the corner from "the shop", which had moved from the lush premises on the Place Vendôme, where I had served Kemsley Newspapers in the late 'Fifties, to the Rue de Castiglione, a matter of 150 metres away.

The new offices looked out onto the Tuileries Gardens alongside the Rue de Rivoli and were opposite the Intercontinental Hotel, which, during the German occupation of France, was used as the headquarters of the Gestapo. They always knew how to pick the best and rob it for themselves. There was a large office with big windows, a smaller office leading from it and another fairly big one which was used by the administration people. In those days, the *Telegraph* spent large amounts of money on its overseas promotion, distribution and circulation. Today, it is doing its utmost to save money and boasts only a showy building next to Victoria Station in London. Overseas coverage has sunk to a disastrously low level.

Michael introduced me to a jolly woman named Denise Beniguel, who acted as PA and general factotum, performing a multitude of tasks for the staff,

The author, while head of The Daily Telegraph offices in Paris, 1986

the office and the *Telegraph* in France, and a secretary, Christiane Gallo, a pretty, dark-haired young woman who would take care of my correspondence, phone calls and the like. A thick-set, jovial, red-cheeked and consistently breathless individual called Jacques was the Louis Herchenroder of the outfit, taking care of the paper's circulation and distribution. He actually knew Louis from way-back, but, like me, had lost touch with my "best man" at my previous Paris wedding.

Michael Field and I got on reasonably well after a couple of weeks but I could feel that there was some slight resentment, not so much with me as with the *Telegraph*'s new administration. Clearly, he had hoped to spend the rest of his days writing for the paper and there's no question that he would have been perfectly capable. But the "new broom" wielded by Max Hastings swept out anyone who was thought to be getting on a bit. New blood was needed in Max's view and as I had shown myself to be a "distinguished" education correspondent and fluent writer, I was to be that new blood in Paris.

I seemed to spend most of the four or so weeks "tasting" the needs of the office and getting to know Paris again. The only real work I did was to establish my credentials with the French authorities. Denise Beniguel wrote the necessary letters to the Ministry of the Interior to arrange my accreditation and I had to go in person to introduce myself, complete with a set of passport photographs and completed forms and receive the valuable rubber-stamped cards. Once again I found out just how bureaucratic the French were. If anything, they had become worse than in the 'Fifties during my first sojourn in the capital.

Home was a small but comfortable hotel – the Pas de Calais – in my beloved Saint Germain des Près on the Left Bank. June joined me there for one or two weekends of good eating, drinking, walking and love-making… lots and lots of it. She would need to hand in her notice and make arrangements to bring children and baggage over, while I searched for a suitable place for us.

This was found fairly quickly with the help of a French estate agent and the advice of Denise. It was a big house on the edge of a lovely forest in L'Etang la Ville, a charming village just half an hour's train journey from St Lazare Station. The house comprised a spacious sitting room, a good-sized and well equipped kitchen, three bedrooms, the usual conveniences and a huge garage cum wine cellar beneath the ground floor. A big garden, complete with BBQ and space for an allotment, surrounded the house. It was perfect.

I immediately signed up for its rental (the *Telegraph* would take care of payments) and went to the local bank – the Banque de Paris (BNP) to open a much-needed account. That's where I encountered the second piece of grotesque bureaucracy.

"I should like to open an account – a sterling account, please," I told a broadly smiling woman behind the counter.

"Oui, Monsieur," she said and waited for me to explain myself and my wishes.

"Well, Madame, I wish to open my account before I move into the village. I can already provide you with my address."

"Très bien, Monsieur. Please fill in this form."

I tackled the four pages of questions at once and filled in every one of them, including the usual name, date and place of birth, address, employment place, names of mother, wife, children etc etc. and handed it back to the woman.

"And how much would Monsieur wish to put into the current account?"

I produced 500 "old" francs from my pocket (just under £50 at the time) and explained that I would be paid monthly by my British employer and that the money would go into that account, so please would she provide me with the account number a.s.a.p.

"Ah, non, Monsieur. First you must give us a copy of your electricity bill – or your telephone bill. It does not matter which."

"My what? Madame, how can I possibly have an electricity, telephone or any other bill? I haven't yet moved into the house, but I can give you a copy of the agreement I have signed with the agent who is renting me the house."

"I am sorry, Monsieur, but we must insist on a bill addressed to you at your new address proving that you live there…"

"Madame," I said, trying to keep my cool, "I am offering to give you money – regular money for the account I wish to open. I am not asking to *borrow* money from the bank…"

"It is the law, Monsieur…"

There were elements of the *Pink Panther* comedy about this and I wondered what Peter Sellers might have made of it. But I had to walk out of the bank without a bank account to my name. The *Telegraph* would have to wait for its details. Denise Beniguel tried her damndest with letters to BNP headquarters and the Ministry without avail.

I had to wait until the telephone company re-connected the phone at the house and accepted some money as an advance payment – in return for a small bill denoting the rental price and connexion charge – in my name. Then all was clear.

France had managed to be a good step in advance of the rest of Europe in producing a security system to prevent money laundering and the like. But at the time it was sheer hell.

On my departure from the education front, several little parties were thrown in my honour. The NUT invited me to a special Press conference. I was told that a "special announcement" was to be made. When I got to Hamilton House, most of my colleagues were already assembled and the special announcement was the opening of a number of decent bottles, the arrival of trayloads of delicious snacks and a vote of thanks to me. I was genuinely deeply moved. General secretary Fred Jarvis, who was about to become chairman of the TUC and retire from the union shortly afterwards to concentrate on his hobby – photography – made a speech that brought tears to my eyes. Max Morris and many other executive members all wished me luck in my new post.

There was a similar "vote of thanks" accompanied by toasts at the National Association of Schoolmasters/Union of Women Teachers and the National Association of Head Teachers. I began to wonder whether I had done the right thing. I would certainly miss them all. But I was inwardly pleased that I would no longer have to miss out on Easter. For years I had to skip Easter and egg hunts at home in order to attend the various teacher conferences. For this relief I was grateful.

At the *Telegraph* there was no "proper" farewell as I was not leaving the ship, merely moving port. But my last column not only allowed me to let my hair down properly but even published a caricature of me by the great Nick Garland, the *Telegraph*'s faithful political cartoonist. It showed a schoolboy on his knees, bearing a bunch of flowers to hand to me, with hearts of love leaping from his head. The caption read: "John Izbicki: A prefect's last day of term". The headline was: **Head boy moves on after 17 years of full-time education**. Alongside my last essay was a single column: **St Telegraph's Preparatory School: End of Term Report...Pupil: Izbicki, J.** This was followed by messages from my many contacts.

Fred Jarvis wrote: *John Izbicki is held in high regard by many teachers – not because he has slavishly supported everything they said or did, but because of his sense of fairness and his total lack of malevolence. Some of his columns and news stories have infuriated teachers; others have inspired and cheered them. That is how it should be if journalism is to retain any sense of professionalism. The NUT wishes him well in Paris.*

Peter Dawson, general secretary of the Professional Association of Teachers, said: *John is one of the most perceptive education reporters that one could come across and also hugely amusing – and anyone who could keep his sense of humour while reporting the education in this country must be some kind of genius.*

Lord Flowers, vice-chancellor of the University of London and the former chairman of what was then still the Committee of Vice-Chancellors and Principals, wrote: *John Izbicki has helped enormously to present the case for higher education and in particular universities at a time when they have not been geared up to reach out to the public and remind everyone what we can contribute to the community.*

David Walker, who was to follow me as education editor, said: *An early and abiding Izbicki achievement was the transatlantic transfer of Sesame Street. He campaigned long and hard for British television to show the unconventional pioneering American programme: if only one child was brought to his or her letters by the programme (and there have been many) then an education writer could not wish for more.*

After a long complimentary message from "Friends at Nottingham University" (my *alma mater*), there was a final word from Carol Coles, my faithful PA who wrote as "Gamesmistress at St Telegraph's": *John should do well in the outside world. He must endeavour to keep up his French and persevere with joined-up writing.*

A separate *Telegraph*-printed page had a big picture showing me walking sadly (one presumes) into the sunset alongside an unidentified vice-chancellor and what one could presume to be a teacher. The page was littered with farewell messages and signatures from scores of colleagues, both male and female.

Did I regret my departure? Possibly. How did the Bard put it? "Parting is such sweet sorrow". Sorrow it certainly was.

Before I left, I was presented with what looked like a slim briefcase. It turned out to be a computer – what later became known as a laptop. It was a Tandy 200. It wasn't so much a gift as a tool to be used in my work. I had never used, or even touched a computer before. Paul Williams, who had been my counterpart on the *Sunday Telegraph* but had resigned to take charge of the so-called new technology on both the *Daily* and *Sunday* papers, took me aside and gave me a 30-minute tutorial on how to use this newfangled machine.

That brief lesson was in itself history-making. No one, but *no one*, had ever used a computer on the *Telegraph*. There was a locked room which was crammed with Tandy 200s and other, bigger, desktop computers. But it was to remain locked for many more months. The print unions ruled the roost and would not allow anyone to touch a single computer key. They were probably justified in feeling that the introduction of computers could only spell redundancies. Printers and typesetters in the hot metal days fought hard to retain their positions of authority: no typesetting – no printing – no printing – no paper. It was as simple as that.

Those were the days when we had people called Mickey Mouse and Donald Duck on the payroll. Their pay would be collected each Friday evening and divided up among an entire team of men who argued that this was the only way of getting a rise. The management knew of this wholly illegal ruse but were powerless to act. The editorial staff knew that to use a computer meant that a union official would simply pull the plug and all machinery would come to a standstill.

Giving me the Tandy was taking a risk but I knew and the management knew that being "abroad" could not interfere with work in Fleet Street. If there had been the slightest hint that my activity with a computer would have broken union rules, I would never have used the Tandy. I was a loyal trade unionist and remain a life member of the National Union of Journalists to this day.

My first story from Paris, a political piece of no great value, nevertheless notched up a small piece of history. It was typed on the Tandy 200 keyboard and transmitted by telephone to some address in Holborn from where it was transferred to the Tape Room of the *Daily Telegraph*. When I finished typing the piece onto the screen, I connected the computer to the telephone on my desk and dialled a given number. There was a beep and the transmission began. All I could see on the screen was a series of dots, each one representing a word. I had no idea what the dots meant. At the end there was another beep and the dots would disappear. Had it been received by the Tape Room and would some messenger be scurrying with it along to the News Room?

Only once was there a mistake when a story was transmitted from the Holborn people to the *Daily Mirror*. There my name was recognised and the piece was forwarded to the *Telegraph*. Obviously the story was not worth cribbing and publishing in the tabloid.

It did not take us long to make new friends at L'Etang la Ville. Our next door neighbours, Jean and his mother Suzanne Fuseau, were French and welcomed us immediately with a bottle of Champagne. We knew we were accepted as soon as they started to address us individually by the more familiar *tu* instead of *vous*. A little further down the road were Bob and Pauline Matthews. Bob worked for Citroën as designer of the cars' interiors. They rapidly became our best friends.

Work ran smoothly for months on end and I soon accumulated a large number of friends in the media. Peter Dewhirst, who was the Paris correspondent of the *London Evening Standard* as well as the *Sunday Express*, lived with his Japanese wife Makiko, in nearby Le Vésinet, just outside Saint Germain, and became a good and lasting friend; then there were Paul Betts of the *Financial Times*, Robin Smythe of the *Observer*, Philip Jacobson and Susan Macdonald of *The Times*, Mary Follain of the *Times Educational Supplement* (who was already known to me from my education days), Thomas Kamm of the *Wall Street Journal* and the dear Clare Hollingworth, the former *Telegraph* foreign correspondent.

She was not just any old foreign correspondent but the doyenne of all those who would call themselves foreign correspondents. Even at 75, as she then was, she continued to work, covering Hong Kong and the Far East for the *Sunday Telegraph*. But towards the end of August 1939, when she was 27 years old and had just started in journalism with a job for the *Daily Telegraph*, she found herself in Poland and had interviewed the British consul-general. He lent her his car to go on a "fact-finding" trip to the Polish border with Germany. In fact, she drove into Germany and bought food and films before turning back. She was a little perturbed to see that the Germans had erected huge sheets of tarpaulin near the border. Just as she was crossing back into Poland, one of the sheets tumbled and she saw that it had been covering a tank. She looked more closely and saw many tanks and an entire army of soldiers bearing weapons.

Clare cabled the office, clever girl, to say that Germany was about to invade Poland. She told the consul-general about it. It was the first he knew of the outbreak of World War Two. Clare Hollingworth had managed to get herself the biggest scoop in modern journalism. As I write this she is reaching the age of 97 and continues hale and hearty. A great journalist.

One other friend was Diana Geddes, whom I had already known in London, where she had been education correspondent for *The Times* before escaping, like me, to Paris. Diana used to live in Brixton and was stopped by the police from entering her street on the night of the infamous riots "But I live there – that house over there," she tearfully told the coppers. Eventually they allowed her to go – but escorted her to the door. Diana used to go everywhere by bicycle and it accompanied her to France. She used it like I used taxis and I would often meet her at rowdy demonstrations (and they can be very noisy in France), clutching her bike with one hand and her notebook with the other. When she took notes she would simply lean her metal steed against her hip and write with the freed hand. She was almost always cheerful but was treated badly by *The Times*, who demanded more and more of her until she felt obliged to resign.

Curiously, Stephen Jessel, who also acted as *The Times'* education correspondent for a while, turned up in Paris as the BBC's man in France – and there he still remains to this day, but only in a freelance capacity. Indeed, freelancing is just about the norm these days. Very few journalists seem to be on permanent staff rolls any more. It is cheaper for companies as they don't need to pay for days off sick, holidays or even national insurance. It has, of course, robbed employees of their long-term security.

I recall a mild row I had with Stephen at the House of Commons. We were attending a Press conference given by one of the Monday Club MPs whose right-wing views were fairly obnoxious to most of us hacks present. He was attacking some learning packs going the rounds of schools for their "socialist leanings". No doubt he would not have complained had they been Tory leanings. Anyway, Jessel suddenly slammed shut his notebook and stamped out, muttering "I've had enough of this…" Later I confronted him. "That was somewhat unprofessional, Steve," I said. "Why? We don't need to listen to such a fucker spouting his fucking venom," he argued. "It's not up to us to make such a choice, Steve. Our job is to report his views whether we like them or not. I don't agree either but what I shall write will probably show him up as a bit of a fool, whereas you won't produce anything for your paper. Well, so be it…"

But I respected Stephen for sticking to his own principles as opposed to the principles of his boss, Rupert Murdoch. He resigned from *The Times* because he could no longer support the Murdoch regime and I could never blame him.

How different from my third successor at the *Telegraph*. David Walker was the first to replace me because Max Hastings insisted on appointing him, despite my decommendations. Max asked me what I thought and I took David to lunch to find out. I later told Max: "He is a superbly intelligent man and would make a first-class leader writer. But as an education correspondent, I think he lacks what it takes – soul. He needs to speak to mums about their little swans and empathise with the woes of teachers. I don't somehow think he will manage that." But Max overruled that view. Fair enough. He was the editor and his word was final. But David Walker lasted about six months. He *was* a superb leader writer – but he was not a hack. And, to give him his due, Max apologised to me. "You were right and I was wrong," he said magnanimously.

Number two replacement was Christopher Rowlands, the education correspondent of the *Daily Mail*. He and I were good mates and he was one of the reasons I refused to go over to the *Mail*, despite their excellent financial offer. At conferences I was often in a hotel telephone booth next to the one being used by Chris filing his story and I could hear the loud voice of his news editor coming across the air waves. Poor Chris was being roundly persecuted by his bosses and I certainly wanted none of that. I fully understood his decision to accept the offer to cross the street to the *Telegraph*. But he, too, went after less than a year. It appears that his copy had often to be rewritten by the subs.

Then came the third man. And to me, he was the biggest surprise of all. John Clare used to be the education correspondent of the BBC and was excellent in that role. He also covered stories dealing with racial problems. He once launched into a tirade of abuse at me during a Press conference at the Department of Education. I don't even recall the subject but I had asked a question, which everyone afterwards agreed was a perfectly reasonable one, but which Clare decided was "racist" and "typical of the *Telegraph*". I was flabbergasted. To openly attack a fellow journalist at a Press conference was unforgivable. Indeed, I wrote him a personal letter saying so. I also explained that he had picked on the wrong person to accuse of racism and that I had probably experienced far more racism than he had had hot dinners etc.

He apologised and we remained good colleagues.

John was full of surprises, not least his cabaret performance featuring Sir Keith Joseph. One surprise was his departure from the BBC to become education correspondent of *The Times*. Why should that have been surprising? Because *The Times* was at the time in the throes of noisy demonstrations following its takeover by Rupert Murdoch and its move to Wapping, the use of computers and the mass redundancies of the print force. Journalists of even the slightest Left-wing persuasion would have nothing to do with a Murdoch newspaper. And John happened to be a card-carrying member of the Labour party.

So I was doubly surprised, even shocked, when he joined the *Telegraph*. It was a case of from the frying pan into the fire. I reckoned that only money would have persuaded him to make both moves. I was proved right. It appears he was a good friend of Max Hastings and that Max had lured him to the *Telegraph* lair at a reputed salary exceeding £100,000 – about three times what I was earning.

His deputy was Paul Marston, a delightful young man and a splendid journalist. It was said that, not long after John made his appearance, the two had a genuine exchange of fisticuffs in the office because John had seduced Paul's sister. It was Paul who left Education to take on the transport correspondent's mantle. John remained firmly in the chair I had occupied for more than 17 years.

In France I was able to cover just about everything from the mundane to the seriously political. Nigel Wade had taken over the foreign editorship and was good at it but he expected everyone to jump at his bidding. I would receive calls at all times of night to follow this or that tupenny-ha'penny story in one of our competitors. I had no objections to doing follows to good reports but baulked at the unimportant. It was like Peter Eastwood's "wanted" stories all over again.

But there were the genuine urgencies – like the sinking of the Townsend-Thoresen ferry, the *Herald of Free Enterprise*. In the evening of March 6, 1987, I received a call from the office to get myself over to Zeebrugge in Belgium, where a roll-on, roll-off car ferry had sunk with "possibly many" passengers feared drowned. I arrived on the scene at dawn the next day and could see the vessel lying on its side, partially submerged by the sea, not more than a few hundred meters from the shore. How could this have happened?

The *Telegraph* had sent not only me but seven other reporters. We made a formidable team and the coverage was, to say the least, thorough. Someone had forgotten to close the doors leading to the car decks and the water had rushed in. It had all happened so quickly that the crew did not even have time to send out a Mayday call.

Someone on shore had seen the tragedy and alerted the emergency services. Of the 533 passengers and crew on board, 193 were drowned. It became the worst passenger shipping tragedy since the sinking of the *Titanic* 75 years earlier. It was a terrible story to have to cover, especially since it was barely credible that a ship of that size could keel over in such comparatively shallow water, so close to the shore, similar to the *Costa Concordia*, sunk in January 2012, with 16 dead and 17 still missing.

On one occasion, the desk wanted me to go to the Central African Republic to cover some trial. I tried to obtain a visa and careered around Paris seeking a permit from the CAR embassy. I was treated like shit by the officials who did not like the Press let alone anyone from the *Daily Telegraph*. I had to report my total failure back to Nigel who, of course, did not believe me, thinking that I simply wanted to skive off the assignment.

It was the beginning of a minor feud with my bosses back home. Max recalled me on one occasion and suggested I return to Education...or the news room. To have done so would have been a real bummer. I said I'd rather stay in France.

June almost walked out on one occasion early on. Although she spoke reasonably good French, she felt it was not good enough to get her through everyday life and L'Etang la Ville was, after all, small compared to Dulwich. She felt trapped and I couldn't blame her.

As for the children, we enrolled them in our local primary school. French was a totally alien language to them and I was worried in case they might be bullied as I was when I came to England and went to the Bartram's Convent School at Belsize Park. I would often come home in tears. Patrick and Anna, however, did not experience anything like that. Luckily, both were helped by their peers. The only bully turned out to be the headteacher, a tall, buxom woman in her fifties who strode about the school in military fashion, firing orders as from a machine gun. She, as bad luck would have it, taught Anna.

French schools are sticklers for learning entire pages of boring text by heart as homework, then having to reproduce it in neat copperplate handwriting the following morning. It was, of course, difficult to say the least, for Anna and Patrick to learn huge chunks of text books by heart – even if they had been written in English.

So every time I went to the school to pick up the children, Madame, whose name I have conveniently forgotten, would accost me at the school gates. "Monsieur Eezbeeky," she would screech. "Why do you not send your children to the Lycée britannique?" "Because," I would reply as softly as possible, "because, Madame, I would prefer them to attend a French school."

"But, Monsieur, they cannot speak a single word of French and they will never learn!"

"Don't be such a nihilist, Madame," I would counter. "You'll see. They will learn!"

"I am not a nihilist, Monsieur Eezbeeky. I am very experienced in these matters and I tell you that they cannot and will never speak French!"

Thus it would go on and on – until, one day, grizzly Madame stopped going through her routine little speech. I had prophesied that both children would be able to speak French within six months. I was proved wrong. By the end of the school year, they were able to converse fairly fluently with their mates.

It was time to withdraw them from the village primary and send them to a decent secondary school. St-Germain-en-Laye, a pretty, affluent town some 10 kms from L'Etang la Ville, had just such a school: the Lycée Internationale. This is a French state school, which has a total of 11 sections to educate students from that number of different nationalities: British, German, Spanish, Danish, Norwegian, Swedish, Dutch, Polish, Portuguese, Italian and Japanese – plus French of course. The school's principle is to allow French students to become bilingual and for the non-French students to master the French language and become bi- or even multilingual. Teachers provide all students with lessons of up to eight hours a week in literature, geography and history – in their mother tongue. All other disciplines are taught in French. In the end, all will sit the International Baccalauréat, a splendid qualification, which to my mind is far superior to our A-levels.

That was the school to which we enrolled both Patrick and Anna. They had first to pass an entrance examination to make sure their French was good enough. Fortunately, it was. Here they made friends quickly and were a great deal happier than at the village school. The head of the British Section was a man who knew how to run a school and how to deal with young people. Their French became lastingly fluent.

At home we built up a good circle of friends, ranging from thoroughly French people – Jean and Suzanne Fuseau next door – to the British pedigreed Bob and Pauline Matthews down the road. The women formed what became known as The Gourmet Group, which would meet once a month at each other's houses, each couple providing a different course for the dinner – from entrée, main course, cheese and dessert. The wines, digestifs and coffee would be provided by whoever hosted the occasion. Conversation, mainly juicy gossip would punctuate the meal, which would stretch late into the night.

Our next door neighbours, the Fuseau's, would be invited separately. Suzanne, an elderly woman, would often disappear to a health farm for a week or so to take *une cure*, a course of treatment to help her arthritis. On such occasions we would invite Jean, a retired rocket scientist to dine (his name – Fuseau – was most appropriate). He knew his wines and had a superb cellar. He would always come laden with decent bottles of claret but on one occasion, when his aged mother was also dining with us out in the garden, I introduced him to a drink that he took to immediately and with gusto. It was called the *Ancienne Alliance* – the Old Alliance – named after the old friendship between Scotland and France. It comprised a goodly measure of Drambuie, a scotch-based liqueur, and an equally decent measure of Pernod-Ricard, a rather fierce French aperitif tasting of aniseed. Personally, I should never have guessed that this mix could have produced anything other than a nasty taste. The contrary is the case. It is beautiful. Jean literally lapped it up and between us we finished more than half a bottle of each. The result was that Jean got completely blotto and had to be helped – almost carried – home by June, me and his totally sober mother.

The next day, Jean was back working in his garden much later than usual and looking a little pale. He waved a half-hearted *bonjour* – then said: "What was that concoction you served after last night's splendid dinner? You must give me the exact mix. Today I shall buy a bottle of that – what is it called?"

"Drambuie," I said.

"Ah, oui, Drahmbouilly! Merci encore!"

CHAPTER NINETEEN:

FAREWELL SQUABBLES

The office in the Rue Castiglione continued to thrive under my direction and the stories I produced were well used. But I started to get the feeling that my lords and masters wanted more. Max Hastings asked me to return to the fold and come back to Education. As I explained in the previous chapter, my successors were not really successful. Even John Clare's output was considered lightweight and it looked as though he might not remain in the job as long as I had done.

Special Reports filled the pages of a special advertising supplement, which the paper used to publish from time to time – and time to time meant whenever the advertising department had succeeded in selling enough space to a company or companies whose products related to a topic that would be covered by a series of features. So there might be supplements on a country (France, for example, with adverts from the French tourist office, hotels, French railways and the like) or on MBA courses (with adverts from universities running them, companies wanting to recruit staff possessing them and so on). The Special Reports department on the top floor of the *Telegraph* building was a true money spinner.

It was also a department which provided refuge for a growing number of editorial refugees – people who had been given the push by Max Hastings or his hatchet man, Jeremy Deedes, who had been appointed the paper's chief executive and who had managed to beat the late Peter Eastwood for unpopularity with the staff. It was difficult to understand how this man could have come from the same DNA as Bill Deedes. Even Bill tended to beat a retreat when he saw Jeremy approaching. Indeed, when I went to the memorial service to my faithful Ettie at one of London's Scottish Presbyterian churches, Max Hastings and Jeremy Deedes turned up and sat in a front pew (Max, whose secretary Ettie had become, spoke a few kind words at the service, which was being celebrated by Ettie's widower, the Rev. Dr Denis Duncan). I was sitting in a seat about the centre of the church, when Bill – who was then already Lord Deedes – arrived and walked down the left-hand aisle. He had almost reached the front when he spotted his son sitting alongside Max. Bill turned smartly round, walked back up the aisle, turned at the top and walked a short way down the right-hand aisle. He clearly did not wish to sit in the limelight.

Anyway, the Special Reports department comprised an entire group of those who had been made redundant. It was brilliantly edited by Clive Barrow, who had been an equally excellent night news editor; he was aided and abetted by the splendid Chris Bramwell, who had been deputy news editor in his previous incarnation. There were also Anthony Marshall, the excellent photographer who covered our wedding, Roy White, deputy features editor, among the most charming of the men I knew, Chris Rowlands – and my old PA, the successor to Ettie's place in my office – Carol Coles.

I could see which way the *Telegraph* was being re-shaped and declined the offer of having my old job back – even though a large number of my former contacts within the teaching unions, schools, universities and polytechnics, as well as one or two in the Palace of Westminster, the DES and Whitehall would have wished me back.

So I continued covering stories in France. One in particular remains clearly in my memory. It was the day I travelled to Lyon to interview the people who were designing the Euro well before its introduction to the EU member countries. The UK was alone in refusing to accept this currency. From the station I took a taxi to the offices of the Euro designers – a large grey stone building outside the centre of the city. I rang the bell and spoke into an intercom. "Ah, yes, Monsieur. We are expecting you. The door will open. Please make your way to the second floor."

The moment I walked in, I felt an uneasy chill pass through me. A door in front of me was obviously leading into a cellar. Somehow, the chill was coming to me from that plain wooden door. It passed the moment I started up the stairs and, once inside the comfortable designers' office where a drink awaited me, the dreadful feeling left me. We chatted for about 20 minutes and looked at various designs of paper notes in different denominations and some coins. "How about some lunch?" the head designer, a Belgian, asked, and he, his partner and I left the office and descended the stairs. As soon as we had reached the ground floor and front door, that chill ran through me again. I somehow felt that I was in the presence of evil.

"It is very strange," I said to my hosts, "but I feel a terrible chill just at this point. Has anything awful happened here?"

The two men stopped and stared at me, their faces suddenly grim. "Good God, you must be psychic," said the chief designer of the Euro. He pointed to the door. "That leads down to the cellar of this building. In that cellar Klaus Barbie tortured his many victims during the Nazi occupation of France."

That experience happened shortly before Klaus Barbie, then 73, was brought to trial in Lyon. At that trial, which I covered for the paper, I learned that "The Butcher of Lyon" had personally tortured the hundreds of prisoners he interrogated in that cellar before having them either killed or deported. He was blamed for 4,000 deaths and for sending 7,500 people, most of them Jews, to the extermination camps of Germany. During the many days I spent in that courtroom I also sought out numerous witnesses to get their heartbreaking stories in readiness for the features I was preparing to write for the aftermath of the trial. Barbie was, of course, found guilty by nine jurors and three judges of the 341 charges listed against him.

The most heinous of his crimes to my mind was the murder on his orders of 44 Jewish children who were found hiding in a farmhouse at Izieu. The evidence from the mouths of witnesses, spoken in tearful tones in a totally silent courtroom, gave me nightmares for weeks to come.

Barbie the Butcher pleaded Not Guilty and sat expressionless in his glass cage throughout the trial, which opened on May 11 and continued until July 3, 1987 when he was at last sentenced to life imprisonment.

The Barbie trial clinched for me my growingly uneasy relationship with the *Telegraph*. The story of how Barbie came to trial was worthy of the piece I wrote well before the trial opened. I interviewed Serge Klarsfeld, the French Jewish lawyer who traced Barbie to his lair in Bolivia; he also discovered that Barbie had been used by American counter-intelligence between 1947 and 1951. This showed just how stupid the CIA has been and still is (viz – the dreadfully inaccurate "discovery" of atomic weapons hidden somewhere in Iraq). America actually apologised for its decision to allow a Nazi murderer to spy for them. Klarsfeld with the help of Israeli intelligence (*real* intelligence!) found Barbie in Bolivia as early as 1972 but the Bolivians, who have given refuge to many high-ranking Nazis, including, it would seem, the arch-killer, Martin Bormann, did not agree to extradite him to France until 1983 – 11 years after his unmasking. It took another four years to prepare the cases for the prosecution and defence.

I was determined to report the trial objectively but I could not help dissolving into tears while dictating some of the gruesome evidence over the telephone to London. The copy takers were marvellous. "Take your time, John. I can wait," one or the other of them would say.

The features I wrote on the case were published but some were poorly subbed, cutting out some important sections. I thought I had better address myself to the features editor – the deceptively attractive Veronica Wadley. She immediately launched into a diatribe of criticisms of the features I wrote on the Barbie affair. I was thunderstruck and decidedly hurt, even insulted. So much so that I forgot my usual good conduct and civil tongue and completely lost my cool. Memory has failed me to a certain extent but I believe I actually said words to the effect: "Look here my dear, I've written more fucking features than you've had hot dinners!"

I somehow forgot to apologise. And anyway, political correctness was still to be born.

It took nearly seven hours to find Klaus Barbie guilty and send him to jail for life. He died in the Lyon prison, to which he had sent hundreds of tortured Jews and Christians, on the 25th September 1991. He was 78.

I did not shed any tears. Indeed, I would have happily danced on his grave.

My little contretemps with Veronica Wadley must have travelled round the "inner circle". I found that Nigel Wade, who had been treating me coldly from well before the Wadley episode, was now breathing solid icicles across the airwaves; no doubt Max Hastings' Master's Voice must have transmitted itself to Nigel. Max hardly spoke to me after I had rejected his offer of a return to Education.

The climax came when the Supremo, Jeremy Deedes, decided to take me to lunch – in Paris. It was all very civilised. I was being laid off, but not quite sacked. The company wanted to save money, so I should continue to write for the *Telegraph* and use the Paris office, and my salary would continue to be paid. So what was different?

They wanted to employ someone else, a woman, to be the Paris correspondent. And so, Suzanne Lowry came onto the scene and took over the office. As it happens, she turned out to be extremely pleasant and we got on exceedingly well. Her writing was good but she never really managed to give the paper the same output that I had. But I suppose it's quality that counts, not quantity. Like me, she was an experienced hack, having started her professional career on the *Belfast Telegraph*. She later worked for the

Guardian and launched their women's page. She did stints for the *Observer* and the *Sunday Times* before moving to the *International Herald Tribune* in 1986. That did not last long before she was picked, presumably by Max, to take over from me as the Paris correspondent of the *Daily* and *Sunday Telegraphs*. She also wrote a number of books, including one on Princess Diana, called *The Cult of Diana: the Princess in the Mirror*.

Her days on the *Telegraph* turned into years – eight of them – before she, too, decided to call it a day, write more books and go and live in the warmth of the Midi. I wish her luck.

I suppose I might have also continued to live in France, had it not been for the visit of two old contacts from the education days. Gerry Fowler was one; Christopher Price the other. Gerry started life as a college lecturer before turning to politics He was a lecturer at Pembroke College, Oxford (he was a graduate of Lincoln College and held the Craven Fellowship of Oxford), then at Hertford and Lincoln Colleges, followed by the University of Lancaster. Gerry was a thorough Socialist and was a city councillor for Oxford as early as 1960 and would later be Leader of the Wrekin district council in 1970.

He then decided to try for the big time and stood as the unsuccessful Labour candidate for Banbury in 1964. But his dream came true in the general election of 1966 and he became Labour MP for the Wrekin, rapidly rising through the backbench ranks to hold a number of important ministerial roles under Harold Wilson and James Callaghan, finally becoming Minister of State for Higher Education. It was then that I got to know and like him. He never sold me a pup, never spinned stories. He was an honest, good humoured politician – and there aren't many of them about the Palace of Westminster. When he eventually lost his seat and came back into "civvy street", he returned to education and in 1970 landed the post of Assistant Director of Huddersfield Polytechnic – a position that began his long love affair with the country's polytechnics.

By the time he came to Paris in 1989 to attend an OECD conference, he was Rector of the Polytechnic of East London and chairman of the Committee of Directors of Polytechnics (CDP).

Christopher Price was also an Oxford man – and also a Socialist, becoming secretary of the Oxford University Labour Student Club and, after his graduation from Queen's College, chairman of the National Association of Labour Student Organisations. Unlike Gerry, he did not immediately take jobs in education, but like Gerry, he went into politics, becoming a Sheffield City councillor in 1962 and deputy chairman of its education committee the year after. Also like Gerry, he wanted to get into Parliament as soon as possible and contested (unsuccessfully) Shipley in 1964, Birmingham Perry Bar in 1970 and Lewisham West in 1983.

But Chris was an educationist at heart and took up journalism, editing *New Education* in 1967-68 and becoming the education correspondent of the *New Statesman* from 1969 until 1974. Meanwhile, he again stood for Parliament, this time successfully, becoming MP for the Perry Barr division of Birmingham in 1966-70 and MP for Lewisham West in 1974 – a seat he held for seven eventful years until he lost it in 1983, also obtaining ministerial posts within education and chairing the Parliamentary Select Committee on Education, Science and the Arts.

When he came to Paris along with Gerry to attend the same conference, they decided to contact their "old mate" Izbicki and take him out to dinner. They caught me at that delicate time when my anger was brewing up against the *Daily Telegraph*. A decent dinner with old friends was exactly what was needed at the time. I didn't know that Chris had also gone into the world of higher education and that, shortly after I had left the *Telegraph* to take over the Paris office, he had become director of Leeds Polytechnic. I knew him more as a hack who was writing for the *Times Educational Supplement* and the *New Statesman*. He, too, was now a member of the CDP.

We went to Fouquet's on the Avenue des Champs-Elysées. The food is always good and although I cannot now recall what dishes we had, I do remember that the wines were excellent and washed down the dishes in welcome succession. Chris had to leave the next day to take his wife to Germany but Gerry and his wife, Lorna, would continue in Paris for the weekend, so I invited them home to L'Etang la Ville for Sunday lunch.

The weather turned out to be warm and sunny so we laid a table in the garden. June produced a meal, which, frankly, was as good if not better than that at Fouquet's although I could not compete with their wines. Nevertheless, it was a splendid meal and a decidedly boozy one. Gerry smoked his awful cigarillos and became increasingly merry. He asked me how I was liking it in Paris and on the paper. I had said nothing on the Friday evening's meal, but now, having been asked directly, I spilled the beans. I told Gerry of my thorough disdain with the paper and its leadership and my sorrow at having been demoted to a freelance position after 23 years with the paper.

I also told him of my love for the *Telegraph*, not for its politics but for the wonderful paper it used to be. "Never once in all the years I was working in Fleet Street did I ever wake up in the morning and say: 'Oh, fuck, it's the *Telegraph* again today!' It was a happy ship and we all worked loyally for the bosses we had. Now for the first time in those 23 years I feel rotten, even in the city I adore!"

Gerry puffed away at his cheroot and sipped the big cognac I had poured. He appeared deep in thought. Then he said: "I've an idea." I topped up his brandy glass.

"As you know, the polytechnics should dearly love to become universities in their own right. Most of them are already running degree courses. For my sins, I am chairing the Committee of Directors of Polytechnics – and the CDP is taking a lead in the campaign to persuade the government to give us university status. But it's not going to be easy. We're no good at promoting ourselves. What we need," he said, puffing vigorously at his cigarillo, "what we desperately need is someone to help us promote ourselves and make the government recognise our value.

"So," he puffed and gulped some more Martell cognac, "we thought we'd appoint a man or woman to take on this task. I don't mind telling you, John, that your name came up but it was thought that you were well entrenched at the Folies-Bergère. Still, from what you've told me today, you might not be so unhappy to kiss the old Torygraph goodbye. What d'you say? Would you consider such a job?"

The offer, for that's what it sounded like, came as a proverbial bolt out of the blue. I thought about it for a full four seconds before replying.

"You bet I'd be interested, Gerry. It sounds right up my street!"

"You'll need to hold on a bit though, dear boy. The thing is the CDP is a public body and as such, the job would have to be advertised and you'd have to apply through the normal channels. In the end you might not get it. You might not beat the competition from other applicants. But I'll say this ol' boy, I'll say this: you stand a fuckin' good chance!"

And so I waited – until a telephone call from Gerry alerted me to the advert that had been published in *The Times* and the *Telegraph*. It was brief and to the point: the CDP, umbrella body of the 32 polytechnics in the country wanted to appoint a Director of Public Affairs who would act as senior spokesperson for the CDP and represent it to the media and to local and national government. Salary to be negotiated.

I applied immediately, explaining that I had already written many reports and features about individual polytechnics – not all of them favourable – and enclosed a well documented CV.

I stuck down the envelope, posted it, sat back and waited.

Before returning to England, I needed to do two things (apart from holding a number of boozy farewell parties). The first was to resign my position as vice-president of the Anglo-American Press Association, of which I had been a member throughout my time in Paris. I had only recently been voted into that role and was in line to becoming president the following year. I would have joined the list of the other *Daily Telegraph* luminaries who had held the presidency: James Ozanne, in 1907, the year the Association was founded; John Bell (1921); John Wallis (1952) the man who had "given Maureen away" at our wedding; Geoffrey Myers (1958) who had also attended the wedding; Anthony Mann (1972); and Michael Field (1976) my predecessor as head of the Paris office. It was a sad farewell.

The other was to buy a house in France. I felt I needed an umbilical cord with the country I had grown to love. June and I chose Normandy for its beauty and its closeness to England So I contacted a few estate agents in the Dieppe area, gave them my budget and awaited their information of houses in the price-range and area.

June and I then travelled to Dieppe at weekends, booked into a hotel close to the beach and the centre and allowed ourselves to be driven by one estate agent after another to view the "typical Normandy style" houses I had stipulated. Over some four or five weeks we tramped round scores of properties, many of them surrounded by acres of land and additional outhouses, sheds and workshops. Houses in France were a great deal cheaper than in the UK but many were in a poor state of repair and I am not in the least bit adept at DIY – unlike June who could probably build a house single-handed and certainly knows how to fill in holes, repair leaks and plaster a wall.

During one of these excursions, I turned to the estate agent driving us around and said: "Tell me – what do the French people think about *les Anglais* invading their country and buying up all their houses?"

"Ah, Monsieur, they love *les britanniques* and welcome you to our country…"

"No, Monsieur, I don't think you understand. I'm not your usual tourist, so please don't give me all that. Just tell me the truth."

He was silent for a moment, then said: "*Alors, bon.* The French do really like the British because you buy all the old houses. These are houses the French do not want. They are only interested in new, modern houses. So you are really doing them a favour. However, I must say in all honesty: they do not like the British house buyers because they have made the price of property go up and up and that affects not only the British but the French as well."

He was, of course, right. But French housing was still much cheaper than at home.

It was when we entered our umpteenth house at a small village called Routes I knew that we had found the right place. It belonged to a Monsieur

Serge Verdier and his wife, Suzanne, and was a typical Norman building with its outside stairs leading to the first floor. Its rooms were spacious and beautiful, with a huge salon and an open fireplace of massive proportions. There were enough bedrooms to sleep as many as 12 people, and a garden at front, side and rear filled with cider apple trees and eaters.

Serge Verdier was a schoolteacher at Doudeville, the town just three kilometres away. He was about to retire and move south to find the sun. He was anxious to sell and get away in order to try and dim the memory of his son who had recently been killed in a motorcycle accident. The boy had loved the house and his room upstairs still reflected his penchant for motorbikes, Georges Brassens and Juliette Greco, whose posters adorned his walls.

The price of the partly furnished house was 530,000 old francs (just over £50,000). We could hardly buy an apartment in or near London for that price in 1989. We have lived there on and off for 21 years, travelling to France, either from Newhaven to Dieppe (Routes is a mere 35 minutes' drive from there) or from Dover to Calais (a two-hour drive down the motorway), Dover to Boulogne (one and a half hours drive) or via Le Tunnel (35-minute crossing plus two-hour drive).

But the house grew too big for the two of us and we sold it in 2010, moving to a smaller, equally comfortable "maison secondaire" at Grainville La Teinturiere, just 8 kms further from Routes and a few kms nearer to the sea.

CHAPTER TWENTY:

FROM POLY TO UNI

My interview at the offices of the Committee of Directors of Polytechnics at Kirkman House in Whitfield Street, a small, insignificant street that runs parallel with Tottenham Court Road, was a hoot.

Until now I had been doing all the interviewing, whether to cross-examine politicians, celebrities or crooks for information for my stories or to employ my secretaries, PAs or others. I had been in journalism for more than 30 years. Now, here I was being interviewed for a job to do something totally new. I had not dealt with public relations since I was a public relations officer in the Canal Zone of Egypt, doing my national service.

I sat in the small waiting room alongside other candidates. To my absolute embarrassment, I knew one of them. I knew him very well. It was John Richards, who had been my colleague at the *Daily Telegraph* twenty years earlier, when I was industrial correspondent, deputy to Blake Baker. John came in as "Number Three" and quickly moved up the ranks once I took on the education mantle. He would be a formidable competitor and I would have to be on top form. I suppose he must have thought just about the same thing about me, so we just exchanged a few pleasantries, then sat back quietly reading the reading materials left lying there for us.

The door opened and Michael Lewis, the CDP's Secretary, walked in looking flustered. A small, rotund man with bright blue, smiling eyes but a nervous manner, came over to me and said quietly: "John – er – sorry to disturb you, but you've forgotten to give us your age in the form you filled in."

I was 59 – the kind of age one is loathe to surrender on such an occasion. Companies, no matter how big or small, were reluctant to take on anyone over 45, let alone over 55. Frankly, I thought my end had come. But I played it for all it was worth and said somewhat haughtily: "Oh, I didn't realise this was an ageist organisation!"

I had hit the right spot. Michael Lewis was about the first person in history to be totally PC. "Oh, dear, no, no, not at all, John, not at all," he stammered. "We only need it for our books – tax and national insurance, that sort of thing. We're certainly not ageist…"

"Oh well," I said with a smile and still playing him along: "In that case I don't mind telling you that I'm approaching 55 but I won't tell you from which direction!"

He laughed, made a note and retreated satisfied.

My interview passed better than I had anticipated. The questions thrown at me were tough but my answers coped with them. After about half an hour, I was asked whether I would accept the post. My salary would be somewhat more than the *Telegraph* had paid me – although at that time, as I was to find out, those who followed me, whether in Paris or in London, were paid considerably more and that John Clare was being paid a three-figure salary, about three times as much as me.

I accepted of course.

The committee still had others, including John Richards to see, so I was asked whether I would mind stepping out through the back of the interview room and down the back stairs. I thought this was like something out of a James Bond movie, but I agreed and shook hands with each of the eight people who had questioned me and floated down and out into the street to telephone June and tell her the good news.

I had entered totally new territory, turning from poacher to gamekeeper. I had to sell the country's polytechnics to a government that considered them at the bottom of the higher education heap and people who thought of them as nothing better than FE colleges where one could take GCSEs and maybe a few diplomas in hairdressing and flower arranging.

After writing a round robin to every poly director, introducing myself and explaining my objectives, I decided to travel the country and visit each of the 32 institutions. I wanted to see them all for myself, meet their heads and information officers. Before undertaking this rather ambitious move, I needed to employ a PA and an assistant.

Among several bright women who applied for the job as PA, a young blonde with an effervescent personality, appealed to me at once. Lucy Grout was talkative but efficient, answered telephones swiftly and brightly, and quickly became not only a loyal employee and efficient worker but a friend. As for an assistant, this position was also easy to fill. A serious young woman who was filled with bright ideas struck me as lacking in experience but sufficiently intelligent to learn quickly. Luckily I was proved absolutely right. Joanne Harris turned out to be exactly right for the job and, once she relaxed, would envelop everyone in sight with a broad smile. As it happened, she was also Jewish – though this had in no way influenced my choice.

The CDP was founded in 1969 just as the first eight of a projected 30 new polytechnics were set up. There were around 40,000 students at those early 1969-70 polys. When I came along not quite 20 years later, there were 32 polytechnics with 500,000 students in them. Somehow I had to tell politicians and public alike that many of those students were into university-standard courses up to postgraduate level and not the Mickey Mouse diplomas the "enemy" imagined.

I started on my whistle-stop tour of the institutions, kicking off at Middlesex Polytechnic which was not more than 10 minutes' walk from the first proper house Maureen and I owned in Belmont Avenue, Cockfosters. Paul and I often used to go there to play tennis on its courts and then nip into the director's house for tea. Raymond Rickett and his charming wife, Naomi were our friends well before I had anything to do with the CDP. In 1990 he was deservedly knighted.

I had often written about Middlesex and praised its magnificent campus whose annual display of daffodils attracted people from throughout Hertfordshire, so it was the obvious place to stop by for some useful information.

One by one, I ticked off the polytechnics, getting to know their directors and their student union presidents.

The visits gave me my first real idea to get the sector more widely known and present it not as a series of different institutions, but as a single family whose members were widely dispersed around England, Scotland and Wales. I decided to launch a National Polytechnics Week. I put this notion to a National Union of Students president at Leicester Polytechnic. I immediately took to this young man and he was quick to suggest half a dozen superb ideas for me to consider.

Mark Walker was about to graduate and I offered him a job to come to the CDP and help me design and launch the Week. I was unable to promise him a permanent appointment (my budget would not allow such an extravagance) but took him on in a freelance capacity. As I rightly foresaw, he proved himself magnificent.

I wrote a round robin to every director, every poly PRO and each union president outlining the National Polytechnic Week and asking whether they had any objections to the week's date I proposed. I wanted each poly to produce "something special" during that week, whether an exhibition of artwork, photographs or paintings, or an Open Day to bring the public in and experience their campus. Some replied that they could not put anything special on as it clashed with their graduation ceremonies.

"So what's wrong with that?" I would respond "Make the graduation ceremony your special event for the Week! Exhibit your wares at the entrance to the theatre where the ceremony is to be enacted."

Mark Walker, who was an ace at the computer, produced some remarkably colourful brochures and posters adorned with great graphics that found their way into polys up and down the country and received favourable mentions in the Press.

Sporting events, plays, concerts, illustrated talks, campus tours, dinners, cocktail parties, exhibitions – and graduation ceremonies — all became part and parcel of NPW, the National Polytechnics Week. Local newspapers throughout the country reported on their own poly's events and mentioned in more than a little detail that this was all part of a national display.

November 19 – 25, 1990 was designated National Polytechnics Week and with some astute lobbying I managed to persuade the *Observer* newspaper to sponsor it. Peat Marwick Management Consultants and the KPMG also joined in helping sponsorship. We were even given a free advert by the *Observer*. Under a colourful picture of graduating students in caps and gowns was the caption: "*There are 317,854 of them...and they have one thing in common: That is how many people currently study at the 32 Polytechnics of England and Wales; on full-time, sandwich and part-time courses in subjects that will produce the well-qualified workforce for tomorrow's world. The Polytechnics...created 21 years ago, now striding into the 21st century...offer over 1,800 courses at diploma, degree and higher degree levels...preparing students for work by providing functional, relevant qualifications.*"

It advised readers wanting more information about the work of the polytechnics to contact either "*your nearest Polytechnic or John Izbicki, Director of Public Affairs, Committee of Directors of Polytechnics...*"

Among the many other things I managed to produce in the few years I was with the CDP was a booklet – *A Parent's Guide to Polytechnics* – which explained exactly what they were, how to choose a course, how to apply and what help parents could give. It was printed by Colibri Press – the printing company of my good friend, Alfred Jeckel (but it was not a matter of favouritism. His quote had been the most reasonable and his production, the very best.) And I persuaded the polys to "go green". They were the first within higher education to do so. Two documents emerged from this initiative: *Greening Polytechnics* (published in October 1990) and *Greening the Curriculum* (May 1991)

But what became known as "Izbicki's biggest coup" in the campaign to promote this little-known sector came early — on November 9, 1989, after I had been with the CDP only a matter of a couple of weeks. I am something of an insomniac and often use those waking hours to listen to the BBC's World Service. In the early hours of November 9, I heard the news that the Berlin Wall was being dismantled. It was wonderful news and I immediately set myself wondering how could this historic event be commemorated, even celebrated by the CDP.

As soon as it was light and late enough to make a telephone call, I contacted Gerry Fowler. After all, he was my chairman and would either agree with my idea or throw it back in my face. He didn't sound exactly pleased to be interrupted at breakfast on a Saturday morning. "What is it John?" he asked tetchily.

"Gerry, have you heard the news about the Berlin Wall?"

"Yes, it was on the eight o'clock news. Wonderful. But what of it?"

"Well, Gerry, what would you say if polytechnics were to offer a one-year scholarship to East German students?"

There was a silence. "Gerry? Gerry, Are you still there?" Had he fallen asleep? The silence continued for a little while. Then: "I'm just thinking," he rasped. He must be smoking one of his awful cheroots, I thought.

Then he said: "John, you've just earned yourself your first month's salary. Well done! It'll cost quite a bit but it might well be worth it."

"Ah, but Gerry, it might not cost us anything. If I put this idea to Maggie Thatcher, she might agree that the Government chips in all or part of the money."

"If you pull this off, you'll get another month as a bonus, ol'boy," he said.

I immediately phoned the DES and asked to be put through to the duty officer. On a Saturday the offices at the Department of Education would not be staffed but there was always someone on duty just in case of emergency. After a lengthy wait, a bored sounding young man came to the phone and I explained the CDP's offer and told him that I wanted the message to be passed on to the Prime Minister. He thought that was hilarious but when I interrupted him with a terse: "It's not funny. It is very serious and she will definitely want to know!" He apologised and said he would do his best.

The same afternoon, I received a call from Number Ten – but not from Herself. It was Downing Street's duty officer. "The Prime Minister received your message and wishes you luck but wanted you to know that this was more of a matter for the Foreign and Commonwealth Office. You should contact them…" John MacGregor, then Secretary of State for Education, also passed the buck to the FCO.

The FCO was indeed interested but balked at the cost which I had worked out at a cool million pounds. After much toing and froing, I was given a rendez-vous with the powers that be at the Foreign Office. Prior to that meeting, I had faxed the directors of every polytechnic in England and Wales and asked each to agree to just one scholarship. Of the 32, I received 31 positive responses. All that was now needed was the money – and a name for the initiative. I invented PECESS. It sounded fairly East European and stood for the Polytechnics Eastern and Central European Scholarships Scheme.

The Government also came up trumps. It agreed to go halves with us. This was indeed good news as it meant that in practise, it would cost the polytechnics nothing. All they needed to do was to provide the scholars with a free course. The real money from the FCO would cover fares, a room on campus and fairly generous pocket money. Scholarships, it was decided, would go only to graduates with a reasonable knowledge of the English language.

The polys were inundated with applications from universities (we had produced the forms and had also asked for a photograph to be submitted with each application) and it proved quite difficult to choose 31 winners. In the end, Gerry Fowler and I flew to Berlin to meet the winners. The British embassy agreed to host the little ceremony and provide the food and drink.

On our arrival in Berlin, Gerry and I decided to pay a visit to the Humboldt University and see a Professor Dr Hass, a chemist and chairman of East Germany's *Rektorenkonferenz*, equivalent of our Committee of Vice-Chancellors and Principals (CVCP). The university's Chemistry Department was in a side street off the Invalidenstrasse, the street where I had spent my childhood. Going back there again after the collapse of that ugly Wall made my heart pound and my eyes smart. Gerry gripped my arm. "God, John, this must be awful for you. Would you rather we turned back?" I think he was almost as moved as I was.

"No Gerry. Let's meet Professor Hass," I said and laughed. "Strange name. It means Hate…Professor Hate." I giggled. "I hope he turns out to be nicer than his name."

We climbed up three ghastly flights of creaking stairs, The walls were damp and their paint peeling away. The whole place looked dilapidated and in need of a good clean and a lick of fresh paint. Gerry suddenly stopped, a little breathless. "If this is a university, then I don't think I want to become one. God, John, it's worse than any of the most run-down polys I've ever seen."

We arrived at the third floor where a receptionist showed us into a small office and asked us to wait. It wasn't so much a request as an order. "I see the East Germans are still living in their old Communist bureaucracy," I said when the stern-faced woman had gone. We sat down to wait for Professor Hate. Gerry spoke reasonable German but said he'd leave me to do the talking as my German was better.

At last, after about ten minutes, the door opened and the professor entered. He was a big man, rotund rather than fat, with grey hair and thick glasses. He wore white overalls as befitted a chemist. His manner was brusque and there was no apology for having kept us waiting. The discussion was entirely in German. I had the feeling that he was not really very happy. But he had accepted the British Embassy's invitation to come to the little ceremony and even say a few words.

As we were making to leave, he suddenly came out with the reason for his attitude.

"Your polytechnics are not universities, are they?" he said with what seemed like a sneer. "Not yet," I replied – "but they soon will be."

He laughed. "Ach so, but their degrees are worthless, is that not so?"

"What nonsense," I replied and Gerry started to say something very quietly, like: "They're a bloody sight better than your bloody degrees…"

Professor Hass (I decided it was a most appropriate name) ignored Gerry's remark, which luckily was made in English, and continued: "Is it true that your students graduate after only three years?"

"Yes," I replied. "Sometimes they take four years for sandwich courses."

"So! Our students have to take seven years for their degrees," he smirked. "So it is clear that our universities must be better than your polytechnics."

"Herr Professor," I retorted. "Do you think that Oxford and Cambridge are bad universities?"

"*Nein*! Of course not. They are excellent universities."

"Well, it might surprise you to learn that their students also take *only* three years for a degree."

"*Ach*, that I did not know. But it is quite different," he said but looked a little shocked.

As we made our farewell, Gerry turned to Hass and, with a broad smile, declared in perfect German: "Quality comes before Quantity, Herr Professor!"

Later, at the British Embassy's excellent knees up, where we met the successful graduates, Professor Hass stood up to deliver his little speech. It was in fluent and faultless English.

He really was a despicable academic.

By the time that original wave of East German students had completed their year successfully, Mrs Thatcher was out and John Major had become Prime Minister. He asked the CDP to repeat the scheme. The FCO would continue to produce the funds. PECESS had proved not only a good piece of publicity for the polytechnics but also for Britain and the Government. What is more, the scheme was enlarged to embrace other countries that had formerly been under Soviet control: Poland, Czechoslovakia, Bulgaria and Rumania.

Although the polytechnics were no longer thought of as the "poor relations" of higher education, that is exactly what in reality they had remained: poor when compared with the country's 48 universities. The Government and the Treasury had treated the polytechnics appallingly, giving them at least £2,000 per student less than for students at universities. In 1979-80 universities spent £3,074 per student, while the polys were able to spend only £2,515. By 1987-88, the difference had grown worse still: £5,719 per university student; £3,356 for the poly student — £2.363 less.

I had to make these figures public as soon as possible after my arrival on the scene and contacted as many of my old Press contacts as possible. I didn't just tell them how the Government was short-changing poly students, but added that, as a result, polytechnic buildings had also suffered the consequences. Many buildings found themselves in a state of abysmal repair, some bordering on the danger level.

I also explained that, whereas the staff-student ratio stood at 1 : 8 only six years earlier, it had slumped to nearly 1 : 15 by the end of the 1980s. "Our students," I told education correspondents, "are being taught for the 21st century and are being obtained on the cheap. It's a total con."

The headlines could almost write themselves: "Polytechnics are being conned by the Government," thundered one.

The CDP was certainly getting the kind of publicity it wanted. Gerry Fowler was delighted. "You're doing a bloody fine job, ol'boy," he said, sucking at his cheroot. His chairmanship had come to an end and John Stoddart, principal of Sheffield Polytechnic took his place. The committee felt it was time to appoint a chief executive to act as front man (or woman – though that thought never entered into the discussions) and speak to Government ministers. Until that time, I had already undertaken such a role.

Just before her reign came to an end, I had spoken to Margaret Thatcher. I knew that she was "fond" of the polytechnic sector, but only because the institutions were "cheap and cheerful" and seemed to be keeping closely to every policy her Government had levelled at higher education. She accepted my argument that polys were being short-changed.

"But John, you must realise that this is only because they don't conduct the very advanced research undertaken by the universities and they don't have medical faculties. Those things are terribly expensive, you know. Terribly expensive," she would repeat, her head slightly leaning to the side and an oh-most-charming smile playing around her lips. Any further argument on my part would have been totally in vain. I didn't bother to tell her that our surveys showing the dreadful discrepancy in the numbers and financing of students in the binary system (universities and polytechnics) were always comparing like with like and that we never included universities with medical faculties.

The CDP debated the question of a CEO *in camera* but I was later given to understand that my name had "come up". I let it be known that I would not be interested. When I was appointed CDP director of public affairs at the age of 59 I calculated that I had about five years in which to turn the polys into unis and retire gracefully from the scene. Becoming chief executive of the organisation would create all kinds of snags once that task was completed satisfactorily. After all, what would happen to the CDP? It would become redundant. The Committee of Vice-Chancellors and Principals, umbrella body of the universities, would almost certainly take it over. I would prove too old to take on the entire HE sector.

So the job was advertised and of the many applicants interviewed, one man stood out above the rest: Roger Brown. He was tall to the point of gangling, wore spectacles and was just 44 years old but looked older due to early baldness having struck. His pedigree was good. Like me, he had many friends in high places but unlike me, he was not a poacher turned gamekeeper. He was already a gamekeeper, having been Secretary of the influential Polytechnics and Colleges Funding Council and prior to that, Assistant Secretary at the Department of Trade and Industry. He had also worked in the Cabinet Office and earlier at the Inner London Education Authority, during which period (1975-76) he had acted as Secretary to the William Tyndale School board of inquiry.

Dr Brown was made welcome by all and immediately managed to make himself unpopular by demanding that every member of staff with the slightest responsibility should produce a report spelling out his/her Aims and Objectives. I have always detested such formal nonsense. I knew exactly what my aim was – to lift the polytechnics into the limelight and help them become universities in their own right. What is more, I was getting there and had no need of civil service bureaucracy. Roger and I got off to what one might call "a bad start".

I felt that everything I undertook, everything I wrote was dissected by this new broom. He would call me into his office and suggest in the sweetest and most syrupy voice that I should write it "this way" or "that way" and let him see it again…

Every Monday morning we had a staff meeting at which plans, appointments and ideas for the week would be discussed. Roger, sitting at the head of the long table, would put on his best teacher's voice and go round the table asking each member for new ideas. As the most senior of the rest of the staff, the finger would come to me first and I would come out with some brilliant proposal.

Roger would laugh. "That's quite ridiculous, John. Quite ridiculous. No use whatsoever." And without further ado, he would go to the next in line. Jo Harris would put forward an idea of hers – and her ideas were good. "Ah, that's most helpful, Jo. I'll make a note of that." And a note of it he would certainly make. Rarely, however, was the idea used.

As the Mondays went by and all my dreams were smashed, I decided on a different ploy. My colleagues had all noticed the Brown bullying tactics and were puzzled by them. All were prepared to come to my assistance. So I slipped an idea – a fairly minor one – to Jo prior to the meeting and asked her to put it forward. When I was asked I put forward a very similar idea but dressed up quite differently. As usual, it was pooh-poohed. Jo, who was sitting towards the other end of the table, waited for her turn, then put forward my differently dressed proposal.

"Very useful, Jo. Very useful as usual. I'll make a note of that."

We knew then that there was no mistake. I felt relieved. I had actually begun to think that my ideas really were rubbish, that I was losing my grip, that I could no longer write. Now at least I knew that it wasn't me but Roger who, for some totally unknown reason, was prejudiced against me.

The real reason became clear some months later, when Roger decided it was time for staff assessments. I went into the torture chamber anticipating the worst. I did not want a fight but was determined not to take any shit but at least try to hold my own. We went through the usual rigmarole of pros and cons and I was surprised that my pros seemed to be better than my cons, neither of which I can now recall in any detail. But I do recall the part where I was invited to put questions. I asked why he was very obviously making my job so difficult for me.

"Oh dear, do you really think so? I had no idea I was doing it."

He then confessed the truth: "You see, I've always considered you as my biggest rival at the CDP and that you were probably after my job…"

I was frankly flabbergasted. "Me? After your job, Roger? That's nonsense. In fact, quite the contrary is the case. I fully supported your appointment and made it clear to both Gerry Fowler and John Stoddart that I did not want to be chief executive. I'm perfectly happy with my position and know in which direction I'm going – and it's not in your direction."

From that moment on things quietened down and I was able to carry out my own task more or less freely. I say more or less because Roger would never allow anyone to forget that he was boss.

Some years later, after the CDP had disappeared, he invited me to lunch at a nearby Bloomsbury club of which we were both members. It was to apologise to me for the aggro he had caused me. I do not bear grudges and readily forgave and forgot.

We remained on excellent terms ever since and still meet every Christmas for a get-together of the old CDP staff for a decent lunch at an inexpensive restaurant in Central London.

Roger later became vice-chancellor of Southampton Solent University and professor in higher education policy and later still co-directed the Centre for Research and Development in Higher Education at Liverpool Hope University.

For once I managed to miscalculate my plans. Instead of taking five years to turn the polytechnics into universities, it had taken a mere three years. I had perhaps promoted them too well and too quickly. There had been a number of decent dinners to which we had invited the *crème de la crème* of the political world. Margaret Thatcher had been ousted and left Number Ten in tears, clutching the arm of Denis. It was, in a way, a sorry sight. She had, after all, been the country's very first woman to lead a major political party and become Prime Minister. She had taken the nation into war to defend and free the Falkland Islands and given Britain a half-hearted victory. But she had also managed to whip up a great deal of antagonism bordering on veritable hatred for her policies and of her as a woman. The closure of the country's main coal mines followed by a long and bitter miners' strike did her no good at all. Her agonisingly brutal poll tax, which inflamed the nation and led to one after another violent demonstration, solidified her unpopularity.

She was followed not by "Tarzan", the blond bombshell Michael

Heseltine, my one-time boss, but by the almost unknown Brixton boy, John Major. For the polytechnics this was good news for Major, like Margaret Thatcher, liked the polys. For her they had been "cheap and cheerful"; for him they were a real "success story". Although he was born close to Wimbledon and went to the Rutlish Grammar School, he left school at 16 because his family was too poor to allow him to continue in education. He tried to join the post office but was rejected because his maths were not good enough, which made it particularly ironic that he went on to become Chancellor of the Exchequer. But his background made him admire a higher education sector that made a point of giving young people a second chance with an "open access" policy.

John Major supported totally our campaign to gain universary status and recommended it to Her Majesty.

No one had expected the Queen to give the Royal Assent for the Further and Higher Education Act as early as March 6, 1992 for England and Wales and on March 16 for Scotland. Major's decision to call a General Election on April 9 brought on a veritable frenzy of activity to push legislation through to the statute books. The new Acts meant the abolition of the so-called binary line, which separated universities and polytechnics. It allowed the polys to present their own degrees after December 1992 instead of having them awarded solely by the Council for National Academic Awards (CNAA).

And the Acts allowed the polytechnics to call themselves universities if they so wished.

If they wished? You bet they wished! On June 4, 1992 the Privy Council permitted the country's polytechnics to award their own degrees and to change their names to University – as long as it did not clash with any existing ("pukka") university. This meant that, for instance, Liverpool Polytechnic could not call itself New University of Liverpool. But it was all right to take on the name that it did: Liverpool John Moores University – a clever move as John Moores owned Littlewood Pools and was expected to leave the old poly something in his will.

Only Anglia Polytechnic retained Polytechnic in its name and became Anglia Polytechnic University, so that they could remain top of an alphabetical list. Birmingham Polytechnic adopted one of the strangest names – University of Central England in Birmingham; Bristol Poly was another: University of the West of England, Bristol.

The Polytechnic of Central London, which was the first ever poly built, wanted to call itself University of Central London, but it was feared that its initials UCL would clash with the "genuine" UCL (University College

London, a college of the University of London) so it became The University of Westminster, one of the best names in the business.

I had produced a regular CDP Newsmagazine called *Direct*, which was sent to all members and the Press. Its last issue, published in November 1992, contained a front page message from the Prime Minister which said:

> *I am delighted to contribute to this final edition of "Direct". The Polytechnic story has been one of enormous success over what, for higher education, has been a very short timescale. The emergence of the Polytechnics as Britain's new universities is a triumph not just for the institutions themselves but for the CDP which has represented them so well over the past 22 years. I would like to thank the CDP most warmly for all their work.*
>
> *The new single sector means that all Britain's universities will now be represented by a single organisation. That is a great step forward and I wish them all the very best.*

John Major

My job was done.

I wondered how long it would be before people would refer to these so-called "New Universities" as universities in their own right and not just as "old polys". I remember telling one or two of the new vice-chancellors to resist the temptation of copying Oxbridge, but to continue their policies of open access and an emphasis on the more vocational type of courses. It was whistling against the wind. Most of them were quick enough to discard the word "director", even "rector" and adopt "vice-chancellor" but explained that it was not really their own choice but the direction of their governors. Hm.

CHAPTER TWENTY-ONE:

HEADHUNTED AT 62

I had no intention of tying myself to the Committee of Vice-Chancellors and Principals (CVCP). I had, after all, only agreed to work for the CDP because there had been a goal to aim for. Helping an entire sector of higher education institutions to be promoted by Royal Charter to the status of university was truly satisfying, even if I often had the feeling that it might have been the wrong thing to have done.

Mea culpa...Mea maxima culpa!

The polytechnics had all performed their tasks not just well but exceptionally well. The change of title was only good for their promotion abroad. Singapore, for instance, would not allow its students to come and study at British polys because they were considered not good enough. The name "polytechnic" was completely misleading. In France, *L'école polytechnique*, represents the *crème de la crème* and is part of the country's *Grandes Ecoles*, whose standing supersedes even the best universities.

Germany had it right when it called its polytechnics *Fachhochschulen* – Technical (or Vocational) Colleges. Yet the leaders of the *Fachhochschulen* invited me to come to Munich and deliver a lecture on how the British polytechnics had managed to become universities. They made no secret of their envy.

Auriol Stevens, the former education editor of the *Observer* and one of those who joined the small Press delegation on a three-week trip to China (described in a previous chapter) had, like me, turned to public relations and was head of PR at the CVCP. She was leaving, having happily married John

Ashworth, the director of the London School of Economics, so there was a vacancy. I agreed to an interview but it was clear that I did not want them – and they didn't want me. I was, after all, in my 63rd year.

But then something surprising happened. I had a telephone call from Leslie Wagner, vice-chancellor of the (new) University of North London. Would I come to see him for some lunch. Lunch? I was always ready to accept a decent meal. Leslie Wagner, among the senior members of the CDP, was always friendly and fair...and he offered me a job: to be public affairs director of the university.

Here I was, being headhunted at the age of 62!

The irony of it all was that the University of North London, which used to be PNL – the Polytechnic of North London – had suffered from my pen more than from anyone else's during the Seventies. It was constantly being occupied by militant students and was under very real threat of closure from the Education Secretary, Sir Keith Joseph. The appointment of Dr Terence Miller caused rioting in the streets (see Chapter 16) and the discovery that one student, Patrick Harrington, was in fact the treasurer of the Fascist National Front movement brought further occupations and led to bloodshed.

Now here I was having to promote a university whose background could not have been worse. Again, this appealed to me. It was a challenge. How can one resist a challenge? The managerial post was offered to me and I accepted.

I admit that it proved a tougher job to "sell" UNL than the CDP. Still, I set to work, touring the "campus", meeting as many of the academic staff as I could in as short a time as was possible. I asked each one to search their minds and their departments for positive stories. "Even if you don't think it'll make a story, tell me about it. Let me be the judge," I would tell one after another head of department.

PNL had a number of buildings, one worse than the others. It was an old establishment, having been opened in 1896 as a poly and a school. Most of it stood in just about the bleakest and noisiest parts of London on the Holloway Road – or, for those who see places in terms of maps – the A1. Its buildings, though not as dilapidated as the one Gerry and I entered at the Humboldt University in Berlin, were in great need of repair and decorating.

It is strange how, again and again, I seemed to be drawn back to places of a past existence. Humboldt was one, since it was a site close to the house we lived in and the shop my parents ran on the Invalidenstrasse; UNL was opposite one of the most misnamed streets in the capital: Eden Grove, where Maureen was taken on as a teacher by the nuns of Our Lady of Sion. The street was certainly no Garden of Eden, nor could it ever be considered a Grove. But UNL was at least a happy ship and Leslie was a pleasure to work for.

As a religious Jew, he would leave early on a Friday afternoon, so as to reach home before sunset and celebrate the Sabbath. Jewish holidays were, of course, also closely observed. He tut-tutted at my irreligious ways. I only ever take off one day in the year – the Yom Kippur – the Day of Atonement, holiest in the Jewish calendar. And I do so, not so much out of religious feelings on my part as out of tradition and in loving memory of my parents and the many of my mother's relations who were murdered in the Nazi camps.

I distributed as many Press releases as I found stories to highlight in them. Some of them even hit the mark. Each month I would produce several pages of "feedback" from the media that have used the stories I had put out. This bulletin was distributed to every head of department. Gradually they saw that the public relations they so badly needed were beginning to get positive results.

There was a time when both the universities and the polytechnics and colleges of higher education had their own umbrella associations. That was clearly no longer necessary and I attended a meeting in Oxford in the summer of 1993 at which it was suggested that we should amalgamate. I was entirely in favour of such a move and was proud to become a founder member of HEERA – the Higher Education External Relations Association.

I am in fact mistaken to say that I was such a member because the members are not individuals but the institutions they represent.

A colleague at UNL, Nigel Curson, and I got together to discuss yet another idea. Nigel was an IT ace and could structure computers to his will. Together we decided to launch a HEERA mailbase so that we could exchange ideas and information with one another. There were many of us and we were able to assist those who needed help. This mailbase is still going strong and is open only to HEERA members and totally confidential. A website, open to the public, provides information about each institution.

I became chairman of HEERA for a couple of years and lectured regularly at annual HEERA conferences, originally shared with CASE – the Council for Advancement and Support of Education – and HEIST, involved in the marketing of HE. Whereas CASE was mainly involved in fundraising, HEERA was more concerned with public relations. But as marketing, development and PR tend to go together, the conferences provided something for everyone and were excellently attended.

It was a friendly organisation and I made many lifelong friends. Some of us continue to meet regularly for lunches in central London, even though we are almost all retired. The gossip and stories recounted at such times keep us all going. For example, Robert Hawker, a superb information officer, who kept London Guildhall University's publicity afloat for years before moving on to other HE institutions, is a regular at these lunches; Barbara Anderson who was London University's director of information and still works on at Gresham College as its academic registrar, is another; Christine Hodgson, who, like me, was a journalist before taking on public relations for East London Polytechnic (later the University of East London), yet another; and Anne McHardy, who edited *Education Guardian* and continues to freelance, was another regular.

Before I joined UNL, Leslie suggested that I might consider the university's centenary, which was coming up in 1986. We discussed a number of possibilities and agreed that I should write a history of the university for publication in time for any other centenary celebrations we would eventually devise. It was true that the university had a fabulous story to tell from its very start in Victorian London right up to the present day.

It was impossible to concentrate on so important and detailed a piece of writing in the office where the telephone rang every few minutes and people came in and out to see me about publicity material, promotional brochures and the like. So it was agreed that, once I was ready to start putting words to paper, I should do so in the peace and quiet of home. There I would be alone for most of the day. Paul had taken himself off to Australia with Sue, his gorgeous New Zealand girl friend and was living and working in Sydney, and June was busy teaching special needs' boys in a Forest Hill comprehensive. So I had the house to myself. But I agreed to come to the office on one day, possibly two, to take care of anything that needed to be done in the PR field.

I spent the next several weeks searching for archive material. The university had no archive as such and it was often a matter of following one's nose and hoping to smell out some morsels. In the bowels of the Holloway Road building I came across a veritable goldmine of "bits and pieces". Nothing was sorted; very few things were dated. But there was a pile of photographs showing the old poly in its early stages.

There were even some sets of programmes of concerts...with dates printed on them.

Holloway Road was not the only building making up the UNL campus. Far from it. If anything the university had branches that spread themselves across north London like some spider's web. The main block could be divided into the Tower Building and, alongside it, the original redbrick edifice with its beautiful clocktower in which the management was housed: the Vice-Chancellor and looking after the academic side, a Deputy Vice-Chancellor, who when I was there was a lovely woman, Sandra Ashman; and a Deputy Vice-Chancellor for finance and resources – one Miles Atchison in my time; and a Secretary and Clerk to the Board of Governors, who was an efficient young man called John McParland. And there was my office. This in itself caused a number of tongues to wag. Was I "management" or was I just Leslie's man?

Among other buildings there was one across the road housing the business school, built over a furniture store, and another smaller one around the corner from the business school in Eden Grove; then there was yet another close to Highbury tube, where one could study art and architecture. The excellent Faculty of Environmental and Social Studies at Ladbroke House in Highbury Grove, whose Dean was another splendid woman, Dr Jennifer Somerville, who became a true friend. Yet another building stood some two miles away at Kentish Town.

It was there, in the Kentish Town building, that I came across a large series of files containing letters and local newspaper reports dating back to 1895 – while the opening of a polytechnic in the area was still being discussed. They proved invaluable and I managed to fill the boot of my car with them for closer study at home.

Newspaper reports using my Press releases were growing in volume. I was careful to put out only the most positive of stories. My policy was simple and echoed the popular song: *accentuate the positive; eliminate the negative.* Journalists would be quick enough to hear and follow up any rumour with the slightest negative in it, so I would always be ready to answer their questions as truthfully as possible and manage to persuade them to add something positive to their stories. The university was rarely in even minor trouble while I was directing its public relations.

After I had been there a little over a year, Louise Slater, Leslie's wonderful PA, phoned me. "John, could you please come in? Leslie wants to see you."

"Oh? What about?" I wanted to know. Louise would normally have given me a clue. But she remained firm. "Just come in, will you John?" She sounded strange. Almost miserable. I immediately started to think the worst. What had I done? Had I fucked up some Press release? Had I annoyed someone? Was I going to be sacked?

I only needed to cross the narrow corridor from my office to his ante-chamber housing Louise and a secretary. Both had grim faces. "Go straight in, John. He's expecting you," said Louise. Now I knew something was definitely wrong. I knocked and entered the large, light room overlooking Holloway Road. Leslie was behind his desk sorting some papers.

I stood there waiting for him to say something. At last he looked up.

"Ah John, sorry, I'm doing a bit of clearing. Do sit down. I need to talk to you. Won't keep you long." He continued for a while sorting papers from his desk and stuffing them into his briefcase. I now felt almost as if waiting for an execution.

Leslie at last came to the little table where I was sitting. "D'you fancy a cuppa…Well, I do," he said and went to the intercom to ask Louise to make some tea.

He sat down alongside me. "I've got some news which you might not like," he began.

"Oh dear," was all I could retort. "What have I done wrong?"

"Nothing. Good Lord, nothing John. But I'm afraid that I'm going to have to leave. I've just been offered to go to Leeds Metropolitan. The offer is so good that I don't think I could refuse it."

My relief must have made itself obvious. "Oh, you look like the news might have pleased you," he said with some disappointment.

"Oh no. No! Leslie, I'm shattered that you'll be leaving. I'm sure the entire university will be. I thought I had committed some awful sin. Now I understand why Louise was looking so downhearted and bleary-eyed. Mazeltov! Wow! Vice-Chancellor of Leeds Metropolitan – I suppose it is as V-C or what?"

"Oh yes, I'm to be its Vice-Chancellor. Chris (Price) is retiring and they've offered the job to me. I'll be sorry to leave here and only hope that my successor will prove to be all right. I'll let you know as soon as there's a shortlist…"

I was, of course, pleased for Leslie. Leeds Met was big and had a better reputation than North London. Like UNL it stands in the middle of the city, almost cheek by jowl with its older brother, Leeds University (founded towards the end of the 19th century, compared with Leeds Met, founded in 1970 as a polytechnic). The result is a mass of buildings belonging to both and forming a veritable student-city. The Met students are certainly far less militant than those who appear constantly to be attracted to UNL, so Leslie would not have to face anything like the aggro he would have experienced at fairly regular intervals on the Holloway Road. Leeds also has a large Jewish community, so Leslie would certainly have been able to continue the various leadership posts he held: vice-president of the United Synagogue in London, trustee of the Chief Rabbinate and of the *Jewish Chronicle* and, most important to him, advisor to the Chief Rabbi. I often wondered how he managed to perform all these tasks and still direct a busy university so brilliantly.

He was greatly missed by staff and students alike.

His successor, a short, slightly tubby, bearded man with a broad grin, was recruited from Oxford Brookes University, which topped the list of so-called New Universities for academic scholarship and student satisfaction. His name: Brian Roper. Oxford Brookes, I later learned during one of my visits to Oxford, was glad to have been deprived of his services.

Dr Roper started at UNL quietly enough but soon began using his broom. My monthly news sheet providing the academic staff with brief accounts of the many articles, radio and television programmes, interviews and the like that had been produced, was axed. Any reports of the Vice-Chancellor's speeches within or outside the university had first to be checked and passed by him. My attempts at subbing such speeches and correcting any poor grammar were treated with disdain.

Roper was a chain smoker and when the university became a smoke-free (i.e. cigarette-free) zone, he would join the hordes of students on the pavement of the Holloway Road and puff away at his fags.

Despite my lack of sympathy for him, I did not disagree with his policy. It was not all that different from the policy conducted by Leslie Wagner. Roper continued UNL's tradition of offering places to students from all walks of life, as long as they showed themselves willing to take advantage of the higher education they were being taught. He did not believe that A-levels were the "gold currency" that helped to buy a university place. He made no bones about the fact that he had "consistently seen excellent results from students who entered our university with no formal academic qualifications or modest A-level scores, yet with active support and guidance, achieved excellent degrees and successful careers."

And he asked the very pertinent question: "Should these students have missed out on an education simply because they did not meet the A-level test?" He added: "It would appear that proponents of such arguments would like us to return to a time when only the privileged were lucky enough to receive a university education."

One could not disagree with such a view, especially when one was able to see many examples of students who proved him one hundred per cent right. Brian Roper was not alone in following such a philosophy. Leslie Wagner, Gerry Fowler, Christopher Price, Raymond Rickett and many others who had turned their polytechnics into fully fledged universities were of exactly the same opinion.

One student who was a superb illustration of this belief was Chris Kitch. I came across her among those in the School of Women's Studies. She was in her Fifties and was pointed out to me by one of her lecturers as "a miracle woman". I started talking to Chris and the whole story came blurting out. She had been expelled from her Yorkshire school for being "lazy and a trouble maker" and had run away from home, making her way to London at the age of 12 or 13. She had no money and started sleeping in the streets. The inevitable happened and she took to drugs and drink. She became an alcoholic and teamed up with another alcoholic woman who used to be a dancer with Covent Garden ballet Both slept in cardboard boxes in one of the underpasses around Tottenham Court Road. Chris stole to pay for her drink and drugs and spent a large proportion of her time sleeping in police cells. On returning from the cells to her pavement home, she found that her partner had topped herself in a public lavatory.

Chris knew that she would either also commit suicide or change her life. She had always regretted having dropped out of education and decided to give up her miserable life. She sought help and was sent into rehab to be dried out and de-drugged. It was the toughest of times for her but she struggled on and, once she was "well again", went to a south London college to take a foundation course in English. There she was provided with some remarkable help and was recognised as having a gift for writing. They suggested she applies to UNL for a degree course.

She was interviewed by Dr Liz Kelly of the Child and Women Abuse Studies Unit, and later told me: "It was the first time anyone, other than a magistrate, actually listened to me." She worked hard and, to no one's surprise, was awarded a 2:1 degree. It made a great story but as is the case with many good stories, it doesn't always hit the right spot. The trouble is that Press releases drop on hacks' desks in great numbers throughout the day and tend to end up at the bottom of a pile – and never seen. I was nevertheless amazed when not a single newspaper spotted this one.

So I tried another scheme. I invited Richard Garner to have lunch. He was at that time the education correspondent of the *Daily Mirror* and was a good friend (he was later to become the education editor of *The Independent*). We chatted about all kinds of things, possible stories and other ideas. Then, over coffee, I said: "By the way, there *is* a story which I think you might like…" and I launched into the tale of the Bag Lady. He loved it and made immediate arrangements to travel to Oxford where Chris had taken a job at the convent of All Saints Sisters of the Poor – helping women in distress. It was a neat rounding of her life's experience. He took a photographer with him and the piece made a page lead in the *Mirror*, as I thought it might.

And, of course, it was then followed up by just about every other newspaper – and television. BBC2 arranged to produce a half hour film about Chris and cover her actual graduation ceremony. The programme was called appropriately perhaps, *Raising Lazarus*. When she climbed the few steps onto the stage at the Barbican, where UNL held its series of graduation ceremonies, and strode towards Brian Roper to receive her scroll, her fellow graduands rose as one to cheer her. Brian shook her hand warmly and congratulated her for having achieved what many might have thought to be the impossible. There was hardly a dry eye in the house.

Chris had accompanied me around her former haunts and met a number of other bag ladies and men, lying in the spots she and her partner had often occupied, down in the tunnel opposite Tottenham Court Road tube station. After that moving experience, she told me: "John, I've not finished yet. I'm going to write it all down and have it published as a book." And she did. *Pavement for My Pillow* was published in November 1997 as "the astonishing story of one woman's climb from pitiful baglady to scholar and writer".

That was not all. Chris later took an MA at Oxford and, later still, after having spent four years as a novice with the All Saints Sisters (which she said she found "harder than the streets") she took the holy vows of Poverty, Chastity and Obedience and became a nun in November 2003. Unfortunately, I did not see her again after *Raising Lazarus* but I have always remembered her with admiration and affection. She proved that it is never too late to succeed in education or anything else as long as one has the will and the stamina to strive for the goal.

It was time for me to start writing the university's history, as I had arranged with Leslie Wagner. Brian Roper was not altogether happy at my suggestion that I would undertake this work in the peace and comparative quiet of home. "Who is going to take care of PR and everything else that you do here?" he demanded to know, and I agreed to come in every Friday to cover anything that needed to be covered. I might have known that this alone would not have worked. I was telephoned at home almost every day to provide some academic with advice or produce press releases. These I would fax to the Communications Office where they would be copied and distributed to the long list of media contacts.

I was able to concentrate on the book after those at the university had shut their offices and gone home. I worked solidly until the early hours and gradually built up a story that told not only the creation and development of UNL but also the history of the polytechnics movement. It turned out to be an opus of almost mammoth proportions and related the turbulent beginnings of the polytechnic on the Holloway Road and its struggle to reach not only designation as a New Polytechnic but the ultimate designation as a university in its own right.

I contacted every former director who was still alive to ask for the accounts of their own time at North London. Each, including Dr Terence Miller, whose appearance as first director of the newly designated poly caused so much strife, provided me with a chapter. Leslie Wagner, of course, wrote a brilliant chapter as first vice-chancellor. I even managed to persuade the chairman of governors, Richard (Dick) Coldwell, to pen a rather good introduction which began: *Few British universities have had as colourful a story to tell as the University of North London. It has been an exciting century and one of which this university is justifiably proud.*

He also said that more than 72 per cent of the students at UNL were mature – i.e. over 21 on entry – and most of them (54 per cent) were women. Four out of ten came from minority ethnic groups and "*all of them without question are intent on improving their skills, their qualifications and certainly their 'well being'.*"

Towards the end of this intro, he wrote: "*This book is dedicated to our students, past and present, without whom neither the Polytechnic of North London nor the University of North London would ever have existed. I hope they will enjoy reading their history. It is their heritage – a heritage they should rightly cherish.*"

So why, then, was this piece of heritage never published? Why, indeed, was it banned from publication?

This unpleasant decision had nothing to do with the title. I had called it *The University of North London – One Hundred Turbulent Years*. Turbulent met with an immediate objection from both Brian Roper and Dick Coldwell. So I changed it to *The University of North London – One Hundred Vibrant Years*. Vibrant was considered all right. Frankly, I didn't care one way or the other. The story it told was certainly vibrant and readers would have found the facts nothing short of turbulent. So why? I had asked Roper for a chapter – I wanted it to be the final chapter (there were 15 in all) and I asked the vice-chancellor to outline his view of the future. I never received this chapter. But after I had virtually pleaded with him to supply the words and reminded him that printing deadlines were getting ever shorter, I was summoned to his presence.

He was clearly embarrassed and began by praising me for the work I had done. "I like the book you have written. It's excellent," he said and I wondered what piece of nastiness was about to follow. "What you have written is good... very readable. But the chapters submitted by my predecessors I didn't like.

And the other thing is the chapters concerning that man – er – Harrington. I think that should be omitted."

"What? Left out altogether?" I retorted. "I couldn't possibly do that, Brian. That's like asking me to write a history of Germany and leave out Auschwitz and the holocaust."

It was a ridiculous, even stupid suggestion. The Polytechnic of North London had undergone a number of violent skirmishes, but none so violent as that which surrounded one of its students, Patrick Antony Harrington, who had applied for a degree course in philosophy in December 1981. He was accepted and came to the Kentish Town building as a fresher the following October. He proved to be a fairly uninteresting student who attended lectures regularly and kept himself to himself. Indeed, he might have gone through the course without the slightest disturbance if it had not been for an article in *Fuse*, the Polytechnic students' magazine. An article in its April 1983 issue bore the title *Who Polices the Nazis?* It dealt with neo-Nazi activities in North London and was illustrated with a picture of two young fascist thugs selling copies of *Bulldog*, a National Front journal at the Chapel Street Market.

One of the two men in the picture was immediately recognised by some students as Patrick Harrington. They stormed to the *Fuse* office to voice their concerns. Two students recalled how this same man had tried to sell copies of *NF News* in the Kentish Town students' bar. Harrington, in fact, was not only a member of National Front but one of its officers. All hell was let loose. Students picketed philosophy lectures and Harrington's life was made a misery. Matters were made worse when a black student's bag was found with a swastika painted on it. Although this incident was never connected to Harrington, it made matters even more explosive.

Pickets were swollen by students from other universities and colleges. Busloads of them came in from as far away as Glasgow and Manchester. Holloway Road became clogged with screaming young men and women. Harrington had managed to find a solicitor, Tessa Sempik of Willesden Green, to act for him. It turned out that she was the wife of Richard Verall, a one-time National Front member who wrote a scurrilous book titled *Did Six Million Really Die?* which attempted to sweep the holocaust under the carpet of time.

On Friday May 11th 1984, an Order was made in the High Court directing its Tipstaff to accompany his agents to the Polytechnic *"for the purpose of bringing any persons participating in any picket against Patrick Harrington before the High Court to show cause why they should not be committed to prison for contempt of Court..."* The picketing did not cease and riots became a daily routine on the Holloway Road. Back at the Department of Education and Science, Sir Keith Joseph was just waiting to shut the entire polytechnic down. But the law was as adamant as the non-budging Harrington. He had been lawfully registered as a student and had the right to be treated as such.

David MacDowall, the then Director of PNL, put the matter bluntly in a memorandum dated 27th September 1984, that he distributed to all heads of department and division. They and their staffs were ordered to report any action by any student which contravened regulations. The actions were listed as:

Assault or serious threatening behaviour; malicious damage to polytechnic property; theft, fighting or any criminal or serious offence on Poly premises; sexual harassment; racist behaviour or activity; a breach of the Polytechnic Equal Opportunity Policies; behaviour which causes fear or distress to others…and many other misdemeanours.

Of course, the matter grew and spread. Unions rapidly became involved. The National Association of Teachers in Further and Higher Education (NATFHE) had this to say: *"This NATFHE branch totally opposes the National Front – a fascist and racist organisation whose policies are incompatible with the anti-racist and open education to which PNL is committed."* The National Union of Students also supported all action preventing Harrington from entering the polytechnic buildings.

Only one thing remained for the polytechnic to do in view of the Court Order. Harrington, despised as his views were, had the right to study and had to be allowed that right. So the polytechnic rented a room above a pub behind the poly and secretly provided lectures and tutorials to Harrington. Amazingly, none of the students were made aware of this ruse.

Harrington was even privately examined and was awarded his BA degree at an equally private ceremony above the pub.

That, in brief, was what became known as *The Harrington Affair*. I reported it briefly in the book (after all, I had actually reported it on an almost daily basis for the *Daily Telegraph* at the time it happened) but I went further and commissioned three academics who were teaching at the poly at the time of the Harrington Affair to let me have their own accounts. It provided three different views of the same event. Dr Denis Judd, Professor of History at UNL, was Subject Tutor for History at the time and ended up in the High Court charged with contempt of court as a member of the so-called 'PNL Fourteen' because he had refused to name photographed student pickets; Michael Newman, course tutor of the BA in Contemporary European Studies, was another member of staff involved in the Harrington Affair; and Alan Haworth, who taught philosophy at UNL and was philosophy subject leader during the Harrington period, recalled being asked to hold a philosophy seminar in the back of a squad car. He refused. All three allowed me to include their accounts in the book.

And all three, as well as the various past directors and past students who contributed to the book, kept asking me when the wretched thing would be published. To the eternal shame of Brian Roper, it never was. I had refused to allow my name to be used as author of a book that deliberately re-wrote history by omitting one of the most important sequences – and in history it was but a brief sequence, yet important nevertheless – of the University of North London's story.

I continued my employment at UNL until my retirement, producing as a celebration of the centenary a concert staged at the Barbican. I used orchestras from local schools that had been found and rehearsed by the versatile and talented Maxwell (Max) Pryce, who ran the Schools Music Association, a similar movement to the equally excellent School Proms. I picked the now late Claire Rayner, the well known agony aunt and nurse, and Trevor Philips, former NUS president and chairman of the Commission for Racial Equality, as compères, and the (also now late) actor David Kossoff, who was an alumnus of the university (having been taught at the Northern Polytechnic before taking to the stage) as narrator of one of the orchestral pieces – *Peter and the Wolf.* The concert was a great success and I believed it to be my swan song.

It was.

I was 66 and had overstepped the official retirement mark. It was high time for me to go and I was glad to take my departure from a university whose Vice-Chancellor had been responsible for the first piece of censorship I had ever experienced. Considering that some 90 per cent of the book had been written in my own time at home, often through much of the night, I felt that the university could not even claim to own the copyright. It ranks as one of my failures and the university's loss.

Tough.

My retirement was interrupted by an offer I could not refuse. Wendy Berliner, a journalist friend who had been education correspondent of *The Guardian* before editing the *Independent*'s excellent education supplement, asked me to write a weekly light hearted gossipy column. I was delighted to accept. It meant a return to the profession I had always loved and with which I had always felt most at ease. My many contacts at universities and schools provided me with as much information as I needed, and more.

This happy period lasted nearly three years. Wendy left the *Indy* and the columns stopped.

But one outlet still remained. *Education,* a magazine that had been going for many years, published by Longman's, was closed and with it, many good friends were made redundant, including Tudor David, its distinguished editor who doubled as the 2,000-volt Welsh composer of satirical "operas" that were regularly performed at the series of education correspondents' cabarets. Also out were its deputy editor and, following Tudor's retirement, editor George Low, and numerous outstanding reporters and writers. One of its regular columnists, Demitri Coryton, decided to pull the magazine out of the flames and resurrect it as a monthly called *Education Journal.* He asked me to contribute a regular column and I have been writing for this magazine ever since. Later, when the *Times Educational Supplement* was foolishly sold (foolishly, because it had become the biggest and most successful money-spinner for *Times Newspapers*) its new bosses made many of its finest members of staff redundant. Some of these joined *Education Journal* including Ian Nash, who had edited its Further Education section for years; Diane Hofkins, who edited its Primary Schools section; Frances Rafferty, its news editor; and Susan Young, assistant editor. Wendy Berliner, who became acting editor of the *TES* but was stupidly overlooked when it came to appointing an editor, also wrote briefly for *E J* before taking a job abroad.

Mike Baker, former education correspondent of the BBC and John O'Leary, former editor of *The Times Higher Education Supplement* and editor of its *Good University Guide*, also joined *Education Journal.* George Low who had edited *E J* for its first few years, remained as a regular contributor. With myself added to that large group, it meant that *Education Journal* was able to boast having an editorial staff that was education's *crème de la crème.*

Perhaps I had come full circle. It has certainly felt like it.

CHAPTER TWENTY-TWO:

EPILOGUE

A t the age of 80, I can look back with a mixture of sorrow and pleasure.

Pleasure, because I have two beautiful grandchildren in Chloe and Tyler, who I hope will one day read all this in the company of Paul, my loving son, and Sue, my gorgeous daughter-in-law. Pleasure, because my super stepchildren, Anna and Patrick, have indeed been super. Patrick married Mary, an attractive Irish general practitioner, and produced a gorgeous baby girl, my step-granddaughter, Robyn, and Anna has taken a commission in the Army. Both Patrick and Anna are excellent linguists, particularly Anna, who, like her brother, speaks fluent French, thanks to our life in France, but also Italian, some German, Spanish, Japanese and even Arabic. Her two-year period of teaching English to Japanese children in Osaka, had certainly helped. Paul has built up a successful business in Australia and travels the world. How could I not take pleasure from all of this?

Pleasure, too, because I have a good wife and an intelligent teacher in June. I am grateful to her for many things, including her corrections of the doubtless abundant number of slips of spelling and grammar perpetrated in these pages. If she has missed any, I apologise.

And pleasure because I have had a generally good life. I enjoyed my two years of National Service in the Army; I certainly enjoyed my several years of study at Nottingham, Paris, Göttingen and Münster.

So what of the sorrow? I weep for the many, far, far too many, who

My wonderful son, Paul and his gorgeous Kiwi wife, Sue in Australia since 1991

My marvelous family today:
L-R: stepson Patrick, me,
my wife, June,
my stepdaughter Anna.

My mother outside her Southport nursing home
in 1990, aged 89. A year later, shortly after her
90th birthday, she died. This is how I shall
always remember her.

perished in the gas chambers and crematoria of Nazi concentration camps, my dear mother's brothers and sister, her mother who died of starvation at Theresienstadt, the many cousins, uncles and aunts and their children who were dragged away in cattle trucks, tortured and murdered at Auschwitz, Belsen and Buchenwald. I weep for my beloved parents who suffered the agony of having to flee from their persecutors in Berlin and start afresh in a strange land whose language and customs they did not know but happily learned. I weep for Maureen whose life was cut short by so deadly a disease as cancer and who had to suffer three years of agony.

How do I sum it all up, this pleasure and this sorrow?

I can still see the little boy who ran out into an empty Berlin street to shout with pride that he was a Jew; the little boy who saw with horror how an old woman was cut down by a large splinter of glass as she screamed abuse against the Jews; I still experience the excitement of seeing the British fleet silhouetted against the sky while a ship of refugees waited to be rescued by the immigration authorities at Harwich.

Could that little boy have guessed that he would one day become the education editor of so famous a quality newspaper as *The Daily Telegraph* and even help a nation's polytechnics become recognised as universities?

Was it all perhaps a dream? And was Horst really a proper name?

My late parents
to whom I owe everything.

INDEX

A

Abbottempo 169-170, 171, 173
Abbotts 169, 170
Adenauer, Dr Konrad 79
Adventure 51
Advertising World 113
Agate, James 165
Agence France-Presse (AFP) 205, 206
Aiglon 277-279
Aiglon College, Chesières-Villars 278
Aldershot 86, 87, 89, 90, 94, 108
Alexander, Beatrix/Beatrice 52, 209
Alexander, Berta (John's maternal
  grandmother) 5, 6, 7, 14, 15, 16, 17,
  19, 20, 22, 24, 25, 26, 52, 60, 61
Alexander, Georg 5, 25, 26, 52, 62, 97,
  209
Alexander, Hedwig 4, 5, 7, 25, 52, 62
Alexander, Hermann (John's maternal
  grandfather) 5
Alexander, Isidor 5, 25, 26, 61, 85, 149
Alexander, Karl 5, 25, 52, 62
Alexander, Liane 6, 7, 15, 24, 25, 40, 61-
  62, 84, 92
Alexander, Mary/Maria 6, 25, 61, 62, 84,
  149
Alexandria 98, 103
All Saints Sisters of the Poor convent
  334, 335
Alte Füchse (Old Foxes) 82, 83
America 25, 26, 59, 178, 229, 313
American Embassy, Paris 134, 158
Amis, Kingsley 221
An Inspector Calls (J. B. Priestley) 98,
  150

Anderson shelter 43-44
Anderson, Barbara 330
Sister Angela (Bartram's Convent School)
  42
Anglia Polytechnic University 325
Anglo-American Press Association 136,
  311
Archer, Nikki 266, 272
Armstrong, John 180
Aryan/Aryanisation 9, 10, 22
Ashman, Sandra 331
Ashworth, John 327-328
Assistant Masters & Mistresses
  Association (AMMA) 249
Assistant Masters Association (AMA)
  225, 249
Associated Newspapers 162
Association of Assistant Mistresses 225,
  249
Association of County Councils 225, 250
Association of Education Committees
  248
Association of Metropolitan Authorities
  225, 250
Association of Scientific, Technical and
  Managerial Staffs (ASTMS) 220
Association of Teachers in Technical
  Institutions (ATTI) 237
Association of University Teachers
  (AUT) 249
Aston University 229
Atchison, Miles 331
Auschwitz 7, 26, 59, 62, 63, 76, 77, 209,
  215, 239, 337, 343
Australia 330, 341

B

Baccalauréat 281, 303
Bagnall, Nicholas 243-244, 249
Baker, Blake 195-196, 197, 198, 199,
    200-201, 217, 314
Baker, Kenneth 287
Baker, Mike 340
Mrs Baldry 265, 279
Banque de Paris (BNP) 294-5
Barbican Theatre 335, 339
Barbie, Klaus 307-308
Barnet 269, 284, 286, 287
    General Hospital 286
Barnett, William 246
Barrow, Clive 306
Bartram's Convent School, Haverstock
    Hill 42-43, 302
BBC 41, 42, 102, 111, 162, 170, 221,
    223, 228-229, 252, 256, 299, 300, 318,
    335, 340
    Children's Television 228
    German Service 41, 221
    television 162
Beano, The 51, 232, 240
Princess Beatrix of the Netherlands 52,
    209
Beaverbrook, Lord (Max) 43, 143
Bedlow, Robert 198, 199
Beech Street, Manchester 52, 53, 57
Beethoven, Ludwig van 76, 80, 103, 215
Belfast Telegraph 308
Belgrade 205, 206, 207, 216
Bell, John 312
Belle Vue Circus 117
Belmont Avenue, Cockfosters 182, 316
Belsize Park Gardens 41, 42, 43
The Belvedere, Venice 119
Beniguel, Denise 292, 293, 295
Benn, Wedgwood 239
Benny, Bill and Enid 119
Bergen Belsen (concentration camp) 7,
    59, 62, 215, 343

Berlin 3, 4, 5, 6, 7, 9, 10, 11, 12, 15, 20,
    26, 27, 29, 32, 37, 40, 52, 62, 76, 80,
    82, 84, 92, 110, 175, 176, 177, 178,
    195, 196, 203, 204, 205, 208, 209, 210,
    216, 318, 319, 328, 343
    East —— 177, 204, 209, 210, 216
    West —— 177, 178, 203, 210
Berlin Wall 177, 203, 210, 318, 319
Berliner Morgenpost 204
Berliner, Wendy 339, 340
Berry, Gomer and William (*see* Kemsley,
    Lord and Camrose, Viscount) 113
Betts, Paul 298
Birkbeck College 230
Birkenfeld, Helga 52
Birkenfeld, Ilse 52, 58
Birmingham Post 190
Black Papers on Education (1969-1977)
    221-223, 254, 282
Black, Conrad 288
Blackburn, Robin 220
Blackpool 58, 135, 248, 249, 259, 265,
    270, 276
Blair, Tony 222
Blake, Tony 230
Bleicher, Hugo 141
Blitz 40, 43, 221
Block, Brian and Hazel 265
The Bloomsbury Hotel 36, 38, 39
Bluebell Girls 127
Bormann, Martin 307
Bonn, Issy 51
Borchert, Wolfgang 80, 81
Boyle, Edward 239
Boyson, Dr Rhodes 222, 281, 282
Boyson, Florette 282
Boyson, Violet 282, 283
Bramall, Ashley 246, 247
Bramwell, Chris 306
Brassens, Georges 313
Brasserie Lipp 131, 149, 150
Brecht, Bertolt 103
Brent North 222, 282

Brevet d'Etudes Professionelles (a
  Certificate of Vocational Aptitude) 281
Brighton 49, 236, 248, 249, 265
Brighton Argus 180
Bristol Polytechnic (latterly University of
  West England, Bristol) 235
British
  army 41, 45, 80, 86, 87, 90, 99, 100,
    106, 112
  Council 72, 81, 83, 84
  Embassy, Berlin 319, 320, 321
  Embassy, Paris 131-132, 136, 147, 155,
    157
  Foreign Office 27, 34, 130, 133, 134,
    284, 319
  International School 278
  Navy 31, 33
  prime minister 25, 37, 55
  visa 28, 30
British Airways 118
British Army of the Rhine (BAOR) 91
British National Party 178
British United Provident Association
  (BUPA) 261, 262
Brittan, Regimental Sargeant-Major 107
Brittany Ferries 290
Britton, Ted 236-238
Brixton 287, 299, 325
Brown, Barry 57
Brown, Roger 322
Die Brücke (the Bridge), Münster 83
Buchenwald (concentration camp) 19,
  59, 80, 215, 343
Bulldog (a National Front journal) 337
Buller Barracks 90
Bullock, Alan and Hilda 229, 230
Bunnell, Stanley and Brigitte 277
Burg, Helene 42
Burnett, J. C. 53, 57
The Burnham Committee 224, 225, 227,
  250
Burr, Raymond 104
Burt, Cyril 221

Busby, Sir Matt 118

C

Cabaret Club 118
Café de Flore 149
Cairo 99, 103, 106
  Military Academy 103
Calder, Richie 162
Callaghan, James 222, 253, 254, 309
Cambridge 88, 320
Cameron, James 162
Camrose, Viscount (William Berry) 114
Camus, Albert 149
Carlisle, Mark 280
Carré, Micheline (La Chatte) 141
Cartier 126
Carus, Andre 170
Casino Royale (Ian Fleming) 130
Castle, Barbara 196, 220
Cattle, Peter 160
Cecile Court 180, 182
Celebrity Service 146
Central African Republic (CAR) 302
The Certificate of Secondary Education
  (CSE) 255, 280
Chamberlain, Neville 25, 37
Chanel, Coco 126
Chapel Street Market 337
Chaplin, Charlie 126
Prince Charles, Prince of Wales 279
Charterhouse Square 166
Chaucer, Geoffrey 273
Checkpoint Charlie 204, 208, 216
Cheetham Hill, Manchester 57, 58, 90,
  116, 136, 169
Cheshire Cheese 179
Chesières-Villars 278
China 289, 327
Chinley, Derbyshire 135, 136, 155, 156,
  169
Christ the King Roman Catholic Church,
  Oakwood 270, 272

Churchill, Winston 25, 178
Circular 10, 65, 235,236
Clare, John 252, 253, 300, 305, 315
Clarke, Sir Kenneth 229
Cleveleys 259, 265, 270
Clifton College 65
Cockfosters 182, 186, 277, 287, 316
Colchester Evening Gazette 101
Coldwell, Richard 336
Coles, Carol 296, 306
Colibri Press 317
Committee of Directors of Polytechnics
   (CDP) 309, 310, 311, 314, 316, 317,
   318, 321, 322, 324, 326, 327, 328
Committee of Vice-Chancellors and
   Principals (CVCP) 296, 319, 322, 327
Connell, David 228
Connolly, Kate 195, 196
Conquest, Robert 221
Conservative 79, 179, 232, 239, 251, 282
Conway, Arthur 118
Cooper, Ken 281
Corlette, John 279
Corpus Christi College, Oxford 255
Coryton, Demitri i, 252, 340
Coulter, Stephen 125, 127, 146, 155, 162, 201
Cox, Brian 221, 222, 282
Coxhead, Peter 181
Crillon (Hotel), Paris 134, 149, 158
Cromford Club, Manchester 118
Crosland, Anthony 235
Crossley, Thomas A. (TAC) 54, 55
Curson, Nigel 329
Cyprus 91, 105
Czech 24, 25, 33, 205, 206, 207, 211,
   216, 257
   Jews 25

D

Dachau (concentration camp) 10, 19, 80
Daily and Sunday Telegraph Chapel 200
Daily Chronicle and Clerkenwell News

(*News Chronicle*) 162, 163, 245
Daily Express 43, 117, 143, 166, 174,
   182, 233, 235, 251
Daily Graphic 114
Daily Mail 190, 199, 253, 300
Daily Mirror 155, 174, 176, 196, 252,
   298, 334
Daily Sketch 114
Dali, Salvador 146
Dandy 51, 232, 240
Dartmoor Hotel, Princetown 187-188
David, Tudor 252, 340
Dawson, James 219
Dawson, Peter (a teacher) 250
Dawson, Peter (general secretary to the
   NATFHE) 296
Deedes, Bill 288, 290, 305
Deedes, Jeremy 305, 306, 308
Department of Education and Science
   (DES) 225, 234, 241, 250, 254, 280,
   300, 318, 338
Department of Trade and Industry 322
Deutsche Reichs Partei (German Empire
   Party) 79
Les Deux Magots, Paris 149
Dewhirst, Peter and Makiko 298
Dieppe 123, 312, 313
Digby, Major Harold 97
Dior Monsieur (Yves Saint Laurent's
   boutique) 139
Dior, Christian 138
Dior, Françoise 139
Direct (CDP Newsmagazine) 326
Disraeli, Benjamin 55
Distressed British Subject (DBS) 131
Doudeville 313
Dournelle, Madeleine 128, 131, 132
Downing Street 231, 253, 319
Dubourg, Alain-Yves 170, 171
Duchess of Windsor 136
Duke of Windsor 137, 138
Duncan, Ettie 230, 271, 277, 284, 290,
   306

Duncan, Rev Dr Denis 230, 271, 277, 306
Durham, Michael 249
Dyson, Antony 221

E

East London Polytechnic (then The University of East London, latterly London Metropolitan University) 330
Eastwood, Peter 161, 182, 183, 185, 196, 197, 199, 201, 224, 255, 258, 271, 277, 289, 301, 305
Eden Grove, London 328, 331
Eden, Sir Anthony 25, 111
Edinburgh 221, 229
Education Act (1944) 238, 250
Education Guardian 260, 330
Education Journal 1, 235, 252, 340
Egypt 91-92, 96, 98, 99, 100, 102, 103, 104, 108, 109, 111, 112, 142, 218, 225, 314
Eicken, Prof Dr Carl von 20
Eickhoff, Dr Louise 223-224
El Alamein 96, 97-98
El Vino 179-180
Elizabeth House 254, 287
England, Rosemary 68, 69
Etang la Ville 294, 298, 302, 303, 310
Euro 306, 307
Evans, Harry 200
Evening Gazette (Middlesborough) 101
Evening News 66, 67, 101, 117, 167, 200

F

Fachhochschulen (German Technical or Vocational Colleges) 327
Fainlight, Mr and Mrs 47
Falkland Islands 261, 288, 324
Fanstone, Elizabeth 144, 159
Fawdrey, Kenneth 228
Feather, Vic 198

Field, Michael 292-293, 312
Financial Times 114, 298
Fishman, Jack 160-161
Fleming, Ian 121, 130, 131, 155, 162
Fletcher, David 219, 227, 230
Flowers, Lord 296
Folies-Bergère, Paris 140, 141, 142, 311
Follain, Mary 298
Fortune 124
Fowler, Gerry 309, 318, 319, 321, 324, 333
Fowler, Lorna 310
Fowler's Modern English Usage 184
France Dimanche 127
Francis, Sam 132, 133, 155, 156
Franck, James 72
Fraser, Jim 203
Fridtjof Nansen Haus (FNH) 74, 78
Fuseau, Jean and Suzanne 298, 303, 304

G

Gaitskell, Hugh 284
Gallo, Christiane 293
Gänsicke, Stefan 203
Gardner, Major Frank 99
Garland, Nick 296
Garner, Richard 334
de Gaulle, Charles 140, 141, 156, 201
Gazette of Nottingham Graduates (*Gong*) 70, 71
Geddes, Diana 299
General Certificate of Secondary Education (GCSE) 239, 255, 280, 315
King George V 180
King George VI 107
George, Lloyd 162
Georgia Augusta (University of Göttingen) 72
Gerhart, Dr Hans 142
German Jews 20, 25, 38, 41, 43
Gestapo (*Geheime Staatspolizei*) 4, 9, 10, 13, 20, 21, 22, 27, 29, 30, 82, 84, 141, 292

Getty, Paul 123, 124, 125
ghibli (Saharan wind also known as the *khamsin*) 101
Give Your Child a Chance (Bruce Kemble) 235
Godfrey, Admiral John 130
Goethe, Johann Wolfgang von 69, 74, 80, 213
Golding, Louis 57
Goldings, Alan and Vicki 265
Gongster (Nottingham University) 71
Good University Guide 340
Gorb, Peter 283
Gordon-Walker (Izbicki), June 284, 285, 286, 290, 291, 292, 294, 302, 304, 310, 312, 315, 330, 341, 342
Gordon-Walker, Anna 285, 291, 302, 303, 341, 342
Gordon-Walker, Mary 341
Gordon-Walker, Patrick 221, 284
Gordon-Walker, Patrick (younger) 285, 291, 302, 303, 341, 342
Gordon-Walker, Robin 284, 285
Gordon-Walker, Robyn 341
Gordonstoun School, Elgin 279
Göttingen 72, 73, 74, 75, 79, 80, 82, 84, 219, 341
  Stadtstheater 81
Gould, Donald 171
Gould, Sir Ronald 227, 236
Goulden, John 106, 111, 114, 117
Grandes Ecoles 327
Great Debate 253-254
Greco, Juliette 313
Green, Horton 69
Green, Maurice 260
Greening Polytechnics (October 1990) 318
Greening the Curriculum (May 1991) 318
Gresham College 330
Griffiths, Charles 69
Grout, Lucy 315
Gruber, Monika 204

Guardian 117, 176, 182, 259-260, 309, 315, 347
Gurion, David Ben 111

H

Hahn, Kurt 279
Halladale (troop carrier) 90, 91, 92
Hallward, Bertrand 65
Hamilton House (NUT Headquarters) 225, 295
Hamilton, Charles Denis 119, 121, 149, 150, 151-155, 162, 172, 181
Harlech Television 228
Harrington Affair 328, 337, 338
Harris, Jo 323
Hart, David 232, 245, 247
Hartwell, Lord 288
Harvey, Michael 142
Harwich 32, 33, 34
Hass, Professor Dr 319-321
Hastings, Max 288, 289, 293, 300, 301, 305, 308
Hawker, Robert 330
Haworth, Alan 338
Haymarket Press 171
Hazlehurst, Alan 281
Heath, Edward 231, 234, 257
Heine, Heinrich 80
HEIST (Higher Education Information Services Trust) 329
Hemingway, Ernest 126
Herald of Free Enterprise 301
Herchenroder, Louis 125, 127, 155, 158, 293
Herder, Johann Gottfried 213
Heseltine, Michael 167, 168, 171, 325
Hess, Rudolf 8
Heywood Street, Manchester 57, 58, 90, 135, 136, 169
Highbury Grove Boys School 281, 331
Higher Education External Relations Association (HEERA) 329

Higher School Certificate (pre-runner of GCE A-levels) 56, 64, 66
Hill, Jack 174, 175, 176, 218, 219
Hilpert, Heinz 80
Hitler Youth 17-18
Hitler, Adolf 8, 20, 24, 25, 32, 33, 27, 40, 42, 61, 73, 80, 120, 142, 215, 279
Hodgson, Christine 330
Hofkins, Diane 340
Höft, Waltraut 203
Hollingworth, Clare 298, 299
Holocaust 61, 337
Hope, Robert 244
Hopkinson, David 190
Hopkinson, Tom 97
Horst/Horstchen 3, 4, 8, 9, 10, 13, 15, 16, 17, 19, 21, 26, 29, 30, 32, 35, 38, 39, 46, 47, 56, 61, 90, 115, 343
Hôtel d'Isley, Paris 123, 127, 201
Hotel Elephant, Weimar 213
Hôtel Ritz, Paris 126, 138, 143, 144, 155, 157, 158, 202
Houfe, Bill 66
Mr Howard (of the Manchester Quakers) 115
Howard, John 115, 137, 185, 186, 189, 197
Huddersfield Polytechnic 309
Hull, General Richard 99
Hulton, Edward 97
L'Humanité 236
Humboldt University, Berlin 319, 328
Hutton, Joe Bernard 266, 267

I

Independent 334, 339
Inner London Education Authority (ILEA) 246, 247, 322
Inner London Teachers' Association 238
International Baccalauréat 303
International Herald Tribune 315
Internationales Institut für Journalismus in Entwicklungsländer 177, 203

Invalidenstrasse, Berlin 3, 6, 8, 13, 14, 15, 17, 37, 44, 319, 328
Isbie, David and Eddie 45
Ismailia, Egypt 93, 94, 99, 102, 103, 106, 225
Israeli 106, 110, 181, 307
ITV 228
Itzig, Benno 7, 25, 26, 52, 62
Itzig, Heini 7, 24, 25, 40, 52, 62
Izbicki (née Alexander), Selma 5, 6, 9, 24, 39, 60, 61, 115
Izbicki (née Jones), Liz 180, 281
Izbicki (née Ryan), Maureen 129, 131-136, 140, 147-149, 153-158, 163, 172, 174-178, 181-182, 186, 191-195, 200-205, 208, 214, 216-220, 227, 245, 259, 261-278, 282-286, 289-290, 292, 312, 316, 328, 343
Izbicki, Asher 26, 27, 181
Izbicki, Chloe 341
Izbicki, Jacob 181, 277, 291
Izbicki, Luzer Ber (Hans/Leonard) 4, 5, 8, 9, 39, 47, 61, 115
Izbicki, Paul Howard 179, 180, 193, 195, 200-201, 205, 216, 217, 219, 220, 227, 228, 240, 241, 245, 248, 259, 261, 262, 265, 266, 271, 272, 274, 277-279, 283, 286, 290, 316, 330, 341, 342
Izbicki, Sue 330, 341, 342
Izbicki, Tyler 341

J

Jackson, Margaret 281
Jacobson, Philip 298
Jaffé, Tony and Joy 286
James Allen's Girls School 286
James Bond (Ian Fleming) 130, 315
Jarrow March (October 1936) 226
Jarvis, Fred 295-296
Jeckel, Alfred 318
Jenkins, Clive 220
Jessel, Stephen 299

Jewish Chronicle 194, 332
Jewish Refugee Committee 36, 38, 44
Jewish Telegraph 67
John Bright's County School 55
Jones, Aubrey 220
Joseph, Sir Keith 252, 253, 281, 300,
   328, 338
Judd, Dr Denis 338

K

Kamm, Thomas 298
Karl Marx Stadt 210, 211
Katz, Dagobert 62
Katz, Flora 25, 60-61
Keele University 256
Kelly, Dr Liz 334
Kelly, Margaret ("Miss Bluebell") 127
Kemble, Bruce 233, 235-236, 247, 251
Kemsley House, Manchester 113, 122,
   130, 144, 150, 154
Kemsley Newspapers 114, 119, 121, 125,
   138, 150, 158, 201, 273, 292
Kemsley, Lady 114, 122, 127, 143-145,
   157, 158, 159, 266
Kemsley, Lord (Gomer Berry) 113-114,
   125-127, 143, 145, 146, 150, 155, 157
Kindertransport 27
King Alfred's School, Golders Green 266
King and Keys 179, 180
King, William 79
King's College Hospital 285
Kitch, Chris 333
Klarsfeld, Serge 307
Kobler, Richard 240
Kossoff, David 339
Kray twins 188
Kristallnacht 3-23, 24, 35, 73

L

Labour
   government 198, 222, 226, 281

New —— 222
Labovitch, Clive 167, 171
The Lancet 264
Lang, Dr (of Aylesbury) 266
Laurent, Yves Saint 139
Lee, Jennie 255
Leicester Polytechnic 316
Lenczyca 4, 34, 194
Lesley (John's secretary) 168
Levison, Dr Victor 263
Lewandowski, Ernst and Hertha 25, 60
Lewis, Essie 119
Lewis, Michael 314-315
Liberal Democrats 255
Libya 107, 111
Lido nightclub, Paris 127
"Lie Sheet" 125, 161
Liese (née Mühl), Lonni 25, 52, 209, 210
Liese, Otto 209
Lincoln College 309
Linke (née Izbicki), Nacia 120
Linke, Ettie (Michelle/Mishka) 121
Linke, Gabriel 120, 121
Linke, Yona 121
Lipski, Lydia Lova de Korczac 140-143
Liverpool Hope University 324
Liverpool John Moores University
   (formerly Liverpool Polytechnic) 325
Liverpool Post 165
Llandudno 46, 47, 48, 49, 50, 51, 53, 55,
   240, 248
Lochner, Robert 177-178, 203
London Business School 283
London Evening News 163
London Evening Standard 134, 155, 288,
   298
London Evening Star 163
London Guildhall University 330
London School of Economics (LSE) 220,
   328
London School of Oriental and African
   Studies 242
Longman's publishing 252, 340

Loshak, David 185, 284, 285
Loshak, Molly 284
Lourdes 272, 273
Love, John 275
Low, George 340
Dr Löwenstein 21
Lowry, Suzanne 308
Lycée Britannique 302
Lycée Internationale 303
Lyte, Charles 252

M

Macdonald, Susan 298
MacDowall, David 338
MacGregor, John 319
Mackenzie, Gordon 122, 125
Mackenzie, Hector 78
Macleod, Iain 256
magnetiseur 144, 266
Major, John 321, 325, 326
Manchester
  Central Library 56, 118
  City Council Scholarship 64, 67
  Excise Office 33
  Food Office 115
  Society of Friends (Quakers) 115
  University 200, 221, 229
Manchester Evening Chronicle 81, 94, 106, 111, 113, 114, 131, 146, 173, 185, 190, 196, 200
Manchester Evening News 66, 101, 117, 200
Manchester Grammar 53
Manchester Guardian 117, 175
Manchester United 118, 216
Mann, Anthony 312
Marceau, Marcel 252
Margaret, Princess 138
Marlowe, Christopher 68
Marsh, E H (Ricky) 195, 201, 203, 207, 289
Marshall, Anthony 291, 306

Marston, Paul 301
Maskell, Norman 167
Matisse, Henri 124
Matthews, Bob and Pauline 298, 303
Matthews, Tim 242
Maude, Angus 221
Maupassant, Guy de 125, 162
Mauthausen-Gusen 80
Maxim's, Paris 145, 149, 158
McCarthy, Senator Joe 132
McHardy, Anne 330
McParland, John 331
Medical News 171
Medical World 171
Mein Kampf (Adolf Hitler) 8
Melcher, Russell 127, 132, 137, 138, 155
Mellor, Harold 112, 115, 116
Mendelbaum, Rabbi 194
Mendelssohn, Felix 80, 153
Middlesex Hospital, London 263, 264-265, 268, 271, 273, 275, 316
Middlesex Polytechnic 316
Militant 251
Miller, Max 251
Miller, Prof Dr Terence 242, 244, 328, 336
Mitchell, Frank 186, 188
Mitterand, François 149
Moascar Players 98, 100, 150
Mohel 193, 194
Mollet, Guy 111
Le Monde 127, 140
Montgomery, Bernard 98
Moores, John 325
Moorfield's Hospital 266
Morden, Michael 180
Morris, Colin 100
Morris, Max 251, 295
Morris, Norman 68
Mother Superior 163-164
Mount, Roger 188
Mountview Theatre Club 181, 218, 219
Mozart, Wolfgang Amadeus 69, 80, 103

Mühlen, Lieselotte 203
Müller, Pinkus 81
Münster 81-85, 341
    University 81
Murdoch, Rupert 200, 300, 301
Myers, Geoffrey 155, 312
Myers, Michael 48-49
Myers, Pauline 48

N

Naked Heroine 140-142
Nansen, Fridtjof 74, 75, 78
Nash, Ian 340
Nash, Roy 245, 247
Nasser, Gamal Abdel 103, 109-111
Nathan, Amelia 170
National Association of Head Teachers
    (NAHT) 220, 231, 234, 235, 245, 249-
    251, 265
National Association of Labour Student
    Organisations 309
National Association of Schoolmasters
    (NAS) 220, 225
National Association of
    Schoolmasters/Union of Women
    Teachers (NASUWT) 225, 249, 250,
    251
National Association of Teachers in
    Further and Higher Education
    (NATFHE) 225, 249-250, 338
National Front 178, 328, 337, 338
National Health Service (NHS) 155, 263-
    264, 274
National Polytechnics Week (NPW) 316-
    317
National Service 86, 137, 139, 225, 314,
    341
National Union of Journalists 200, 297
National Union of Students (NUS) 230,
    316, 338
National Union of Teachers (NUT) 220,
    224, 225, 227, 236, 237, 238, 245, 248,

249, 250, 251, 252, 281, 295, 296
National Viewers and Listeners'
    Association 223
National Westminster Bank, Paris 126
Nationalist Party (NPD), Germany 79
Nazi (German National Socialist) 7, 8, 9,
    10, 16, 17, 18-19, 22, 25, 28, 30, 31,
    33, 37, 41, 42, 43, 62, 63, 72, 73, 75,
    ,76, 79, 80, 90, 120, 139, 141, 142, 149,
    178, 204, 208, 209, 215, 221, 239, 279,
    307, 329, 337, 343
    Party (the NSDAP) 8
Nelson, Peter 124
Neuengamme 80
Neustadt, Professor Richard 255
New College, Oxford 198
New Education 310
New Statesman 3106
Newcastle Journal 101, 114, 146
Newman, Michael 338
News Chronicle 162, 163, 245
News of the World 162
Newsweek 124
NF News 337
Nietzsche, Friedrich 213
Night of the Long Knives 8
No More Peace (Ernst Toller) 59, 68
Noah (André Obey) 55
Nobel Prize 72
Nobel Prize for Peace 74
Norman, Margot 249, 265
North Manchester Grammar School 54,
    64, 119
North Manchester High School for Boys,
    New Moston 53, 55
North Middlesex Hospital 262-263
North Western Polytechnic 242, 243
Northampton Chronicle 101
Northern Polytechnic 244, 339
Nottingham Evening Post 114
Nottingham Guardian 69
Nottingham University 65-71
Nuffield Hospital 261

O

O'Leary, John 340
O'Sullivan, Grainne 181
Observer 298, 309, 317, 327
Oliver, Vic 51
Olivier, Laurence 165
Opa, Charles 120
Opa, Lisette 120, 121
Opatowski (née Izbicki), Genia 120
Opatowski, Oscar 120
Open University 235, 253, 255, 256, 258
Oranienburger Tempel, Berlin 19
Order of Sion 164
Organisation for Economic Co-operation
    and Development (OECD) 309
Organisation for Rehabilitation through
    Training (ORT) 280, 281, 283
Orpheus (cruise ship) 261
Our Lady of Sion (grammar school) 163,
    164, 171, 178, 272, 277, 328
Out of this World (Joe Bernard Hutton)
    267
Oxford University 98, 229, 239, 254,
    255, 309, 320, 329, 333, 334, 335
Oxford Brookes University 333
Ozanne, James 312

P

Palace of Westminster 306, 309
Paradiso e Inferno (Italian Restaurant,
    The Strand) 288
Parliament 220, 222, 309-310
Parliamentary Select Committee on
    Education, Science and the Arts 310
Parsons, Philip and Inge 278
Pas de Calais (hotel), Paris 294
Paul, Gerda 179
St Paul's Cathedral 36, 159
Pavement for My Pillow (Chris Kitch)
    335

Pawley, "Pop" 175, 184, 186, 196, 197,
    203
Payne, Ronnie 126, 165, 201, 208
Pays des Galles (hotel), Paris 171
Pearson, May 270
Perry Mason 104, 105
Peter Simple column 217-218
Peterborough column 249, 278
Prince Philip, Duke of Edinburgh 279
Philips, Trevor 339
Piaf, Édith 143
Picture Post 97
Pioneer Corps (British Army) 41
Place Vendôme, Paris 125, 129, 134, 153,
    176, 202, 292
Play School 228
Polytechnic of Central London (latterly
    The University of Westminster) 325
Polytechnic of North London (PNL; later
    the University of North London (UNL)
    and latterly London Metropolitan
    University) 242-243, 328, 336, 337
polytechnics 1, 235, 242, 253, 306, 309,
    311, 315, 316, 317, 318, 319, 320-327,
    329, 333, 335, 343
Polytechnics and Colleges Funding
    Council 322
Polytechnics Eastern and Central
    European Scholarships Scheme
    (PECESS) 319, 321
Port Said 91-92, 93, 107, 111
Povey, Terence 244
Press Association 136, 247, 311
Price, Christopher 309, 333
Priestley, J. B. 98-99
Private Eye 288
Privy Council 198, 325
Professional Association of Teachers
    (PAT) 250, 296
Prüfert, Peter 203
Pryce, Maxwell (Max) 339
Psychic News 266, 267

Q

Queen's School, Bushey 277

R

R U R 55
rabbi 110, 121, 193, 194, 295, 340
  -nate 121, 332, 340
Radio Fun 51
Rafferty, Frances 340
Rais, Guy 185
Raising Lazarus 335
Raising of the School Leaving Age
  (ROSLA) 253
Rank REC 240-241
rationing 46, 59, 72
Ratisbon brothers 164
Ravensbrück 141
Rayner, Claire 339
Reading University 243
Red Cross 60, 63
Rees, Edwin 169
Rehmer, Otto Ernst 79
Rektorenkonferenz 319
Reluctant Heroes (Colin Morris) 100-
  101, 218
Renoir, Pierre-Auguste 124
Renton, Sir David 258
Requiem Mass 103, 277
Reuters 130
Revolutionary Socialist League 251
RIAS radio station, Berlin 177, 203
Richard III (William Shakespeare) 68, 83
Richards, John 199, 201, 314, 315
Richards, Morley 166
Richardson, Ralph 165
Rickett, Naomi 316
Rickett, Raymond 316, 333
Ridsdale, Julian 258
Ring, Len and Polly 45
Risa (Lady Kemsley's maid) 144
Risley, Manchester 47, 53

Ritz, César 126
Robbins, Lord 220
Robert Montefiore Secondary School,
  281
Roberts, Alfred 238
Roberts, Brian 243, 244
Mrs Rogers 44-46
Rolls Royce 136-137
Rommel, General Erwin 74, 98
Roper, Brian 333, 335, 336, 339
Rose, Kenneth 230
Round Square Schools 279
Rowlands, Christopher 300, 306
Roxan, David 162
Royal Academy of Dramatic Arts
  (RADA) 55, 56, 218
Royal Army Service Corps (RASC) 87,
  94, 107, 108, 109
Royal Ordnance Factories (ROFs) 47, 53
Rudden, Jim 246, 247
Rutherford, Margaret 128, 132
Rutlish Grammar School 325
Ryan, Harry 135
Ryan, Margaret 276
Ryan, Nell 135, 155, 156, 193, 259, 262,
  276

S

Sachsenhausen (concentration camp) 19,
  80
Sagan, Françoise 149
St Nicholas Hotel, Scarborough 231, 233
Salem school, Germany 279
Salgado, Gamini 68
Sandler, Albert 40
Sankey (soap manufacturer), Salford 53
Sartre, Jean-Paul 149
Saunders, Arthur 117
Scheffold, Horst 177
Schicklgrüber 7, 40
Schiller, Friedrich 74, 80, 213, 215
Schmidt, Peter 185

Schnabel, Günter 210-216
School Certificate 66, 239
School of Women's Studies 333
School Proms 339
Schools Council 281
Schools Music Association 339
Schopenhauer, Arthur 215
Schramm, Professor Ernst von 74-75
Schultz, Aneliese 185
Schumacher, Kurt 79-80
Schwantze, Helmut 208, 211, 214, 215-216
Schweizer, Dr (Nottingham don) 69
Scotsman 158, 199
Scott, John 247
Searle, Christopher 246
Secondary Heads Association (SHA) 249, 251
Sellers, Peter 170, 295
Sempik, Tessa 337
Seraphim, Barbara 81, 82
Seraphim, Ulli 82
Sesame Street 227-229, 296
Sheffield Polytechnic 321
Sheffield University 229
Short, Edward 221, 222, 226, 234, 235, 240, 247
Sibson, R. M. 57
Silber, Bernhardt 75
Silver Spirit (Rolls Royce) 137
Simple, Peter 217, 218
Simpson, Wallis (Duchess of Windsor) 136
Sims, Monica 228
Slater, B. V. 238
Slater, Louise 331
Smythe, Robin 298
Snowdon, Lord (Mr Antony Armstrong-Jones) 138
Social Democratic Party (SDP) 255
Socialist Workers Party 251
Society of Friends (the Quakers) 115
Socrates 59, 60

Somerville, Dr Jennifer 331
Sorbonne, Paris University 1119, 121, 202
South Bank Polytechnic 242
Southampton University 324
Southgate School, Enfield 245, 277
Southgate Technical College 266
SPD (Germany's socialist party) 79
Spearman, Neville 142
Springer 204
Stage and Radio Club, Manchester 119
Stalingrad 80
Stanmore Hotel, Brighton 49
Stasi (East German secret police) 210, 211, 216
Steen, Sergeant David 97, 101
Stephens, H J C 196
Stephens, Peter 155
Stettiner Bahnhof, Berlin 5, 6, 18, 29
Stevens, Auriol 327
Steventon (village near Abingdon) 44-45
Stiller (German Jewish refugee) 41
Stiller (leatherware shop), Berlin 17, 44
Stockport 56, 135, 156
The Stockport Players 56
Stoddart, John 321, 324
Stoicjovic, Serge 205
Stone of Scone 78
Straubenzee, William Van 257, 258
Striker (Izbicki family dog) 259, 265, 272, 277, 286
Stubbs, Colonel John 95-96, 97, 107, 108
Sturmabteilung (the SA) 19
Der Stürmer 10
Suez 93, 111, 117
Suez Canal 96, 98, 111
Sulzbach, Herbert 41-42, 43
Sunday Empire News 122, 124, 133, 139, 146, 160-163, 201, 273
Sunday Express 298
Sunday Graphic 122, 138-140, 146, 154, 160, 161, 173, 201
Sunday People 102

Sunday Times 114, 121-122, 125, 131, 138, 146, 150, 158, 160, 162, 201, 309
Sussex University 229
Sutton, Maurice 263
Swann, Michael 221
swastika 9, 10, 17, 36, 337
Sweetwater Canal, Egypt 102, 142

T

Talking Books 242
Talking Page 240-242
Tandy 200 (laptop computer) 297
Targett, Peter and Val 277
Tausend Worte Englisch (One Thousand Words English) 27
Tavistock 187, 189
Tavistock Hotel 187
The Teacher (the NUT's journal) 237-238
Telegraph, The Daily 1, 58, 114, 126, 155, 161, 174, 175, 176, 177, 178, 179-180, 181, 182, 183, 184, 186, 187, 188, 191, 195, 196, 198, 200, 202-203, 206, 217, 221, 224, 227, 228, 230, 234, 238, 240, 243, 238, 243, 244, 245, 246, 249, 250, 255, 256, 259, 260, 261, 271, 274, 277, 278, 284, 287, 288, 290, 291, 292, 293, 294, 296, 297, 298, 301, 302, 305-306, 307, 308, 309, 310, 311, 312, 314, 315, 338, 343
  Sunday —— 200, 201, 230, 243, 288, 297, 298, 309
Tempelhof 28, 84
  Airport 24
Terence Miller – a Conscientious Objector (Tim Matthews) 242
Tewson, Vincent 198
Thames Polytechnic 242
Thatcher, Carol 240
Thatcher, Denis 239, 255, 324
Thatcher, Margaret 200, 222, 231, 231, 235, 236-238, 241, 242, 247, 253, 257, 281, 282, 322, 324, 325

the "Finchley Nightingale" 239
  the Iron Lady 200, 247
Thatcher, Mark 240
Theresienstadt (concentration camp) 7, 26, 60, 343
Thirty Years' War 74
Thompson, Sarah 265
Thomson, Roy (First Baron Thomson of Fleet) 158, 159, 161
Thorndike, Dame Sybil 55, 68, 218
Times 159, 165, 174, 176, 182, 183, 184, 188, 195, 298, 299, 300, 301, 311
Times Educational Supplement 163, 222, 249, 260, 310, 340
Times Higher Education Supplement 340
Times Newspapers 260, 340
Timpson, Major John 108
Toller, Ernst 59, 68
Tomlinson, John 281
Topic 166-170, 266
Tour d'Argent (restaurant), Paris 145
Townsend-Thoresen ferries 301
Trades Union Congress (TUC) 196, 197, 198, 199, 220, 237, 295
Transport and General Workers Union (TGWU) 196-199, 220
Travers, Paddy 180
Treasury 231, 248, 253, 254, 256, 321
Trent Building, Nottingham University 65, 66, 67
Trinder, Tommy 51
Trotskyism 255
Tucker, Sophie 146-147
Turatsky, Mary 45
Turner-Warwick, Richard 263-264
Tynan, Kenneth 239

U

U-Bahn (Berlin's underground trains) 210
Uganda SS (cruise ship) 260-261
Ulbricht, Walter 203

Umpire, The 161
Understanding Mrs Thatcher (John Izbicki) 238
Undotheboys Hall (Robert Conquest) 221
Union of Women Teachers (UWT) 225, 249, 295
United Nations Educational, Scientific and Cultural Organization (UNESCO) 132
United Press International 165
University College London (UCL) 325
University College of Rhodesia 242
University of Central England in Birmingham (formerly Birmingham Polytechnic) 325
University of East Anglia 221, 282
University of East London (formerly East London Polytechnic) 330
University of Kent, Canterbury 229
University of Lancaster 309
University of London 296, 326
University of North London (UNL) (formerly the Polytechnic of North London, then London Metropolitan University) 328-344
– *One Hundred Turbulent Years* 336
– *One Hundred Vibrant Years* 336
University of Singapore 172
University of the West of England, Bristol (formerly Bristol Ploytechnic) 325
University of Westminster (formerly Polytechnic of Central London) 326
Utley, Peter 249

V

Verall, Richard 337
Verbindungen (German fraternities) 82
Verdier, Serge and Suzanne 313
Volpone (Ben Jonson) 69, 83

W

Wade, Nigel 289, 301, 308
Wadley, Veronica 289, 308
Wagner, Leslie 328, 333, 335, 336
Walker, David 296, 300
Walker, Mark 316-317
Walker, Molly 67
Wall Street Journal 125, 298
Wallis, John 125, 155, 156, 202, 292, 312
War Office Selection Board (WOSB) 88
Ward, Corporal Frank 87
Warlingham County Secondary School 237
Warsaw Pact 207, 211, 216
Warwick University 229
Weaver, Maurice 199
Wedekind, Franz 69, 218
Weill, Kurt 103
Welch, Colin 217, 218
Wesker, Arnold 83
Western Mail (Cardiff) 114
Westminster Abbey 78, 79
Westminster Bank, Paris 126, 129, 202
Wharton, Michael 217, 218
White, Roy 306
White, Sam 134, 155
Whitehouse, Mary 223-224
Whithy Grove, Manchester 113
Whittington Hospital, Archway 191, 194
Why teachers are militant (*Telegraph* feature) 226
Wiedergutmachung 63
Wig and Pen (pub), London 179
Wilcox, Annette 132, 155
Wilde, Oscar 123, 127, 201
Willems Barracks, Aldershot 86, 87, 108
William Tyndale School 322
Williams, Bernard 255
Williams, Paul 297
Williams, Shirley 222, 253, 254
Sister Williams (Jewish Hospital ward sister) 58

Wilson, Harold 196, 231, 237, 247, 255, 258, 309
Wilson, Mary 231
Winslade, Harry 185
Woodcock, George 197, 198
Workers Revolutionary Party 251
World Medicine 171, 174, 178, 266
World Press News 163

Y

Yinglish (a mixture of Yiddish and English) 39
Yom Kippur (the Jewish Day of Atonement) 329
Young, Susan 340
Your Write (The Gazette of Nottingham Graduates) 70

Z

Zionist 106
Zyklon B gas 78